The Meaning of Culture

W9-AWJ-167

The Meaning of Culture

A Reader in Cultural Anthropology

Edited by
MORRIS FREILICH
Northeastern University

Xerox College Publishing
Lexington, Massachusetts / Toronto

ACKNOWLEDGMENTS

I am grateful to the following authors, journals, and publishers for permission to reproduce previously published works:

FREDRIK BARTH

JOHN W. BENNETT

S. N. GERBER

A. IRVING HALLOWELL

GEORGE PETER MURDOCK

MORRIS OPLER

RICHARD J. PRESTON

The American Anthropologist

American Sociological Review

The American Scientist

Anthropos

Human Organization

Institute of Caribbean Studies (University of Puerto Rico)

Quarterly Review of Biology

Southwestern Journal of Anthropology

GILBERT SHAPIRO

LAURA THOMPSON

FRED W. VOGET

ANTHONY F. C. WALLACE

MURRAY WAX

LESLIE A. WHITE

DAVID WILSON

For committed assistance in the pragmatics of typing, proofing, and bibliographical work, I am grateful to Evelyn Hulda Barchi and Elaine Standke.

Copyright © 1972 by Xerox Corporation.
All rights reserved. Permission in writing must be obtained from the publisher before any part of this publication may be reproduced or transmitted in any form or by any means, electronic or mechanical, including photocopy, recording, or any information storage or retrieval system.
ISB Number: 0-536-00699-7
Library of Congress Catalog Card Number: 70-143629
Printed in the United States of America.

To Cantor Harry Freilich
in loving memory

Preface

Science, to paraphrase Newton, involves climbing, seeing, and reporting: we climb on the backs of older scientists, see further than they did, and then report on the wonderful visions so obtained. Science, we are being told, is a game of addition, of integration, of building on top of structures others have laid down. Today, as perhaps never before, the world needs good social science: we need to understand man, society, and culture, before all of these phenomena disappear in the war that *will* end all wars. Poetic analogies of scientific progress, therefore, are usefully translated into practical, operational terms. How does one "climb on the backs of others"? And, precisely what does one do when one reaches the heights? The answer, at first sight, sounds simple and the work appears rather boring; in actuality neither is the case.

The scientist begins by reading the works of others. He then summarizes their conclusions, generalizations, and conceptual ideas in a way which makes this information quickly retrievable. A useful and frequently used method for storing information is to put it on 5″ × 7″ file cards. As one develops an ever larger card collection it is necessary to *pull together* the ideas on the various cards in order to develop more general notions upon which to base one's own research. This "pulling-together" labor is a tricky enterprise: many ideas do not add up; they do not easily permit synthesis. That is, there are some ideas (let us call them "X") which are contradictory to other ideas (let us call them "Y"). Here, integration can occur only after the scientist has allowed X and Y to engage in intellectual conflict. Differently put, proper sciencing includes the scheduling of a series of "debates" between the cards. In the course of such debates it will become clear what data is "critical" and which is marginal; what ideas are stronger and which are weaker; what parts of a theory can be utilized profitably for future research, and which parts should be discarded. Decision-making on the data and ideas of fellow scholars is an activity surrounded by intellectual traps and psychological snares. Today, as perhaps never before, we need to gather deep insights into this process, for the consequences of doing a poor job are far-reaching and serious.

In supervising debates between the cards the scientist can play one of two quite distinct roles: *judge or arbitrator.* Scientists who play judge consider these "fights between the cards" as purely a matter of ritual. For the judge these are mock battles, since he considers himself *the* intellectual giant who will carry his science toward great progress. The judge broadcasts his superiority in many ways. One ploy is to misrepresent what the cards are saying and then brilliantly cut up "their" arguments. Another more artful technique is to show how scholars, generally considered wise and profound, were actually fools, ninneys, or even racists. Judge-scientists rarely make lasting contributions to their fields; they constantly throw out babies (valuable ideas) with the dirty waters (irrelevancies). Arbitrators, however, generally do far better. Unfettered by megalomaniacal views, these scholars are free to work in ways likely to generate a little inspiration.

Arbitrators do science in ways quite different from the judges. Every card is considered valuable: it has important information. Every card-combat is an exciting event; it brings truth closer. Arbitrator-scientists have an unwritten charter with four basic principles: (1) fellow scientists, almost invariably, are honest, able, and dedicated; (2) most of them produce very valuable work; (3) most of them overemphasize one aspect of the problem they are working on, and underemphasize other aspects; and (4) truth is a patchwork, consisting of the ideas of many. Some very few scientists play the role of judge; fortunately for science most are arbitrators.

Truth is a patchwork; and the final garment is a mosaic—made up of threads contributed by many. Scientists and other truth-seekers must therefore learn the weaver's art. My concluding essay is an attempt at idea-weaving. My conclusions, hopefully, will meet with some measure of approval from fellow professional anthropologists. The main goal however is something quite different; it is to help the neophyte, the introductory anthropology student, to grasp the deep complexities inherent in a small word—"culture." To such a student I say: For more than one hundred years the concept of culture has been a subject of considerable debate among professional anthropologists. That these scholars have considered such argumentation worthwhile clearly indicates that "culture" ranks as a major contribution to human knowledge. The papers presented herein indicate some of the main issues around which intellectual combat has occurred. It is very much worth your while to study this argumentation; indeed it would be well if you become an active participant in these debates. Take your arguments out of the classroom and continue them on and off campus. Become an arbitrator and make your own synthesis!

The message "become an arbitrator" is a challenge rather than a piece of advice. First, to become an arbitrator will require that you become intimately familiar with the various ideas presented. Such work, while immensely rewarding, is arduous. A second and greater difficulty is the temptation to be a judge. Being a judge over the ideas of many has obvious charms; egos weakened by constant pressures to succeed are instantly and magically recharged. The temptations are yet stronger and more social than our own ego needs. We live in a world where "strength" is often represented by "an extreme position," and where truth is often discovered through the style of a message rather than in its content. Often what people say means less to us than how they say it: "The medium is the message." Predictably, in such a milieu idea-judges keep springing up like weeds in an unattended garden. From the anarchist, who demonstrates his truth with bombs, to high-placed political figures who wrap their truths up with the flag, little notice is taken of arbitrators.

By developing and popularizing the role of arbitrator, we can all help transform the world into a healthier place. By using this strategy to arrive at the meaning of culture, we can slowly climb out of this age of neo-barbarism and develop a real, worldwide civilization. Man's most important goal in the 1970s is to seize control of his destiny, of his culture.

M.F.
Boston, Massachusetts

Contents

Introduction
Culture: A Concept in Search of Meaning

How is human behavior to be explained? Why do some people continually search for new challenges, while others live more like rabbits or cows? Why will some men kill gladly and with obvious enjoyment, while others would give their lives not to have to take another's life? The history of man reads like a long, stranger-than-science-fiction story; what wisdom makes it understandable? Answers that have been given show how imaginative man can be when faced with a puzzle that really grabs his interest: (1) Race determines behavior—it makes some people smart, others crafty, yet others stupid or selfish or lazy; (2) Environment is *the* cause—heat saps your energy, cold makes you like hard work, and mountains lead to lofty ideas, while deserts bring out deep thoughts; (3) Body type controls behavior: fat people are jovial, thin and lanky ones are thoughtful; (4) Higher powers control people's lives—gods and angels, planets, good magic and bad magic.

Anthropologists reject these explanations and provide an answer of their own: man's behavior is fully explained by culture. Man learns to think, feel, believe, and strive for that which his culture considers proper. The student who is initially unfamiliar with social sciences will find this explanation hard to accept. His own behavior, quite clearly, appears to be "his own." Yet slowly doubts begin to enter; particularly as the instructor continues to hammer away the anthropological theme: "Your eating habits, waking and sleeping hours, friendships, sexual life, economic and political activities, all follow the patterns of your culture." Finally, the student capitulates, culture does seem to rule. It is the final explanation of human behavior.

Like most simple explanations for complex problems, this one too raises more questions than it answers. If culture rules, then mighty man with his big brain and tremendous technological toys is but a slave—a slave to culture. How did man manage to get into such a mess? From where does "culture" derive its powers to subjugate? Man revolts against all kinds of oppression; why has he not revolted against this master? These and similar questions receive various and conflicting answers in the essays that follow. Why are these questions so troublesome? An illustration here may be illuminating.

In some parts of India a rich man, who plans an extended trip away from home, must hire a poor man to sleep in his bed. This custom is known as *Khutmul Kilao;* literally, "feeding the bedbugs." How is *Khutmul Kilao* to be explained, anthropologically?[1] Superficially, the whole matter is quite simple: In parts of India (particularly down south around Madras) the status "rich man" includes among its obligations the duty of keeping his bedbugs fed at all times, even when he himself sleeps away from home. However, the essential question is left untouched by this superficial answer. Namely, why is it necessary to "feed" bedbugs? Many societies have the status "rich man"; many have large populations of bedbugs, yet only in some Indian subcultures do we hear about feeding bedbugs with sleeper-substitutes.

Anthropologists faced with finding a reasonable explanation would begin to argue and present a variety of different, "reasonable" explanations for *Khutmul Kilao.* Each explanation in actuality represents one view of the meaning of culture:

1. *Culture is a historical phenomenon:* Cultural patterns are little more than accidents of history. In X A.D., a Hindu mystic concerned with the welfare of bedbugs inspired rich and powerful Hindu Indians to practice *Khutmul Kilao.* Thereafter rich men have taught it to their sons as the "proper thing to do."
2. *Culture is essentially in the "hands of" the establishment:* The rich wish to maintain their prestige and power. *Khutmul Kilao* must help them do so. By following this custom, a rich man broadcasts to the multitude that he can afford to house, feed, and pay a poor man while spending money on travels. This is conspicuous consumption for the maintenance of power and prestige.
3. *Culture helps a society adapt to its natural and social environment:* Indian society is well-stocked with poor people. Feeding the poor is a major social problem. Now, *Khutmul Kilao* is really concerned with the poor, and with

---

[1] Somehow, *Khutmul Kilao* has managed to escape much anthropological analysis. It is discussed, however, in a charming and humorous novel by Aaron Juda, *Clown on Fire,* New York: Dial Publishers, 1967.

ways of feeding them. By hiring a man to sleep in his bed (ostensibly to feed the bedbugs), a rich man provides a poor man with food, lodging, and income. This custom allows a poor man to "save face," transforming him from a beggar into a productive worker.

4. *Culture is a simple phenomenon and its customs are frequently self-explanatory:* If a custom's name clearly describes its meaning why search further? Bedbugs, like anything else alive, require feeding. When the owner of a house is away from his bed, the bugs lose a source of sustenance. Hindu Indian culture is concerned with the welfare of all living things, even bedbugs, hence *Khutmul Kilao.*

5. *Culture forms a pattern or configuration around one or more themes:* The argument here would start like number 4, and would continue by showing how *Khutmul Kilao* fits in with (a) the concern for life, (b) the belief in the holiness of life, and (c) the belief in re-incarnation (the bedbug you feed may be your own great-grandfather or may become an important person in some future life). These themes form a pattern which could be called: *Life is eternal and holy; respect it.*

6. *The materialistic position:* Culture serves man, and, therefore, if the rich practice *Khutmul Kilao*, it has immediate benefits for them. The benefits are clear, and are twofold. First, if you leave a bed which houses bedbugs empty, you will return to find lots of very hungry bedbugs ready to feast on you. Better then to keep someone sleeping in your bed at all times. Second, what is it that a rich man has around his house? Obviously, lots of valuable possessions. When he is away from home, he needs someone to guard his valuables, particularly during the night when they are most likely to be stolen. To make sure the guard is around at night, he is told to sleep in the owner's bed.

Two things should be clear from the *Khutmul Kilao* analysis: first that the anthropological proposition "culture explains human behavior" is far more complex than it seems to be. Second, that when six (or sixty) anthropologists use the word "culture," they probably have six (or sixty) slightly different ideas in mind. The current situation can be best understood if looked at historically, and a good starting place is a book written by E. B. Tylor, in 1871—*Primitive Culture*. Tylor's definition of culture makes it include everything that humans learn as members of a society. In his words, "Culture or civilization, taken in its wide ethnographic sense, is that complex whole which includes knowledge, belief, art, morals, law, custom, and any other capabilities and habits acquired by man as a member of society."

Tylor's definition of culture presents us with another puzzle; most anthropologists consider it the "classic" definition, yet most anthropologists no longer accept this definition as "the best." Leslie White, a prominent theorist on culture, finds this situation quite distressing. He writes:

> Thirty years ago most anthropologists in the United States—at least—knew what they meant by culture. And most of them meant, I believe, what Tylor meant in 1871 when he formulated his "classic" definition. . . . But who knows what Mr. X means by culture today? Culture is "learned behavior"; it is not behavior at all but an "abstraction from behavior"; it is "intangible," a "logical construct"; it is a "psychic defense system," a "precipitate of social signals that are correlated with social responses," etc. One anthropologist has gone so far as to question the "reality" of culture.[2]

How do we escape from the intellectual mess depicted by Leslie White? George Peter Murdock provides some valuable clues when he tells us that the various approaches to culture are actually not contradictory, but supplementary; that their adherents err, not in what they assert, but in what they deny; that, in short, a true conception of culture will flow, not from the rejection of divergent points of view, but from their acceptance and reconciliation.[3] Following Murdock's advice we should make attempts to reconcile the various views on culture, to attempt an integration. This, essentially, is the strategy to be assumed in this book: to study various views of culture and finally attempt a reconciliation. I say "finally" because at first I wish to highlight the differences that separate many cultural anthropologists and keep them in intellectual conflict. For a real reconciliation does not sweep differences away quickly; rather it delves into and seeks to comprehend the essential ideas on which such differences are based. In order to understand properly the different views of culture, various cultural theorists will be pitted against each other in an "open to the public" debate. Since the theorists discussed in this work cannot be brought into one room to debate each other, the "debate" will have to be simulated. I will present a position, as an introduction to a paper, the paper itself will then follow (often in a shortened form to highlight its essential arguments), and then I will have some final comments. The concluding comments will attempt to link the position presented in the first paper to that of the next paper, and so on. The student who carefully follows the readings and the editorial comments will slowly discover answers to the following questions:

1. To what extent did a few anthropological "great men" determine the meaning of culture, and thus indirectly determine the goals and methods of cultural anthropology?
2. Is the study of culture part of history, science, neither, or both?
3. In considering man's relationship to culture, what is the direction of

[2] Leslie White, in "Review of Culture: A Critical Review of Concepts and Definitions," by A. L. Kroeber and C. Kluckhohn, *American Anthropologist,* 1954, Vol. 56, pp. 461–486.
[3] George Peter Murdock, "The Science of Culture," *American Anthropologist,* 1932, Vol. 34, pp. 200–215.

determination; does culture determine human action, or does man determine culture?

4. Is culture a phenomenon that tends to change or one that tends to persist? That is, should we consider cultural change to be something strange, requiring special types of explanations, or something "normal"?

5. What is the research value of the concept of culture?

6. What is the pragmatic value of the concept of culture? That is, how can a good understanding of this concept help us solve major world problems: racism, conflicts, wars, population explosion, and ecological rape.

Why should a student waste his time going through the arguments of the professionals? Surely, it is simpler and quicker to provide the neophyte with conclusions rather than arguments; with areas of agreement rather than with heated conflicts. I use the Socratic method to communicate anthropological understanding of culture for various reasons. The modern student is completely disenchanted with the "I know it, you learn it" approach. Their distrust of professionals on all governmental levels is *not* what many of our leaders with pious platitudes would like to think—the contagious ideas of college "bums." With double-talk such as, "We had to kill all the people of P village to save them from the Communists;" with constant military support of dictatorial regimes the world over, which leave large populations starving, while war spending is increased; and with a business-as-usual attitude, while we race toward what will be the war to end all wars, the credulence of most professional politicians is gone.

The young respond ever more loudly with "I do not believe you." This distrust has been generalized to all professionals; indeed towards all the "old ones": those over 30. There is but one way to handle this communication breakdown; complete honesty. In complete honesty, we must admit that *solid* conclusions and brief, well accepted generalizations are hard to find when the problem is, what does "culture" mean? A viable alternative is, therefore, to present arguments about the meaning of culture, and permit the student to listen in and join the discourse. This "look behind the scenes and join us" approach includes an important ingredient missing from many other approaches—excitement. The excitement intrinsic to the learning process is not achieved by pedantic presentation and authoritarian rigidities. It is obtained by showing the intellectual conflicts which exist. This then is a presentation of science as it really is: argumentation (hot and cold) between humans with different views concerning the nature of reality and man's place therein. Our subject matter is complex, our science is yet in its infancy; what meaning can culture have today other than the arguments surrounding it?

1 Tylor's Views of Culture and Evolution

MORRIS E. OPLER

Most discussions of "culture" begin with Tylor's classic definition, go on to show some inadequacies therein, and make suggestions for improvements. Before we improve on Tylor's views of culture, we must really understand them. Such understanding will include a knowledge of his ideas on the stages of cultural evolution, progress, and the relationships between cultural evolution and biological evolution. These and related matters are thoughtfully discussed by a scholar who has spent many years studying and creating cultural theory, Morris E. Opler.

Despite the fact that Tylor introduced the definition of culture that most social scientists accept and repeat today and thus paved the way for a sharp distinction between physical inheritance and cultural acquisitions, he himself was not completely emancipated from notions of the superior cultural attainments and potentialities of "gifted breeds." For instance, in his last general book he still could say:

> ... It cannot be at present made out how far the peculiarities of single ancestors were inherited by their descendants and became stronger by in-breeding; how

SOURCE: Abridged and adapted from "Cause, Process and Dynamics in the Evolutionism of E. B. Tylor" by Morris Opler, *Southwestern Journal of Anthropology*, 1964, Vol 20, pp. 123–143, by permission of the author and the publisher.

> far, when the weak and dull-witted tribes failed in the struggle for land and life, the stronger, braver, and abler tribes survived to leave their types stamped on the nations sprung from them; how far whole migrating tribes underwent bodily alteration through change of climate, food, and habits, so that the peopling of the earth went on together with the growth of fresh races fitted for life in its various regions.[1]

Because of the very inclusiveness of his evolutionary doctrine, this type of thinking, with its benevolence toward colonialism, was extremely difficult to avoid, for evolution to Tylor meant concomitant physical, mental, and cultural changes. I call attention, also, in this quotation, to the hint of strong dependence on Darwinian natural selection as an explanation of the physical differences between groups of men and of the results of the clashes between peoples for "land and life."

Despite these physical differentiations between human groups and the related cultural potentials which he believed accompanied them to some degree, Tylor saw a much greater gap between man and other primates than between one variety of man and any other. He was therefore inclined, within limits, to consider all mankind as one basic unit; and he tended, in the main, to emphasize the similarities of human physiological response and need rather than the differences.

Tylor was sure that man's biological unity was more than matched by his underlying psychic unity. He was impressed by the fact that any human child of sound mind, given the opportunity early enough, could learn any language spoken on earth. It seemed to him that similarities in gesture language the world over and the existence of comparable institutions, symbols, and myths in areas widely separated could not easily be explained unless some fundamental unity of the human mind were postulated. Moreover, Tylor saw in man's natural environment a reasonably uniform background of challenge and opportunity. In spite of climatic differences and variations in resources, life could be maintained in most regions into which man had penetrated. Everywhere there was need for protection against the elements and foes, human and nonhuman. Throughout most of the world nature provided materials to be utilized for shelter, dress, and artifacts, and in nearly all regions sufficient animal and vegetable food existed to support human groups. The world and its people appeared to Tylor to be a vast laboratory in which uniform causes operating in similar settings might be expected to yield comparable results, and he felt confident that he had isolated factors sufficiently stable and objective to serve for a science of culture.

It was almost inevitable that Tylor's science of culture should be actively

---

[1] Edward B. Tylor, *Anthropology: an Introduction to the Study of Man and Civilization,* 1881, p. 5. (Page references taken from the 1904 edition, published by J.A. Hill and Company, New York.)

concerned with issues of history and process. Paleontology, geology, and archeology had raised questions concerning the duration and sequence of epochs of the strata of the earth, of plant forms, of animals (including man), and of culture. It was the triumph of Darwinism in biology to offer a generally acceptable explanation of the manner in which animal life had developed and differentiated over time. Tylor addressed himself to comparable problems with special reference to culture and utilized most of the same postulates which had proved so helpful in charting inorganic and organic evolution.

One of the postulates of biological evolution of his day which Tylor felt applied quite as well to cultural evolution was that developments on the whole occurred slowly over immense spans of time. A related postulate was that the changes were minute rather than large and that their effect was cumulative rather than abrupt. In the third place Tylor held that the changes were of significance; they did not cancel each other out but moved culture in a direction which was, despite minor fluctuations and disruptions, irreversible in principle. In the fourth place, Tylor argued that this movement is prevailingly a progressive one involving more knowledge, greater efficiency, extended control over nature, and higher morality. According to this view, all aspects of culure share in this advance. In successive evolutionary stages family life becomes more secure, thinking more logical, knowledge more detailed, artifacts more efficient, religion more firmly wedded to morality, and abundance more general. Tylor applied this conception of evolutionary progress through stages of Savagery, Barbarism, and Civilization to world culture as such in the first instance; but he also believed that any given group that maintained its existence and vitality for any great length of time could be expected to pass through the defined stages seriatim. He asserted time and again that the ancestors of members of complex civilizations must be presumed to have passed through stages of less exalted practice and must have resembled, at earlier points of history, the barbarians and savages of his day.

One does not have to winnow out the postulates I have named or attempt any elaborate analysis to arrive at them. Tylor's works are generously sprinkled with clear summary statements of his premises. In one place he writes:

> . . . The thesis which I venture to sustain, within limits, is simply this, that the savage state in some measure represents an early condition of mankind, out of which the higher culture has gradually been developed or evolved, by processes still in regular operation as of old, the result showing that, on the whole, progress has far prevailed over relapse. . . . That the tendency of culture has been similar throughout the existence of human society, and that we may fairly judge from its known historic course what its prehistoric course may have been, is a theory clearly entitled to precedence as a fundamental principle of ethnographic research.[2]

[2] Edward B. Tylor, *Primitive Culture: Researches into the Development of Mythology,*

Another well-known and much-quoted passage reads:

> On the whole, it appears that wherever there are found elaborate arts, abstruse knowledge, complex institutions, these are results of gradual development from an earlier, simpler, and ruder state of life. No stage of civilization comes into existence spontaneously, but grows or is developed out of the stage before it.[3]

Even Tylor's articles and shorter pieces, as the following quotations indicate, seldom fail to provide the evolutionary overview within which he worked. I call particular attention, moreover, to the primary position in cultural evolution which Tylor, in the first selection, ascribes to increased knowledge and mental accomplishments.

> The teaching of history, during the three to four thousand years of which contemporary chronicles have been preserved, is that civilisation is gradually developed in the course of ages *by enlargement and increased precision of knowledge,* invention and improvement of arts, and the progression of social and political habits and institutions towards general well-being. . . . Starting from the recorded condition of such barbaric nations [as the older Jews, Greeks, and Germans—M.E.O.], and following the general course of culture into the modern world, all the great processes of *mental* and social development may be seen at work. Falling back or decay also takes place, but only to a limited extent destroys the results of growth in culture. It is thus a matter of actual record, that the ancestors of civilised nations were barbaric tribes, and the inference seems reasonable that the same process of development had gone on during previous ages outside the domain of direct history, so that barbaric culture itself arose out of an earlier and ruder condition of primitive culture, more or less corresponding with the state of modern savage tribes.[4] [my emphasis]

> . . . Even the diagrams of this paper may suffice to show that the institutions of man are as distinctly stratified as the earth on which he lives. They succeed each other in series substantially uniform over the globe, independent of what seem the comparatively superficial differences of race and language, but shaped by similar human nature acting through successively changed conditions in savage, barbaric, and civilised life.[5]

To give the flavor of Tylor's dicta concerning the universal stages and the unilinear progression of human groups through them, we quote two passages from his last general treatise, *Anthropology:*

Philosophy, Religion, Language, Art, and Custom, 2 vols., London: John Murray, 1871, Vol. 1, pp. 32–33.

[3] Tylor (1881), p. 16.

[4] Edward B. Tylor, "Anthropology," *Encyclopedia Britannica,* 9th ed., 1878, Vol. 2, p. 121.

[5] Edward B. Tylor, "On a Method of Investigating the Development of Institutions: Applied to Law of Marriage and Descent," *Journal of the Royal Anthropological Institute,* 1889, Vol. 18, p. 269.

. . . This classification of three great stages of culture is practically convenient, and has the advantage of not describing imaginary states of society, but such as are actually known to exist. So far as the evidence goes, it seems that civilization has actually grown up in the world through these three stages, so that to look at a savage of the Brazilian forests, a barbarous New Zealander or Dahoman, and a civilized European, may be the student's best guide to understanding the progress of civilization, only he must be cautioned that the comparison is but a guide, not a full explanation.

In this way it is reasonably inferred that even in countries now civilized, savage and low barbaric tribes must have once lived.[6]

. . . As the foregoing chapters have proved, savage and barbarous tribes often more or less fairly represent stages of culture through which our own ancestors passed long ago, and their customs and laws often explain to us, in ways we should otherwise have hardly guessed, the sense and reason of our own.[7]

Well before this, in his first general book, Tylor had delineated his unilinear evolutionary theory:

. . . The state of things which is found is not indeed that one race does or knows exactly what another race does or knows, but that similar stages of development recur in different times and places. There is reason to suppose that our ancestors in remote times made fire with a machine much like that of the modern Esquimaux, and at a far later date they used the bow and arrow, as so many savage tribes do still.[8]

Since we shall be mentioning Darwinism, it is interesting that Tylor, in an encyclopaedia article, refers to his formulation as "the natural development-theory of civilisation." It is most unlikely that he would have used such terminology unless he had been markedly and consciously influenced by the formulations of that other notable evolutionist, Charles Darwin.

. . . It has been especially the evidence of prehistoric archaeology which, within the last few years, has given to the natural development-theory of civilisation a predominance hardly disputed on anthropological grounds. . . . The finding of ancient stone implements buried in the ground in almost every habitable district of the world, including the seats of the great ancient civilisations, such as Egypt, Assyria, India, China, Greece, etc., may be adduced to show that the inhabitants of these regions had at some time belonged to the stone age. This argument goes far to prove that the ancestors of all nations, high and low, were once in that uncultured condition as to *knowledge,* arts, and manners generally, which within our experience accompanies the use of stone implements and the want of metals.[9]

---

[6] Tylor (1881), p. 19.

[7] Tylor (1881), p. 313.

[8] Edward B. Tylor, *Researches into the Early History of Mankind and the Development of Civilization,* London: John Murray, 1865, p. 371.

[9] Tylor (1878), p. 121.

[my emphasis. Note once more the precedence of "knowledge" in the arrangement of cultural materials]

Because he had such progressions in mind, we are not surprised to find that Tylor in one place defined civilization as "the general improvement of mankind by higher organization of the individual and of society, to the end of promoting at once man's goodness, power, and happiness."[10] Yet Tylor was not content merely to indicate the direction of change or to stop at a description of the stages through which he believed culture had passed. He sought to provide an identification of the dynamics—the causative agent or agents—which moved culture from Savagery toward Civilization.

Tylor found the key to cultural evolution in what I would call "cultural Darwinism," a process of competition and selection through which was guaranteed the perpetuation of the fittest among artifacts and customs contending for recognition as the most useful and adaptive in their categories. As I hinted above, there is little doubt in my mind that this was a considered utilization of Darwin's "natural selection," for the appearance of a concept so completely parallel to Darwinism in the work of a scholar so well acquainted with Darwinism and so friendly to that doctrine is rather strong presumptive evidence of the influence of Darwin's theories of biological evolution upon this formulation. Tylor's position is unmistakably what is termed social or cultural Darwinism today, and we can find it summarized pointedly in his own words:

> . . . It will be seen again and again, by examining such topics as language, mythology, custom, religion, that savage opinion is in a more or less rudimentary state, while the civilized mind still bears vestiges, neither few nor slight, of a past condition from which savages represent the least, and civilized men the greatest advance. Throughout the whole vast range of the history of human thought and habit, while civilization has to contend not only with survival from lower levels, but also with degeneration within its own borders, it yet proves capable of overcoming both and taking its own course. History within its proper field, and ethnography over a wider range, combine *to show that the institutions which can best hold their own in the world gradually supersede the less fit ones, and that this incessant conflict determines the general resultant course of culture.*[11] [my emphasis]

Tylor's writings, from first to last, are peppered with expressions of cultural Darwinism of this kind. I should like to make this very explicit, for in some branches of neo-evolutionism there is a tendency, as we have seen, to picture Tylor as endorsing a technological, rather than a cultural Darwinian, explanation of cultural development. Perhaps a few additional excerpts will help us appreciate Tylor's position on this matter:

---

[10] Tylor (1871), Vol. 1, p. 27.
[11] Tylor (1871), Vol. 1, pp. 68–69.

. . . But arts which belong to the daily life of the man or the family and cannot be entirely suppressed by violent interference, do not readily disappear *unless superseded by some better contrivance,* or made unnecessary by a change of life and manners.[12] [my emphasis]

. . . On the other hand, though arts which flourish in times of great refinement or luxury, and complex processes which require a combination of skill or labour hard to get together and liable to be easily disarranged, may often degenerate, yet the more homely and useful the art, and the less difficult the conditions for its exercise, the less likely it is to disappear from the world, *unless when superseded by some better device.*[13] [my emphasis]

Tylor does not merely flourish his doctrine of the survival of the culturally fittest in a general way. He applies it to specific aspects and institutions of culture. Of legal and political institutions he declares:

. . . the history of judicial and administrative institutions may be appealed to for illustrations of the modes in which old social formations are reshaped to meet new requirements, new regulations are made, and new officers are constituted to perform the more complex duties of modern society, while from time to time institutions of past ages, which have lost their original purpose, and become obsolete or hurtful, are swept away.[14]

Language, too, according to Tylor, goes through a process of selection and elevation in order to fit it for its modern tasks:

. . . Ethnography reasonably accounts at once for the immense power and the manifest weakness of language as a means of expressing modern educated thought, by treating it as an original product of low culture, gradually adapted by ages of evolution and selection, to answer more or less sufficiently the requirements of modern civilization.[15]

Religion is likewise constantly subjected to tests of purpose and of fitness and can maintain itself only by adaptation and improvement. As Tylor puts it:

. . . Unless a religion can hold its place in the front of science and of morals, it may only gradually, in the course of ages, lose its place in the nation, but all the power of statecraft and all the wealth of the temples will not save it from eventually yielding to a belief that takes in higher knowledge and teaches better life.[16]

. . . Looking at each doctrine by itself and for itself, as in the abstract true or untrue, theologians close their eyes to the instances which history is ever holding up before them, that one phase of a religious belief is the outcome of another,

---

[12] Tylor (1865), p. 185.
[13] Tylor (1865), p. 373.
[14] Tylor (1878), p. 122.
[15] Tylor (1871), Vol. 1, p. 239.
[16] Tylor (1881), p. 291.

> that in all times religion has included within its limits a system of philosophy, expressing its more or less transcendental conceptions in doctrines *which form in any age their fittest representatives,* but which doctrines are liable to modification in the general course of intellectual change, whether the ancient formulas still hold their authority with altered meaning, or are themselves reformed or replaced.[17] [my emphasis]

Nor is science exempt from the evolutionary spiral. Savage conceptions have to give ground and yield to more serviceable knowledge based on careful observation and reasoning:

> . . . In the evolution of science the new knowledge ever starts from the old, whether its results be to improve, to shift, or to supersede it. . . . Beginning with this first stage of the science, there lies before us the whole record of the exacter observation and closer reasoning which have gradually replaced these childlike savage conceptions by the most perfect of physical theories.[18]

It must not be supposed that, because Tylor conceived of evolution as a many-sided process, he considered every facet of it to be of equal importance. Actually he believed that developments in one sphere in particular are of greatest moment, that attainment in this area makes possible a wide range of advance, and that failure here constitutes an effective bar to general evolutionary progress. This was a determinism of sorts, but it was not economic determinism, technological determinism, social determinism, or (if culture be viewed in a holistic sense) cultural determinism. Because it hinges on the importance that Tylor attributes to the evolution of mind and to man's development of a certain level of intellectual achievement as a prelude to his successful control over natural forces and his own destiny, it can perhaps be named "rationalistic determinism."

It is essential to understand the significance and primacy that Tylor attached to the acquisition of rational thought and logic and, in addition, the degree to which he saw in this the gateway to knowledge and to the control of life forces. Historical materialists and technological determinists subordinate mind to matter and see mental life as the consequence or "superstructure" of the mode of production. In Tylor's view, mental life has an evolution of its own and one that has enormous implications for all the rest of culture and for the further progress of culture. I emphasize this because Tylor's attention to progress in the material arts is sometimes taken to mean that he was a materialist and because his references to man's increasing control over nature are interpreted as evidence of his espousal of technological determinism. Yet Tylor's general position is obviously one of philosophical idealism. It is true that he said that man's first need "is to get his daily food." But, as we have seen, he also taught—and this is central to his evolutionism—that man's food quest and all his other

---

[17] Tylor (1871), Vol. 2, pp. 450–451.
[18] Tylor (1878), p. 121.

endeavors remain on a humble, brutish level until certain intellectual goals are reached and obstructing mental confusions are eliminated.

Early in his very first general book Tylor gives some indication of the import he attaches to the evolution of mind when he writes:

> . . . In the following chapter on "Images and Names," an attempt is made to refer a great part of the beliefs and practices included under the general name of magic, to one very simple mental law, as resulting from a condition of mind which we of the more advanced races have almost outgrown, and in doing so have undergone one of the most notable changes which we can trace as having happened to mankind.[19]

Tylor does not leave us in doubt about the nature of the "condition of mind which we of the more advanced races have almost outgrown." It is the tendency of man in early stages of mental evolution to confuse an object with the image of it, the word with what it represents, dream with reality. As Tylor phrases it:

> . . . It needs no very large acquaintance with the life and ways of thought of the savage, to prove that there is to be found all over the world, especially among races at a low mental level, a view as to this matter which is very different from that which a more advanced education has impressed upon us. Man, in a low stage of culture, very commonly believes that between the object and the image of it there is a real connexion, which does not arise from a mere subjective process in the mind of the observer, and that it is accordingly possible to communicate an impression to the original through the copy.[20]

After introducing some examples of the type of thinking among aboriginal peoples which he considers characteristic, Tylor again asserts:

> Such cases as these bring clearly into view the belief in a real connexion existing between an object and its image. By virtue of their resemblance, the two are associated in thought, and being thus brought into connexion in the mind, it comes to be believed that they are also in connexion in the outside world.[21]

Philosophy, religion, language, and thought are all vastly affected by the inability to distinguish between the object and its representation during the earlier stages of mental evolution, an evolution which, according to Tylor, is still proceeding:

> It may be said in concluding the subject of Images and Names that the effect of an inability to separate, so clearly as we do, the external object from the mere thought or idea of it in the mind, shows itself very fully and clearly in the superstitious beliefs and practices of the untaught man, but its results are by no

---

[19] Tylor (1865), p. 3.
[20] Tylor (1865), pp. 119–120.
[21] Tylor (1865), p. 125.

means confined to such matters. It is not too much to say that nothing short of a history of Philosophy and Religion would be required to follow them out. The accumulated experience of so many ages has indeed brought to us far clearer views in these matters than the savage has, though after all we soon come to the point where our knowledge stops, and the opinions which ordinary educated men hold, or at least act upon, as to the relation between ideas and things, may come in time to be superseded by others taken from a higher level. But between our clearness of separation of what is in the mind from what is out of it, and the mental confusion of the lowest savages of our own day, there is a vast interval. . . . Lower down in the history of culture, the word and the idea are found sticking together with a tenacity very different from their weak adhesion in our minds, and there is to be seen a tendency to grasp at the word as though it were the object it stands for, and to hold that to be able to speak of a thing gives a sort of possession of it, in a way that we can scarcely realize.[22]

Whatever their appearance and physical characteristics, avers Tylor, those who have not advanced sufficiently far along the path of mental evolution are bound to be childish and ineffective:

The trite comparison of savages to "grown-up children," is in the main a sound one, though not to be carried out too strictly. In the uncivilized American or Polynesian, the strength of body and force of character of a grown man are combined with a mental development in many respects not beyond that of a young child of a civilized race. It has been already noticed how naturally children can appreciate and understand such direct expressions of thought as the gesture-language and picture-writing. In like manner, the use of dolls or images as an assistance to the operations of the mind, is familiar to all children, though among those who grow up under the influences of civilized society, it is mostly superseded and forgotten in after life. Few educated Europeans ever thoroughly realize the fact, that they have once passed through a condition of mind from which races at a lower state of civilization never fully emerge; but this is certainly the case, and the European child playing with its doll, furnishes the key to several of the mental phenomena which distinguish the more highly cultivated races of mankind from those lower in the scale.[23]

Tylor's conviction that a certain level of mental evolution has to be attained by a human group before it can enter creatively into civilization or fully appreciate its benefits leads him to a certain smugness and paternalism concerning native peoples. In one place he writes:

In the comparison of man with other animals the standard should naturally be the lowest man, or savage. But the savage is possessed of human reason and speech, while his brain-power, though it has not of itself raised him to civili-

---

[22] Tylor (1865), pp. 150–151.
[23] Tylor (1865), p. 108.

zation, enables him to receive more or less of the education which transforms him into a civilized man.[24]

In fact Tylor tends to take a rather negative view of the fruits of contact when a marked discrepancy in the evolutionary position of the groups in question exists:

> . . . It is a general rule that original and independent progress is not found among a people of low civilization in presence of a higher race. It is natural enough that this should be the case, and it does not in the least affect the question whether the lower race was stationary or progressing before the arrival of the more cultivated foreigners. Even when the contact has been but slight and temporary, it either becomes doubtful whether progress made soon afterwards is original, or certain that it is not so.[25]

The pre-eminence of mind and its stimulus value for the development of all other aspects of culture are fundamental premises of Tylor, to which he returns again and again and from which he never strays very far. Of man's "brain-organisation" and his ability to use symbols he says: "Man's power of using a word, or even a gesture, as the symbol of a thought and the means of conversing about it, is one of the points where we most plainly see him parting company with all lower species, *and starting on his career of conquest through higher intellectual regions*."[26] In another place he declares: "Man's power of accommodating himself to the world he lives in, and even of controlling it, *is largely due to his faculty of gaining new knowledge*."[27] "History," he tells us, "is an agent powerful and becoming more powerful, in shaping men's minds, and *through their minds their actions in the world* . . . ."[28] The key to man's achievements, as Tylor saw it, lay in his "power of coordinating the impression of his senses, which enables him to understand the world he lives in, and *by understanding* to use, resist, and even in a measure rule it."[29] [Emphases in quotations in this paragraph are mine]

Moreover, as Tylor viewed it, science and higher developments of culture could not be attained until "one of the most pernicious delusions that ever vexed mankind, the belief in Magic," was surmounted by advanced branches of mankind in the course of mental development. Tylor's account of this chapter of mental evolution is as follows:

> . . . Looking at Occult Science from this ethnographic point of view, I shall instance some of its branches as illustrating the course of intellectual culture.

[24] Tylor (1881), p. 42.
[25] Tylor (1865), p. 162. See also (1878), p. 121.
[26] Tylor (1881), p. 42.
[27] Tylor (1881), p. 40.
[28] Tylor (1871), Vol. 2, p. 447.
[29] Tylor (1878), p. 109.

> Its place in history is briefly this. It belongs in its main principle to the lowest known stages of civilization, and the lower races, who have not partaken largely of the education of the world, still maintain it in vigour. From this level it may be traced upward, much of the savage art holding its place substantially unchanged, and many new practices being in course of time developed, while both the older and newer developments have lasted on more or less among modern cultured nations. But during the ages in which progressive races have been learning to submit their opinions to closer and closer experimental tests, occult science has been breaking down into the condition of a survival, in which state we mostly find it among ourselves.[30]

In several other passages Tylor describes the evolution of mind from magical associations at one extreme to reasoning, logic, observation, and experiment at the other:

> The student who wishes to compare the mental habits of rude and ancient peoples with our own, may look into a subject which has now fallen into contempt from its practical uselessness, but which is most instructive in showing how the unscientific mind works. This is magic. In the earlier days of knowledge men relied far more than we moderns do on reasoning by analogy or mere association of ideas.[31]

In order to demonstrate how magic has been arrested and superseded by rational thought, Tylor traces the history of science. As he pictures it, in the various branches of science "progress has been made in age after age by facts being more fully observed and more carefully reasoned on." Reasoning or logic is now itself a science but "began as an art which man practiced without stopping to ask himself why or how." Man thought and talked for untold ages "before it occurred to him to lay down rules how to argue." Reasoning reached a scientific stage when the Greek philosophers, and especially Aristotle, brought argument "into a regular system by the method of syllogisms." By applying exact reasoning to mathematics the Greeks "brought on a general advance in knowledge." The "so-called scholastic period" was a setback, but the "great movement of modern philosophy with which the name of Bacon is associated as a chief expounder, brought men back to the sound old method of working experience and thought together, only now the experience was more carefully sought and observed, and thought arranged it more systematically." Tylor's survey ends on this optimistic, cultural Darwinian note: "Thus man has but to go on observing and thinking, secure that in time his errors will fall away, while the truth he attains to will abide and grow."[32]

In Tylor's opinion, it is not that the savage or barbarian does not reason

---

[30] Tylor (1871), Vol. 1, pp. 112–113.
[31] Tylor (1881), p. 264.
[32] Tylor (1881), pp. 263–267.

sensibly about some things but rather that in "matters beyond his limited knowledge, he contents himself with working on resemblances or analogies of thought, which thus become the foundation of magic."[33] When mental evolution has cleared the way for a systematic application of rules of reason to all observed phenomena, the opportunity is at hand for striking and progressive changes, which Tylor envisages in these words:

> There have been indeed few more important movements in the course of the history of mankind, than this change of opinion as to the nature and relations of what is in the mind and what is out of it. To say nothing of its vast effects upon Ethics and Religion, the whole course of Science, and of Art, of which Science is a principal element, has been deeply influenced by this mental change. Man's views of the difference between imagination and reality, of the nature of cause and effect, of the connexion between himself and the external world, and of the parts of the external world among themselves, have been entirely altered by it.[34]

As one would expect from his preoccupation with rationalism and with the growth and transformation of mind, Tylor was especially impressed by arts and practices which bore upon the accumulation and transformation of knowledge. The written word seemed to him to be such a factor; and whereas he held that agriculture ushers in the stage of Barbarism, it is writing by which he identifies the onset of Civilization, for in his eyes it is this discovery, as we have already had occasion to note, which best preserves the information wrung painfully from experience.[35] And in still another place he refers to the same subject in these words:

> In the growth of systematic civilisation, the art of writing has had an influence so intense, that of all tests to distinguish the barbaric from the civilised state, none is so generally affective as this, whether they have but the failing link with the past which mere memory furnishes, or can have recourse to written records of past history and written constitution of present order.[36]

There is another dimension of Tylor's thinking to which attention should be called, namely, his applied interests. Since he considered civilized man to be much more rational than the savage or the barbarian, Tylor advised that he strive to be even more completely so. He urged his fellow men to assess their opinions, and their customs and to cast out or to reform any that were found to be shoddy and burdensome survivals of a past stage of culture. No area of culture, not even religion, should be exempt from this rational scrutiny:

---

[33] Tylor (1881), p. 265.
[34] Tylor (1865), pp. 378–379.
[35] Tylor (1881), p. 19.
[36] Tylor (1878), p. 123.

> . . . Should the doctrine or rite in question appear to have been transmitted from an earlier to a later stage of religious thought, then it should be tested, like any other point of culture, as to its place in development. The question has to be raised, to which of these three categories it belongs;—is it a product of the earlier theology, yet sound enough to maintain a rightful place in the later;—is it derived from a cruder original, yet so modified as to become a proper representative of more advanced views?—is it a survival from a lower stage of thought, imposing on the credit of the higher by virtue not of inherent truth but of ancestral belief? These are queries the very asking of which starts trains of thought which candid minds should be encouraged to pursue, leading as they do toward the attainment of such measure of truth as the intellectual condition of our age fits us to assimilate.[37]

Obviously, anthropology, with its knowledge of the past and its conception of the totality and integration of each stage of culture, should take a leading role in this cultural housecleaning. It is small wonder that Tylor was able to speak of anthropology as "essentially a reformer's science" and as a discipline "active at once in aiding progress and in removing hindrance."[38]

In the distant past, according to Tylor, knowledge was unconsciously acquired, but the garnering, organization, and interpretation of facts has become a science in itself, entered upon deliberately and boldly. Use that knowledge in the interests of progress, and man becomes the architect of his future. It is on this benign, hopeful, and practical note that Tylor ended the last of his general studies:

> . . . Acquainted with events and their consequences far and wide over the world, we are able to direct our own course with more confidence toward improvement. In a word, mankind is passing from the age of unconscious to that of conscious progress. Readers who have come thus far need not be told in many words of what the facts must have already brought to their minds—that the study of man and civilisation is not only a matter of scientific interest, but at once passes into the practical business of life. We have in it the means of understanding our own lives and our place in the world, vaguely and imperfectly it is true, but at any rate more clearly than any former generation. The knowledge of man's course of life, from the remote past to the present, will not only help us to forecast the future, but may guide us in our duty of leaving the world better than we found it.[39]

We can say, in summary, that although Tylor occasionally applied the principles of biological evolutionism to human culture and wrote of struggles be-

---

[37] Tylor (1871), Vol. 2, pp. 451–452.
[38] Tylor (1871), Vol. 2, p. 453. See also Robert H. Lowie, *The History of Ethnological Theory,* New York: Farrar and Rinehart, 1937, p. 83.
[39] Tylor (1881), p. 342.

tween physically distinctive types of man for land and survival, this was not a marked feature of his thinking. Sometimes he seems to accept a doctrine of physical or racial determinants of cultural development by associating superior psychological and intellectual qualities with certain physical strains; yet he did not carry this line of reasoning very far or depend upon it to any great extent in tracing the course of cultural evolution. Though he made room in his theoretical system for minor physical differences in human groups and their possible consequences, in the main he considered mankind one basic organic unit. Even more firm was his belief in the psychic unity of all mankind, in the sense of a common substratum of mind or intelligence from which higher developments could proceed. He set himself resolutely against doctrines of degeneration and sudden catastrophe in human affairs and taught that over an immense period of time, by minute, cumulative additions and changes, world culture has developed in a progressive manner through universal stages of Savagery, Barbarism, and Civilization. Though a few individual peoples may not move with the tide, the mainstream of culture is one-directional and irreversible. In form the evolution is from simple to complex, and in function it is from less efficiency and lower morality to greater scientific and technological control and more advanced ethical precepts. Although individual peoples and nations are found at different points in the evolutionary sequence of stages, they are advancing, if they advance at all, along the same cultural highway; the progression is unilinear.

The driving force or causative agent which Tylor uses to explain the evolutionary spiral is what he terms the "natural-development theory of culture." Upon examination we find it to be a transfer of Darwin's biological natural selection to the cultural realm, a doctrine of competition for survival among cultural traits and institutions, ending in the retention and continuance of the most appropriate and useful. By this incessant struggle and selection, the cultural engine inches forward. All aspects of culture—intellectual, material, and ethical—share in the hard-won advances, and so a certain unity and internal fitness characterizes each stage. But advance along one particular front has special significance for all the rest of culture; it determines the pace at which progress will take place and, indeed, whether progress is possible at all. This is the evolution of mind, the development of rational thought. Upon rationalistic determinism or progress in this sphere depends a view of man and nature which sets the stage for the correct formulation of problems and attempts at their solution. Therefore, control, science, invention and discovery, and all material benefits are contingent upon the evolution of the mind and the impetus it gives to the rest of culture. Many scholars, Lowie and Stocking among them, have noted Tylor's stress on rationalism and the attention he gives to magic and impediments to clear reasoning. But these scholars have not related Tylor's rationalism to the dynamics of his evolutionism and to his cutural Darwinism. And this is the core of Tylor's theoretical work. Once this relationship is established, Tylor's emphasis on magic, animism, logic, language, and survivals falls into place.

The central place of the evolution of the mind in Tylor's theory stamps him as a philosophical idealist and invalidates any attempt to select passages to prove him a materialist. Tylor gave ample attention to material culture not because he was a philosophical materialist but because his conception of culture was many-sided and complete. He never granted to material factors the determinative qualities that he saw in the evolution of mind. He was confident of future material abundance because he believed that a rational being who had achieved logical thinking and the ordered knowledge and control which stemmed from it would inevitably use his information and the related skills in his own best economic interests. If he were here today, he would doubtless be saddened by the "survivals" and the magical thinking that still beset us.

2 The Anthropology of Boas

MURRAY WAX

Tylor, the armchair theoretician of cultural theory, believed in cultural evolution depicted by a slow, cumulative, and irreversible progress. Franz Boas, who masterminded the development of cultural anthropology in America, believed in empirical research. Boas' contribution to the development of cultural theory has been hotly debated by many anthropologists. The following paper presents the critical views of Murray Wax, a scholar who has had the courage to look at Boas as a fellow scientist, and not as a legend.

This paper will examine the dominant convictions of Franz Boas on a variety of subjects. We will show that whatever their individual merits, they formed, when linked together, a chain that constricted creative research in cultural anthropology.

SOURCE: Abridged and adapted from "The Limitations of Boas' Anthropology" by Murray Wax. Reproduced by permission of the author and the American Anthropological Association from *American Anthropologist,* Vol. 58, No. 1, February 1956, pp. 63–74.

The Aims of Inquiry

The form of a typical ethnographical study by Franz Boas was as follows: A general hypothesis about culture or about culture processes had been advanced by some scholar. Boas would then collect a considerable mass of data of the most objective kind—material objects or texts. He would describe these succinctly and with little or no interpretation. The data, so presented, would speak for themselves; they were an exception to the general hypothesis and it was therefore refuted. Then Boas would present his own point of view; the situation was a complex one; the refuted hypothesis had ignored the complexities; a full analysis, if humanly possible, would reveal many factors in operation.

The logic of his argument was simple and potent. The hypothesis advanced could be framed in the form, "All A is B." Boas would present an entity that was clearly an A yet equally clearly not a B. Accordingly, the hypothesis was false.

This logic was and is frequently utilized by natural scientists, but the aim there is usually not to discredit completely but to test the limits, to discover the region where the hypothesis applies and that where it fails. Then the scientist attempts to reformulate the hypothesis so that in its revised form it fits both regions. But Boas was not interested in the partial truth that might be implicit in the refuted generalization; as a generalization it was wholly false and should no longer receive any respect whatsoever from the scientist. He would, therefore, attack it over and over again in his publications and in his classes.

At Columbia Boas preached empiricism to his students almost as a crusade. Science was a holy vocation, and the young men who entered it would be subjected to many temptations: Speculation, Theory, (traditional) Philosophy. The intelligence of the scientist would desire to generalize on the basis of inadequate data or would be attracted by the seductive phrases of an armchair theorist. He must train himself to resist such impulses and not to stray from the path of strictest empiricism. Boas' preaching, reinforced by his tremendous abilities and his sincere dedication to science, converted his students and decisively influenced the character of American anthropology. Even when his students, as mature scholars, could perceive that Boas' empiricism was so extreme as to be hurtful to the progress of the discipline, they still defended their teacher in emotionally and morally toned words. For example, Lowie wrote of his teacher Boas:

> His critics suggest an incapacity for synthesis; his intimates know that he forms opinions on all anthropological questions but refrains from utterance when the evidence seems indecisive. That even the provisional synthesis of this

independent and erudite thinker would shed floods of light is unquestionable; it is not, however, Boas' method of procedure.

> The craver of systems cannot understand a scientist's progress from problem to problem without at once generalizing a particular solution achieved. . . . (His) attitude is the scientist's as opposed to the philosopher's.[1]

In replying publicly to the foreign scholars whose works he had so often attacked and who had responded with criticism of his anti-theoretical position, Boas emphasized in 1920 a more positive attitude toward "ultimate problems."

> It may seem to the distant observer that American students are engaged in a mass of detailed investigations without much bearing upon the solution of the ultimate problems of a philosophic history of human civilization. I think this interpretation of the American attitude would be unjust because the ultimate questions are as near to our hearts as they are to those of other scholars, only we do not hope to be able to solve an intricate historical problem by formula.[2]

Feeling, perhaps, that more than this verbal statement was necessary, he listed some of the "general conclusions" deriving from the American studies. Among them we note the following (the alphabetical labelling is my own):

> (a) . . . a surplus of food supply is liable to bring about an increase of population and an increase of leisure, which gives opportunity for occupations that are not absolutely necessary for the needs of everyday life. In turn the increase of population and of leisure, which may be applied to new inventions, gives rise to a greater food supply and to a further increase in the amount of leisure so that a cumulative effect results.[3]
>
> (b) . . . the sequence of industrial inventions in the Old World and in America, which I consider as independent. A period of food gathering and of the use of stone was followed by the invention of agriculture, of pottery, and finally of the use of metals. Obviously, this order is based on the increased amount of time given by mankind to the use of natural products, of tools and utensils, and to the variations that developed with it. Although in this case parallelism seems to exist on the two continents, it would be futile to follow out the order in detail.[4]
>
> (c) A similar consideration may be made in regard to the development of rationalism. It seems to be one of the fundamental characteristics of the development of mankind that activities which have developed unconsciously are gradually made the subject of reasoning. We may observe this process everywhere.[5]

The extracts demonstrate that Boas could not only refute significant hypothe-

[1] Robert H. Lowie, *The History of Ethnological Theory*, New York: Farrar and Rinehart, 1937, pp. 151–152.
[2] Franz Boas, *Race, Language and Culture*, New York: Macmillan, 1940, pp. 283–284.
[3] Boas (1940), p. 285.
[4] Boas (1940), p. 287.
[5] Boas (1940), p. 288.

ses, he could advance them. Taken together and integrated, they constitute a good part of the basis for a neo-evolutionary or developmental schema in the style of V. Gordon Childe or of Robert Redfield. But Boas was unwilling to direct his own and his students' attention toward such a positive goal. As a matter of fact, he had no real warrant for describing (a) and (c) as general conclusions deriving from the American studies; the American students made no systematic studies of those phenomena. Boas preferred to attack the simple-minded, rigid, and ethnocentric evolutionary schemes to framing accurate, flexible, and humanistic ones.

How, then, shall we classify and understand the labors of Boas in cultural anthropology? In 1935 Kroeber proposed an ideal typical dichotomy between *history* and *science*, which he evidently modeled after the German distinction between *Geisterwissenschaft* and *Naturwissenschaft*. In these terms he classified Boas as a scientist. Is this correct?

Both history and science seek the truth, but their typical methods of investigation are different and their typical end-products are different. The methods we shall discuss in a later section; here we confine ourselves to end-products. Science seeks the general statement, the universal proposition true of every situation yet not truly descriptive of any single situation. History seeks to understand the particular events of a past with their human ("historical") significances, and to convey this understanding to others. Thus conceived, science is epitomized by a treatise in mathematical physics; history (to use Kroeber's epitome) by Burckhardt's *The Renaissance*. On the one hand, the highest abstraction and the greatest universality; on the other hand, the depiction of a particular epoch with its particular, and yet general, human significances and values.

Many disciplines have, limitedly, the goals of both history and science. Thus, astronomy seeks to generalize about the behavior of galactic systems and also to describe the history of our solar system. Cultural anthropology seeks to generalize about human culture and society and also to describe particular human groups and their human significances. In such cases, the differently directed activities within the discipline may fruitfully assist each other, and a joint store of particular facts, generalizations about process, and insightful interpretations and understandings come to be accepted as valid. In its happier intervals, cultural anthropology has this appearance.

In terms of his history/science dichotomy Kroeber asserted that Boas was not an historian. Boas agreed that he did not write history.

By default, then, Boas appeared as a scientist. Yet, Boas not only did not prepare scientific systems, he did not seek generalizations. As we have observed, he gave verbal allegiance to the pursuit of generalizations, but in fact his interest in them was confined to demonstrating their invalidity. At times, he contended that he was interested in a limited type of generalization about cultural processes, and it was on this basis, apparently, that Kroeber labelled him a scientist. But, again, no systematic pursuit of cultural processes is evident in his research; rather, he seemed to use the term "process" as an *ad hoc* slogan in his attack upon the rash proposers of scientific laws.

Thus, the history/science dichotomy seems to fail to classify Boas. This is not surprising, since the two concepts are not logical contradictories but only contraries; they are not mutually inclusive of the field. A moment's reflection reminds us that there are many researchers although few of the stature of Boas, who are neither historians nor scientists as Kroeber and we have defined them.

If, now, we were to establish a typology of investigators on the basis jointly of Kroeber's and Boas' analyses, we would have three archetypes: scientist, historian, and (let us call him) phenomenalist. The chief function of the last would be, *à la* Boas, to concentrate on individual phenomena and to criticize scientists and historians for careless and rash generalizations.

As an anthropologist Boas was intensely loyal to the individual phenomenon, whether by temperament (affective desires) or by epistemological conviction (radical empiricism), and this devotion gave his studies their scientific rigor. Boas is difficult to type, hence it will be useful to postpone judgment until we have discussed other aspects of Boas' work—his conception of cultural anthropology and his methods.

The Individual and Culture

If one knew of Franz Boas only that he had been trained in the natural sciences, one might have expected his to be a generalizing, abstracting method like that of Durkheim, in which society is considered a reality *sui generis* and where purely social, superindividual laws are sought. But only occasionally, and especially in opposition to racist and environmental doctrines, did Boas stress the autonomy of culture and the passivity of the individual:

> The influence of an individual upon culture depends not only upon his strength but also upon the readiness of society to accept changes. During the unstable conditions of cultural life produced by contact between European and primitive civilizations many native prophets have arisen who have with more or less success modified the religious beliefs of the people. Their revelations, however, were reflexes of the mixed culture. The new ideas created in society are not free, but are determined by the culture in which they arise. The artist is hemmed in by the peculiar style of the art and the techniques of his environment; the religious mind by current belief; the political leader by established political forms.[6]

Strikingly enough, in the revised edition of the same work (1932), this

[6] Franz Boas, *Anthropology and Modern Life*, New York: W. W. Norton, 1928, p. 162.

passage was omitted, and instead there were several pages of examples of cultural changes and the roles played by individuals in the changes.

It fitted with his adherence to radical empiricism that Boas emphasized the reality of the individual and warned against reifying culture. Thus, in both the first and revised editions of *Anthropology and Modern Life* he declared:

> It seems hardly necessary to consider culture a mystic entity that exists outside the society of its individual carriers, and that moves by its own force. The life of a society is carried on by individuals who act singly and jointly under the stress of the tradition in which they have grown up and surrounded by the products of their own activities and those of their forebears. . . .
>
> The forces that bring about the changes are active in the individuals composing the social groups, not in the abstract culture.[7]

Even in his earliest essays on anthropological theory, Boas was oriented social-psychologically. In 1888, when he was still a believer in evolutionary theory, he thought of ethnology as discovering the laws of folk psychology, the laws governing the development of the human mind. And this approach remained when he rejected evolutionary theory. Benedict is in agreement:

> It has never been sufficiently realized how consistently throughout his life Boas defined the task of ethnology as "the study of man's mental life," "fundamental psychic attitudes of cultural groups," "man's subjective worlds."[8]

Boas' theoretical orientation to cultural anthropology was quite clearly social-psychological rather than sociological or culture-historical.

The same emphasis upon the individual appeared in Boas' political liberalism. His book, *Anthropology and Modern Life,* was written "to show that some of the most firmly rooted opinions of our times appear from a wider point of view as prejudices,"[9] and the opinions he singled out all bore the stamp of illiberalism. Six of the nine chapters are largely criticisms of the various forms of belief in the overwhelming social importance of heredity. They attacked the belief in the superiority of one race over others; the belief that race and nationality are one; the belief in eugenics; and the belief in the inheritance of criminal traits. In opposition to the belief in the social importance of heredity, Boas urged the importance of social environment, culture. But, cultures could be better or worse, confining to the individual or liberating him. He advocated such (early twentieth-century) liberal notions as: the desirability and inevitability of a world federation of nations; the desirability of individual freedom and the importance of designing education so that it liberates the mind of the child

[7] Boas (1928), pp. 235–236. See also Boas (1928), rev. ed., New York: W. W. Norton, 1932, pp. 245–246.

[8] Ruth Benedict, "Franz Boas as an Ethnologist," *American Anthropologist*, 1943, Vol. 45, p. 31.

[9] Boas (1932), p. 5.

rather than confines it; the lack of tradition and therefore greater wisdom of the urban masses as against the classes; and the unnecessary harshness of contemporary sexual conventions.

Freedom of the individual is the central theme running throughout the book, and it places Boas' liberalism in the tradition of John Stuart Mill. From this perspective we can better appreciate the attacks in this book, and elsewhere, upon certain kinds of anthropological generalizations. Racist theories, evolutionary theories, geographical, economic, or cultural determinisms, all these minimize the importance, power, and value of the individual. In opposition, Boas felt that the individual was the actor in the adventure of mankind and that, accordingly, each individual should be judged by his actions, not by his nonvoluntary membership in some group or placement in some physical or historical situation.

Thus, when Boas studied say, North American art, he focused on the individual craftsman, and how he, or she, worked within the givens of tradition, tools, and raw material. For example:

> I have noticed that here, where in a fine imbricated technique color bands are produced, the basket weavers tend to use with great regularity certain groupings of the number of stitches belonging to each color, although, owing to the irregularity of the size of the stitches, these modifications can hardly be observed. If these facts have a wider application, it would seem that on the whole the pleasure given by much of the decorative work of primitive people must not be looked for in the beauty of the finished product, but rather in the enjoyment which the maker feels at his own cleverness in playing with the technical elements he is using.[10]

From this focus on the social psychology of the individual craftsman Boas was able to attack sociological generalizations such as the assertion that in the decorative arts conventional designs develop from the degeneration of representational designs.

Clearly, the power of a social psychological approach, like that of Boas, depends directly upon the adequacy of the social psychology that is employed and elaborated in the course of research. If the anthropologist wishes to study "man's subjective worlds," or "fundamental psychic attitudes of cultural groups," he must have both excellent data and a rich psychological conceptual scheme or theory for handling and interpreting the data. Boas had access to the data. But the tragic flaw in his approach to cultural anthropology was that he operated with a simpleminded, mechanical psychology.

The influence of that psychology was expressed in many areas of his work, but one of the few places where he explicitly sketched it was in the chapter on "Stability of Culture" in *Anthropology and Modern Life:* Men act largely

---

[10] Boas (1940), p. 592.

according to habit. The earlier in life the habit is inculcated, the more difficult it is to alter, the more automatic is its action, and the stronger are the emotions associated with it. Habit is fundamentally activity, not thought; and thought about habitual activity is usually rationalization.

This psychology was not the product of the research of Boas or of his students; it was never tested explicitly in the field or elaborated in consequence. It was one of the psychologies popular in the first quarter of this century, but it was far from being the best social psychology he might have selected. The great contribution of the American interactionalist psychologists, Charles H. Cooley and George H. Mead, the conception of human interaction as mediated by symbols and as internalized in the form of the *self*, had escaped him. He was aware of psychoanalysis and accepted the notion that the first few years of life are critical for personality formation, but otherwise he was skeptical of its findings and methods. With such an impoverished view of human nature and human interaction as schematized by his habit psychology, Boas was unable to cope with [complex] social phenomena such as the Inquisition.[11]

Since, on the whole, he was dealing with simpler situations than that, and since he was so reluctant to advance a hypothesis publicly, Boas made no glaring errors in his handlings of ethnological materials. But, equally, he contributed no dazzling insights.

The Methods of Inquiry

Kroeber typified history and science as seeking contrary goals, and in the first section of this paper we followed his lead. We saw history as seeking to understand the events of a past with their human significance and to convey this understanding to others; science as seeking to describe abstractly and with economy and elegance the processes of any situation of a certain class. But history and science differ not only in goals, they differ typically also in *methods*.

Since science seeks to generalize about the members of an indefinitely large class, its method emphasizes the notion of replicability. In theory, a scientist can duplicate the manipulations and observations of any other scientist in his discipline and, allowing for the vagaries of chance, emerge with identical findings. If two sets of observations are not in agreement, then the two observers were not really studying events belonging to the same class. Thus, it is a typical problem of science to discover, by criticism of observational techniques, by more refined observation, and by theoretical analysis, why the observations of a class of apparently identical events are at variance with each other.

The historian wishes to understand particular events of human significance (and then to convey this understanding to his audience). This means that his

[11] Boas (1932), pp. 142–143.

is primarily a task of insightful interpretation of whatever evidence has come to him from the particular past. Since it is a past, and since the events were not conceived of as especially significant until the passage of a long period of time, the evidence desired is usually meager, and the historian must develop his ability to wring the last drop of information from the documents at his disposal. He relies upon his knowledge of human nature generally and of the character of the particular people being studied to aid him in his interpretation. Historians frequently disagree as to the meanings of particular facts and, accordingly, as to the character of the events that occurred. A disagreement between historians is often attributed to the differences in their basic conceptions of man and society, and such disagreements are not simply resolvable by appeals to the facts.

While much of the data of cultural anthropology is essentially historical in character, the methods by which they are and can be handled are both scientific and historical. A study of the diffusion of, say, pottery styles leans toward the scientific pole. Here the ethnographer is dealing with the objects which can be arranged into large classes and considered within each class as substantially identical. The proportions and design of any one pot in a class are the same as those of any other. In contrast, a study of the function and emotional meaning of poetry in the traditional culture based on interviews with a few aged women is essentially historical. The ethnographer, ideally, weighs each informant's testimony against her character, the interview situation, and the testimony of others.

Boas thought of his task in scientific terms even when it was clearly historical. For example: he realized the value of collecting as much information as possible from living informants about the vanished or vanishing customs of American Indian groups. Furthermore, as a scientist, he realized that the best data were those which were independent of the observer; this meant exact texts in the language of the native. But, as Radin pointed out, he did not realize that the value of these texts was greatly reduced by the lack of historical method, the lack of background data as to who was the informant, what sort of individual he was, what was the nature of the interview situation, etc.[12] Boas the scientist presented his readers with hundreds of pages of texts—the product of the most intensive labor—without the commentary that would have increased their (historical) value and reliability manyfold. Moreover, he did not nor did he encourage his students to draw the texts and field observations together into a carefully wrought description of the way of life of a people.

If we now link these various convictions of Boas together, we will find that they form a chain of conditions so divergent and opposing and so rigid that they make systematic, positive research in cultural anthropology all but impos-

---

[12] Paul Radin, *The Method and Theory of Ethnology*, New York: McGraw-Hill, 1933.

sible. Boas was a scientist in method and temper but not in his goals. He was interested in the individual phenomenon and the individual person, but he rejected historical method, which is adapted to such studies (e.g., the open interview, the biography), in favor of scientific method, and he attempted to work with an impoverished, "scientific" social psychology. His radical empiricism and scientific bent made him comfortable with only the "hardest" of data: skeletal proportions, material objects, texts. But his political liberalism was antagonistic to positive hereditary findings, and he was always seeking to demonstrate that differences apparently due to heredity had actually other causes. Pure distribution studies of designs and of folktales smacked of the superorganic and of reifying cultural processes; he insisted that we needed to find the individuals active behind the cultural process and the reasons for their behavior. Style and folktales are evidences about man's subjective worlds and the life of the individual but only when interpreted with the aid of historical insight and a rich social psychology. Thus, his divergent, conflicting, iron convictions added up to a set of limiting preconditions for ethnological work that might have broken the spirit of a lesser man.

We can illustrate by a consideration of one of the few works in which his positive, rather than critical, efforts are predominant, *Primitive Art.*[13] Boas' drive for knowledge of man's subjective worlds led him to investigate the decorative aspects of primitive art. His habit psychology and his refusal to make insightful interpretations handicapped him severely, but he doubtless feared that better vehicles would prove less governable and would propel him willy-nilly into the morass of aesthetic criticism or the quicksands of culture history.

Let us trace the principal argument of the chapter on "Style": Boas began by considering the influence of traditional or habitual motor habits on the design of various artifacts. Weapons, household furniture, clothes, and tools are designed to consonance with the habitual acts of which they are an element. When an act has been habitual since childhood, there is an emotional attachment to it and resistance to change; so, too, there will be an emotional attachment to the design of the attachment customarily utilized, even when the design of the artifact is not critical to the execution of the action. When the raw material from which the artifact has been made is changed, there will be an attempt to impose the old designs upon the new material. Boas then recalled an argument of the preceding chapters; as a craftsman works upon an object, he modifies or produces a surface; if he is a highly skilled virtuoso, the surface produced is so regular as to be aesthetically pleasing. Moreover, the virtuoso will often play with his material, thus producing an intricate pattern. Such patterns may then, later, be transferred to a new medium, e.g. from cloth to pottery.

Here the principal argument of the chapter ended. Boas admitted that he had

---

[13] Franz Boas, *Primitive Art,* Oslo: Instituttet for Sammenlignende Kulturforskning, 1927.

not explained the variation from group to group, technical conditions being otherwise similar. But, in his usual fashion, he concluded that the subject was complex, and that it was doubtful whether all the factors would be fully elucidated.

We note how this analysis mirrored his social psychology in its emphasis upon ingrained habit, upon the dominance of motor habits over intellectual processes, and upon the emotional attachment to tradition. Boas' approach was adequate, perhaps, to a discussion of the craftsman who amuses himself with his own dexterity, but it fails completely in interpreting styles or genuine artistry. The artist, in contrast to Boas' craftsman, is aware of himself and of an audience for his creation. He looks at his work from the point of view of his audience, and he directs his virtuosity toward the creation of forms that, he anticipates, will have certain kinds of impact upon the audience. (Of course, many craftsmen will possess artistic self-consciousness although in weaker degree than the true artist.) But Boas could not perceive or discuss this essential ingredient of art; in his psychology the individual is dominated by habit; the individual has no self and cannot interact with himself in order to so control his actions as to produce forms whose impact he can anticipate.

Since he would not interpret historically, with insight, Boas could not cope with the richness of emotional and intellectual meanings in a cultural style. Even in the case of the Indians of the Northwest coast, whom he had studied for so many years, he could not discuss the significances, values, meanings, and functions of their dramatic carvings. Viewed objectively, as the product of great labor by a distinguished anthropologist, *Primitive Art* was a failure. But, when we understand the self-imposed restraints, it was a triumph that he produced anything at all on the subject.

Given these restraints, Boas' *forte* was criticism. He was a master at exposing the generalization that was false to the phenomena, or that explained away a serious problem by reifying culture, or that was constructed in violation of the canons of scientific method. Insofar as his targets were would-be scientists relying upon inadequate data and slipshod methods, his criticism was healthful for the growing discipline. But cultural anthropology also required positive leadership, and here Boas failed.

3 The Anthropology of Sapir

RICHARD J. PRESTON

Boas found anthropology while it was yet an infant and attempted to point the young discipline in directions which would lead to growth and maturation. Clearly, his self-assumed role was a most difficult one and quite often he equivocated. His writings show some interest in generalization, but he maintained a steady flow of criticisms of the generalizations of others. Culture, he said, appears to determine the individual, yet he warns against reifying culture, and emphasizes the creative role of the individual.** Boas has the strong empirical bent of the scientist but is constantly wary of the goals of science—the development of laws and theories. Enigmatically, his notions of the individual as a free agent are found alongside a habit psychology. Free from slavery to culture, man is, for Boas, still chained to his habits. To pinpoint what culture means for Boas becomes a difficult exercise in uniting contradictions. Two leading spokesmen for cultural anthropology, Alfred Kroeber and Clyde Kluckhohn, have said that "directly he (Boas) contributed little to Tylor's attempt to isolate and clarify the concept of culture; indirectly he hindered its progress by diverting attention to other problems."†*

Other scholars have been more sympathetic in evaluating Boas' contribution to culture theory. George Stocking, for example, believes that Boas was inconsistent in the way he discussed and worked with the concept culture because he was a transitional figure. However, (according to Stocking) Boas' contribution was enormous and involved "the rejection of simplistic models of biological or racial determinism; it involved the rejection of ethnocentric standards of cultural evaluation; it involved a new appreciation of the role of unconscious social processes in the determination of human behavior; it implied a conception of man not as a rational *so much as a* rationalizing *being."‡*

SOURCE: Abridged and adapted from "Edward Sapir's Anthropology: Style, Structure and Method" by Richard J. Preston. Reproduced by permission of the author and the American Anthropological Association from *American Anthropologist,* Vol. 68, No. 6, October 1966, pp. 1105–1128.

* To reify "is to make a thing of that which is not a thing, such as hope, honesty, or freedom." See Leslie White's essay, Chapter 8.

** Franz Boas, *Anthropology and Modern Life,* New York: W. W. Norton, 1928.

† A. L. Kroeber and Clyde Kluckhohn, *Culture: A Critical Review of Concepts and Definitions,* Papers of the Peabody Museum of American Archaeology and Ethnology, 1952, Vol. 47, No. 1, p. 15.

‡ George Stocking, "Franz Boas and the Cultural Concept in Historical Perspective," *American Anthropologist,* August 1966, Vol. 68, No. 4, pp. 867–882.

That Boas should have difficulty in clearly identifying the nature and meaning of culture is quite understandable. This problem remains unanswered a half-century later.

A central question with which Boas grappled has lost none of its allure over the decades—colloquially, who is senior partner in Life Incorporated, man or culture? No cultural theorist of any stature has evaded this question, and none have provided an answer that is completely acceptable to the rest of the scientific community. The dialectic continues to bear useful fruits, however, and few who have engaged in it have surpassed the brilliant insights of Edward Sapir. For Sapir, anthropology must center its interest on man. Only through our deeper understandings of man can we attain clear conceptualizations of man's unique achievement: culture. How is man to be studied so that we can best understand him and his culture? Sapir provides an answer in the essay that follows, and along with it, we get his views of anthropology as a humanistic science.

Two main tenets in the position of traditional scientific anthropology have proved to contain theoretical weaknesses or to be problematic in the development of method: (1) it holds culture to be the most fundamental concept, and (2) it holds this culture-based scientific ethos adequate to cope with the demands of a problem as complex and diverse as man. Sapir was hardly the first to face these problems; probably every field worker has sensed them, on a more or less conscious level. This idea seems to be implied when Frazer speaks of "man in the round" and in Malinowski's concern with the "imponderabilia of everyday life." Sapir consciously and deliberately organized his efforts to account for man in the round.

His attempt was undoubtedly facilitated by the emergence of psychodynamic theory. If offered an approach to the study of man *qua* individual that had not been available before. That Sapir understood basic psychodynamic theory is evident from his reviews of psychoanalytic writings and his skillful and clearly conceived use of psychoanalytic concepts in his original writings. From the insights of psychiatry comes his plea for a "psychiatric science," a science adapted to dealing with a kind of complexity not found in the physical sciences, due to man's individually variable and personally dynamic qualities.

Sapir's vision of a true psychiatric science looks to the "total personality as the central point of reference in all problems of behavior and in all problems of 'culture' (analysis of socialized patterns)."[1] The science will utilize psychiatric concepts and methods as well as those of anthropology and the other social

[1] Edward Sapir, *Selected Writings of Edward Sapir in Language, Culture and Personality*, ed. David G. Mandelbaum, Berkeley: University of California Press, 1958, p. 579n.

sciences, in a more humanistic, comprehensive, individual-oriented framework than has yet been realized.

Sapir's programmatic writing constitutes an exhortation to anthropologists to break their avoidance relationship with the systematic analysis of their own professional ethos. He urges a self-conscious examination of commitment to the traditional scientific ethos and recommends a more sophisticated and powerful, yet more difficult, scientific ethos.

His psychiatric science finds the true locus of culture in the individual. Culture is not discarded as a useful concept *or* as a psychological reality; it is rather seen in an inclusive frame of reference that Sapir feels will give the concept a more vital importance to social thought than it has heretofore enjoyed. Rather than do without the culture concept, as Voget suggests, Sapir wants to *personalize* the concept, to find the psychological reality of culture patterns. And on the academic side, Sapir wants to personalize the way in which the professional understands and uses his concepts, as expressions of his own value system, not as expressions of a supposed objective validity. For, as Maquet's recent paper demonstrates, anthropology is a good deal more culture-bound than anthropologists are wont to acknowledge or even to perceive.[2] With the benefit of personalized insight into the psychological reality of culture patterns and into the role of the anthropologist, anthropology will be in a position to cope, on a vital level, with the relationship of human nature to culture.

> In short, the application of the personality point of view tends to minimize the bizarre or exotic in alien cultures and to reveal to us more and more clearly the broad human base on which all culture has developed. The profound commonplace that all culture starts from the needs of a common humanity is believed in by all anthropologists, but it is not demonstrated by their writings.[3]

The difficulty of grasping all of what Sapir is doing in his programmatic writing stems from at least two kinds of "strangeness." One is his style of writing. The other, and most difficult to cope with, is his style of thinking. And because these two styles may be independently perceived (one without the other), and the literary style is more obvious, it is easy to see how the reader might react by admiring the brilliance, flair, and perception with which Sapir expressed his ideas, yet be unable to integrate Sapir's ideas effectively into the framework of concepts and ideas that the reader already holds. This difficulty is heightened by the fact that Sapir's style of thinking—his intellectual world view—is qualitatively distinct from what the reader is likely to be accustomed to. What, then, was Sapir's style of thinking?

Sapir expressed himself holistically in his writings; he expressed his intellect plus his feelings and attitudes. This hardly makes Sapir unique among

---

[2] J. J. Maquet, "Objectivity in Anthropology," *Current Anthropology*, 1964, Vol. 5, pp. 47–55.
[3] Sapir, p. 595.

anthropologists, but Sapir does it on a clearer and more conscious level than many of his colleagues. The *personal holism* that Sapir expresses also extends to men as his reading audience, and still further to men as subjects for scientific study. In other words, Sapir thinks in terms of men as total personalities, whether he is thinking of his own self-expression, of the readers to whom he wishes to communicate, or of the scientific study of man. This is an impressive clue to the broad scope of his approach. Even more, it testifies to the degree of coherent understanding he commands. Sapir's scientific ethos is expressed at each of these levels of holistic, personalistic thinking. In summary, Sapir has made a plea for a personalistic science of man, in a very comprehensive sense of the word "personalistic."

The history of anthropology has seen different types of primary models or "basic analogies" used as devices for dealing with man and culture. Mechanistic and organismic models have proved useful, but their extension and development have revealed weaknesses. Sapir is suggesting a personalistic model. He has formulated his basic analogy to be as close to man himself as possible—the "total personality" or whole individual, including biological, sociological, and psychological attributes, but from the personal point of reference.

The rational appeal of a development from mechanistic through organismic to personalistic, as an evolutionary progression of the conceptual orientation to the study of man, is quite compelling.

The personalistic approach takes culture to be fundamentally and exclusively composed of a group of total personalities who interact with each other and develop as culture carriers through the selection (often unconscious) of experiences that the individual values or perceives as significant.

From the point of view of the individual, culture can be regarded as a complex of demands to which the individual responds in his own personal way; in doing so, he defines, or at least expresses, his personality structure and at the same time extends his personality by responding to demands in a way that he has not done before. This is a test, in a sense, that the individual is called upon to demonstrate his own response to the micro-milieus he perceives in the course of his everyday experience, not only to express the structure of his subconscious (which psychiatrists seek to discover) but also to show how he can respond in a reinterpretive or creative way to his perceptions.

> The true locus of culture is in the interactions of specific individuals and, on the subjective side, in the world of meanings which each one of these individuals may unconsciously abstract for himself from his participation in these interactions.[4]

Taking the individual as the true locus of culture, one can see that in all

[4] Sapir, p. 515.

cultures (although to varying degrees) the individual has a very great range of possible, personally significant perceptions with which to experience his existence. Sapir saw the task of his proposed psychiatric science to be the analysis of particular personality-in-culture perceptions of individuals, assessed in depth and over time, including the study of the conventional categories of ethnography as they have meaning, both conscious and unconscious, for the individual.

We now turn to the method for field work suggested by Sapir's personalized approach. Sapir himself offers rather little specific advice on the subject, and if he ever did field work with this conceptual basis clearly in mind, he never published it. On the other hand, some personalized qualities do appear in his early ethnography.

In a Nootka life history, Sapir demonstrates the meaning that events in the life of a specific individual have for that person. Sapir's writing points to a way of life as it is actually lived and valued by the individual.

> Tom is now old and poverty-stricken, but the memory of his former wealth is with his people. The many feasts he has given and the many ceremonial dances and displays he has performed have all had their desired effect—they have shed luster on his sons and daughters and grand-children, they have "put his family high" among the Ts'isha'ath tribe and they have even carried his name to other, distant Nootka tribes, and to tribes on the east coast of the island that are of alien speech.[5]

Sapir's presentation is not couched in exotic terms. Rather than contrast the culture of the observer and the culture of the observed, he dismisses the exotic element by presenting the material as it is seen by the individual in the culture. More than that, Sapir presents the material in such a way that the reader is easily caught up in the empathetic relationship between Sapir and the man he tells us about. Tom's former wealth serves the purpose of putting his family 'high" in the eyes of the people of his own neighboring tribes. Sapir's task as an anthropologist was not simply to provide quantitative reports of the amount of wealth displayed or distributed by members of the tribe, but also to discover what wealth, as a category, means to people in this cultural milieu, and further, to find out what it means to Nootka individuals to want to put their family "high."

In other words, the categories the anthropologist attempts to deal with cannot realistically be defined for him before he enters the particular cultural milieu. To be realistic, the categories must be distinctively meaningful in, and therefore derived from, the particular milieu, so that they will accurately describe the milieu. For example, wealth as a category of Nootka culture is clearly not the

---

[5] Edward Sapir, "Sayach'apis, a Nootka Trader," *American Indian Life*, ed. Elsie C. Parsons, New York: Viking Press, 1922, p. 29. Re-issued: Bison Books, 1967.

same thing as wealth in American middle-class culture; and the significant difference lies in what culturally defined categories of wealth mean to the Nootka individual and to the American individual.

> No West Coast Indian, so far as we know, ever amassed wealth as an individual pure and simple, with the expectation of disposing of it in the fullness of time at his own sweet will. This is a dream of the modern European and American individualist, and it is a dream which not only brings no thrill to the heart of the West Coast Indian but is probably almost meaningless to him. The concepts of wealth and the display of honorific privileges . . . which have been inherited from legendary ancestors are inseparable among these Indians. . . . We may go so far as to say that among the West Coast Indians it is not the individual at all who possesses wealth. It is primarily the ceremonial patrimony of which he is the temporary custodian that demands the symbolism of wealth.[6]

The two citations above show certain personalized attributes. Sapir's life history of Tom is a directly personal method of ethnography (not all life histories deal so directly with personal significances or meanings). The second citation is an illustrative example used in a theoretical paper, "The Unconscious Patterning of Behavior in Society," and is an example of how personalized information may be presented on a rather high level of generality, showing an individually understood and culturally patterned meaning of wealth. The fact that the individual is not autonomous or somehow independent of culture is shown in two ways: (1) the significant recognition of wealth in the eyes of Tom's people depends upon what Redfield calls "shared understandings" of the meaning of wealth, and (2) the true locus of wealth, as perceived by individuals, is actually the ceremonial patrimony, not the individual per se. Put another way, the psychological reality of wealth, in Nootka culture, is not acquisition for the individual, but rather a display for the honor of the patrimony of which the individual is temporary custodian. In order to "put his family high," Tom maintained the honor of his patrimony, and even increased the esteem the patrimony enjoyed in the eyes of other members of the tribe, for "the memory of his former wealth is with his people." Tom's poverty in old age is not a detriment to the esteem that the patrimony commands, for the patrimony has moved to a new custodian. Tom has fulfilled his obligation successfully, and this fact is a source of enduring satisfaction to him in his old age.

The point to this extended treatment of the Nootka individual-in-culture is simply to illustrate, by example, what Sapir thought to be significant to the individual-in-culture, and therefore to the anthropologist. The illustration is not an attempt to show Sapir's whole concept of a psychiatric science, but only to give an example of one way in which the psychiatric science may be applied.

---

[6] Sapir (1958), pp. 557–558.

The life-history approach, which Sapir directs at "the ever more minute analysis and comparison of individual personality pictures,"[7] is but a part of the broadly conceived psychiatric science. Sapir gives us an idea of the breadth and place of his approach:

> When the cultural anthropologist has finished his necessary preliminary researches into the overt forms of culture and has gained from them an objectivity of reference by working out their forms, time sequences, and geographical distribution, there emerges for him the more difficult and significant task of interpreting the culture which he has isolated in terms of its relevance for the understanding of the personalities of the very individuals from whom he has obtained information.[8]

The citation illustrates what Singer calls Sapir's "bifocal" approach to anthropology.[9] The first focus, on overt forms, might include such information as census figures, language, material culture, geographical environment, and economic flow. The second focus was Sapir's personalistic method, and it is this method that Sapir feels is so vitally important, yet so badly neglected. As anthropology attempts to implement the personalistic method,

> we shall have to operate as though we know nothing about culture but were interested in analyzing as well as we could what a given number of human beings accustomed to living with each other actually think and do in their day to day relationship. We shall find that we are driven, willy-nilly, to the recognition of certain permanencies, in the relative sense, in these interrelationships, permanencies which can reasonably be counted on to endure but which also must be recognized to be eternally subject to serious modification of form and meaning with the lapse of time and with those changes of personnel which are unavoidable in the history of any group of human beings.[10]

In speaking of different foci, we are speaking of a difference that is, as Sapir tells us, merely imposed by the interests of the observer, not a difference that is inherent in the phenomena. Sapir differentiates between overt forms and personalistic interpretations as different methods employed by the anthropologists for imposing structure on their data. There is no set rule for the use of either focus, but certain phenomena, such as inanimate objects, are normally more appropriately studied as overt forms. On the other hand, people are more normally studied with a personalistic approach. There are occasions that call for a change of focus, such as when artifacts are studied as expressing the ideas of their makers or users, or when a census is being taken, or when the language is

---

[7] Sapir (1958), p. 563.
[8] Sapir (1958), p. 595.
[9] Milton Singer, "A Survey of Culture and Personality Theory and Research," *Studying Personality Cross-Culturally*, ed. Bert Kaplan, Evanston, Ill.: Row, Peterson and Co., 1961, p. 63.
[10] Sapir (1958), p. 574.

studied to find how the symbolic content is related to the personality-in-culture of the speakers.

Sapir does not deal at length with his psychiatric or personalistic science on the level of method, but he does offer occasional suggestions. I have extracted several of these suggestions, or hints, which I will relate and interpret into somewhat more specific detail.

The first of these suggestions is the most general, and subsumes the other, more specific ideas. Sapir calls for "translating social and cultural terms into that intricate network of personalistic meanings which is the only conceivable stuff of human experience."[11] Sapir is pleading here for the reinterpretation of traditional academic terms into a context of the personal, since these very terms purport to describe, and to be derived from, the actual experience of human beings. A personalistic interpretation gives a working vocabulary for a more vital (directly appropriate) description of meaningful human experience. An example of this is the description of the Nootka conception of wealth discussed above. While this reinterpretive method is highly conceptual (dealing with the process of perceiving old concepts in a new frame of reference), it is nonetheless a method used, at least in part, in the field. That is, part of this reinterpretation is in a framework of "typical psychic mechanisms," or "relational ideas . . . in the domain of pure psychology."[12] This part of the framework deals with human nature, and may be classed as theoretical anthropology, insofar as this work is done by anthropologists. The second part of the framework is a field method, which involves the description of the different personality-in-culture *elaborations upon* typical psychic mechanisms. The Nootka life history is a description of such an elaboration. The field method involved, then, is the description of social and cultural terms as they are defined in the lives of specific individuals-in-culture.

Closely related to the method indicated above is the next suggestion for method, which is to find "through an analysis of variation . . . the reality and meaning of norm."[13] Sapir illustrates this idea in his discussion of the dissenting Indian "Two Crows." Sapir was impressed by J. O. Dorsey's parenthetical comment that "Two Crows denies this."[14] In a hypothetical illustration, Sapir shows that the deviant is actually never wrong in any absolute sense, but only in the sense that his perception differs from the perception of his fellows. Sapir then points out that an analysis of variations in perception may well lead to very significant understandings of the subject of the disagreement, "the reality and meaning of a norm."

---

[11] Edward Sapir, "The contribution of psychiatry to an understanding of behavior in society," *American Journal of Sociology,* 1937, Vol. 42, p. 867.
[12] Sapir (1958), p. 529.
[13] Sapir (1958), p. 576.
[14] Sapir (1958), p. 569ff.

Now if we look at the same situation, that of Two Crows, from the cultural rather than the personal point of reference, we may seek to find the "varying degrees of compulsiveness which attach to (a culture's) many expectations and implications."[15] That is, we want to know how closely Two Crows, as an individual in his culture, feels pressed to conform to culturally patterned actions, thoughts, and feelings. How far does he feel obliged to agree rather than to express his individual-defining perceptions of a given idea or event? Again, when the individual does express himself, to what extent is this expression individual-defining and to what extent culturally defined? This question leads to the next method suggested by Sapir.

"An important field for investigation is that of personal symbolisms in the use of cultural patterns. Personal symbolisms are often the more valuable as they are hidden from consciousness and serve as the springs of effective behavior."[16] In other words, Sapir wants to know the personal meanings, the distinctively individual personality dynamics, that lie behind the use of culturally defined actions, thoughts, or feelings. For example: why did Two Crows make his denial? or why did Tom, as a particular Nootka individual want to put his family high? Tom saw the goal of putting his family high in a partially distinctive way, as compared with the similar perception on the part of other Nootka individuals. Insofar as Tom or Two Crows or any individual expresses his own personal self in the use of cultural patterns, he is expressing the personal symbolisms that Sapir sees as important to understanding individuals-in-culture. We might find, for instance, that Two Crows tended to deny a rather substantial portion of the culturally patterned ideas held by most of his fellow Omaha—perhaps his own personality organization was rather out of joint with his cultural milieu.

This last possibility leads to the next idea for field method, ". . . to relate the patterns of culture to germinal personality patterns . . . (involving) the intimate study of personality."[17] Again, the examples of Tom and Two Crows may be cited, except that Sapir does not furnish enough of an intimate study of the two personalities to allow for more than a partial illustration. The life-history approach, using concepts from psychiatry or "pure psychology," is clearly a part of this method. Note that the goal here is to relate, not to equate, the two types of patterns. Personality is not simply a cultural microcosm, nor is culture simply personality writ large. Nevertheless, a relationship exists, and the nature of the relationship demands understanding. Germinal personality patterns, I take it, are more than the typical psychic mechanisms of human nature, yet less than the whole complexity of an aggregate of total personalities

---

[15] Sapir (1958), p. 517.

[16] Sapir (1958), p. 568.

[17] Sapir (1958), p. 563.

(possibly close to Kardiner's idea of basic personality structure). Sapir does not develop this idea further. The thing that Sapir does repeatedly emphasize about the proper study of individuals is the humanistic personalistic element. This emphasis is his most important point, and he indicates some attributes of the personalistic method for the study of individuals-in-culture.

Anthropologists should direct their interest to "the interactions of specific individuals and . . . the world of meanings which each one of these individuals may unconsciously abstract for himself from his participation in these interactions."[18] Perhaps this method could be labeled "personalistic social psychology." Whatever the label, the job of the anthropologist is not only to observe interactions, but also to obtain an understanding of the world of meanings that individuals abstract from their interactions. The interaction has then a subjective side, and it is this subjective side that gives vital significance to the overt behavior in interaction. The personal side of interaction is the "reason why" of interaction; without it we have only the hollow shell of an event. The importance of the world of meanings that each individual abstracts leads to the final suggestion for method.

"The acquirement of culture by the child"[19] is much less of a problem to explain since we are dealing with the familiar subject of socialization. Of all the fields for research that Sapir suggested, this is the one that has enjoyed the greatest popularity among anthropologists. Yet not all socialization studies adhere to Sapir's personalistic, holistic approach. In socialization, as in all other suggested fields, the area of study is not all Sapir is interested in. The theme in all his culture and personality writings is the application of his psychiatric science, his total (holistic) personality approach. He does not explain his approach in specific detail. In fact we do not know, at this early point in the history of anthropology, how to "do" anthropology in these terms.

Sapir's suggestions, presented above, are so schematic that they must be viewed as expressing a general direction for field work rather than as indicating specific field methods per se. With regard to method, Sapir tells us that psychiatry has yet to furnish us with the necessary tools.[20] Yet it is unfortunate that Sapir, with his extraordinary insight and feel for the problem and his proven skills as a field worker, did not make more of an effort to apply his programmatic ideas, even without the benefit of the psychiatric tools he refers to. Apparently, during the years that he made his personalistic approach known, Sapir came to think of himself as a theoretical anthropologist[21] and was content to let the application wait for the psychiatric tools, or for other field workers.

---

[18] Sapir (1958), p. 515.
[19] Sapir (1958), pp. 595–596.
[20] Sapir (1958), pp. 575–576.
[21] Sapir (1958), p. 596.

With respect to what these tools are, Sapir implies that what is needed is not a set of specific categories, but rather a better grasp of the "typical psychic mechanisms" upon which individuals build culturally patterned elaborations and individual-defining elaborations. Sapir rejects the specific categories of psychoanalysis (e.g., the Oedipus complex) as tending to be "either ill-founded or seen in distorted perspective," but finds Freud's "immense service . . . in his revelation of . . . relational ideas [such] as the emotionally integrated complex, the tendency to suppression under the stress of a conflict, the symptomatic expression of a suppressed impulse, the transfer of emotion and the canalizing or pooling of impulses, [and] the tendency to regression."[22] These examples of relational ideas are the beginnings of the psychiatric tools that the anthropologist needs. If anthropologists choose not to wait for the development of these ideas into a usable concept of human nature, then we are faced with the need for a method for applying the personalistic approach.

In my opinion, this approach involves a field method that makes the most of participation in the cultural milieu under study. The anthropologist should participate so far as he is able in the activities and interrelationships that constitute the culturally patterned life-way. Sapir tells us, in defining an element of one's own culture, that "you must put yourself in a behavioral relationship to a thing before it becomes an element of culture."[23] I suggest that this method may also be taken as the proper way for the anthropologist to define, or to understand, the elements of the culture he is studying. Such a method might be called personalized, since the anthropologist puts himself in a personal, not simply intellectual or analytical, relationship to the ideas and events he witnesses. Anthropologists have long acknowledged the value of reports by men who have lived as participant members of so-called primitive societies, for they often have a depth of rapport and a grasp of the imponderabilia that the more objective anthropologist lacks. The failing of these men is usually a lack of the sense of the relativity of cultures and a lack of the analytical habits of observation that are necessary to the serious anthropologist.

Yet one wonders: perhaps many anthropologists prefer to hold themselves in analytical detachment from their opportunities for fuller participation, if only because of their consciousness of the great personal strain of maintaining, on a personal and intensive level, a sort of deliberate double personality in which one lives by the patterns of the anthropologist's culture simultaneously with the patterns of the culture being studied. Every field worker must enter into this to some degree. But the line tends to be drawn, I suspect, rather close to the home culture. This is perhaps even more true in the published reports

[22] Sapir (1958), p. 529.

[23] Anne M. Smith, class notes from Sapir's "Psychology of Culture" seminar, 1936–1937, p. 17.

than in the actual field situation. Sapir's personalizing approach pushes the anthropologist closer to the people he is studying, and demands a personal holism in analysis and in publication. In other words, what is needed is personalized ethnography, combined with psychiatric sophistication and depth of participation. This permits the understanding of personal relationships that, in turn, are intimate enough to reveal the personal meanings of ideas and events in the cultural milieu.

Beyond this, I suspect that there cannot be any *one* specific field method for personalistic ethnography, for the personality of the anthropologist and of the individuals with whom he interacts must structure the method at this highly specific level. This is similar to the way in which the psychiatrist and his patient structure their relationship, except that interaction in ethnography is more active and lacks the sense of urgent need that motivates the psychiatric patient to project the major part of the situational structure. In ethnography, the relationship is necessarily a reciprocal one, since the informant will not likely feel the same sense of urgency to express his world view to the anthropologist. This highly personal relationship in field work requires sincerity and personal consideration on the part of the anthropologist, not only to avoid the two extremes of technicality and sentimentality, but also to maintain an ethical human quality in relationships with the people involved.

Such a methodology ill suits those anthropologists who place a premium on quantifiable and replicable data and analysis. Sapir's method is no more precise in definition than Sapir's concept of structure, yet it offers the reward of a similar type of perceptually precise and highly relevant understanding that I have claimed for the structure concept. Here again, we are faced with a choice between striving for precision in the definition of terms, with its attendant advantages of economy and elegance, and striving for precision in the perception of people-in-culture, with the very real complexity and obscurity that inhere in the phenomena. This is not a choice between mutually exclusive opposites so much as a choice of emphasis and style, in which precise definition is clearly and consistently subordinate to, and styled by, precise perception.

4 The Anthropology of Malinowski

BRONISLAW MALINOWSKI

For Sapir, any piece of observable behavior (activities, expressions, etc.) has a dualistic quality. On the one hand it points to some cultural norm or norms; either by affirming them or by denying them. On the other hand, it points to personal meanings, a personality expressing his thoughts and feelings as he relates to the norm. Man and culture, according to Sapir, are inseparable; one can no more develop conceptions of culture without including man and his personality, than one can discuss humans without relating them to a cultural milieu.

Sapir's views gain substance and richer meaning when related to the work of a renowned European anthropologist, Bronislaw Malinowski. Malinowski, one of the fathers of functionalism, discusses the biological determinants—hunger, thirst, sex appetite, etc.—which every culture refashions and molds. Culture here becomes a set of formalized responses to basic needs. But, it is more than that, as Malinowski himself explains in the paper which follows.*

The legitimate subject matter of anthropology, as well as of other social sciences, is culture. The experimental approach to this subject matter must be based on direct observation of collective, organized behavior through field work. By field work I mean the study of living communities and their material culture, whether at a low level of development or within our own civilizations. Such study must be guided by the general theory of culture, whereas observation has to be stated in terms of general principle. As in all sciences, so also here, we shall have to inquire whether the final test of applicability through planned social engineering is possible in the case of social studies.

Considering culture as a whole, that is, at all levels and in any environment, recognition must first be given to its instrumental character. We might survey the organization of an arctic community, a tribe living in the tropical jungle, a horde of lowest primitives, such as the Australian aborigines, and anywhere and

SOURCE: Abridged from "Man's Culture and Man's Behavior" by Bronislaw Malinowski, *Sigma Xi Quarterly*, Vol. 29, Autumn 1941, pp. 182–197, and Vol. 30, Winter 1942, pp. 70–78, by permission of the publishers and the estate of Bronislaw Malinowski.

* When the precise origin of a mode of analysis is in doubt, it is best to speak of "one of the fathers." Models, like humans, may have many competing fathers, but only one mother!

everywhere we would find them wielding a body of implements, following rules of behavior, cherishing ideas and beliefs, engaging through all this in activities which integrate into a vast and complex instrumental apparatus. At higher levels of development, in the New World civilizations of Mexico or Peru, in ancient Egypt or in modern Europe, the apparatus and the activities are more highly developed, but the total effect is instrumental and so is every one of the differential phases. Man everywhere is maintained by his culture, allowed to reproduce, as well as instructed and assisted in this, supplied with techniques, knowledge, recreation, art, and religion.

Were one to look more closely at any particular culture, every activity would be found to be related to some organization or other. In each we would find a group cooperating, linked by common interests and a purpose. Members of such a group or institution own conjointly a portion of the environment, some implements or machines, and dispose of a quota of national wealth. They obey prescribed norms of conduct and are trained in particular skills. Through their activities thus normed and implemented, they achieve their purpose or intentions, known to everybody and socially recognized. They also produce an impression on the environment, social and physical; they achieve results which can be revealed through a sociological analysis.

We would find such groups in the homes of the people as family groups and domestic institutions, and that the food supply and the production of goods and implements is the result of such organized cooperative work. The temples and the courts of law are maintained and run by groups of people organized for a purpose, moved by definite motives or values, and having a special function in public life.

This surface impression, dictated by sound common sense, might lead the observer to the statement of a few generalizations. Culture as a whole is an extensive instrumental system of organized activities. It is exercised by a system of related institutions, that is, groups of people united by common interest, endowed with material equipment, following rules of their tradition or agreement, and contributing towards the work of the culture as a whole. The interests that supply the motive power and dictate the tasks of the group are at times physiological, as in food production, domestic life, and defense mechanisms. There are, however, other interests, values, and motives connected with science or with art which transcend any biological determinism. We are thus led to the fuller analysis as to what the drives or motives of human beings are, and also as to the principles and forces of human organization.

As regards the drives, man is obviously an animal; hence his organic needs will always give rise to a permanent biological determinism in all behavior. Men eat, sleep, reproduce, and protect their body from excessive temperature, as well as from physical destruction. There is a minimum of elementary conditions that has to be fulfilled so that the individual organism survives and the group retains its numbers. Even a slight, but progressive, deterioration of the healthy organic state would inevitably lead to cultural extinction.

It is equally important to realize that human beings live not by biological drives alone, but also by physiological drives molded and modified by culture. As regards nutrition, food and its intake are not a mere exchange between man and environment. In a primitive tribe or a civilized community, there is an organized system of production, distribution, storing, and preparing, which provides each member with his meals. Here again, consumption, that is, the intake of food, is fashioned by the taste, taboos, and hygienic rules, which partly limit and partly redirect the normal appetite. Propagation is determined, in its very impulse, by the ideals of beauty and desirability in which the sex impulse integrates with aesthetic, economic, and social considerations. The rules of specific taboo, such as incest and exogamy, as well as of preferential mating, dictate the type of courtship, whereas the production of children is universally defined by the law of marriage. Nor are the results of propagation merely biological. The extensive systems of kinship ties and grouping into clans, so prevalent in primitive communities, are the translation into sociological norms of the results of biological propagation. Bodily exercise is determined by economic labor and by systems of sports, recreational pursuits, or even artistic activities. Thus, man everywhere acts under culturally determined incentives; he submits to the norms prescribed by tradition; he cooperates and pools, or redistributes, the produce of his labor.

There are certain phases in human behavior even more removed from biological fact than those here described. In a primitive tribe there are objects of magical virtues or religious sanctity or economic value: the famous bull-roarers of central Australia, the totemic poles of the northwestern American tribes, or the millstones known from Micronesia. In order to understand the value attached to such objects and the activities that surround them, it would be necessary to enter a world of mythological antecedents or social and economic conventions. We would have to learn the meaning of the dogmatic principles and see how they are expressed in ritual, or economic transaction, or ethics. To understand why certain people indulge in head-hunting and others practice cannibalism, why in certain cultures valuable objects are produced only in order to be destroyed, would obviously require consideration of the formation of cultural value, of legal principle, as well as the native conceptions of wealth, social ranking, and the realities of magical or religious belief.

Accordingly, man is not merely impelled by hunger and thirst, by love, and the desire to sleep. There are other motives connected with ambition, rank, doctrine, and mythology which establish as powerful incentives for conduct as do those of an innate drive. Instrumentality obtains throughout. In other words, it is always found that a human being is impelled to a specific activity in order to attain a desired end. It is obvious, however, that culture solves not merely the simple organic problems, but creates new problems, inspires new desires, and establishes a new universe in which man moves, never completely free from his organic needs, but also following new ends and stimulated to new satisfactions.

All this does not imply that cultural determinism introduces a mere chaos of relativity in which we would have to resort to the arbitrary biddings of a *deus ex machina* of some specific tribal or cultural genius. We shall be able to give a clear definition and catalogue of the biological needs that are the prime movers of human behavior. We shall also clearly establish what we mean by derived needs or instrumental imperatives. Finally, it will be possible to show that the integrative values, such as ideas, belief, moral rule, are also determined and significant through their relation to culture as a whole. The needs of the organism and the raw materials supplied by the environment are the elements of the primary, or biological, determinism. The indirect cultural situation, however, in which the raw materials are obtained and elaborated and the human organism adjusted imposes new cultural, that is, instrumental and integrative imperatives, which are subject to determinism, hence also to scientific analysis.

The ability to establish and to maintain the cultural apparatus confers enormous advantages on mankind, advantages that consist, on the one hand, in a safer and fuller satisfaction of organic needs; and, on the other hand, in the gift of new impulses and new satisfactions. Culture thus satisfied first the minimum standard of living, that of organic survival. It also adds an increased artificial standard of enjoyment, in which man reaches what usually is described as intellectual, artistic, and ethical pleasures and satisfactions.

For all this there is a price to be paid in terms of obedience to tradition. Man must submit to a number of rules and determinants that do not come from his organism but from submission to his own artifact and machinery, to cooperation, and to the tyranny of words and other symbols. The oft-repeated opposition as between man and machine, in which man is often described as the slave of his self-produced mechanism, his Frankenstein monster, contains an essential truth. Even when man is not enslaved beyond the limits of real necessity, he becomes permanently dependent on his artifacts, once he has started to use them. Cooperation, the social give and take, implies a determined quota of contribution for which man receives, generally, a larger return, but has to remain bound to his social contract. As regards symbolic tradition, it does not always enslave, but it invariably redirects, limits, and determines human behavior.

The Biological Determinism of Culture

We have seen that the biological determinants appear in every culture and that they are invariably refashioned and intertwined with other motives. The problem arises in what sense is it possible to isolate and define biological deter-

FIGURE 1. Permanent vital sequences incorporated in all cultures.

A. *Impulse* ——→	B. *Act* ——→	C. *Satisfaction*
drive to breathe; gasping for air	intake of oxygen	elimination of CO in tissues
hunger	ingestion of food	satiation
thirst	absorption of liquid	quenching
sex appetite	conjugation	detumescence
fatigue	rest	restoration of muscular and nervous energy
restlessness	activity	satisfaction of fatigue
somnolence	sleep	awakening with restored energy
bladder pressure	micturition	removal of tension
colon pressure	defecation	abdominal relaxation
fright	escape from danger	relaxation
pain	avoidance by effective act	return to normal state

minism? And further, in what way is it related to more complex cultural phenomena? The answer is contained in Figure 1, in which the main types of biological determinism have been summed up severally and concretely. A set of vital sequences is there listed which, it is maintained, are always incorporated into every culture. The concept of vital sequence means that the central activity or biological act, listed in column B, must be performed regularly and permanently in every culture. This part of the performance is integrally incorporated into culture, with modifications, to be discussed later, as regards certain prerequisites and the conditions under which it is allowed to happen. The drive, listed in column A, invariably receives a profound modification, different from one culture to another. But although modified, the drive can be determined partly in its physiological character, partly in that it is always connected with the biological act. The items listed in column C are again definable in terms of biological fact: satiation, detumescence, the freeing of the organism of waste matter, the restoration of muscular energy, and the using up of biochemical tensions through muscular exercise and breathing.

The three phases can be defined by the biochemist, the physicist, and the ecologist. The actual intake of air or food; the act of conjugation; sleep, rest, nutrition, or excretion, are clearly defined activities, in which several branches of natural science are interested. Thus, the concept of vital sequence is neither vague nor devoid of substance. It refers to happenings within the human organism as related to physical and cultural environment. However much the drive or satisfaction might be refashioned by culture, both drive and satisfaction must be of such a nature as to lead to the performance of each physiological act, adequate in terms of biology. We see here that the concept of form and function of human behavior is included, since each can be defined in terms of natural science.

The vital sequence is thus the projection of a complex cultural reality onto the physiological plane. We can now also define the concept of basic need over and above that of drive. In each culture there must be systems of standardized arrangements which allow of full, regular, and general satisfaction of all the individual drives. The basic need in its several varieties can, then, be defined as including all individual drives that have to be satisfied so as to keep the organisms of a community in a normal state of healthy metabolism. The non-satisfaction of any or every basic need would imply the gradual biological deterioration of the group, which, if cumulative, would lead to extinction. As regards procreation, the basic need here requires that a sufficient incidence of effective reproduction should occur to maintain the numerical strength of a community. In any culture where celibacy, chastity, vows, abstinences, or castration exceeded restricted numerical limits, we would have a process of gradual extinction. The concept of basic need differs from that of drive, in that it refers to the collective exercise of individual drives, integrated with reference to the community as a whole. The satisfaction of basic needs is predicated with reference to all the organisms, to environmental conditions, and to the cultural setting of the community. It need not be, perhaps, stressed that in the study of cultural realities, whether through field work or in theoretical analysis, we do not resort any more to our analysis in terms of individual drive, but have to rely on the concept of basic need. The drive → activity → satisfaction analysis contains an abstraction of great importance for the foundations of a sound theory of culture. In actual research, however, we do not meet this abstraction, but are faced always with culturally organized satisfactions of integral basic needs.

Figure 2 summarizes concretely and in a highly simplified manner the basic needs and the cultural responses to them. Its meaning will become clearer in detail as our argument advances. For the present, it is clear that it corresponds to a large extent to the list of drives. Several of them, however, have been compressed into one entry in this figure as, for instance, the need of solid foods, liquids, and intake of oxygen. All these are associated with the process of metabolism. Another important point is that each entry is to be considered as integrally related with reference to need and its linked responses. For, as we already know, in the human species biological motive never occurs in a pure and isolated form. Human beings breathe in closed rooms or caves; they have

FIGURE 2. Basic needs and cultural responses.

A. *Basic needs:* 1, metabolism; 2, reproduction; 3, bodily comforts; 4, safety; 5, movement; 6, growth; 7, health.

B. *Cultural responses:* 1, commissariat; 2, kinship; 3, shelter; 4, protection; 5, activities; 6, training; 7, hygiene.

to combine breathing with rules of politeness or taboo, since human breath is, in some cultures, regarded as sacred and in others as dangerous. Nutrition, propagation, or bodily comforts occur as formed habits. Human beings eat according to a definite daily sequence. They conjugate in accordance with rules of law and morals, or else against them, and thus under cultural conflict. The need for bodily comforts does not arise in an environmental vacuum and then send off the organism in search of a satisfaction. Savages and more sophisticated beings alike wear clothes, carry out a routine of cleanliness, live in habitations, and warm themselves at some permanent sources of warmth. Thus it is clear that the stream of necessities of motives arising out of each need flows, as it were, parallel to the stream of culturally obtainable satisfactions. In the daily round of life, as well as in the seasonal cycle, the human being normally passes through a routine of instrumental effort and of prepared satisfaction in which biological stimulus and organic effort are not hooked up by *ad hoc*, short-circuited links of desire and satisfaction, but are interwoven into two long chains: one of large-scale organized work on culture and for culture; the other, a systematic drawing upon or consuming of already prepared cultural benefits and goods.

The Instrumental Phase of Human Behavior

To make the last argument more concrete and precise, let us again embody it into a diagrammatic presentation:

FIGURE 3. Instrumentally implemented vital sequence.

Drive (1)——Instrumental performance——Culturally defined situation——
Drive (2)——Consummatory act——Satisfaction (meta-physiological).

This is obviously a much more accurate and less abstract representation than the vital sequence previously shown (Figure 2). Certain similarities between the two obtain. We are here still dealing with the vital sequence, one which includes a biological activity. There are in culture, as will be seen later, sequences that do not include such a link. In this figure there is a definite linkage in which all the phases are determined by the relationship between a biological drive and its satisfaction.

There are however differences. To be true to the reality of typical culture concatinations, it was necessary to split the drive into two parts. Drive (1) is the instrumental motive, the impulse to take the round-about way that man follows when he produces or purchases his food, prepares it, and places it on his table. In this he acts to a certain extent like the learning animal in a maze, who has to discover and to use the devices which supply it with food. Sex leads the human animal not to conjugation directly, but to courtship and, in many cases, to marriage. In short, the entire training of the human organism teaches the individual to obtain biological ends through the recognition, appreciation, and the handling of the appropriate means.

Drive (2) represents the culturally determined appetite. Man very often does not eat by hunger, hardly ever by hunger alone. He eats at the right time, the right place, and in the right company. His tastes and values are highly shaped, and even when hungry, he will not touch food defined in his own culture as disgusting, unpalatable, or morally repugnant. "One man's meat is another man's poison": my cannibal friends in New Guinea would have developed a healthy appetite if confronted with missionary steak, but turned away in disgust from my tinned Camembert cheese, sauerkraut, or frankfurters, which latter they regarded as gigantic worms. Again, the impulse of sex which, in animal societies, occurs between any two healthy organisms, is culturally inhibited by such taboos as those of incest, of caste prejudice, and to a lesser extent, by appreciation of rank, class, and professional or racial discrimination. What is a comfortable means of sleeping to an African or a South Sea native would be torture to a pampered Parisian or New Yorker. Nor would our beds, bathtubs, and sanitary arrangements be convenient or even usable to a native from the jungle. Thus there is a two-fold redetermination of physiological drives. Cultural drive occurs in two forms, and each of them is determined by the tradition in which an organism is trained.

Satisfaction in this series has been modified by an adjective. It appears invariably as a cultural appetite rather than as the satisfaction of a pure physiological drive. Breathing, as carried on by certain European communities within the non-ventilated and heavily modified atmospheres of enclosed rooms, would not satisfy an Englishman accustomed to a super-abundance of fresh air. The satisfaction of appetite by food discovered to be unclean ritually, magically, or in terms of what is repugnant in a culture does not lead to a normal state of satiety, but to a violent reaction, including often sickness. The satisfaction of the sex impulse in an illicit or socially dangerous manner produces detumescence, but also conflicts which may lead, in the long run, to functional disease.

Thus culture determines the situation, the place, and the time for the physiological act. It delimits it by general conditions as to what is licit or illicit, attractive or repulsive, decent or opprobrious. Although the act itself, as defined in terms of anatomy, physiology and interaction with the environment, is constant, its prerequisites as well as its consequences change profoundly.

The greatest modification, however, in this new diagram consists in the insertion of the two terms: Instrumental phase—culturally defined situation. The instrumental phase, as we shall see in a closer analysis, is always an integral part of a largely organized system of activities. The instrumentalities of food production would have to be connected with agriculture or hunting or fishing. The storing, preparing, and consuming of food happen in a home or a club or a restaurant. The instrumental phase is also the open door through which such elements of culture as artifacts, norms, and cooperative habits enter as essential constituents of human behavior.

Let us consider any instrumental phase. Primitive fire-making subserves the needs of cooking, warmth, and light. It implies the element of artifact, the knowledge and techniques of friction, and also the appreciation of the value of these objects and activities. In any food-producing instrumental phase we would discover the use of the digging-stick, the hoe, the plough; weapons, nets, or traps; and also the whole system of technique and knowledge, of cooperation and distribution with its legal and customary basis. In every instrumental phase of preparatory activities, the following factors are disclosed: (1) artifacts; (2) normed behavior; (3) organized cooperation; (4) symbolic communication by means of language or other signs. These four cardinal constituents of culture are present in each phase at any level of civilization.

One simple inference occurs immediately: the existence of culture depends upon the mechanisms and activities through which every one of these four constituents is produced and maintained, as well as generally distributed. First, therefore, there must exist in every culture forms or organization through which the material substratum of culture, that is, the body of artifacts, are produced, distributed, and consumed. The economic aspect of a culture is omnipresent.

The norms of behavior have to be known and they have to be enforced. Hence again we can postulate that some mechanisms for the statement, the interpretation, and the sanction of law and order must exist in every community. Accordingly at higher levels there exist everywhere legislative bodies, courts of law, and forces of police. In primitive communities such special institutions may be absent or rudimentary. Nevertheless, the equivalents of codifications, of adjudication, and enforcement are never absent. The essence of custom or norm is that it coordinates behavior; hence it has to be known by all those who cooperate. Many norms curb innate tendencies, define privileges and duties, limit ambition, and circumscribe the use of wealth. There is invariably a tendency to circumvent them. Together with the need of force implied in the imperative of social order, we have in authority a principle which implies the existence of force socially determined and physically implemented. We find everywhere, therefore, the political principle, that is, the socially or culturally determined distribution of force and the right to use it.

Finally, we found that communication, through language and other symbolic means, and the transmission of culture are essential parts of our extended instrumental sequence. Both can be subsumed under the concept of training, insofar as the skills, technical and social rules of conduct have to be implanted

FIGURE 4. Table of instrumental imperatives.

1.	2.	3.	4.
The cultural apparatus of implements and consumers' goods must be produced, used, maintained, and replaced by new production. *Economics.*	Human behavior, as regards its technical, customary, legal, or moral prescription must be codified, regulated in action and sanctioned. *Social control.*	The human material by which every institution is maintained must be renewed, formed, drilled, and provided with full knowledge of tribal tradition. *Education.*	Authority within each institution must be defined, equipped with powers, and endowed with means of forceful execution of its orders. *Political organization.*

in the growing organism and maintained through precept and exhortation. Education, at all levels, can be differentiated into schooling and adult education. Thus the derived need of training or fashioning of the organism for its cultural tasks is one which can be listed as the fourth derived imperative of culture.

Figure 4 gives a condensed presentation of the instrumental needs of culture and of the organized responses to them. We have only to add that the instrumental imperatives have the same degree of cogency as those derived directly from biological needs. We have shown that all vital sequences occur in culture through instrumental implementation. Hence no biological need, that is, no need of the community as a whole, can be normally and regularly satisfied without the full and adequate working of the instrumental responses. These latter constitute together the integral mechanism through which the whole set of basic need receives its regular flow of satisfaction in every culture. Since even the simplest culture raises the level of the quantitative and qualitative standard of living and thus alienates any human group from the direct hand-to-mouth satisfaction by contact with environment, the breakdown of the cultural machinery would imply at least gradual extinction.

Confirmation of this fact is evident when we look at the evidence of historical facts. A serious breakdown in the economic, political, or legal order which usually also implies deterioration in the systems of knowledge and ethics, leads human groups to disorganization and to the sinking of the cultural level. The breakdown of many simpler cultures under the impact of western civilization and the extinction of many racial groups supply one sample. The ever-recurrent decay of once flourishing cultures, which are then replaced by others or else enter a period of Dark Ages, is another case in point. Even today we are faced with a serious threat to culture, that of total war, which is waged not merely in terms of destruction and physical aggression, but also as economic war against the systems of production and, above all, nutritive maintenance. As propaganda, it aims at the breaking down of moral and social resistance through the sapping of the constitutional principles of organization, both as regards defense and the normal working of institutions.

The Emergence of Culture

A clear definition of the symbolic process is still lacking. Its existence was implied throughout, especially in our statements concerning the codes of human behavior, the rules of conduct, the educational processes which largely consist in verbal instruction, and the inculcation of systems of value.

It will be helpful to turn once more to very simple cultural conditions, that are on the borderline between the precultural behavior of man, the animal, and the emergence of truly cultural conduct. From the well-known facts of animal training, which have been now raised to a system of principles embodied in the psychology of stimulus and response, it is established that apes and lower animals can acquire habits and be taught to use artifacts. It is a fair assumption that precultural man, living under conditions of nature, was led frequently to the instrumental use of material objects. Whenever he was placed, with a fair degree of regularity, under conditions resembling those of an experimental maze in which the rat or the guinea pig is being trained, he probably developed individual habits. An individual habit implies at least the development of a skill, the appreciation of the instrumental value of an object and, finally, the retention of both skill and appreciation. This integral retention, diagrammatically embodied in our presentation of instrumentally implemented series, corresponds to the concept of reinforcement, so fruitfully used by Clark Hull and other contemporary psychologists, as the pivotal principle of animal learning. It is not difficult to see that reinforcement, which means the integral retention by an animal organism of a definite sequence in instrumental activities, contains two concepts of great importance to the student of culture, the concept of symbol and that of value.

Reinforcement, however, accounts only for the formation of habits, that is, of individual acquired types of behavior. As long as habit is not infectious or public, it is not a real unit of culture. Culture begins when the transition between habit and custom is made. Custom can be defined as a habit made public by communication from one individual to others and transferable, that is, capable of being ingrained by one generation on to the next.

We have to introduce two more factors as indispensable prerequisites for the transformation of habits into customs. First, the existence of a group in permanent contact and related on the genealogical principle must be assumed. We have further to assume the existence of means of communication which would make possible discourse and symbolic training. The means of communication, moreover, have to be linked and standardized into traditional statements that can be transmitted from the elder generation to the younger. Thus it is necessary to add two more factors to those previously listed.

And once more we come upon the same list of the cardinal constituents of culture: artifacts; skills, that is, norms of behavior; organized groups; and means of communications, that is, symbols and theoretical systems of precept and value.

The raw materials of both sociability and symbolism can also be assumed as pre-existent to the actual emergence of culture. The long infancy of the human species and the formation of families and of family groups was undoubtedly precultural. These are mere assumptions for which proof need not be given, but which are essentially plausible.

The same condition is evident with respect to the raw materials of symbolism. If precultural man were occasionally driven into developing habits, his behavior was determined by what the modern psychologist calls conditioned stimuli. Finding himself regularly within a context of situation and under the urge of a biological drive with no direct satisfaction, he would resort to instrumental behavior. In this the instrument, a piece of wood or stone, and the association of previous effective activity with this object would provide the cue or the conditioned stimulus to action. The fact that an environmental sign directs the organism to action, is essentially symbolic.

Thus we can say that the artifact itself, the typical context of circumstance, the habitual technique, all these functioned symbolically, as well as instrumentally. It may also be assumed that the example of a performance was an act instilled with demonstrative symbolism. When this is added to such symbolic raw material as the bodily or facial expression of emotions, the deictic or otherwise significant gesture, and the natural sound symbols characteristic of many animal performances, it is apparent that symbolism, as significant direction of activity between one organism and another, may, indeed, must have been, precultural.

This allows us to define our idea of cultural emergence by relating a number of empirically substantial facts. The birth of culture probably occurred as a gradual, maybe age-long, process. It was not the miraculous occurrence of sudden speech or intelligence or invention or social organization. It consisted instead of the all-round systematic and effective integration of the partial increments of cultural behavior. As soon as the use of artifacts, the employment of skills gradually tended to become cooperative; in the measure as cooperation led to the development of significant signs and sounds, entering into concerted work as an integral system of links; and these systems of behavior became fixed into tradition; culture was born. The pervading principle of cultural behavior might perhaps be subsumed under the concept of value.

Value means a deep change in the whole organism, especially, no doubt, in the nervous system. It refers to all those attitudes which make for the retention of habits, the submission to traditional rules, the appreciation of and permanent grip upon material objects, and the adequate action and reaction in terms of an articulate sound or formally determined symbol. This latter aspect became, from the very outset, embodied in systems of theoretical knowledge, of belief, and of mythological or historical tradition. Principles of human knowledge based on true experience and on logical reasoning and embodied partly in verbal statements, partly in the context of situation to which these refer, exist even among the lowest primitives. They must have existed from the very beginning of cultural tradition. Had this at any moment lapsed into mysticism or false interpretation of fact; or had it sinned against logic—that is, the principle of identity—human actions, techniques, and economic routine would have become false and useless, and the culture would have been destroyed in its very foundations. Knowledge then, as the symbolic system organizing all the phases of reasonable human behavior—that is, behavior in which experience is logically integrated—is a permanent and essential imperative of human culture.

Knowledge, however, introduces certain new elements into the organic diathesis of man. Knowledge implies foresight, calculation, and systematic planning. In this it not only reveals to man how to achieve certain ends, but also lays bare the fundamental uncertainties and limitations of human planning, of his calculations, and, indeed, of his very existence. The very fact that man, however primitive, becomes accustomed to thinking clearly, to looking ahead, and also to remembering the past, makes him also aware of failures and potential dangers.

We have constantly emphasized that the birth and development of symbolism always occurs under the control of organic drives. Man becomes reasonable because his instrumental actions contain a strong dynamic, that is, emotional, tone. The principles of knowledge are always controlled by desire, by anticipation, and by hope. Their counterpart, the apprehension of failure, is equally strongly charged with emotions of fear, anxiety, or potential frustration. Man, even as his knowledge increases, becomes more and more aware of the fact that his desire is often thwarted, his expectations subject to chance, that there are always grave, incalculable potential dangers lurking ahead.

Man experiences ill health and physical disability in his own life. He sees kinsmen, friends, and neighbors removed by death or disabled by disease. He often finds that the best laid plans are crossed and disorganized by the unexpected intervention of chance and fate. Calamity or misfortune affect the individual and disorganize the group.

What new integrative imperative could be assumed to arise under such circumstances? The need arises from the conflict between hope—that is, positive expectation—and anxiety, or anticipation of possible failure. Any positive affirmations of success, stability, and continuity would satisfy this need. Here again we can indicate psychological foundations for the occurrence of such hopeful signs. A chance association, which might act as prognostic or be interpreted as good augury, could be described as the secondary symbolism of good omen. The normal reliance of the individual, especially the infant, on the protection of the group, might provide the prototype of the assumption of supernatural powers in those who are older, stronger, and more familiar with tradition. As regards death, the assumption of its being but an imaginary event whereas reality consists in the survival of the soul, is brought near not only by the natural strength of the general impulses of "self-preservation," but also by the collateral evidence of dreams, visions, and strong emotional memories.

Thus the dogmatic affirmations of religion and magic are brought near to us simply as standardized natural reactions of the human organism under conditions of conflict. The essence of much religious belief is the affirmation of man's dependence on Providence; that is, on some powerful, partly benevolent, partly dangerous principle pervading the universe. The other equally important source of religious attitudes is the affirmation of human immortality. Magic is, in its substance, the reinterpretation of the secondary causation in terms of good as against bad luck; is thus the ritual production of favorable antecedents of luck and success.

Clearly, neither religion nor magic are mere dogmatic affirmations. Man believes in order to act with greater confidence. He also has to enact his belief. Accordingly to understand any magico-religious system it is necessary to study ritual as the enactment of dogmatic reality, and ethics as the moral consequences of man's dependence upon supernatural powers.

This is not the place to enter into the details of the various religious systems from Totemism to Christianity, or to study minutely the varieties of magic, sorcery, and witchcraft.[1]

We are here interested primarily in the definition of knowledge, religion, and magic, as integrative systems in culturally regulated behavior. Let me briefly sum up the place of integrative imperatives within the theory of the hierarchy of needs here developed. The biological need was defined as the conditions imposed by the interaction of the human organism and environment upon behavior. These conditions determine the permanent incorporation of refashioned vital sequences into every particular culture. These needs are definable in terms of biology, and we have to put them on the map of anthropological studies insofar as they are all invariably incorporated, and also to the degree that they impose definite limits upon human conduct. The concept of instrumental need corresponds to the regular occurrence, and the permanent

[1] The principles here developed will be found more fully documented in *The Foundations of Faith and Morals,* Oxford University Press, 1936.

incorporation in every culture, of those types of activity which we have defined as economic, educational, legal, and political.

The concept of integrative need declares that in every culture coherent systems of a symbolic nature are found. There exist fixed and standardized texts, verbal or written. These texts are closely related with recurrent organized performances. These texts also appear in the processes of training the young and adolescent members; that is, the processes of their incorporation into organized groups or institutions. The continuity of culture, its transmission, and its maintenance depend upon the existence of those residues of action, crystallized into symbolic texts, diagrams, or inscriptions. The real functional identity of such symbolic systems is due to their having been developed as a by-product of experience and action. It may be the experience of training or the gradual adjustment of symbolic instrumental ability and activity in cooperation. Once formed, symbols can and have to be used, both in the context of the pragmatic situation and outside it.

It is thus evident that what is usually described as tradition closely corresponds to our concept of integrative imperatives. We have here linked up this concept with the other determinants of human behavior, and assigned it a definite place and function within the hierarchy of needs. The integrative imperatives are clearly as stringent as the instrumental ones. A lapse in knowledge and deterioration thereof would undermine the techniques of production, as well as the organization of all productive enterprise. The deterioration of belief and of ethics derived from it would mean the gradual disorganization of groups, as well as the occurrence of conflicts and disruptive forces. If knowledge, belief, and ethics were progressively lowered in any culture, then individual initiative and responsibility, the social loyalties, and the organization of the institutions would perforce disappear, and thus leave the organism exposed to starvation, discomfort, and dangers. We see clearly that all three classes of imperative—basic, instrumental, and integrative—are linked, supplementary, and equally stringent.

It may be profitable to supplement the previous two diagrams of vital sequences, plain and instrumentally implemented, by diagrammatic representations of cultural sequence in which there is no physiological link, and the act itself is of a purely cultural nature. This obviously does not mean that such cultural sequences are not related to basic needs. Such a relationship invariably does exist. Yet, if we were to envisage a culture in which specialization has reached the point where a large number of people live exclusively by instrumental contributions, it would be seen that a great many sequences of activities start with a motive and move through an instrumental phase to a performance which has only a derived or instrumental value. The individual satisfaction as well as the drive, in such a case, are determined by the fact that achievements and contributions of this type receive an economic reward from their realization,

FIGURE 5. Culturally instrumental sequence.

Motive (economic interest)——Cultural setting of instrumental institution——Act (professional service or contribution of labor)——Satisfaction (economic and social reward).

by which the individual can satisfy all his basic necessities. If we think of the professional activities of a doctor or a lawyer or a clergyman, or of the type of work done in a factory by the business members, overseers, and workers, it would be found that it fits directly into our diagram of culturally instrumental sequence.

In this series we obviously have simplified matters. The motive often includes elements of ambition, advancement, constructive interest. The satisfaction is invariably in terms of economic reward, since no man can work without maintenance. But it includes also the satisfaction of self-regard, the admiration enjoyed by a good worker, a constructive engineer, or creative scientist or artist. The middle links of our series mean that in order to satisfy the motive for employment, the workman, the professional, or the business man have to find some organized place of work. They can perform their act of professional or labor service only in a consulting room, business office, laboratory, workshop, or factory; in short, an institution. All such series of purely instrumental contributions obviously fit into our concept of vital, instrumentally implemented sequence. They are really part of the extremely complex instrumental phase, which, as already noted, becomes in highly differentiated cultures a long chain of linked instrumental cooperation.

We could have slightly modified our present diagram in order to apply it to certain acts, mostly found in religion and art, in which the act itself is not instrumental, but rather a direct satisfaction of spiritual needs corresponding to the integrative type of interest. When a believer repairs to a temple in order to participate in a sacramental act, a slight reinterpretation of the series is necessary. The sacrament of communion or of confession, like the enjoyment of a symphony or a theatrical performance, is to the believer or the artistically hungry man of culture an end in itself. To a certain extent, the concept of function breaks down in its instrumental character when some of the most highly derived spiritual needs of human beings are considered. The satisfaction felt by the mystic in complete union with Divinity, as also the satisfaction experienced by the composer or by the musical fanatic when he listens to the symphony, may be related in some ways to the general integration of culture. They have certain indirect influences on cohesion, solidarity, and unity of the group. The other aspect, however, their self-contained character of an end in itself, has to be put on record as well. This argument, as previously, can be set forth in a diagram.

FIGURE 6. Cultural sequence of direct spiritual satisfaction.

Motive (religious or artistic)——Cultural setting——Act (communion with the Supernatural; artistic experience)——Satisfaction (mystical ecstasy or artistic pleasure).

The Organized Systems of Human Behavior

In our analysis we certainly have not thrown overboard considerations of individual psychology or organic physiology. At the same time we were constantly faced by the fact of human organization. The cultural fact starts when an individual interest becomes transformed into public, common, and transferable systems of organized endeavor. It will be necessary to define the nature of such systems.

In the principle of prepared opportunities, previously discussed, it was evident that man never has to seek for the satisfaction of any of his needs, bodily, instrumental, or spiritual; they are awaiting him, stored and prepared. We spoke of the two streams of requirement and satisfaction flowing parallel. Man finds his food, his shelter, the remedies for ill health, the redress of injuries, and spiritual comforts in definite places and within organized groups. Those are the home, the workshop, the hostelry, the school, the hospital, or the church. We shall describe such standardized systems of cooperation, as well as their material embodiment and the groups running them, by the term *institution.*

This reality was encountered in our analysis of the instrumental phase of a sequence. It was stated that such a phase was always the integral part of a larger unit of organization. Fire-making, as an instrumental phase, can happen at home and for the household, or during an organized enterprise or else ritually, in a temple. Stone implements are produced to build a house or to pound the raw material of food or to engage in some organized agricultural work.

At a much higher level, we can see that no individual initiative is ever culturally relevant unless incorporated into an institution. The man who conceives a new scientific idea has to present it before an academy, publish it, teach it at a school, and compel its recognition by the organized profession before it becomes an accepted part of science. The inventor has to take out a patent, and thus obtain a charter. He has to organize the group of engineers and workmen, to finance them, and thus to implement the production of his practical device. He then has to find the market of consumers by creating new wants or redirecting old ones, and make the productive activity of his organization perform a function in satisfying a need.

In the analysis of the concrete structure of the instrumental phase of behavior, it was shown that it always consists in the concurrence of artifacts, organization of the personnel, norms of conduct, and a symbolic factor which functions in the establishment of that phase and in its coordination. From this we can proceed to a fuller definition of the concept of organized activities or institutions.

It is clear that the essence of organization implies *prima facie* three factors: a group of people engaged in the common performance of a task. These people must be equipped with instruments and have a definite environmental basis for their activity. We know also that in technique, law, and ethics, rules are the essence of human organization. As shown above, however, human groups do not organize for nothing. They have a purpose in common, they pursue an end, and thus they are bound together by a charter defining the purpose of their collaboration and its value. Right through our analysis it is evident that humanity, primitive and civilized alike, engages in work not only under the impulse of motives, but also towards the satisfaction of their real needs. This we have called function.

The function of an institution is the effect which it produces in the satisfaction of human needs. To the three concepts of personnel, norms, and material apparatus, we must add those of charter and function. Figure 7 summarizes

FIGURE 7. Outline of an institution.

CHARTER

PERSONNEL NORMS

MATERIAL APPARATUS

ACTIVITIES

FUNCTION

this argument in associating the several co-effective factors of human organization. It can be read as follows: human beings organize under a charter that defines their common aims and that also determines the personnel and the norms of conduct of the group. Applying these norms and with the use of the material apparatus, the members engage in activities, through which they contribute towards the integral function of the institution.

Let us briefly define the concepts used in our institutional analysis. The charter is the system of values for the pursuit of which the group have organized. It may consist simply of a legal document, or, in the case of traditional institutions, it may be based on history, legend, or mythology. The personnel of an institution is the group organized on definite principles of authority and division of work and distribution of privilege and duty. The rules or norms consist, as we know, in all the acquired skills, habits, legal norms, and ethical commands. The distinction here made between norms and activities is justified. The norms represent the ideal standard of behavior, the activities their actual realizations. The distinction between charter and norms is based on the more fundamental character of the former. It defines the constitution of the group, its value and purpose for the members, as well as the command, permission, or acquiescence of the community at large.

The diagram would be as useful in ethnographic field work as in comparative studies where it supplies the common measure of comparison. It is related to our previous analysis in that the entries *personnel, norms, material apparatus* correspond to the instrumental phases of culture. The charter, as well as the verbal prescriptions referring to the norms, belong to the integrative class in our hierarchy of imperatives. The function is related to the theory of hierarchical needs in general.

The importance of the concept of institution as the legitimate concrete isolate of cultural analysis is seen also through the fact that we can draw up a list of the main types of institutions valid for all cultures. At first sight such a list does not look impressive, in that it appears entirely common sense. In reality it supplies the student with one of the most valuable proofs that universal laws of structure and process can be established in his field. The main types of institutional organization can be listed briefly under the following headings:

1. Family and derived kinship organizations
   (Extended family; kindred groups; clan).
2. Municipality
   (Local group; horde; village; township; city).
3. Tribe as the political organization based on territorial principle
   (Primitive tribe; polis; state; state-nation; empire).
4. Tribe as the culturally integrated unit
   (Primitive homogeneous tribe; nation).
5. Age-group
   (Age-grades; age hierarchies; professional age distinctions).
6. Voluntary associations
   (Primitive: secret societies and clubs; advanced: benevolent, political and ideological societies).
7. Occupational groups
   (Primitive: magical organizations; advanced: economic teams; artisan guilds; professional associations; religious congregations).
8. Status groups based on the principle of rank, caste, and economic class.

The analysis of this list would obviously require a textbook of cultural anthropology in full comment. Here I only want to point out that an institution like the family may change considerably from one culture to another. It is possible, nevertheless, to give a minimum definition that would serve in any comparative study as a common measure and for any type of ethnographic or sociological field work as a general guide. The family is the group consisting of husband and wife, parents and children. It is based on the charter of marriage contract, concluded on the foundation of the marriage law and religious sanctity of this bond as it is concretely formulated in each particular culture. This contract implies not only the definition of the relation between the consorts; it also determines the legitimacy and the status of the children.

The combination of the law of marriage and the law of kinship prevalent in any culture constitutes the minimum definition of the family. It is obvious that the family fulfils several functions: reproductive, educational, economic, legal, and often also religious and magical. Nevertheless, it is clear that the main function of the family is the culturally redefined production not merely of human infants, but the supply of young citizens of the tribe. The economic appurtenances, the legal prerogatives, the definition of authority and distribution of authority are all contingent on the main function. We can, therefore, define this briefly as the transformation of biological reproduction into culturally defined continuity of the group. We could supply analogous definitions in terms of charter and function of all the other entries in our table. This example must suffice. It shows that in each case we can define the integral function of an institution, while it would also be possible to show that the aggregate working of the community as a whole, that is, its culture, is carried along by the combined activity of all the institutions. These problems, however, refer already to the detailed and specialized province of social anthropology, and cannot be more fully developed here.

Conclusions

An attempt has been made in the present discussion to define cultural determinism; the influence of man's culture on man's behavior. We have seen that human beings act within the framework of institutional organization, and that the determinants of their activities can be defined in terms of what was described here as the hierarchy of needs. Our analysis of the various needs and, particularly, their relations proves that although cultural determinism supplies all the final motives of behavior, culture, in turn, is determined all along the line. We were not driven into the assumption of such concepts as cultural relativism, nor is it necessary to resort to research for specific tribal or racial geniuses or entities. It is evident that the driving forces of all behavior are biologically conditioned. The indirect instrumental satisfaction through culture engenders new needs of an instrumental and symbolic character. As shown, however, both the instrumentalities and the symbolic systems, again, submit to certain general principles which we were able to formulate.

Does this mean that we are denying here the diversity of cultural phenomena as encountered in various types of environment, at various levels of evolution, and even within nearly related cultures? By no means. The stress which was laid here on the uniformity is due primarily to the fact that we are here concerned with methods of approach, with common measures of comparison, and with instruments of research. These had to be built upon elements which are constant, recurrent, and which, therefore, lead to generalizations of universal validity.

The very concept of function, which was dominant throughout our analysis, however, opens the way for the introduction of variety and differentiation, as well as for the assertion that there is a common measure in this variety. In a fuller descriptive statement of what anthropology teaches about human nature, such differential characteristics would obviously have to be introduced. Some of them would undoubtedly lead us back to the differential influences of environment. We would find that the very basic needs have to be satisfied differentially in a desert, in an arctic environment, in a tropical jungle, or a fertile plain, respectively. Other divergencies are accounted for by the level of development. Over and above such distinctions, we have to register fully and clearly that there occur in human cultures strange hypertrophies of custom, specific types of value, or else dominant interests in one or the other of the instrumental imperatives. In some cases they can be accounted for by a gradual integration of accidental events which gave to the development of a culture a specific twist. In such cases we could say that an historic explanation of such a hypertrophied economic institution as the Melanesian *kula* or the northwestern American *potlatch* can be given. In many cases the anthropologist, following the famous student of physics, has to admit simply and honestly his ignorance: *Ignoramus ignorabimus.*

As in all other studies, however, it is first necessary to establish the basis of research in formulating the universal principles of cultural analyses and thus providing a thoroughgoing classification of facts. On this basis it is then easier and more profitable to discuss the minor or partial problems of the subject matter: the deviations and the regional characteristics of cultures.

5 Kroeber's Superorganic

A. L. KROEBER

Kroeber's "Superorganic" was published in 1917 and soon thereafter became recognized as a tour de force. *The great appeal of this essay stemmed from many bases. First, its author had an obvious command of a wide range of scholarship. Second, by considering culture* as if *man did not exist, Kroeber appeared to have made anthropology susceptible to real scientific analysis. The Boasian problem, so well discussed by Professor Wax, appeared settled: anthropology was a science capable of identifying regularities of a universal nature. Third, Kroeber's writing style facilitated communication: a large and varied audience could quickly respond to Kroeber's messages. By artfully interweaving theoretical ideas with examples drawn from many fields, the central point was hammered home: to understand man, we must look to his creations. A study of man's creations indicates that man is a messenger carrying information across the generations. And, such information (i.e. man's culture), is the prime determinant of human action.*

Kroeber develops his argument from a discussion of the basic difference which exists between organic things and superorganic (social, cultural) things. We pick up Kroeber's thesis when he contrasts animal speech (an organic process) with human speech (a superorganic process).

On the surface, human and animal speech, in spite of the enormously greater richness and complexity of the former, are much alike. Both express emotions, possibly ideas, in sounds formed by bodily organs and understood by the hearing individual. But the difference between the so-called language of brutes and that of men is infinitely great; as a homely illustration will set forth.

A newly-born pup is brought up in a litter of kittens by a fostering cat. Familiar anecdotes and newspaper paragraphs to the contrary, the youngster will bark and growl, not purr or miaow. He will not even try to do the latter. The first time his toe is stepped on, he will whine, not squeal, just as surely as when thoroughly angered he will bite as his never-beheld mother did, and not even attempt to claw as he has seen his foster-mother do. For half his life seclusion may keep him from sight or sound or scent of another dog. But then

SOURCE: Abridged from "The Superorganic" by A. L. Kroeber. Reproduced by permission of the author's estate and the American Anthropological Association from *American Anthropologist*, Vol. 19, No. 2, April–June, 1917.

let a bark or a snarl reach him through the restraining wall, and he will be all attention—far more than at any voice ever uttered by his cat associates. Let the bark be repeated, and interest will give way to excitement, and infallibly he will answer in kind, as certainly as, put with a bitch, the sexual impulses of his species will manifest themselves. It cannot be doubted that dog speech is as ineradicably part of dog nature, as fully contained in it without training or culture, as wholly part of the dog organism, as are teeth or feet or stomach or motions or instincts. No degree of contact with cats, or deprivation of association with his own kind, can make a dog acquire cat speech, or lose his own, any more than it can cause him to switch his tail instead of wagging it, to rub his sides against his master instead of leaping against him, or to grow whiskers and carry his drooping ears erect.

Let us take a French baby, born in France of French parents, themselves descended for numerous generations from French-speaking ancestors. Let us, at once after birth, entrust the infant to a mute nurse, with instructions to let no one handle or see her charge, while she travels by the directest route to the interior heart of China. There she delivers the child to a Chinese couple, who legally adopt it, and rear it as their son. Now suppose three or ten or thirty years passed. Is it needful to discuss what the growing or grown Frenchman will speak? Absolutely not a word of French; and absolutely pure Chinese, without a trace of accent and with Chinese fluency; and nothing else.

Now there is something deep going here. No amount of association with Chinese would turn our young Frenchman's eyes from blue to black, or slant them, or flatten his nose, or coarsen or stiffen his wavy, oval-sectioned hair; and yet his speech is totally that of his associates, in no measure that of his blood kin. His eyes and his nose and his hair are his from heredity; his language is nonhereditary—as much so as the length to which he allows his hair to grow, or the hole which, in conformity to fashion, he may or may not bore in his ears. It is not that speech is mental and facial proportions physical; the distinction that has meaning and use is that human language is non-hereditary and social, eye-color and nose-shape hereditary and organic. By the same criterion, dog speech, and all that is vaguely called the language of animals, is in a class with men's noses, the proportions of their bones, the color of their skin, and the slope of their eyes, and not in a class with any human idiom. It is inherited, and therefore organic. By a human standard, it is not really language at all, except by the sort of metaphor that speaks of the language of the flowers.

There is in human life a series of utterances that are of the type of animal cries. A man in pain moans without purpose of communication. The sound is literally pressed from him. A person in supreme fright may shriek. We know that his cry is instinctive, unintended, what the physiologist calls a reflex action. The true shriek is as liable to escape the victim pinned before the approaching engineerless train, as him who is pursued by thinking and planning enemies.

The woodsman crushed by a rock forty miles from the nearest human being, will moan like the run-over city dweller surrounded by a crowd waiting for the speeding ambulance. Such cries are of a class with those of animals. In fact, to really understand the "speech" of brutes, we must think ourselves into a condition in which our utterances would be totally restricted to such instinctive cries—"inarticulate" is their general though often inaccurate designation. In any exact sense, they are not language at all.

As a matter of fact however the purely animal element in human speech is small. Apart from laughter and crying, it finds rare utterance. Our interjections are denied by philologists as true speech, or at best but half admitted. It is a fact that they differ from full words in not being voiced, generally, to convey a meaning—nor to conceal one. But even these particles are shaped and dictated by fashion, by custom, by the type of civilization to which we belong, in short by social and not by organic elements. When I drive the hammer on my thumb instead of on the head of the nail, an involuntary "damn" may escape me as readily if I am alone in the house, as if companions stand on each side. Perhaps more readily. So far, the exclamation does not serve the purpose of speech and is not speech. But the Spaniard will say "carramba" and not "damn"; and the Frenchman, the German, the Chinaman, will avail himself of still different expression. The American says "outch" when hurt. Other nationalities do not understand this syllable. Each people has its own sound; some even two—one used by men and the other by women. A Chinaman will understand a laugh, a moan, a crying child, as well as we understand it, and as well as a dog understands the snarl of another dog. But he must learn "outch," or it is meaningless. No dog, on the other hand, ever has given utterance to a new snarl, unintelligible to other dogs, as a result of having been brought up in different associations. Even this lowest element of human speech, then, this involuntary half-speech of exclamations, is therefore not indeed caused but at any rate shaped by social influences.

The mental activity of the animals is instinctive; the content, at least, of our own minds comes to us through tradition, in the widest sense of the word. Instinct is what is "pricked in"; an unalterable pattern inherent in the goods; indelible and inextinguishable, because the design is nothing but the warp and the woof, coming ready-made from the loom of heredity.

But tradition, what is "given through," handed along, from one to another, is only a message. It must of course be carried; but the messenger after all is extrinsic to the news. So, a letter must be written; but as its significance is in the meaning of the words, as the value of a note is not in the fiber of the paper but in the characters inscribed on its surface, so tradition is something superadded to the organisms that bear it, imposed upon them, external to them. And as the same shred can bear any one of thousands of inscriptions, of the most diverse force and value, and can even be tolerably razed and reinscribed, so it is with the human organism and the countless contents that civilization can pour into it. The essential difference between animal and man, in this illustration, is not that the latter has finer grain or the chaster quality of material; it is that his structure and nature and texture are such that he is inscribable, and that the animal is not.

There have been many attempts to make precise the distinction between instinct and civilization, between the organic and the social, between animal and man. Man as the clothing animal, the fire-using animal, the tool-using or tool-making animal, the speaking animal, are all summations that contain some approximation. But for the conception of the discrimination that is at once most complete and most compact, we must go back, as for the first precise expression of so many of the ideas with which we operate, to the uniquely marvelous mind that impelled Aristotle. "Man is a political animal." The word political has changed in import. We use instead the Latin term social. This, both philosopher and philologist tell us, is what the great Greek would have said were he speaking in English today. Man is a social animal, then; a social organism. He has organic constitution; but he has also civilization. To ignore one element is as short-sighted as to overlook the other; to convert one into the other, if each has its reality, is negation. The attempt today to treat the social as organic, to understand civilization as heredity, is as essentially narrow-minded as the alleged medieval inclination to withdraw man from the realm of nature and from the ken of the scientist because he was believed to possess an immaterial soul.

But, unfortunately, the denials, and for every denial a dozen confusions, still persist. They pervade the popular mind; and thence they rise, again and again, into the thoughts of avowed and recognized science. It seems, even, that in a hundred years we have retrograded. A century and two centuries ago, with a generous impulse, the leaders of thought devoted their energies, and the leaders of men their lives, to the cause that all men are equal. With all that this idea involves, and with its correctness, we need not here concern ourselves; but it certainly implied the proposition of equality of racial capacity. Possibly our ancestors were able to maintain this liberal stand because its full practical imports did not yet face them. But, whatever the reason, we have certainly gone back, in America and in Europe and in their colonies, in our application of the assumption; and we have receded too in our theoretic analysis of the evidence. Hereditary racial differences of ability pass as approved doctrine, in many quarters. There are men of eminent learning who would be surprised to know that serious doubts were held in the matter.

And yet, it must be maintained that not a single piece of evidence has yet been produced to support the assumption that the differences which one nation shows from another—let alone the superiority of one people to another—are racially inherent, that is organically founded. It does not matter how distinguished the minds are that have held such differences to be hereditary—they have only taken their conviction for granted. The historian can, and occasionally does, turn the case inside out with equal justification; and he then sees every event, every inequality, the whole course of human history, confirming his thesis that the distinctions between one group of men and another, past and present, are due to social influences and not in any measure to organic causes. Real proof, to be sure, is as wanting on one side as on the other. Experiment, under conditions that would yield satisfying evidence, would be difficult, costly, and perhaps contrary to law. A repetition of Akbar's interesting trial, or some modification of it, intelligently directed and followed out, would yield results of the greatest value; but it would not be tolerated by any civilized government.

There have been some attempts to investigate so-called racial distinctions with the apparatus of experimental psychology. The results incline clearly toward confirmation of the doctrine of the non-existence of organic differences. But too much stress may not as yet be laid on this conclusion, because what such investigations have above all revealed is that social agencies are so tremendously influential on every one of us that it is very difficult to find any test that, if distinctive racial faculties were inborn, would fairly reveal the degree to which they are inborn.

It is also well to remember that the problem of whether the human races are or are not in themselves identical, has innumerable practical bearings, which relate to conditions of life and to views that have intense emotional relations, so that an impartially abstract predisposition is rather rarely to be encountered. It is practically futile, for instance, to even touch upon the question with an American from the Southern states, or one tinged by Southern influences, no matter what his education or standing in the world. The actual social cleavage which is fundamental to all life in the South, and which is conceived of mainly as a race question, is so overshadowing and inevitable, that it compels, for the individual almost as firmly as for his group, a certain line of action, an unalterable and conscious course of conduct; and it could not well be otherwise than that opinions which flagrantly clash with all one's activities and with all the associated ideals, should arouse hostility.

The problem being in the present state of our knowledge unprovable, is really also not arguable. What is possible, however, is to realize that a complete and consistent explanation can be given, for all so-called racial differences, on a basis of purely civilizational and non-organic causes; and to attain also to the recognition that the mere fact of the world in general assuming that such differences between one people and another are inborn and ineradicable except by breeding, is no evidence whatever in favor of the assumption being true.

The final argument, that one can actually *see* such national peculiarities born into each generation, and that it is unnecessary to verify the assumption because its truth is obvious to every one, has the least weight of all. It is of a kind with the contention that might be made that this planet is after all the fixed central point of the cosmic system because everyone can see for himself that the sun and stars move and that our earth stands still. The champions of the Copernican doctrine had this in their favor: they dealt with phenomena to which exactitude was readily applicable, about which verifiable or disprovable predictions could be made, which an explanation either fitted or did not fit. In the domain of human history this is not possible, or has not yet been found possible; so that an equal neatness of demonstration, a definitiveness of proof, a close tallying of theory with the facts to the exclusion of all rival theories, is not to be hoped for at present. But there is almost as fundamental a shifting of mental and emotional point of view, as absolute a turning upside down of attitude involved when the current thought of today is asked to view civilization as a wholly non-organic affair, as when the Copernican doctrine challenged the prior conviction of the world.

Most ethnologists, at any rate, are convinced that the overwhelming mass of historical and miscalled racial facts that are now attributed to obscure organic causes, or at most are in dispute, will ultimately be viewed by everyone as social and as intelligible only in their social relations. That there may be a residuum in which hereditary influences have been operative, it would be dogmatic to deny; but even this residuum of organic agencies will perhaps be found to be operative in quite other manners than those which are customarily adduced at present.

The opinion may further be uncompromisingly maintained, that for the historian—him who wishes to understand any sort of social phenomena—it is an unavoidable necessity, today, to disregard the organic as such and to deal only with the social. For the larger number who are not professional students of civilization, insistence upon these articles would be an unreasonable demand, under our present inability to substantiate them by proof. On the other hand, the social as something distinct from the organic is an old enough concept, and is a plain enough phenomenon about us in daily life, to warrant the claim that it cannot be outright dispensed with. It is perhaps too much to expect any one wedded, deliberately or unknowingly, to organic explanations, to discard these wholly before such incomplete evidence as is available to the contrary of these explanations. But it does seem justifiable to stand unhesitatingly on the proposition that civilization and heredity are two things that operate in entirely separate ways; that therefore any outright substitution of one for the other in the explanation of human group phenomena is crass; and that the refusal to recognize at least the logical possibility of an explanation of human achievement totally different from the prevailing tendency toward a biological one, is an act of illiberality. When once such recognition, of the rationality of this attitude of mind which is diametrically opposed to the current one, shall have become general, far more progress will have been made on the road towards a useful agreement as to the truth, than by any present attempts to win converts by argument.

One of the minds endowed with as eminent power of perception and formulation as any of our generation, Gustave Le Bon explains civilization on the basis of race.[1]

When he says that "cross breeding destroys an ancient civilization" he affirms only what many a biologist would be ready to maintain. When he adds: "because it destroys the soul of the people that possesses it," he gives a reason that must inspire any true scientist with a shudder. But if we change "cross breeding," that is, the mixture of sharply differentiated organic types, into "sudden contact or conflict of ideals," that is, mixture of sharply differentiated social types, the profound effect of such an event is indisputable.

Again, Le Bon asserts that the effect of environment is great on new races, on races forming through cross breeding of peoples of contrary heredities; and that in ancient races solidly established by heredity the effect of environment is nearly nil. It is obvious that in an old and firm civilization the actively changing effect of geographical environment must be small because the civilization has long since had ample opportunity to utilize the environment for its needs; but that on the other hand when the civilization is new—whether because of its transportation, because of its proceeding fusion from several elements, or from mere internal development—the renewing of relationship between itself and the surrounding physical geography must go on at a rapid rate. Here again good history is turned into bad science by a confusion that seems almost deliberately perverse.

A people is guided far more by its dead than by its living, Le Bon says. He is trying to establish the importance of heredity on national careers. What, though unrecognized by himself, lies at the bottom of his thought, is the truth that every civilization rests in the past, that however much its ancient elements are no longer living as such, they nevertheless form its trunk and body, around which the live sap-wood of the day is only a shell and a surface. That imposed education, a formal and conscious thing, can not give the substance of a new or another civilization to a people, is a verity that Le Bon has seized with vigor. But when he deduces this maxim as an inference from the unbridgeable abyss that eternally exists between races, he rests an obvious fact, which no person of discrimination has yet disputed, upon a mystical assertion.

It might nearly have been foreseen, after the above citations, that Le Bon would lay the "character" of his "races" to "accumulation by heredity." If there is anything that heredity does not do, it is to accumulate. If, on the other

[1] Gustave Le Bon, *The Crowd*, 2nd ed., London: T. F. Unwin, 1897.

hand, there is any one method by which civilization may be defined as operating, it is precisely that of accumulation. We add the power of flight, the understanding of the mechanism of the aeroplane, to our previous accomplishments and knowledges. The bird does not; he has given up his legs and toes for wings. It may be true that the bird is on the whole a higher organism than his reptilian ancestor, that he has traveled farther on the road of development. But his advance has been achieved by a transmutation of qualities, a conversion of organs and faculties, not by an increasing summation of them.

The whole theory of heredity by acquirement rests upon the confusion of these two so diverse processes, that of heredity and that of civilization. It has been nourished, perhaps, by unsatisfied needs of biological science, but it has never obtained the slightest unchallengeable verification from biology, and has in fact long been assailed, by a sound and vigorous instinct, as well as in consequence of the failure of observation and experiment, from within that science. It is a doctrine that is the constant blazon of the dilettante who knows something of both history and life, but has no care to understand the workings of either. Le Bon's studies being an attempt to explain one by the other, his utilization, sooner or later, of the doctrine of heredity by acquisition or accumulation, could almost have been predicted.

The reason why mental heredity has nothing to do with civilization, is that civilization is not mental action but a body or stream of products of mental exercise. Mental activity, as biologists have dealt with it, being organic, any demonstration concerning it consequently proves nothing whatever as to social events. Mentality relates to the individual. The social or cultural, on the other hand, is in its very essence non-individual. Civilization, as such, begins only where the individual ends; and whoever does not in some measure perceive this fact, though as a brute and rootless one, can find no meaning in civilization, and history for him must be only a wearying jumble, or an opportunity for the exercise of art.

All biology necessarily has this entire reference to the individual. A social mind is as meaningless a nonentity as a social body. There can be only one kind of organicness: the organic on another plane would no longer be organic. The Darwinian doctrine relates, it is true, to the race; but the race, except as an abstraction, is only a collection of individuals; and the bases of this doctrine, heredity, variation, and competition, deal with the relation of individual to individual, from individual, and against individual. The whole key of the success of the Mendelian methods of studying heredity lies in isolating traits and isolating individuals.

But a thousand individuals do not make a society. They are the potential basis of a society; but they do not themselves cause it, and they are also the basis of a thousand other potential societies.

The findings of biology as to heredity, mental and physical alike, may then, in fact must be, accepted without reservation. But that therefore civilization can be understood by psychological analysis, or explained by observations or experiments in heredity, or, to revert to a concrete example, that the destiny of nations can be predicted from an analysis of the organic constitution of their members, assumes that society is merely a collection of individuals; that civilization is only an aggregate of psychic activities and not also an entity beyond them; in short, that the social can be wholly resolved into the mental as it is thought this resolves into the physical.

It is accordingly in this point of the tempting leap from the individually mental to the culturally social which presupposes but does not contain mentality, that the source of the distracting transferences of the organic into the social is to be sought. A more exact examination of the relation of the two is therefore desirable.

According to a saying that is also almost proverbial, and true to the degree that such commonplaces can be true, the modern schoolboy knows more than Aristotle; but this fact, if a thousand times so, does not in the least endow him with a fraction of the intellect of the great Greek. Socially—because knowledge must be a social circumstance—it is knowledge, and not the greater development of one individual or another, that counts; just as, to measure the true force of the greatness of the person, the psychologist or geneticist disregards the state of general enlightenment, the varying degree of civilizational development, to make his comparisons. A hundred Aristotles among our cave-dwelling ancestors would have been Aristotles in their birthright no less; but they would have contributed far less to the advance of science than a dozen plodding mediocrities in the twentieth century. A super-Archimedes in the ice age would have invented neither firearms nor the telegraph.

If this is true, it follows that all so-called inventors of appliances or discoverers of thoughts of note were unusually able men, endowed from before birth with superior faculties, which the psychologist can hope to analyze and define, the physiologist to correlate with functions of organs, and the genetic biologist to investigate in their hereditary origins until he attains not only system and law but verifiable power of prediction. And, on the other hand, the content of the invention or discovery springs in no way from the make-up of the great man, or that of his ancestors, but is a product purely of the civilization into which he with millions of others is born as a meaningless and regularly recurring event. Whether he in his person becomes inventor, explorer, imitator, or user, is an affair of forces that the science of mechanical causality is concerned with. Whether his invention is that of the cannon or the bow, his achievement a musical scale or a system of harmony, his formulation that of the soul or that of the categorical imperative, is not explainable by the medium of mechanistic science—at least, not by any methods at the command of biological science—but finds its meaning only in such operations with the material of civilization as history is occupied with.

Knowing the civilization of an age and a land, we can then substantially affirm that its distinctive discoveries, in this or that field of activity, were not directly contingent upon the personality of the actual inventors that graced the period, but would have been made without them; and that, conversely, had the great illuminating minds of other centuries and climates been born in the civilization referred to, instead of their own, its first achievements would have fallen to their lot. Ericsson or Galvani eight thousand years ago would have polished or bored the first stone; and in turn the hand and mind whose operation set in inception the neolithic age of human culture, would, if held in its infancy in unchanging catalepsy from that time until today, now be devising wireless telephones and nitrogen extractors.

Some reservations must be admitted to this principle. It is far from established, rather the contrary, that extraordinary ability, however equal in intensity, is identical in direction. It is highly unlikely that Beethoven put in Newton's cradle would have worked out calculus, or the latter have given the symphony its final form. We can and evidently must admit congenital faculties that are fairly specialized. Everything shows that the elementary mental faculties, such as memory, interest, and abstraction, are by nature very uneven in individuals of equivalent ability but distinctive bent; and this in spite of cultivation. The educator who proclaimed his ability to convert a native memory for absolute numbers or for mathematical formulas into an equally strong retention of single tones or of complex melodies, would be distrusted as a charlatan or a fanatic. But it does not essentially matter if the originating faculty is one or several in mind.

If, therefore, any one's interpretation of mentality is disturbed by some of the particular equivalences that have been suggested, he can easily find others that seem more just, without dissenting from the underlying principle that the march of history, or as it is current custom to name it, the progress of civilization, is independent of the birth of particular personalities; since these, apparently averaging alike, both as regards genius and normality, at all times and places, furnish the same substratum for the social.

Here, then, we have an interpretation which allows to the individual, and through him to heredity, all that the science of the organic can legitimately claim on the strength of its actual accomplishments; and which also yields the fullest scope to the social in its own distinctive field. The accomplishment of the individual measured against other individuals depends, if not wholly then mainly, on his organic constitution as compounded by his heredity. The accomplishments of a group, relative to other groups, are uninfluenced by heredity because sufficiently large groups average alike in organic make-up.

The difference between the accomplishments of one group of men and those of another group is of another order from the difference between the faculties of one person and another. It is through this distinction that one of the essential qualities of the nature of the social is to be found.

The physiological and the mental are bonded as aspects of the same thing, one resolvable into the other; the social is, directly considered, irresolvable into the mental. That it exists only after mentality of a certain kind is in action, has led to confusion of the two, and even to their identification. The error of this identification is a fault that tends to pervade modern thinking about civilization, and which must be overcome by self-discipline before our understanding of this order of phenomena that fill and color our lives can become either clear or serviceable.

If the relation of the individual to culture here outlined is a true one, a conflicting view sometimes held and already alluded to, is unentertainable. This view is the opinion that all personalities are, while not identical, potentially equal in capacity, their varying degrees of accomplishment being due solely to different measures of accord with the social environment with which they are in touch. This view has perhaps been rarely formulated as a generic principle; but it seems to underlie, though usually vaguely and by implication only, many tendencies toward social and educational reform, and is therefore likely to find formal enunciation at some time.

This assumption, which would certainly be of extensive practical application if it could be verified, seems to rest ultimately upon a dim but profound perception of the influence of civilization. More complete that this influence of civilization is upon national fortunes than upon individual careers, it nevertheless must influence these latter also. Mohammedanism—a social phenomenon—in stifling the imitative possibilities of the pictorial and plastic arts, has obviously affected the civilization of many peoples; but it must also have altered the careers of many persons born in three continents during a thousand years. Special talents which these men and women possessed for delineative representation may have been suppressed without equal compensation in other directions, in those whose endowment was unique. Of such individuals it is undoubtedly true that the social forces to which they were subject depressed each of them from successful attainment to more mediocre. And without question the same environment elevated many an individual to high rank above his fellows whose special abilities, in some other age and country, would have been repressed to his private disadvantage. The personality born with those qualities that lead to highly successful leadership of religious brigands, for instance, is undoubtedly assured of a more prosperous and contented career in Morocco than in Holland of today.

Even within one nationally limited sphere of civilization, similar results are necessarily bound to occur constantly. The natural logician or administrator born into a caste of fishermen or street sweepers is not likely to achieve the satisfaction in life, and certainly not the success, that would have been his lot had his parents been Brahmins or Kshatriyas; and what is true formally of India holds substantially for Europe.

But, that a social environment may somewhat affect the fortunes and career of the individual as measured against other individuals, does not prove that the individual is wholly the product of circumstances outside of himself, any more than it means that the opposite is true and that a civilization is only the sum total of the products of a group of organically shaped minds. The concrete effect of each individual upon civilization is determined by civilization itself. Civilization appears even in some cases and in some measure to influence the effect of the individual's native activities upon himself. But to proceed from these realizations to the inference that all the degree and quality of accomplishment by the individual is the result of his moulding by the society that encompasses him, is pure assumption, extreme at that, and directly at variance with all observation, both as immediate apperception and as it survives critical analysis.

Therefore it is possible to hold to the historical or civilizational interpretation of social phenomena without proceeding to occupy the position that the human beings that are the given channels through which civilization courses, are only and wholly the products of its stream. Because culture rests on specific human faculty, it does not follow that this faculty, the thing in man that is supra-animal, is of social determination. The line between the social and the organic may not be randomly or hastily drawn. The threshold between the endowment that renders the flow and continuance of civilization possible and that which prohibits even its inception, is the demarcation—doubtful enough once, in all probability, but gaping for a longer period than our knowledge covers—between man and animal. The separation between the social itself, however, the entity that we call civilization, and the non-social, the pre-social or organic, is the diversity of quality or order or nature which exists between animal and man conjointly on the one hand, and the products of the interactions of human beings on the other. In the previous pages the mental has already been subtracted from the social and added to the physically organic which is subject to the influence of heredity. In the same way it is necessary to eliminate the factor of individual capacity from the consideration of civilization. But this elimination means its transfer to the group of organically conceivable phenomena, not its denial. In fact nothing is further from the path of a just prosecution of the understanding of history than such a negation of differences of degree of the faculties of individual men.

In short, social science, if we may take that word as equivalent to history, does not deny individuality any more than it denies the individual. It does refuse to deal with either individuality or individuals. And it bases this refusal solely on its denial of the validity of either factor for the achievement of its proper aims.

It is true that historical events can also be viewed mechanically, and expressed ultimately in terms of physics and chemistry. Genius may prove definable in unit characters or the constitution of chromosomes, and its particular achievements in osmotic reactions of nerve cells. The day may come when what took place in the tissue of Darwin's brain when he first thought the concept of natural selection, can be profitably studied, or even approximately ascertained, by the physiologist and chemist. Such an achievement, shockingly destructive as it may seem to those whom revelation appals, would be not only defensible, but worth while—of enormous interest, even, and possibly of the highest utility. Only, it would not be history; nor a step toward history or social science.

To know the precise reactions in Darwin's nervous system at the moment when the thought of natural selection flashed upon him in 1838, would involve a very genuine triumph of science. But it would mean nothing historically, since history is concerned with the relation of doctrines such as that of natural selection to other concepts and social phenomena, and not at all with the relation of Darwin himself to social phenomena, or other phenomena. This is not the current view of history; but, on the other hand, the current view rests upon the endlessly recurring but obviously illogical assumption that because without individuals civilization could not exist, civilization therefore is only a sum total of the psychic operations of a mass of individuals.

There are those, of mechanistic proclivities and interests, who hold that it is only when historical events are explained on a basis like that assumed in our example, that history will have any significance. They have pressed their view, sometimes by assertion, more often by implication, until it has come to be widely accepted. But it is true only if a single method of thought is the sole one to be accorded validity and justifiability. If the ability to weigh the moon renders Shelley's poetry a useless superfluity, well and good: there is nothing more to be said. There actually are people fanatic enough to take such a stand. But if scientific methods give science, and artistic exercise yields literature, and the two do not exclude each other because they do not come into conflict and are not even comparable; if the justification of each is in its results and not in any toleration extended by the other; and if the truly unforgivable sin with the crown of futility is not to practise one without regard to the other but to try to practise one by means of the other;—then, too, it is at least conceivable that there may be a third activity, neither science nor art in their strict senses, but history, the understanding of the social, which also has an aim that cannot be denied and whose justification must be sought in its own results and not by the standard of any other activity. That is all that history as an intellectual manifestation can ask; but that it must ask. Mechanistic science has accomplished wonders in a brief space by adhering ever more rigidly to its own peculiar methods, and allowing no limits to be set to its application of these methods. Yet that a tool has proved its service for a purpose, does not affect the value of other purposes or the utility of other tools for these other purposes. Whenever the mechanistic scientist proposes to accomplish all the work of the human understanding by his science, he is taking the stand either of his predecessor of ruder days who mingled the objects and means of science and theology, or science and art, or science and morals; or of that other often cited but perhaps imaginary predecessor who, when spiritual power made him arrogant, denied the right of existence of science as a goal or science as a method; proclaiming that divine truth was the only and sufficient truth. Intolerance is ever born anew. But science has escaped from alleged persecution, and then from timid servility, only so recently, that it should remember not to attempt oppression and negation in its turn.

History, then, justifies itself in proportion that it is mechanistically "unscientific"; that it has its own method, its own equivalent to the causality of science; and, in one sense, its own material. Not that there is a range of subjects that can be delimited and assigned respectively to science and to history. In fact, the applicability of science to any and all domains of human cognizance must be expressly affirmed. But the same phenomenon can after all be viewed with different ends. The social is scientifically resolvable; but it is resolvable through the individual—the organic and psychic individual. History deals with the social by resolving it into the social without the medium of the individual.

Science will attack historical material—social material—by converting it into organic terms—whether psychical or physical does not matter, so long as the ever present individual physiological aspect or basis of the social phenomena is dealt with. These organic results will then be ready for interpretation by the methods of physics and chemistry. Thus the material will be made part of that great unit, the system that justifies and elevates science to its high plane—the system that is pervaded by the principle of mechanical causality as its essence. But history, without denying this principle, without concerning itself with it or with the methods that flow from it, keeps its intent fixed upon the unaltered and irresolved facts of the social plane, upon historical data apperceived and utilized directly.

As, then, there are two lines of intellectual endeavor in history and in science, each with its separate aim and set of methods; and as it is only the confounding of the two that results in sterile negation; so also two wholly disparate evolutions must be recognized: that of the substance which we call organic and that of the other substance called social. Social evolution is without antecedents in the beginnings of organic evolution. It commences late in the development of life—long after vertebrates, after mammals, after the primates even, are established. Its exact point of origin we do not know, and perhaps shall never know; but we can limit the range within which it falls. This origin occurred in a series of organic forms more advanced, in general mental faculty, than the gorilla, and much less developed than the first known race that is unanimously accepted as having been human, the man of Neandertal and Le Moustier. In point of time, these first carriers of the rudiments of civilization must antedate the Neandertal race by far, but must be much posterior to other extinct human ancestors of the approximate intellectual level of the modern gorilla and chimpanzee. Evidence fails, and in the present connection the determination would be of little moment.

The beginning of social evolution, of the civilization which is the subject of history, thus coincides with that mystery of the popular mind: the missing link. But the term "link" is misleading. It implies a continuous chain, a strand that is the same in texture before and beyond the break in knowledge. But with the unknown bearers of the primeval and gradually manifesting beginnings of civilization, there took place a profound alteration rather than an improved passing on of the existing. A new factor had arisen which was to work out its own independent consequences, slowly and of little apparent import at first, but gathering weight, and dignity, and influence; a factor that had passed beyond natural selection, that was no longer wholly dependent on any agency of organic evolution, and that, however rocked and swayed by the oscillations of the heredity that underlay it, nevertheless floated unimmersibly upon it.

The dawn of the social thus is not a link in any chain, not a step in a path, but a leap to another plane. It may be likened to the first occurrence of life in the hitherto lifeless universe, the hour when that one of infinite chemical combinations took place which put the organic into existence, and made it that from that moment on there should be two worlds in place of one. Atomic qualities and movements were not interfered with when that seemingly slight event took place; the majesty of the mechanical laws of the cosmos was not diminished; but something new was inextinguishably added to the history of this planet; as when a perpetually reeling thread becomes two from one.

Or, one might compare the inception of civilization to the end of the process of slowly heating water. The expansion of the liquid goes on a long time. Its alteration can be observed by the thermometer as well as in bulk, in its solvent power as well as in its internal agitation. But it remains water. Finally, however, the boiling point is attained. Steam is produced: the rate of enlargement of volume is increased a thousand fold; and in place of a glistening percolating fluid, a volatile gas diffuses invisibly. Neither the laws of physics nor those of chemistry are violated; nature is not set aside; but yet a saltation has taken place: the slow transitions that accumulated from zero to one hundred have been transcended in an instant, and a condition of substance with new properties and new possibilities of effect is in existence.

Such, in some manner, must have been the result of the appearance of this new thing, civilization. We need not consider that it abolished the course of development of life. It certainly has not in any measure done away with its own substratum of the organic. And there is no reason to believe that it was born full fledged. All these incidents and manners of the inception of the social are after all of little consequence to an understanding of its specific nature, and of the relation of that nature to the character of the organic substance that preceded it in absolute time and still supports it. The point is, there was an addition of something new in kind, an initiation of that which was to run a course of its own.

Here, then, we have to come to our conclusion; and here we rest. The mind and the body are but facets of the same organic material or activity; the social substance—or unsubstantial fabric, if one prefers the phrase—the existence that we call civilization, transcends them utterly for all its being forever rooted in life. The processes of civilizational activity are almost unknown to us. The self-sufficient factors that govern their workings are unresolved. The forces and principles of mechanistic science can indeed analyze our civilization; but in so doing they destroy its essence, and leave us without understanding of the very thing which we seek. The historian as yet can do little but picture. He traces and he connects what seems far removed; he balances; he integrates; but he does not really explain, nor does he transmute phenomena into something else. His method is not science; but neither can the scientist deal with historical material and leave it civilization, nor anything resembling civilization, nor convert it wholly into concepts of life and leave nothing else to be done. What we all are able to do is to realize this gap, to be impressed by its abyss with reverence and humility, and to go our paths on its respective sides without self-deluding attempts to bridge the eternal chasm, or empty boasts that its span is achieved.

6 Sapir's Views of the Superorganic

EDWARD SAPIR

Looked at from one point of view Kroeber's essay simplified *the study of man by getting down to the essentials of human behavior. By focusing on culture as a superorganic process it is not necessary to deal with the complexities*

SOURCE: Reprinted from "Do We Need a 'Superorganic'?" by Edward Sapir. Reproduced by permission of the author's estate and the American Anthropological Association from *American Anthropologist,* Vol. 19, No. 3, 1917, pp. 441–447.

of human decision-making. The human animal received a culture, saw reality through his culture's "eyes," and acted accordingly. The powerful message of "The Superorganic" was a milestone in anthropological thinking because whether or not one completely agreed with the views presented, such views had to be taken into account: the serious student of social life was forced to re-think his conclusions as to the nature of reality. In re-thinking reality, new conceptual and analytic doors are opened; novel questions force themselves into our consciousness. Is man but a machine, programmed by culture and fated to act out such a program throughout his life? Are all men (and women) equally enslaved? Do we all, genius and fool, knave and saint, share this destiny? What then is the meaning of free will, and of deviance?

From another point of view, that espoused by Sapir, a superorganic approach oversimplifies *reality. Man is more, much more, than a carrier of information. Man is not just an unimportant messenger. From within this framework it seems logical to ask Sapir's question: "Do we need a superorganic?"*

Nothing irritates a student of culture more than to have the methods of the exact sciences flaunted in his face as a salutary antidote to his own supposedly slipshod methods. He feels that he deals with an entirely different order of phenomena, that direct comparison between the two groups of disciplines is to be ruled out of court. It is some such irritation that seems to have served as the emotional impetus of Dr. Kroeber's very interesting discussion of "The Superorganic." Many anthropologists will be disposed to sympathize with him and to rejoice that he has squarely taken up the cudgel for a rigidly historical and anti-biological interpretation of culture. His analysis of the essential difference between organic heredity and social tradition is surely sound in the main, though doubts suggest themselves on special points in this part of the discussion. The common fallacy of confounding the cultural advancement of a group with the potential or inherent intellectual power of its individual members is also clearly exposed. There is little in Dr. Kroeber's general standpoint and specific statements that I should be disposed to quarrel with. Yet I feel that on at least two points of considerable theoretical importance he has allowed himself to go further than he is warranted in going. I suspect that he may to some extent have been the victim of a too rigidly classificatory or abstractionist tendency.

In the first place, I believe that Dr. Kroeber greatly overshoots the mark in his complete elimination of the peculiar influence of individuals on the course of history, even if by that term is understood culture history, the history of social activities with practically no reference to biographical data as such. All individuals tend to impress themselves on their social environment and, though generally to an infinitesimal degree, to make their individuality count in the direction taken by the never-ceasing flux that the form and content of social activity are inevitably subject to. It is true that the content of an individual's mind is so overwhelmingly moulded by the social traditions to which he is heir that the purely individual contribution of even markedly original minds is apt to seem swamped in the whole of culture. Furthermore the dead level of compromise necessitated by the clashing of thousands of wills, few of them of compelling potency, tends to sink the social importance of any one of them into insignificance. All this is true in the main. And yet it is always the individual that really thinks and acts and dreams and revolts. Those of his thoughts, acts, dreams, and rebellions that somehow contribute in sensible degree to the modification or retention of the mass of typical reactions called culture we term social data; the rest, though they do not, psychologically considered, in the least differ from these, we term individual and pass by as of no historical or social moment. It is highly important to note that the differentiation of these two types of reaction is essentially arbitrary, resting, as it does, entirely on a principle of selection. The selection depends on the adoption of a scale of values. Needless to say, the threshold of the social (or historical) *versus* the individual shifts according to the philosophy of the evaluator or interpreter. I find it utterly inconceivable to draw a sharp and eternally valid dividing line between them. Clearly, then, "individual" reactions constantly spill over into and lend color to "social" reactions.

Under these circumstances how is it possible for the social to escape the impress of at least certain individualities? It seems to me that it requires a social determinism amounting to a religion to deny to individuals all directive power, all culture-moulding influence. Is it conceivable, for instance, that the dramatic events that we summarize under the heading of the Napoleonic Period and which are inextricably bound up with the personality of Napoleon are a matter of indifference from the point of view of the political, economic, and social development of Europe during that period and since? Would the administration of the law in New Orleans be what it now is if there had not existed a certain individual of obscure origin who hailed from Corsica? It goes without saying that in this, as in similar cases, the determining influence of specific personalities is, as a rule, grossly exaggerated by the average historian; but a tendency to deprecate too great an insistence on the individual as such is not the same thing as the attempt to eliminate him as a cultural factor altogether. Shrewdly enough, Dr. Kroeber chooses his examples from the realm of inventions and scientific theories. Here it is relatively easy to justify a sweeping social determinism in view of a certain general inevitability in the course of the acquirement of knowledge. This inevitability, however, does not altogether reside, as Dr. Kroeber seems to imply, in a social "force" but, to a very large extent, in the fixity, conceptually speaking, of the objective world.

This fixity forms the sharpest of predetermined grooves for the unfolding of man's knowledge. Had he occupied himself more with the religious, philosophic, aesthetic, and crudely volitional activities and tendencies of man, I believe that Dr. Kroeber's case for the non-cultural significance of the individual would have been a far more difficult one to make. No matter how much we minimize exaggerated claims, I fail to see how we can deny a determining and, in some cases, even extraordinarily determining cultural influence to a large number of outstanding personalities. With all due reverence for social science, I would not even hesitate to say that many a momentous cultural development or tendency, particularly in the religious and aesthetic spheres, is at last analysis a partial function or remote consequence of the temperamental peculiarities of a significant personality. As the social units grow larger and larger, the probabilities of the occurrence of striking and influential personalities grow vastly. Hence it is that the determining influence of individuals is more easily demonstrated in the higher than in the lower levels of culture. One has only to think seriously of what such personalities as Aristotle, Jesus, Mahomet, Shakespeare, Goethe, Beethoven mean in the history of culture to hesitate to commit oneself to a completely non-individualistic interpretation of history. I do not believe for a moment that such personalities are merely the cat's-paws of general cultural drifts. No doubt much, perhaps even the greater part, of what history associates with their names is merely an individually colored version of what they found ready to hand in their social, philosophic, religious, or aesthetic milieu, *but not entirely*. If such an interpretation of the significance of the individual introduces a repugnant element of "accident" into the history of culture, so much the worse for the social scientists who fear "accident."

The second point in Dr. Kroeber's essay that I find myself compelled to take exception to concerns his interpretation of the nature of social phenomena. If I understand him rightly, he predicates a certain social "force" whose gradual unfolding is manifested in the sequence of socially significant phenomena we call history. The social is builded out of the organic, but is not entirely resolvable into it, hence it implies the presence of an unknown principle which transcends the organic, just as the organic, while similarly builded out of the inorganic, is not resolvable into it but harbors a new and distinctive force that works itself out in organic phenomena. I consider the analogy a false one. Moreover, I do not believe that Dr. Kroeber has rightly seized upon the true nature of the opposition between history and non-historical science.

The analogy is a false one because, while the organic can be demonstrated to consist objectively of the inorganic plus an increment of obscure origin and nature, the social is merely a certain philosophically arbitrary but humanly immensely significant *selection* out of the total mass of phenomena ideally resolvable into inorganic, organic, and psychic processes. The social is but a name for those reactions or types of reaction that depend for their perpetuation on a cumulative technique of transference, that known as social inheritance. This technique, however, does not depend for its operation on any specifically new "force," but, as far as we can tell at present, merely implies a heightening of psychic factors. No doubt the growth of self-consciousness is largely involved in the gradual building up of this technique of social transference. While we may not be able to define satisfactorily the precise nature of self-consciousness or trace its genesis, it is certainly no more mysterious a development in the history of mind than earlier stages in this most obscure of all evolutions. In short, its appearance involves no new force, merely a refinement and complication of an earlier force or of earlier forces. Hence social activities, which I define as a selected group of reactions dependent at last analysis on the growth of self-consciousness, do not result from the coming into being of a new objective principle of being. The differential characteristic of social science lies thus entirely in a modulus of values, not in an accession of irresolvably distinct subject matter. There seems to be a chasm between the organic and the inorganic which only the rigid mechanists pretend to be able to bridge. There seems to be an unbridgeable chasm, in immediacy of experience, between the organic and the psychic, despite the undeniable correlations between the two. Dr. Kroeber denies this *en passant*, but neither his nor my philosophy of the nature of mind is properly germane to the subject under discussion. Between the psychic and the social there is no chasm in the above sense at all. The break lies entirely in the principle of selection that respectively animates the two groups of sciences. Social science is not psychology, not because it studies the resultants of a superpsychic or superorganic force, but because its terms are differently demarcated.

At this point I begin to fear misunderstanding. It might almost appear that I considered, with certain psychological students of culture, the fundamental problem of social science to consist of the resolution of the social into the psychic, of the unraveling of the tangled web of psychology that may be thought to underlie social phenomena. This conception of social science I have as much abhorrence of as Dr. Kroeber. There may be room for a "social psychology," but it is neither an historical nor a social science. It is merely a kind of psychology, of somewhat uncertain credentials, for the present; at any rate, it is, like individual psychology, a conceptual science. It is quite true that the phenomena of social science, as claimed by Dr. Kroeber, are irresolvable into the terms of psychology or organic science, but this irresolvability is not, as Dr. Kroeber seems to imply, a conceptual one. *It is an experiential one.* This type of irresolvability is *toto caelo* distinct from that which separates the psychic and the organic or the organic and the inorganic, where we are confronted by true conceptual incommensurables.

What I mean by "experiential irresolvability" is something that meets us at every turn. I shall attempt to illustrate it by an example from a totally different science. Few sciences are so clearly defined as regards scope as geology. It would ordinarily be classed as a natural science. Aside from palaeontology, which we may eliminate, it does entirely without the concepts of the social, psychic, or organic. It is, then, a well-defined science of purely inorganic subject matter. As such it is conceptually resolvable, if we carry our reductions far enough, into the more fundamental sciences of physics and chemistry. But no amount of conceptual synthesis of the phenomena we call chemical or physical would, in the absence of previous experience, enable us to construct a science of geology. This science depends for its *raison d'être* on a series of unique experiences, directly sensed or inferred, clustering about an entity, the earth, which from the conceptual standpoint of physics is as absurdly accidental or irrelevant as a tribe of Indians or John Smith's breakfast. The basis of the science is, then, firmly grounded in the uniqueness of particular events. To be precise, geology looks in two directions. In so far as it occupies itself with abstract masses and forces, it is a conceptual science, for which specific instances as such are irrelevant. In so far as it deals with particular features of the earth's surface, say a particular mountain chain, and aims to reconstruct the probable history of such features, it is not a conceptual science at all. In methodology, strange as this may seem at first blush, it is actually nearer, in this aspect, to the historical sciences. It is, in fact, a species of history, only the history moves entirely in the inorganic sphere. In practice, of course, geology is a mixed type of science, now primarily conceptual, now primarily descriptive of a selected chunk of reality. Between the data of the latter aspect and the concepts of the former lies that yawning abyss that must forever, in the very nature of things, divorce the real world of directly experienced phenomena from the ideal world of conceptual science.

Returning to social science, it is clear that the leap from psychology to social science is just of this nature. Any social datum is resolvable, at least theoretically, into psychological concepts. But just as little as the most accurate and complete mastery of physics and chemistry enables us to synthesize a science of geology, does an equivalent mastery of the conceptual science of psychology —which, by the way, nobody possesses or is likely to possess for a long time to come—enable us to synthesize the actual nature and development of social institutions or other historical data. These must be directly experienced and, as already pointed out, selected from the endless mass of human phenomena according to a principle of values. Historical science thus differs from natural science, either wholly or as regards relative emphasis, in its adherence to the real world of phenomena, not, like the latter, to the simplified and abstract world of ideal concepts. It strives to value the unique or individual, not the universal. "Individual" may naturally here mean any directly experienced entity or group of entities—the earth, France, the French language, the French Republic, the romantic movement in literature, Victor Hugo, the Iroquois Indians, some specific Iroquois clan, all Iroquois clans, all American Indian clans, all clans of primitive peoples. None of these terms, *as such*, has any relevancy in a purely conceptual world, whether organic or inorganic, physical or psychic. Properly speaking, "history" includes far more than what we ordinarily call historical or social science. The latter is merely the "historical" (in our wider sense), not conceptual, treatment of certain selected aspects of the psychic world of man.

Are not, then, such concepts as a clan, a language, a priesthood comparable in lack of individual connotation to the ideal concepts of natural science? Are not the laws applicable to these historical concepts as conceptually valid as those of natural science? Logically it is perhaps difficult, if not impossible, to make a distinction, as the same mental processes of observation, classification, inference, generalization, and so on, are brought into play. Philosophically, however, I believe the two types of concepts are utterly distinct. The social concepts are convenient summaries of a strictly limited range of phenomena, each element of which has real value. Relatively to the concept "clan" a particular clan of a specific Indian tribe has undeniable value as an historical entity. Relatively to the concept "crystal" a particular ruby in the jeweler's shop has no relevancy except by way of illustration. It has no intrinsic scientific value. Were all crystals existent at this moment suddenly disintegrated, the science of crystallography would still be valid, provided the physical and chemical forces that make possible the growth of another crop of crystals remain in the world. Were all clans now existent annihilated, it is highly debatable, to say the least, whether the science of sociology, in so far as it occupied itself with clans, would have prognostic value. The difference between the two groups of concepts becomes particularly clear if we consider negative instances. If, out of one hundred clans, ninety-nine obeyed a certain sociological "law," we would justly flatter ourselves with having made a particularly neat and sweeping generalization; our "law" would have validity, even if we never succeeded in "explaining" the one exception. But if, out of one million selected experiments intended to test a physical law, 999,999 corroborated the law and one persistently refused to do so, after all disturbing factors had been eliminated, we would be driven to seek a new formulation of our law. There is something deeper involved here than relative accuracy. The social "law" is an abbreviation or formula for a finite number of evaluated phenomena, and rarely more than an approximately accurate formula at that; the natural "law" is a universally valid formulation of a regular sequence observable in an indefinitely large number of phenomena selected at random. With the multiplication of instances social "laws" become more and more blurred in outline, natural "laws" more and more rigid. However, the clarification of the sphere and concepts of social science in its more generalized aspects is a difficult problem that we can not fully discuss here.

I strongly suspect that Dr. Kroeber will not find me to differ essentially from him in my conception of history. What I should like to emphasize, however, is that it is perfectly possible to hold this view of history without invoking the aid of a "superorganic." Moreover, had the uniqueness of historical phenomena been as consistently clear to him as he himself would require, it would be difficult to understand why he should have insisted on eliminating the individual in the narrow sense of the word.

7 The Human Being and Culture

MORRIS E. OPLER

Advance or progress in science follows a rather strange path; the more illuminating an analysis, the more likely that it will lead directly to its own demise. The work that gives birth to new questions leads to novel research and novel data, and thus creates the obvious need for novel frameworks. Hence, the ideas of those who merit the label "brilliant" contain within them the seeds of their own destruction. Sapir's question is thus fruitfully subdivided into two questions: (1) Did we need a superorganic? and, (2) Do we still need a superorganic? In the paper that follows, Professor Opler relates to these questions and raises a number of important issues. Where does the "superorganic" come from? Why did those who developed this concept believe in it? Was the invention of culture man's last *creative act? Is man, now, just a puppet on cultural (superorganic) strings?*

*The belief that man's actions are determined by culture is traced historically, and quite critically by Opler, starting from the views of William Graham Sumner.**

SOURCE: This is an abridged version of the presidential address delivered November 23, 1963 at the 63rd Annual Meeting of the American Anthropological Association, and first published in *American Anthropologist* as "The Human Being in Culture Theory." Reproduced by permission of the American Anthropological Association from *American Anthropologist*, Vol. 66, No. 3, 1964. Professor Opler's help in the preparation of this shortened version is gratefully acknowledged.

* William Graham Sumner, *Folkways: A Study of the Sociological Importance of Usages, Manners, Customs, Mores, and Morals*, Boston: Ginn and Company, 1906.

In Sumner's view superorganic elements (social forms, language, beliefs, etc.) arose when man, driven to cooperation for the sake of security and to experimentation by his stark needs in the struggle for survival against natural forces and other organisms, found crude solutions to his pressing problems. Continued trial and error in an unplanned and spontaneous effort to achieve more suitable means to ends resulted in the production of variant ways of behaving and thinking. Those that reduced discomfort and danger were accepted, and they replaced the older, less satisfactory customs. When a folkway or custom was felt by all to be particularly useful and important, it was supported by sentiment as well as by habit, and activities that challenged or opposed it were frowned upon and penalized. Folkways invested with such an aura of righteousness and truth became mores. The folkways and mores came to constitute a system of beliefs and practices external to the individual and coercive upon him. Over time the totality of folkways and mores has become so impersonal, vast, external, entrenched, and automatic that individuals cannot hope to influence it. In fact, just the opposite is true. It impresses itself upon the individual from his earliest years and shapes and controls his thoughts and actions until he dies.

Although Sumner made liberal use of anthropological materials and sources in *Folkways,* he is identified professionally with the discipline of sociology. It was not until nine years after the publication of *Folkways* that a professional anthropologist dealt as forthrightly with the question of the autonomy of culture and its relationship to the individual. When this anthropological contribution did come, in the form of A. L. Kroeber's "Eighteen Professions," its message was actually not too much different in principle from Sumner's.[1] Kroeber calls for a clear distinction between history, in which he also includes sociology and historical anthropology (cultural anthropology in present terminology), and biology, under which he subsumes psychology and physical anthropology. He then proceeds to characterize history and to differentiate it from the study of man and of individual minds. He comes to a number of conclusions which have remained with us in one guise or another to this day. The material to be studied by history or anthropology, he declares, is not man, but his works. Although a certain mental constitution of man must be assumed by the historian or anthropologist, the individual and personal have no value save as an illustration. Civilization, though carried by men and existing through them, is an entity in itself and of another order from life. Geography, or physical environment, is material made use of by civilization, not a factor which shares or explains civilization. Historic events are conditioned by preceding

[1] A. L. Kroeber, "Eighteen Professions," *American Anthropologist*, 1915, Vol. 17, pp. 283–288.

historic events; cause in history or anthropology must be sought in the flow of historic events.

In 1917, Kroeber published his classic article, "The Superorganic."[2] In it the terminology of "Eighteen Professions" is somewhat revised. The terms "culture" and "the superorganic" take the place of "history" and "historical anthropology"; "civilization" is used synonymously with "culture." There is still no clear distinction made between the "cultural" and the "social." But the main arguments are refinements, in a slightly subdued vein, of those presented in "Eighteen Professions." Culture is represented as being an emergent entity occupying a sphere or level of its own. It was in this article that Kroeber first considered the bearing of instances of genius and duplicate inventions upon his theories. The genius is likely to have some accomplishments to his credit whenever he appears, Kroeber concludes, but the culture and its state and needs will dictate what his contribution is to be. Genius is determined by the culture.

In 1919 Kroeber published the results of a study of changes which had taken place from 1844–1917 in women's fashions in the Western world. He reported that in respect to certain basic measurements such as skirt length and width there were cycles which took long periods to complete. From this he inferred a principle of regularity or order in social change. Moreover, he counted this a refutation of the notion that individual preferences could have been effectively involved, for "when a swing of fashion requires a century for its satisfaction, a minimum of at least several personalities is involved."[3] This led him to a discussion of social change in general, and he concluded that the individual "is of negligible consequence." "In short, monotheism arises, an iron technique is discovered, institutions change, or dresses become full at a given period and place—subsequent to other cultural events and as the result of them, in other words—because they must."[4]

In 1940, in collaboration with Jane Richardson, Kroeber again analyzed women's dress fashions in the Western world, this time with data covering a much longer time span. Again the results were interpreted as a confrontation between overriding cultural forces and the individual. Again the influence of the individual was considered to be negligible. In their conclusions the authors said: ". . . we think that we have shown that through behavioristic and inductive procedures operating wholly within the sociocultural level, func-

---

[2] A. L. Kroeber, "The Superorganic," *American Anthropologist*, 1917, Vol. 19, No. 2, pp. 163–213.

[3] A. L. Kroeber, "On the Principle of Order in Civilization as Exemplified by Changes in Fashion," *American Anthropologist*, 1919, Vol. 21, p. 260.

[4] Kroeber (1919), p. 262.

tional correlations can be established for such supposedly refractory cultural manifestations as style and fashion changes."[5]

What correlations are here established between culture and fashion? The correlations are primarily with time, which is rather impartial with respect to the issue. It is demonstrated that measurements of women's dresses in the Western world moved from extremes of length and shortness, width and narrowness, in fairly regular cycles in the more than 300-year period between 1605 and 1937. But what of the rest of Western culture during this same time period? During these years pure science was moving in one general direction, technology was moving in one general direction, medicine was moving in one general direction, political forms were in general moving toward the limitation of the prerogatives of kings and nobles and the enlargement of the governing group and the electorate. But skirts, we are told, went from one extreme to another and back again with supreme indifference for the one-directional drift of major segments of the culture. It would seem that this raises more questions about the nature of culture and of fashion too, for that matter, than it answers. One wonders whether the authors (and this is a chronic failing of cultural determinists) were not so intent upon minimizing the psychological and the individual that they neglected to test for the cultural. In fact it could be argued that the only convincing functional correlations supplied are with psychological factors, brought in by the back door, for it appears that the greatest periods of pattern "strain" and variability coincide with periods of popular distress, dislocation, and instability occasioned by war and revolution.

The superorganic or cultural had been named by Spencer,[6] utilized in principle by Lippert,[7] and defined by Tylor,[8] but the extended and concentrated treatment given it by Sumner and then Kroeber gave it a vitality and a currency that was to make it a familiar word by the early 1930's. In 1929 Malcolm Willey, in a paper that made acknowledgements to Sumner and defended Kroeber against the criticisms of Allport, furnished a statement of cultural autonomy and determinism, and of individual impotence that was quite as drastic as anything found in either of his sources.[9] By 1932, in his paper, "The Science of Culture," Murdock is prepared to assert: "That culture, a uniquely human phenomenon independent of the laws of biology and psychology,

[5] Jane Richardson and A. L. Kroeber, "Three Centuries of Women's Dress Fashions: A Quantitative Analysis," *Anthropological Records,* Berkeley and Los Angeles: University of California Press, 1940, Vol. 5, p. 150.

[6] Herbert Spencer, *Principles of Sociology,* 3 vols., New York and London: D. Appleton & Co., 1923 (first pub. 1874–1896).

[7] Julius Lippert, *The Evolution of Culture*, New York: Macmillan, 1931.

[8] Edward B. Tylor, *Primitive Culture,* 2 vols., London: John Murray, 1871.

[9] Malcolm M. Willey, "The Validity of Cultural Concept," *American Journal of Sociology*, 1929, Vol. 35, pp. 204–219.

constitutes the proper subject of the social sciences, is a proposition accepted with practical unanimity by social anthropologists today."[10]

The view of man and culture that has been illustrated here from the writings of Sumner, Kroeber, and Murdock is present in the works of many others as well. There is a generous component of it even in the productions of those, such as Ralph Linton, who have been charged with excessive interest in the role of the individual and with psychologizing.[11]

The doctrine we have outlined of autonomous, dynamic, and external culture, and of dependent and impotent man can, as we have seen, be put in very compelling and persuasive terms. It has been and is held by some of the most prominent and influential social scientists of our time. This has given it a prestige that makes it difficult to resist and an appearance of well-founded tradition. But these premises and terms call for a closer examination than some have been willing to give them.

My misgivings concerning an extreme and unrelieved doctrine of cultural autonomy and determinism begin at the source, with the very conception of the origin and early period of culture. We are told that the primate which was to become man was probably making and using tools in an inefficient, discontinuous manner at the time when he invented symbols or arbitrary labels for artifact and concept, and, by organizing them into a system of references and linking ideas, gave birth to language. This was a glorious achievement, making possible the communication of experience and discovery, and the retention of their fruits. This transition from prehuman to human existence occurred between one and two million years ago, we now believe. The being involved in the process was not *Homo sapiens* but a form ancestral to our present species and considered to be inferior to it in potential intelligence and culture-serving capacities. By definition, then, man preceded and originated culture. He was the primal mover. But, according to the cultural determinists, the invention of the first elements of culture constitutes the last creative act in which man ever engaged. The continuation of culture, the development of culture, the proliferation of culture allegedly then went on automatically and quite apart from him. Yet the capacities that enabled him to invent culture are still present in him. He continues to make and use tools, and he can assign verbal (and today even written) symbols to objects, events, and attitudes. But the lazy fellow has for over a million years resisted any further involvement in creative acts; he is said to be content to let culture do everything for him. Obediently, he eats enough of what culture prescribes for him and pumps enough air into his lungs so that he can remain what some choose to call a

---

[10] George Peter Murdock, "The Science of Culture," *American Anthropologist*, 1932, Vol. 34, p. 200.
[11] Ralph Linton, *The Tree of Culture*, New York: Alfred A. Knopf, 1955, pp. 29–37.

thermodynamic system through which culture can work. If this is a true picture of man, something should be done for him. Perhaps culture has distilled some strong brew or some new kind of hormonal substance that can be administered to him to stir him from his lethargy. For this is the most mysterious, serious, and protracted case of arrested development in the annals of medical history. It may be that the explanation is a psychoanalytic one. We have all heard of "the trauma of birth." Perhaps this complete suspension of creativity and will was a consequence of "a trauma of giving birth."

Obviously something is wrong with the doctrine of the complete subordination of man to culture and the reasoning that supports it. In fact, quite a few things are wrong with it. In the first place, it is based in part on a curious and all-too-convenient double use of the word "individual." The individual is sometimes considered a member of a cultural group; but when it serves the purpose of contrasting the biological and the superorganic, all the culture is instantly leached out of him by some secret process. Then he becomes one of the most tropistic physical organisms ever produced by semantics.

The truth is that no human being is a mere organism unless he is a foetus or an imbecile. Perhaps it would be helpful if we restricted our use of the term "organism" to the context of physical anthropology and biology. When we are talking about man in relation to culture, it might be well to employ the terms "human being" or "human individual" or at least to make some attempt to see that employment of the term "individual" carries the correct implication.

The heart of the difficulty, as I see it, is that when Kroeber reacted against racist and biological explanations of culture and called for a clear distinction between the organic and the superorganic, he threw the human being out with the amniotic fluid. His motives were generous and humanistic and his effort magnificent; but in his enthusiasm he oversimplified and took a hazardous short cut. He forgot that there is not merely one emergent culture, at the dawn of the human and cultural horizon, but two. He forgot that a human being intelligent enough, perceptive enough, inquisitive enough, retentive enough, and manipulative enough to create culture was as much a break with the organic past as were the first symbols or deliberately taught cultural processes in which man engaged. Clearly, it is as important to study man in his culture-building and culture-manipulating roles as it is to examine the consequences and products of his actions. Then we will not need to repeat the dreary formulas of technological determinism and dialectical materialism as though they were our own bright invention. We will be something more than intellectual beggars, living on the crumbs that fall from the tables of physicists.

It is a doubtful tribute to the resilience of the human mind and its capacity for irrationality that this doctrine of a cultural realm, separate or separable from man, where invisible strings are pulled to make the human puppets dance, is embraced mainly by materialists who, because they hesitate to grant man too much in the way of will, creativity, and control, are sure they constitute a bulwark against mysticism and supernaturalism. But they have managed to develop their own up-dated brand of visional experience and have been permitted to gaze on a shadow world in which cultural ideas and artifacts jostle each other, breed, take direction, and determine man's course.

When cultural determinists portray the molding influence of a culture on its carriers, the culture is invariably represented as something monolithic and undeviating, and one would think, from the uniform picture drawn of them, that people roll from the relationship like pieces of dough stamped out by a cookie cutter. Where is this culture of such uniformity of practice or person? I have carried on research in so-called simple hunting and gathering cultures, and I have found that they permit many different constellations of activity and interest. Culture is to be thought of less as a rigid cast than as a plastic border against which men strain.

Some of the proofs offered in support of the overwhelming force of culture on the individual—for instance, that he speaks a language also spoken by others—seem naïve indeed. One has to have points of reference in respect to other people to be significantly and understandably different from them. There is no need to press for individuality in a state of anarchy. Those things that we all do in much the same way to initiate communication, to facilitate movement, to avoid friction when nothing important is at stake, lie at the peripheries of culture, not at its heart. And these are ordinarily what the cultural determinist fastens on to demonstrate that the human being has no choice and no effect. The fact that culture has a ground plan, a structure, and roles to be filled does not necessitate bloodless conformity. There are admirable and remiss husbands, fathers, teachers, students, and plumbers, as we all know. Even the roles change over time.

Let us return for a moment to the human being in cultural context. We have heard him referred to as the hapless recipient of the cultural impress. Either he does not protest or he protests in vain, we are told. In my opinion this assertion is just as oversimplified and unconvincing as the depiction of the irresistible cultural juggernaut. Unless they are informed of it by an anthropologist, human beings seldom are aware that they have a culture and that they are supposed to enact and re-enact its terms. What they are really trying to do is to live as fully and as well as they can. The symbols, tools, and understandings that constitute the culture act in a multiple capacity for the human being. They acquaint him with the ordinary possibilities. This the cultural determinist understands. They indicate to him the outer limits of permissible conduct. This too, the cultural determinist understands and even exaggerates. They provide him with materials and avenues by means of which he can fashion something personal and unique for himself. But this idea, that man manipulates and uses his culture for his own ends quite as much as he is subject to it, the cultural determinist resists and ignores. And because he does so, much of the richest data of anthropology passes by him, unrecognized and unappreciated. But this is the theater of our most varied and probing activities. It may bring the painter to New York City, the moon-faced girl to Hollywood, and the adventurous into anthropology. One man uses his work as an escape from his family, and another his family as an escape from his work. Theoretically, the political dimension is here for all; but one man votes regularly, another doesn't even bother to vote, and a third resolves to try to make a career of politics. Even as every Indian cook has a favorite combination of spices that marks her culinary efforts, each of us savors life through culture in a somewhat different way.

"But," it may be asked, "isn't it true that, although man experiences and uses culture differentially, culture can be studied separately from him in its own right? Cannot grammar, for instance, be studied quite apart from the people who respond to its rules when they speak?" This is more apparent than true. We forget that every grammar was worked out in a human context and implies that human context. How did we come to know that one form connotes a command and another a plea? The symbols themselves tell us nothing; neither are the regularities revealing. It is only because we have some reason to think that man will respond in the appropriate manner if these forms are used that we dare speak confidently of them. The human being and human reaction are always inferred. Nor can these forms be taken for granted; there is a continuous test in the human environment of any grammar which still has speakers, and we know that both the meanings and forms change over time.

The subject matter of cultural anthropology began to accumulate when man invented the first elements of culture many hundreds of thousands of years ago. Man and culture have coexisted ever since. The impress of each is on the other. They are not found in isolation from each other, and they are so interdependent that it is doubtful that they can be entirely extricated from each other for research purposes or in the process of living. Those who suppose that they can consistently study man without reference to culture, or culture without reference to man, are about a million and a half years too late. The arguments over how many geniuses culture can juggle on the head of a pin, or the debate over the contributions of this individual or that individual are pathetic *non sequiturs*. How will you distribute your praise of blame among the 75,000 generations of man? Culture is the work of humanity; we have the impression that it is autonomous only because it is anonymous. It is the story, not of impersonal forces or prime movers and shakers, but of countless millions, each of whom has left a trace. Our subject is the study of *man*—of the human being—in every possible cultural context. If we need a word for this, perhaps we could call it "humanology," for the study of the human being includes the study of his culture.

With over 200 years of the industrial revolution behind us and the multiplying might of the new technology before us, it becomes increasingly difficult for some of us to believe that we still control our tools and are not their blind servants. Perhaps we need to be reminded of the words of a wise and witty man who wrote, "If you fall in love with a machine there is something wrong with your love-life. If you worship a machine there is something wrong with your religion."[12]

If it is difficult to refrain from adulation of the machine, it is very easy in these times to lose confidence in man, who has limped along from war to war, from crisis to crisis, and from moral dilemma to moral dilemma. The contempt for man himself and his kind has its manifestations today in political life, in philosophy, in art, and in all the intellectual and practical reaches of our life. It has both direct and symbolic expression. In anthropology it has taken the form of doctrines of the separation of man from his works and of his subordination to technologically shaped culture. If this shows little faith in man's capabilities, it at least puts him beyond responsibility or censure for his fate. It makes of him the grey wake of an impersonal technological wave.

I hope that we will not accept without protest any shallow, mechanical, and cynical assessment of man. I hope that any necessary protest we make will take the form, in our professional work, of maintaining the human being in his cultural undertakings as a central subject of interest and investigation. We shall want to make statistical studies. We shall want to make comparative studies. We shall want to learn as much as we can about culture. We shall seek and apply improved methods. But in whatever we do we shall make it clear that we are men, not computers, and that the primary concern of an anthropologist is with the human being in relation to his cultural creations and not with his machines alone.

---

[12] Lewis Mumford, *Art and Techniques,* New York: Columbia University Press, 1952.

8 The Concept of Culture

LESLIE A. WHITE

For those who are now convinced that man—rather than culture—rules, the paper which follows will come as something of a shock. The superorganic approach appears to be rescued by Leslie White's arguments for a separate science called "culturology." Or is it? "The Concept of Culture" is a definitive statement on "culture" by a scholar whose theoretical writings have achieved international repute.

Virtually all cultural anthropologists take it for granted, no doubt, that *culture* is the basic and central concept of their science. There is, however, a disturbing lack of agreement as to what they mean by this term. To some, culture is learned behavior. To others, it is not behavior at all, but an abstraction from behavior—whatever that is. Stone axes and pottery bowls are culture to some anthropologists, but no material object can be culture to others. Culture exists only in the mind, according to some; it consists of observable things and events in the external world to others. Some anthropologists think of culture as consisting of ideas, but they are divided upon the question of their locus: some say they are in the minds of the peoples studied, others hold that they are in the minds of ethnologists. We go on to "culture is a psychic defense mechanism," "culture consists of *n* different social signals correlated with *m* different responses," "culture is a Rohrschach of a society," and so on, to confusion and bewilderment. One wonders what physics would be like if it had as many and as varied conceptions of energy!

There was a time, however, when there was a high degree of uniformity of comprehension and use of the term culture. During the closing decades of the nineteenth century and the early years of the twentieth, the great majority of cultural anthropologists, we believe, held to the conception expressed by E. B. Tylor: "Culture . . . is that complex whole which includes knowledge, belief, art, morals, law, custom, and any other capabilities and habits acquired by man as a member of society."[1] Tylor does not make it explicit in this statement that culture is the peculiar possession of man; but it is therein implied, and in other places he makes this point clear and explicit, where he deals with the

---

SOURCE: Reproduced by permission of the author and the American Anthropological Association from *American Anthropologist*, Vol. 61, No. 1, 1959, pp. 227–251.

[1] Edward B. Tylor, *Primitive Culture*, London: John Murray, 1871.

"great mental gap between us and the animals."[2] Culture, to Tylor, was the name of all things and events peculiar to the human species. Specifically, he enumerates beliefs, customs, objects—"hatchet, adze, chisel," and so on—and techniques—"wood-chopping, fishing . . . , shooting and spearing game, fire-making," and so on.[3]

The Tylorian conception of culture prevailed in anthropology generally for decades. In 1920, Robert H. Lowie began *Primitive Society* by quoting "Tylor's famous definition." In recent years, however, conceptions and definitions of culture have multiplied and varied to a great degree. One of the most highly favored of these is that *culture is an abstraction*. This is the conclusion reached by Kroeber and Kluckhohn in their exhaustive review of the subject: *Culture: a Critical Review of Concepts and History*.[4] It is the definition given by Beals and Hoijer in their textbook, *An Introduction to Anthropology*.[5] In a more recent work, however, *Cultural Anthropology*, Felix M. Keesing defines culture as "the totality of learned, socially transmitted behavior."[6]

Much of the discussion of the concept of culture in recent years has been concerned with a distinction between culture and human behavior. For a long time many anthropologists were quite content to define culture as behavior, peculiar to the human species, acquired by learning, and transmitted from one individual, group, or generation to another by mechanisms of social inheritance. But eventually some began to object to this and to make the point that culture is not itself behavior, but is an abstraction from behavior. Culture, say Kroeber and Kluckhohn, "is an abstraction from concrete human behavior, but it is not itself behavior." Beals and Hoijer and others take the same view.[7]

Those who define culture as an abstraction do not tell us what they mean by this term. They appear to take it for granted (1) that they themselves know what they mean by "abstraction," and (2) that others, also, will understand. We believe that neither of these suppositions is well founded; we shall return to a consideration of this concept later in this essay. But whatever an abstraction in general may be to these anthropologists, when culture becomes an

---

[2] Tylor, *Anthropology*, London: John Murray, 1881, pp. 54, 123.

[3] Tylor, *Primitive Culture*, 5th ed., London: John Murray, 1913, pp. 5–6.

[4] Alfred L. Kroeber and Clyde Kluckhohn, *Culture, a Critical Review of Concepts and Definitions*, Papers of the Peabody Museum of American Archaeology and Ethnology, 1952, Vol. 47, No. 1, pp. 155, 169.

[5] Ralph L. Beals and Harry Hoijer, *An Introduction to Anthropology*, New York: Macmillan, 1953.

[6] Felix M. Keesing, *Cultural Anthropology*, New York: Rinehart and Co., 1958, pp. 16, 427.

[7] One of the earliest instances of regarding culture as an abstraction is Murdock's statement: "realizing that culture is merely an abstraction from observed likenesses in the behavior of individuals . . . ." George P. Murdock, Editorial preface to *Studies in the Science of Society, presented to Albert Galloway Keller*, New Haven: Yale University Press, 1937.

"abstraction" it becomes imperceptible, imponderable, and not wholly real. According to Linton, "culture itself is intangible and cannot be directly apprehended even by the individuals who participate in it."[8] Herskovits also calls culture "intangible."[9] Anthropologists in the imaginary symposium reported by Kluckhohn and Kelly[10] argue that "one can see" such things as individuals and their actions and interactions, but "has anyone ever seen 'culture'?" Beals and Hoijer say that "the anthropologist cannot observe culture directly; . . ."

If culture as an abstraction is intangible, imperceptible, does it exist, is it real? Ralph Linton raises this question in all seriousness: "If it [culture] can be said to exist at all. . . ." Radcliffe-Brown[11] declares that the word culture "denotes, not any concrete reality, but an abstraction, and as it is commonly used a vague abstraction." And Spiro[12] says that according to the predominant "position of contemporary anthropology . . . culture has no ontological reality. . . ."

Thus when culture becomes an abstraction it not only becomes invisible and imponderable; it virtually ceases to exist. It would be difficult to construct a less adequate conception of culture. Why, then, have prominent and influential anthropologists turned to the "abstraction" conception of culture?

A clue to the reason—if, indeed, it is not an implicit statement of the reason itself—is given by Kroeber and Kluckhohn.

> Since behavior is the first-hand and outright material of the science of psychology, and culture is not—being of concern only secondarily, as an influence on this material—it is natural that psychologists and psychologizing sociologists should see behavior as primary in their field, and then extend this view farther to apply to the field of culture also.

The reasoning is simple and direct: if culture is behavior, then (1) culture becomes the subject matter of psychology, since behavior is the proper subject matter of psychology; culture would then become the property of psychologists and "psychologizing sociologists"; and (2) nonbiological anthropology would be left without a subject matter. The danger was real and imminent; the situation, critical. What was to be done?

---

[8] Ralph Linton, *The Study of Man,* New York: Appleton-Century, 1936, pp. 288–289.
[9] Melville J. Herskovits, "The Processes of Cultural Change," *The Science of Man in the World Crisis,* ed. Ralph Linton, New York: Columbia University Press, 1945, p. 150.
[10] Clyde Kluckhohn and William H. Kelly, "The Concept of Culture," *The Science of Man in the World Crisis,* ed. Ralph Linton, New York: Columbia University Press, 1945, pp. 79, 81.
[11] A. R. Radcliffe-Brown, "On Social Structure," *Journal of the Royal Anthropological Institute,* Vol. 70, pp. 1–12. Reprinted in *Structure and Function in Primitive Society,* Glencoe, Ill.: The Free Press, 1940, p. 2.
[12] Melford E. Spiro, "Culture and Personality," *Psychiatry,* 1951, Vol. 14, p. 24.

The solution proposed by Kroeber and Kluckhohn was neat and simple: let the psychologists have behavior; anthropologists will keep for themselves abstractions from behavior. These abstractions become and constitute *culture.*

But in this rendering unto Caesar, anthropologists have given the psychologists the better part of the bargain, for they have surrendered unto them real things and events, locatable and observable, directly or indirectly, in the real external world, in terrestrial time and space, and have kept for themselves only intangible, imponderable abstractions that "have no ontological reality." But at least, and at last, they have a subject matter—however insubstantial and unobservable—of their own!

Whether or not this has been the principal reason for defining culture as "not behavior, but abstractions from behavior," is perhaps a question; we feel, however, that Kroeber and Kluckhohn have made themselves fairly clear. But whatever the reason, or reasons—for there may have been several—may have been for the distinction, the question whether culture is to be regarded as behavior or as abstractions from it is, we believe, the central issue in recent attempts to hammer out an adequate, usable, fruitful, and enduring conception of culture.

The present writer is no more inclined to surrender culture to the psychologists than are Kroeber and Kluckhohn; indeed, few anthropologists have taken greater pains to distinguish psychological problems from culturological problems than he has.[13] But he does not wish to exchange the hard substance of culture for its wraith, either. No science can have a subject matter that consists of intangible, invisible, imponderable, ontologically unreal "abstractions"; a science must have real stars, real mammals, foxes, crystals, cells, phonemes, gamma rays, and culture traits to work with.[14] We believe that we can offer an analysis of the situation that will distinguish between psychology, the scientific study of behavior, on the one hand, and culturology, the scientific study of culture, on the other, and at the same time give a real, substantial subject matter to each.

Science makes a dichotomy between the mind of the observer and the ex-

---

[13] Several of the essays in *The Science of Culture* (1949)—"Culturological vs. Psychological Interpretations of Human Behavior," "Cultural Determinants of *Mind*," "Genius: Its Causes and Incidence," "Ikhnaton: The Great Man vs. the Culture Process," "The Definition and Prohibition of Incest," etc.—deal with this distinction.

[14] I made this point in my review of Kroeber and Kluckhohn, "Culture: a Critical Review . . . ," *American Anthropologist,* 1954, Vol. 56, pp. 461–468. At about the same time Huxley was writing: "If anthropology is a science, then for anthropologists culture must be defined, not philosophically or metaphysically, nor as an abstraction, nor in purely subjective terms, but as something which can be investigated by the methods of scientific inquiry, a phenomenal process occurring in space and time." Julian S. Huxley, "Evolution, Cultural and Biological," *Yearbook of Anthropology,* ed. Wm. L. Thomas, Jr.

ternal world[15]—things and events having their locus outside the mind of this observer. The scientist makes contact with the external world with and through his senses, forming percepts. These percepts are translated into concepts which are manipulated in a process called thinking[16] in such a way as to form premises, propositions, generalizations, conclusions, and so on. The validity of these premises, propositions, and conclusions is established by testing them in terms of experience of the external world.[17] This is the way science proceeds and does its work.

The first step in scientific procedure is to observe, or more generally to experience, the external world in a sensory manner. The next step—after percepts have been translated into concepts—is the classification of things and events perceived or experienced. Things and events of the external world are thus divided into classes of various kinds: acids, metals, stones, liquids, mammals, stars, atoms, corpuscles, and so on. Now it turns out that there is a class of phenomena, one of enormous importance in the study of man, for which science has as yet no name: this is the class of things and events consisting of or dependent upon symboling.[18] It is one of the most remarkable facts in the recent history of science that this important class has no name, but the fact remains that it does not. And the reason why it does not is because these things and events have always been considered and designated, not merely and simply

---

[15] "The belief in an external world independent of the perceiving subject is the basis of all natural science," says Einstein. Albert Einstein, *The World as I See It,* New York: Covici, Friede, 1934.

[16] Thinking, in science, means "operations with concepts, and the creation and use of definite functional relations between them, and the co-ordination of sense experiences to these concepts," according to Einstein. Albert Einstein, "Physics and Reality," *Journal of the Franklin Institute*, 1936, Vol. 221, pp. 313–347 in German, pp. 349–382 in English; p. 6. Einstein has much to say in this essay about the manner and process of scientific thinking.

[17] Einstein (1936), p. 350.

[18] By "symboling" we mean bestowing meaning upon a thing or an act, or grasping and appreciating meanings thus bestowed. Holy water is a good example of such meanings. The attribute of holiness is bestowed upon the water by a human being, and it may be comprehended and appreciated by other human beings. Articulate speech is the most characteristic and important form of symboling. Symboling is trafficking in nonsensory meanings, i.e., meanings which, like the holiness of sacramental water, cannot be comprehended with the senses alone. Symboling is a kind of behavior. Only man is capable of symboling.

We have discussed this concept rather fully in "The Symbol: the Origin and Basis of Human Behavior," originally published in *The Philosophy of Science,* 1940, Vol. 7, pp. 451–463. It has been reprinted in slightly revised form in *The Science of Culture.* It has also been reprinted in *Etc., A Review of General Semantics,* 1944, Vol. 1, pp. 229–237; *Language, Meaning, and Maturity,* ed. S. L. Hayakawa, New York, 1954; *Readings in Anthropology,* eds. E. Adamson Hoebel et al., New York, 1955; *Readings in Introductory Anthropology,* ed. Elman R. Service, Ann Arbor, Mich., 1956; *Sociological Theory,* eds. Lewis A. Coser and Bernard Rosenberg, New York, 1957; and in *Readings in the Ways of Mankind,* ed. Walter Goldschmidt, 1957.

as the things and events that they are, in and of themselves, but always as things and events in a particular context.

A thing is what it is; "a rose is a rose is a rose." Acts are not first of all ethical acts or economic acts or erotic acts. An act is an act. An act becomes an ethical datum or an economic datum or an erotic datum when—and only when—it is considered in an ethical, economic, or erotic context. Is a Chinese porcelain vase a scientific specimen, an object of art, an article of commerce, or an exhibit in a lawsuit? The answer is obvious. Actually, of course, to call it a "Chinese porcelain vase" is already to put it into a particular context; it would be better first of all to say "a glazed form of fired clay is a glazed form of fired clay." As a Chinese porcelain vase, it becomes an object of art, a scientific specimen, or an article of merchandise when, and only when, it is considered in an esthetic, scientific, or commercial context.

Let us return now to the class of things and events that consist of or are dependent upon symboling: a spoken word, a stone axe, a fetich, avoiding one's mother-in-law, loathing milk, saying a prayer, sprinkling holy water, a pottery bowl, casting a vote, remembering the sabbath to keep it holy—"and any other capabilities and habits [and things] acquired by man as a member of [human] society."[19] They are what they are: things and acts dependent upon symboling.

We may consider these things-and-events-dependent-upon-symboling in a number of contexts: astronomical, physical, chemical, anatomical, physiological, psychological, and culturological, and, consequently, they become astronomic, physical, chemical, anatomical, physiological, psychological, and culturological phenomena in turn. All things and events dependent upon symboling are dependent also upon solar energy which sustains all life on this planet; this is the astronomic context. These things and events may be considered and interpreted in terms of the anatomical, neurological, and physiological processes of the human beings who exhibit them. They may be considered and interpreted also in terms of their relationship to human organisms, i.e., in a somatic context. And they may be considered in an extrasomatic context, i.e., in terms of their relationship to other like things and events rather than in relationship to human organisms.

When things and events dependent upon symboling are considered and interpreted in terms of their relationship to human organisms, i.e., in a somatic context, they may properly be called *human behavior*, and the science, *psychology*. When things and events dependent upon symboling are considered and interpreted in an extrasomatic context, i.e, in terms of their relationships to one another rather than to human organisms, we may call them *culture*, and the science, *culturology*. This analysis is expressed diagrammatically in Fig. 1.

[19] Tylor (1913), p. 1.

FIGURE 1

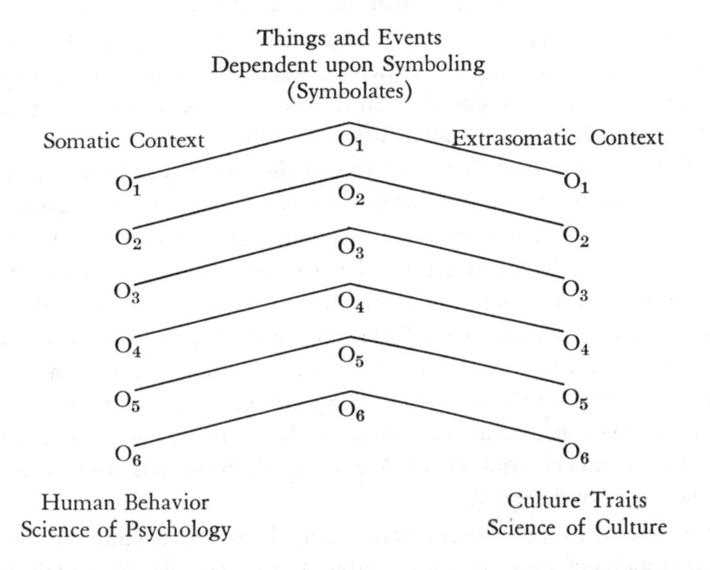

In the middle of the diagram we have a vertical column of circles, O_1, O_2, O_3, etc., which stand for things (objects) and events (acts) dependent upon symboling. These things and events constitute a distinct class of phenomena in the realm of nature. Since they have had heretofore no name we have ventured to give them one: *symbolates.* We fully appreciate the hazards of coining terms, but this all-important class of phenomena needs a name to distinguish it from other classes. If we were physicists we might call them "Gamma phenomena." But we are not physicists, and we believe a simple word would be better—or at least more acceptable—than a Greek letter. In coining our term we have followed a well-established precedent: if an *isolate* is something that results from the process or action of isolating, then something that results from the action or process of symboling might well be called a symbolate. The particular word with which we designate this class of phenomena is not of paramount importance, and perhaps a better term than symbolate can be found. But it is of paramount importance that this class have a name.

A thing or event dependent upon symboling—a symbolate—is just what it is, but it may become significant in any one of a number of contexts. As we have already seen, it may be significant in an astronomic context: the performance of a ritual requires the expenditure of energy which has come from the sun. But within the sciences of man we may distinguish two significant contexts: the somatic and the extrasomatic. Symbolates may be considered and interpreted in terms of their relationship to the human organism, or they may be considered in terms of their relationships to one another, quite apart from their relationship to the human organism. Let us illustrate with some examples.

I smoke a cigarette, cast a vote, decorate a pottery bowl, avoid my mother-in-law, say a prayer, or chip an arrowhead. Each one of these acts is dependent upon the process of symboling;[20] each therefore is a symbolate. As a scientist, I may consider these acts (events) in terms of their relationships to me, to my organism; or, I may treat them in terms of their relationships to one another, to other symbolates, quite apart from their relationship to my organism.

In the first type of interpretation I consider the symbolate in terms of its relationship to my bodily structure: the structure and functions of my hand, for example; or to my stereoscopic, chromatic vision; or to my needs, desires, hopes, fears, imagination, habit formation, overt reactions, satisfactions, and so forth. How do I feel when I avoid my mother-in-law or cast a ballot? What is my attitude toward the act? What is my conception of it? Is the act accompanied by heightened emotional tone, or do I perform it in a mechanical, perfunctory manner? And so on. We may call these acts *human behavior;* our concern is *psychological.*

What we have said of acts (events) will apply to objects (things) also. What is my conception of a pottery bowl, a ground axe, a crucifix, roast pork, whisky, holy water, cement? What is my attitude and how do I react toward each of these things? In short, what is the nature of the relationship between each of these things and my own organism? We do not customarily call these things human behavior, but they are the embodiments of human behavior; the difference between a nodule of flint and a stone axe is the factor of human labor. An axe, bowl, crucifix—or a haircut—is congealed human labor. We have then a class of objects dependent upon symboling that have a significance in terms of their relationship to the human organism. The scientific consideration and interpretation of this relationship is *psychology.*

But we may treat symbolates in terms of their relationships to one another, quite apart from their relationship to the human organism. Thus, in the case of the avoidance of a mother-in-law, we would consider it in terms of its relationship to other symbolates, or symbolate clusters, such as customs of marriage—monogamy, polygyny, polyandry—place of residence of a couple after marriage, division of labor between the sexes, mode of subsistence, do-

---

20 "How is chipping an arrowhead dependent upon symboling?" it might be asked. I have answered this question in "On the Use of Tools by Primates," *Journal of Comparative Psychology,* 1942, Vol. 34, pp. 369–374; reprinted in White, *The Science of Culture;* in *Man in Contemporary Society,* prepared by the Contemporary Civilization staff of Columbia University, New York, 1955; and in *Readings in Introductory Anthropology,* ed. E. R. Service, Ann Arbor, Mich., 1956. There is a fundamental difference between the tool process in the human species and the tool process among subhuman primates. This difference is due to symboling.

mestic architecture, degree of cultural development, etc. Or, if we are concerned with voting we would consider it in terms of forms of political organization (tribal, state), kind of government (democratic, monarchical, fascist); age, sex, or property qualifications; political parties and so on. In this context our symbolates become *culture*—culture traits or trait clusters, i.e., institutions, customs, codes, etc., and the scientific concern is *culturology*.

It would be the same with objects as with acts. If we were concerned with a hoe we would regard it in terms of its relationships to other symbolates in an extrasomatic context: to other instruments employed in subsistence, the digging stick and plow in particular; or to customs of division of labor between the sexes; the stage of cultural development, etc. We would be concerned with the relationship between a digital computer and the degree of development of mathematics, the stage of technological development, division of labor, the social organization within which it is used (corporation, military organization, astronomical laboratory), and so on.

Thus we see that we have two quite different kinds of sciencing[21] with regard to things and events—objects and acts—dependent upon symboling. If we treat them in terms of their relationship to the human organism, i.e., in an organismic, or somatic context, these things and events become *human behavior* and we are doing *psychology*. If, however, we treat them in terms of their relationship to one another, quite apart from their relationship to human organisms, i.e., in an extrasomatic, or extraorganismic, context, the things and events become *culture*—cultural elements of culture traits—and we are doing *culturology*. Human psychology and culturology have the same phenomena as their subject matter: things and events dependent upon symboling (symbolates). The difference between the two sciences derives from the difference between the contexts in which their common subject matter is treated.[22]

The analysis and distinction that we have made with regard to things and events dependent upon symboling in general is precisely like the one that linguists have been making for decades with regard to a particular kind of these things and events, namely, words.

A word is a thing (a sound or combination of sounds, or marks made upon some substance) or an act dependent upon symboling. Words are just what they are: words. But they are significant to scientific students of words in two different contexts: somatic or organismic, and extrasomatic or extraorganismic. This distinction has been expressed customarily with the terms *la langue* and *la parole*, or language and speech.[23]

---

[21] "Sciencing," too, is a kind of behavior. See our essay, "Science is *Sciencing*," *Philosophy of Science*, 1938, Vol. 5, pp. 369–389; reprinted in *The Science of Culture*.

[22] Importance of context may be illustrated by contrasting attitudes toward one and the same class of women: as mothers they are revered; as mothers-in-law, reviled.

[23] "According to [Ferdinand] de Sassure the study of human speech is not the subject

Words in a somatic context constitute a kind of human behavior: speech behavior. The scientific study of words in a somatic context is the psychology (plus physiology, perhaps, and anatomy) of speech. It is concerned with the relationship between words and the human organism: how the words are produced and uttered, the meanings of words, attitudes toward words, perception of and response to words, and so on.

In the extrasomatic context, words are considered in terms of their relationships to one another, quite apart from their relationship to the human organism. The scientific concern here is linguistics, or the science of language. Phonetics, phonemics, syntax, lexicon, grammar, dialectic variation, evolution or historical change, etc., indicate particular focuses, or emphases, within the science of linguistics.

The difference between these two sciences may be illustrated by citing two books: *The Psychology of Language* by Walter B. Pillsbury and Clarence L. Meader (New York, 1928), and *Language* by Leonard Bloomfield (New York, 1933). In the former we find chapter titles such as "The Speech Organs," "The Senses Involved in Speech," "Mental Processes in Speech," etc. In the latter the chapter headings are "The Phoneme," "Phonetic Structure," "Grammatical Forms," "Sentence-Types," etc. We illustrate the distinction between these two sciences in Figure 2.

Figures 1 and 2 are fundamentally alike. In each case we are concerned with a class of things and events dependent upon symboling. In Fig. 1, we are concerned with a general class: symbolates; in Fig. 2 we are dealing with a particular class: words (a subclass of the class symbolates). In each case we refer the things and events to a somatic context on the one hand, and to an extrasomatic context on the other, for purposes of consideration and interpretation. And in each case we have two distinct kinds of science, or sciencing: the psychology of human behavior or of speech; and the science of culture or of language.

Culture, then, is a class of things and events, dependent upon symboling, considered in an extrasomatic context. This definition rescues cultural anthropology from intangible, imperceptible, and ontologically unreal abstractions and provides it with a real, substantial, observable subject matter. And it distinguishes sharply between behavior—behaving organisms—and culture; between the science of psychology and the science of culture.

---

matter of *one* science but of two sciences. . . . De Sassure drew a sharp line between *la langue* and *la parole*. Language (*la langue*) is universal, whereas the process of speech (*la parole*) . . . is individual." Ernst Cassirer, *An Essay on Man,* New Haven: Yale University Press, 1944, p. 122. Huxley (1955), p. 16, citing Cassirer's discussion of de Sassure's distinction between *la langue* and *la parole,* speaks of the former as "the super-individual system of grammar and syntax," and of the latter as "the actual words or way of speaking used by particular individuals." He goes on to say that "we find the *same distinction in every cultural activity*—in law, . . . ; in art . . . ; in social structure . . . ; in science . . ." (emphasis ours).

FIGURE 2

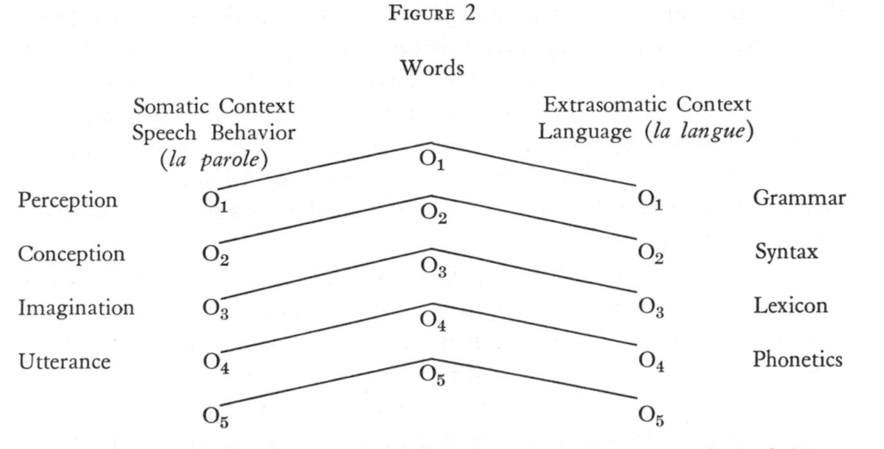

It might be objected that every science should have a certain class of things per se as its subject matter, not things-in-a-certain-context. Atoms are atoms and mammals are mammals, it might be argued, and as such are the subject matter of physics and mammalogy, respectively, regardless of context. Why therefore should cultural anthropology have its subject matter defined in terms of things in context rather than in terms of things in themselves? At first glance this argument might appear to be a cogent one, but actually it has but little force. What the scientist wants to do is make intelligible the phenomena that confront him. And very frequently the significant thing about phenomena is the context in which they are found. Even in the so-called natural sciences we have a science of organisms-in-a-certain-context: parasitology, a science of organisms playing a certain role in the realm of living things. And within the realm of man-and-culture we have dozens of examples of things and events whose significance depends upon context rather than upon the inherent qualities of the phenomena themselves. An adult male of a certain animal species is called a man. But a man is a man, not a slave; a man becomes a slave only when he enters a certain context. So it is with commodities: corn and cotton are articles of use-value, but they were not commodities—articles produced for sale at a profit—in aboriginal Hopi culture; corn and cotton become commodities only when they enter a certain socioeconomic context. A cow is a cow, but she may become a medium of exchange, money (*pecus*, pecuniary) in one context, food in another, mechanical power (Cartwright used a cow as motive power for his first power loom) in another, and a sacred object of worship (India) in still another. We do not have a science of cows, but we do have scientific studies of mediums of exchange, of mechanical power, and of sacred objects in each of which cows may be significant. And so we have a science of symboled things and events in an extrasomatic context.

The locus of culture. If we define culture as consisting of real things and events observable, directly or indirectly, in the external world, where do these things and events exist and have their being? What is the locus of culture? The answer is: the things and events that comprise culture have their existence, in space and time, (1) within human organisms, i.e., concepts, beliefs, emotions, attitudes; (2) within processes of social interaction among human beings; and (3) within material objects (axes, factories, railroads, pottery bowls) lying outside human organisms but within the patterns of social interaction among them.[24] The locus of culture is thus intraorganismal, interorganismal, and extraorganismal (see Fig. 3).

But, someone might object, you have said that culture consists of extrasomatic phenomena and now you tell me that culture exists, in part, within human organisms. Is this not a contradiction? The answer is, No, it is not a contradiction; it is a misunderstanding. We did not say that culture consists of extrasomatic things and events, i.e., phenomena whose locus is outside human organisms. What we said is that culture consists of things and events considered within an extrasomatic context. This is quite a different thing.

Every cultural element has two aspects: subjective and objective. It might appear that stone axes are "objective," and ideas and attitudes are "subjective." But this is a superficial and inadequate view. An axe has a subjective component; it would be meaningless without a concept and an attitude. On the other hand, a concept or an attitude would be meaningless without overt expression, in behavior or speech (which is a form of behavior). Every cultural element, every culture trait, therefore, has a subjective and an objective aspect. But conceptions, attitudes, and sentiments—phenomena that have their locus within the human organism—may be considered for purposes of scientific interpretation in an extrasomatic context, i.e., in terms of their relation to other symboled things and events rather than in terms of their relationship to the human organism. Thus, we may consider the subjective aspect of the mother-in-law taboo, i.e., the conceptions and attitudes involved, in terms of their relationship, not to the human organism, but to other symbolates such as forms of marriage and the family, place of residence after marriage, and so on. On the other hand, we may consider the axe in terms of its relationship to the human organism—its meaning; the person's conception of it; his attitude toward it—rather than to other symboled things and events such as arrows, hoes, and customs regulating the division of labor in society.

We shall now pass in review a number of conceptions of culture, or conceptions with regard to culture, widely current in ethnological literature, and

---

[24] "The true locus of culture," says Sapir, "is in the interactions of . . . individuals and, on the subjective side, in the world of meanings which each one of these individuals may unconsciously abstract for himself from his participation in these interactions." Edward Sapir, "Cultural Anthropology and Psychiatry," *Journal of Abnormal and Social Psychology,* 1932, Vol. 27, 229–242, p. 236. This statement is like ours except that it omits objects: material culture.

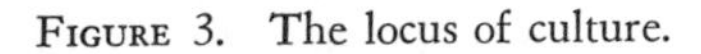

FIGURE 3. The locus of culture.

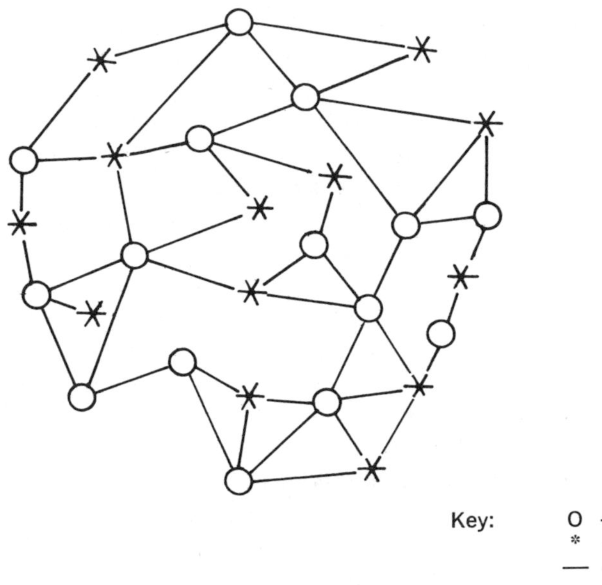

comment critically upon each one from the standpoint of the conception of culture set forth in this paper.

"Culture consists of ideas." Some anthropologists like to define culture in terms of ideas only. The reason for this, apparently, is the notion that ideas are both basic and primary, that they are prime movers and as such originate behavior which in turn may produce objects such as pottery bowls. "Culture consists of ideas," says Taylor,[25] it "is a mental phenomenon . . . not . . . material objects or observable behavior. . . . For example, there is present in an Indian's mind the idea of a dance. This is the trait of culture. This idea influences his body so that he behaves in a certain way," i.e., he dances.

This conception of sociocultural reality is a naive one. It is based upon a primitive, prescientific, and now obsolete metaphysics and psychology. It was Thought-Woman among the Keresan Pueblo Indians who brought about events by thinking and willing them to happen. Ptah created Egyptian culture by objectifying his thoughts. And God said "Let there be light," and there was light. But we no longer explain the origin and development of culture by simply saying that it has resulted from man's ideas. To be sure, an idea was involved in the invention of firearms, but we have explained nothing when we

[25] Walter W. Taylor, *A Study of Archeology,* American Anthropological Association Memoir No. 69, 1948, pp. 98–110.

say that firearms are the fruit of thought, because the ideas themselves have not been accounted for. Why did the idea occur when and where it did rather than at some other time and place? And, actually, ideas—matter of fact, realistic ideas—enter the mind from the outside world. It was working with soils that gave man, or woman, the idea of pottery; the calendar is a by-product of intensive agriculture. Culture does indeed consist in part of ideas; but attitudes, overt acts, and objects are culture, also.

"Culture consists of abstractions." We return now to the presently popular definition: "culture is an abstraction, or consists of abstractions." As we observed earlier, those who define culture in these terms do not tell us what they mean by "abstraction," and there is reason to believe that they are not very clear as to what they do mean by it. They make it emphatically clear, however, that an abstraction is not an observable thing or event. The fact that doubts have been raised as to the "reality" of an abstraction indicates that those who use this term are not sure what "it means," i.e., what they mean by it. We do have some clues, however.

Culture is "basically a form or pattern or way," say Kroeber and Kluckhohn,[26] "even a culture trait is an abstraction. A trait is an 'ideal type' because no two pots are identical nor are two marriage ceremonies ever held in precisely the same way." The culture trait "pot" therefore appears to be the ideal form of which each particular pot is an exemplification—a sort of Platonic idea, or ideal. Each and every pot, they reason, is real; but the "ideal" is never realized in any particular pot. It is like the "typical American man": 5′8½″ high, weighs 164.378 pounds, is married, has 2.3 children, and so on. This is, we suppose, what they mean by an abstraction. If so, we know it well: it is a conception in the mind of the observer, the scientist.

There is a slightly different way of looking at an "abstraction." No two marriage ceremonies are ever held in precisely the same way. Well, let us tabulate a large sample of marriage ceremonies. We find that 100 percent contain element *a* (mutual acceptance of spouses). Ninety-nine percent contain element *b*. Elements *c, d,* and *e* appear in only 96, 94, and 89 percent, respectively, of the cases. We construct a distribution curve and determine an average or norm about which all particular instances are distributed. This is the typical marriage ceremony. But, like the typical American who has 2.3 children, this ideal is never fully and perfectly realized in any actual instance. It is an "abstraction," that is, a conception, worked out by the scientific observer and which exists in his own mind.

The failure to recognize the fact that abstractions are conceptions has led to confusion both as to their locus and their reality. Recognition of the fact that the so-called abstractions of science (such as a "rigid body" in physical

[26] Kroeber and Kluckhohn (1952), pp. 155, 169.

theory; rigid bodies do not exist in actuality) are conceptions in the mind of the scientist clears up both these points: cultural "abstractions" are conceptions ("ideas") in the mind of the anthropologist. And as for their "ontological reality," conceptions are none the less real for being in the minds of men—nothing is more real, for example, than an hallucination.

This point was well made by Bidney[27] in his review of *Culture, a Critical Review etc.*:

> The real crux of the problem centers about what is meant by abstraction and what is its ontological import. Some anthropologists maintain that they are dealing only with logical abstractions and that culture has no reality other than that of an abstraction, but they can hardly expect other social scientists to agree with them, conceding that the objects of their sciences have no ontological, objective reality. *Thus Kroeber and Kluckhohn have confused the concept culture, which is a logical construct, with the actual existential culture* . . . [emphasis ours].

It is interesting to note in this connection that one anthropological theorist, Cornelius Osgood,[28] has defined culture explicitly as consisting of ideas in the minds of anthropologists: "Culture consists of all ideas of the manufactures, behavior, and ideas of the aggregate of human beings which have been directly observed or communicated to one's mind and of which one is conscious." Spiro,[29] also, holds that "culture is a logical construct, abstracted from human behavior, and as such, it exists only in the mind of *the investigator*" (Spiro's emphasis).

"There is no such thing as 'material' culture." Those who define culture in terms of ideas, or as an abstraction, or as behavior, find themselves obliged logically to declare that material objects are not, and cannot be, culture. "Strictly speaking," says Hoebel,[30] "material culture is really not culture at all." Taylor[31] goes farther: ". . . the concept of 'material culture' is fallacious" because "culture is a mental phenomenon." Beals and Hoijer[32]: ". . . culture is an abstraction from behavior and not to be confused with acts of behavior or with material artifacts, such as tools. . . ." This denial of material culture is rather awkward in view of the long established tradition among ethnographers,

---

[27] David Bidney, "Review of Culture, a Critical Review of Concepts and Definitions," by Kroeber and Kluckhohn," *American Journal of Sociology*, 1954, Vol. 59, pp. 488–489.
[28] Cornelius Osgood, "Culture: Its Empirical and Non-Empirical Character," *Southwestern Journal of Anthropology,* 1951, Vol. 7, pp. 202–214.
[29] Spiro (1951), p. 24.
[30] E. Adamson Hoebel, "The Nature of Culture," *Man, Culture and Society,* ed. Harry L. Shapiro, New York: Oxford University Press, 1956, p. 176.
[31] Walter W. Taylor, *A Study of Archeology,* American Anthropological Association Memoir No. 69, 1948.
[32] Beals and Hoijer (1953), p. 210.

archeologists, and museum curators of calling tools, masks, fetiches, and so on, "material culture."[33]

Our definition extricates us from this dilemma. As we have already seen, it would not be absurd to speak of sandals or pottery bowls as behavior; their significant attribute is not mere deer hide or clay, but human labor; they are congelations of human labor. But in our definition, symboling is the common factor in ideas, attitudes, acts, and objects. There are three kinds of symbolates: (1) ideas and attitudes, (2) overt acts, and (3) material objects. All may be considered in an extrasomatic context; all are to be reckoned as culture. This conception brings us back to long established usage in cultural anthropology: "Culture is that which is described in an ethnographic monograph."

"Reification of culture." There is a kind of conception of culture held by some anthropologists that is much deplored by others who call it "reification." As one who has been especially singled out as a "reifier" of culture,[34] I may say that the term is singularly inappropriate. To reify is to make a thing of that which is not a thing, such as hope, honesty, or freedom. But it is not I who have made culture things. I have merely found real things and events in the external world which are distinguishable as a class by being dependent upon symboling, and which may be treated in an extrasomatic context, and I have called these things and events culture. This is precisely what E. B. Tylor did. It is what Lowie, Wissler, and most early American anthropologists have done. To Durkheim[35] "the proposition which states that social facts [i.e., culture traits] are to be treated as things" lay "at the very basis of our method." It is not we who have reified culture; the elements comprising culture, according to our definition, were things to start with.

To be sure, if culture is defined as consisting of intangible, imponderable, ontologically unreal "abstractions," then to transform these wraiths into real, substantial bodies would indeed be to reify them. But we do not subscribe to such a definition.

---

[33] It is interesting to note that Durkheim, who uses the term "society" when many an American anthropologist would say culture, or socio-cultural system, remarks that "it is not true that society is made up only of individuals; it also includes material things, which play an essential role in the common life." He cites as examples such things as houses, instruments and machines used in industry, etc. "Social life . . . is thus crystallized . . . and fixed on material supports . . . externalized. . . ." Emile Durkheim, *Suicide, A Study in Sociology,* ed. George Simpson, Glencoe, Ill.: The Free Press, 1951.

[34] Max Gluckman "reifies structure in precisely the way that White reifies culture . . ." says Murdock. George P. Murdock, "British Social Anthropology," *American Anthropologist,* 1951, Vol. 53, p. 470. Strong feels that "White reifies, and at times almost deifies, culture. . . ." Wm. Duncan Strong, "Historical approach in Anthropology," *Anthropology Today,* ed. A. L. Kroeber, Chicago: The University of Chicago Press, 1953, p. 392. See also C. Judson Herrick, *The Evolution of Human Nature,* Austin: University of Texas Press, 1956.

[35] Emile Durkheim, *The Rules of Sociological Method,* ed. George E. G. Catlin, Chicago: The University of Chicago Press, 1938, p. xliii.

"Culture: a process sui generis." "Culture is a thing *sui generis* . . ." said Lowie many years ago.[36] This view has been held also by Kroeber, Durkheim, and others (for citation of examples see White[37]). It has been misunderstood and opposed by many. But what Lowie meant by this statement is made clear in the rest of the passage cited above: "Culture is a thing *sui generis* which can be explained only in terms of itself . . . the ethnologist . . . will account for a given cultural fact by merging it in a group of cultural facts or by demonstrating some other cultural fact out of which it has been developed." For example, the custom of reckoning descent patrilineally may be explained in terms of customs of division of labor between the sexes, customs of residence —patrilocal, matrilocal, or neolocal—of a married couple; mode of subsistence; rules of inheritance, and so on. Or, to express it in terms of our definition of culture: "a symbolate in an extrasomatic context (i.e., a culture trait) is to be explained in terms of its relationship to other symbolates in the same context."

This conception of culture, like "reification" with which it is closely related, has been much misunderstood and opposed. In general, it has been regarded as "mystical." How can culture grow and develop by itself? ("Culture . . . seems to grow of itself."[38]) "It seems hardly necessary," says Boas, "to consider culture a mystic entity that exists outside the society of its individual carriers, and that moves by its own force."[39] Bidney brands this view of culture as a "mystical metaphysics of fate."[40] And it has been opposed by Benedict,[41] Hooton,[42] Spiro,[43] and others.

But no one has ever said that culture is an entity that exists and moves by, and of, itself, quite apart from people. Nor has anyone ever said, as far as we know, that the origin, nature, and functions of culture can be understood without taking the human species into consideration. Obviously, if one is to understand culture in these aspects he must consider the biological nature of man. What has been asserted is that, given culture, its variations in time and place, and its processes of change are to be explained in terms of culture itself. This is precisely what Lowie meant when he said that "culture is a thing

[36] Robert H. Lowie, *Culture and Ethnology,* New York: Boni and Liveright, 1917, pp. 17, 66.
[37] Leslie A. White, *The Science of Culture,* New York: Farrar, Straus and Cudahy, 1949, pp. 89–94; paperbound, New York: The Grove Press, 1958.
[38] Robert Redfield, *The Folk Culture of Yucatan,* Chicago: The University of Chicago Press, 1941, p. 134.
[39] Franz Boas, *Anthropology and Modern Life,* New York: W. W. Norton, 1928, p. 235.
[40] David Bidney, "The Concept of Cultural Crisis," *American Anthropologist,* 1946, Vol. 48, p. 535.
[41] Ruth Benedict, *Patterns of Culture,* Boston and New York: Houghton Mifflin Co., 1934, p. 231.
[42] Earnest A. Hooton, *Crime and the Man,* Cambridge, Mass.: Harvard University Press, 1939, p. 370.
[43] Spiro (1951), p. 23.

[process would have been a better term] *sui generis,"* as the above quotation from him makes clear. A consideration of the human organism, individually or collectively, is irrelevant to an explanation of processes of culture change. "This is not mysticism," says Lowie, "but sound scientific method."[44] And, as everyone knows, scholars have been working in accordance with this principle of interpretation for decades. One does not need to take human organisms into account in a scientific explanation of the evolution of currency, writing, or of Gothic art. The steam engine and textile machinery were introduced into Japan during the closing decades of the nineteenth century and certain changes in social structure followed; we add nothing to our explanation of these events by remarking that human beings were involved. Of course they were. And they were not irrelevant to the events which took place, but they are irrelevant to an explanation of these events.

"It is people, not culture, that does things." "Culture does not 'work,' 'move,' 'change,' but is worked, is moved, is changed. It is people who do things," says Lynd.[45] He supports this argument with the bold assertion that "culture does not enamel its fingernails . . . but people do . . . ." He might have clinched it by demonstrating that culture has no fingernails.

The view that "it is people, not cultures, that do things" is widely held among anthropologists. Boas tells us that "the forces that bring about the changes are active in the individuals composing the social group, not in the abstract culture."[46] Hallowell[47] remarks that "in a literal sense cultures never have met nor will ever meet. What is meant is that peoples meet and that, as a result of the processes of social interaction, acculturation—modifications in the mode of life of one or both peoples—may take place. Individuals are the dynamic centers of this process of interaction." And Radcliffe-Brown pours fine scorn on the notion that cultures, rather than peoples, interact:

> A few years ago, as a result perhaps of re-defining social anthropology as the study, not of society, but of culture, we were asked to abandon this kind of investigation in favor of what is now called the study of "culture contact." In place of the study of the formation of new composite societies, we are supposed to regard what is happening in Africa as a process in which an entity called African culture comes into contact with an entity called European or Western culture, and a third new entity is produced . . . which is to be described as Westernized African culture. To me this seems a fantastic reification of abstractions. European culture is an abstraction and so is the culture of an African

---

[44] Lowie (1917), p. 66.
[45] Robert S. Lynd, *Knowledge for What?* Princeton, N.J.: Princeton University Press, 1939, p. 39.
[46] Boas (1928), p. 236.
[47] A. Irving Hallowell, "Sociopsychological Aspects of Acculturation," *The Science of Man in the World Crisis,* ed. Ralph Linton, New York: Columbia University Press, 1945, p. 175.

tribe. I find it fantastic to imagine these two abstractions coming into contact and by an act of generation producing a third abstraction.[48]

We call this view, that people rather than culture do things, the fallacy of pseudo-realism. Of course culture does not and could not exist independently of people.[49] But, as we have pointed out earlier, cultural processes can be explained without taking human organisms into account; a consideration of human organisms is irrelevant to the solution of certain problems of culture. Whether the practice of mummification in pre-Columbian Peru was indigenous or the result of Egyptian influence is an example of a kind of problem that does not require a consideration of human organisms. To be sure the practice of mummification, its invention in Peru, or its diffusion from Egypt to the Andean highlands, could not have taken place without the action of real, flesh-and-blood human beings. Neither could Einstein have worked out the theory of relativity without breathing, but we do not need to take his respiration into account when we trace the history, or explain the development, of this theory.

Those who argue that it is people, not culture, that do this or that mistake a description of what they see for an explanation of these events. Seated in the Senate gallery they see men making laws; in the shipyards men are building freighters; in the laboratory human beings are isolating enzymes; in the fields they are planting corn, and so on. And, for them, a description of these events, as they observe them, is a simple explanation of them: it is people who pass laws, build freighters, plant corn, and isolate enzymes. This is a simple and naive form of anthropocentrism.

A scientific explanation is more sophisticated. If a person speaks Chinese, or avoids his mother-in-law, loathes milk, observes matrilocal residence, places the bodies of the dead on scaffolds, writes symphonies, or isolates enzymes, it is because he has been born into, or at least reared within, an extrasomatic tradition that we call culture which contains these elements. A people's behavior is a response to, a function of, their culture. The culture is the independent, the behavior the dependent, variable; as the culture varies so will the behavior. This is, of course, a commonplace that is usually expounded and demonstrated during the first two weeks of an introductory course in anthropology. It is indeed people who treat disease with prayers and charms or with vaccines and antibiotics. But the question, "Why does one people use charms while another uses vaccines?" is not explained by saying that "this people

---

[48] Radcliffe-Brown (1940), pp. 10–11.

[49] "To be sure, these cultural events could not have taken place had it not been for human organisms . . . the culturologist knows full well that culture traits do not go walking about like disembodied souls interacting with each other. . . ." White, *The Science of Culture,* pp. 99–100.

does this, that people does that." It is precisely this proposition that needs to be explained: why do they do what they do? The scientific explanation does not take the people into account at all. And as for the question, Why does one extrasomatic tradition use charms while another uses vaccines, this also is one to which a consideration of people, of human organisms, is irrelevant; it is answered culturologically: culture, as Lowie has observed, is to be explained in terms of culture.

Culture "cannot be realistically disconnected from those organizations of ideas and feelings which constitute the individual," i.e., culture cannot be realistically disconnected from individuals, says Sapir.[50] He is quite right, of course; in actuality culture is inseparable from human beings. But if culture cannot be realistically (in actuality) disconnected from individuals it most certainly can be disconnected in logical (scientific) analysis, and no one has done a better job of "disconnecting" than Edward Sapir: there is not a single Indian—or even a nerve, muscle, or sense organ—in his monograph, *Southern Paiute, a Shoshonean Language*.[51] Nor are there any people roaming about in his *Time Perspective in Aboriginal American Culture*.[52] "Science must abstract some elements and neglect others," says Morris Cohen "because *not all things that exist together are relevant to each other*"[53] (emphasis ours). Comprehension and appreciation of this fact would be an enormous asset to ethnological theory. "Citizenship cannot be realistically disconnected from eye color," i.e., every citizen has eyes and every eye has a color. But, in the United States at least, color of eyes is not relevant to citizenship: "things that exist together are not always relevant to each other."

And so it is perfectly true, as Hallowell, Radcliffe-Brown, and others say, that "it is *peoples* who meet and interact." But this should not keep us from confining our attention, in the solution of certain problems, to symbolates in an extrasomatic context: to tools, utensils, customs, beliefs, and attitudes; in short, to culture. The meeting and mixing of European culture with African culture and the production thereby of a mixture, Euro-African culture, may seem "a fantastic reification of abstractions" to Radcliffe-Brown and others. But anthropologists have been concerned with problems of this sort for decades and will continue to deal with them. The intermingling of customs, technologies, and ideologies is just as valid a scientific problem as the intermingling of human organisms or genes.

We have not asserted, nor do we imply, that anthropologists in general have

[50] Sapir (1932), p. 233.
[51] Proceedings of the American Academy of Arts and Sciences, 1930, Vol. 65, pp. 1–296.
[52] Geological Survey Memoir 90, Ottawa: Canada Department of Mines, 1916.
[53] Morris R. Cohen, "Fictions," *Encyclopedia of the Social Sciences,* 1931, Vol. 7, p. 226.

failed to treat culture as a process sui generis, i.e., without taking human organisms into account; many, if not most, cultural anthropologists have in fact done this. But some of them, when they turn to theory, deny the validity of this kind of interpretation. Radcliffe-Brown himself provides us with examples of purely culturological problems and culturological solutions thereof —in "The Social Organization of Australian Tribes,"[54] "The Mother's Brother in South Africa,"[55] etc. But when he dons the philosopher's cap he denies that this procedure is scientifically valid.[56]

However, some anthropologists have recognized, on the theoretical level, that culture can be scientifically studied without taking human organisms into account, that a consideration of human organisms is irrelevant to the solution of problems dealing with extrasomatic traditions. We have cited a number—Tylor, Durkheim, Kroeber, Lowie, et al.—who have done this.[57] But we may add one or two new references here. "The best hope . . . for parsimonious description and 'explanation' of cultural phenomena," say Kroeber and Kluckhohn "seems to rest in the study of cultural forms and processes as such, largely . . . abstracted from individuals and personalities."[58] And Steward remarks that "certain aspects of a modern culture can best be studied quite apart from individual behavior. The structure and function of a system of money, banking, and credit, for example, represents supraindividual aspects of culture." Also, he says: "form of government, legal system, economic institutions, religious organizations, educational systems," and so on, "have aspects which are national . . . in scope and which must be understood apart from the behavior of the individuals connected with them."[59]

There is nothing new about this; anthropologists and other social scientists have been doing this for decades. But it seems to be difficult for some of them to accept this as a matter of theory and principle as well as of actual practice.

"It takes two or more to make a culture." There is a conception, not uncommon in ethnological theory, that whether a phenomenon is an element of culture or not depends upon whether it is expressed by one, two, or "several" individuals. Thus Linton says that "any item of behavior . . . which is peculiar to a single individual in a society is not to be considered as a part of the society's culture. . . . Thus a new technique for weaving baskets would not be

[54] *Oceania,* 1930–31, Vol. 1, pp. 34–63, 206–246, 322–341, 426–456.
[55] *South African Journal of Science,* 1924, Vol. 21, pp. 542–555. Reprinted in *Structure and Function in Primitive Society.*
[56] See White, *The Science of Culture,* pp. 96–98, for further discussion of this point.
[57] In our essays "The Expansion of the Scope of Science" and "The Science of Culture," in *The Science of Culture.*
[58] Kroeber and Kluckhohn (1952), p. 167.
[59] Julian H. Steward, *Theory of Culture Change,* Urbana, Ill.: University of Illinois Press, 1955, pp. 46, 47.

classed as a part of culture as long as it was known only to one person."[60] Wissler,[61] Osgood,[62] Malinowski,[63] Durkheim,[64] et al., have subscribed to this view.

Two objections may be raised against this conception of culture: (1) if plurality of expression of learned behavior be the significant distinction between culture and not-culture, then the chimpanzees described by Wolfgang Köhler in *The Mentality of Apes* (New York, 1925) had culture, for innovations made by a single individual were often quickly adopted by the whole group. Other subhuman species also would have culture according to this criterion. (2) The second objection is: if expression by one person is not enough to qualify an act as a cultural element, how many persons will be required? Linton says that "as soon as this new thing has been transmitted to and is shared by even one other individual in the society, it must be reckoned as a part of culture."[65] Osgood requires "two or more."[66] Durkheim needs "several individuals, at the very least."[67] Wissler says that an item does not rise to the level of a culture trait until a standardized procedure is established in the group.[68] And Malinowski states that a "cultural fact starts when an individual interest becomes transformed into public, common, and transferable systems of organized endeavor."[69]

Obviously such a conception does not meet the requirements of science. What agreement could one find on the point at which an "individual interest becomes transformed into public, common, and transferable systems of organized endeavor"? Or, suppose an ornithologist said that if there were but one specimen of a kind of bird it could not be a carrier pigeon or a whooping crane, but that if there were an indefinite number then they could be pigeons or cranes. Or, suppose a physicist said that if there were but one atom of a certain element that it could not be copper, but if there were "a lot of such atoms" then it might properly be called copper. One wants a definition that says that item *x* belongs to class *y* or it does not, regardless of how many items of *x* there may be (and a class, in logic, may have only one member, or even none).

---

60 Ralph Linton, *The Cultural Background of Personality,* New York: Appleton-Century, 1945, p. 35.
61 Clark Wissler, *Introduction to Social Anthropology,* New York: Henry Holt and Co., 1929, p. 358.
62 Osgood (1951), pp. 207–208.
63 Bronislaw Malinowski, "Man's Culture and Man's Behavior," *Sigma Xi Quarterly,* 1941, Vol. 29, pp. 170–196, p. 73.
64 Durkheim (1938), p. lvi.
65 Linton (1936), p. 274.
66 Osgood (1951), p. 208.
67 Durkheim (1938), p. lvi.
68 Wissler (1929), p. 358.
69 Malinowski (1941), p. 73.

Our definition meets the requirements of a scientific definition: an item—a conception or belief, an act, or an object—is to be reckoned an element of culture (1) if it is dependent upon symboling, and (2) when it is considered in an extrasomatic context. To be sure, all cultural elements exist in a social context; but so do such nonhuman (not dependent upon symboling) traits as grooming, suckling, and mating exist in a social matrix. But it is not sociality, duality, or plurality that distinguishes a human, or cultural, phenomenon from a nonhuman or noncultural phenomenon. The distinguishing characteristic is symboling. Secondly, whether a thing or an event can be considered in an extrasomatic context does not depend upon whether there is only one such thing or event, or two, or "several." A thing or event may be properly considered an element of culture even if it is the only member of its class, just as an atom of copper would still be an atom of copper even if it were the only one of its kind in the cosmos.

And, of course, we might have pointed out in the first place that the notion that an act or an idea in human society might be wholly the work of a single individual is an illusion, another one of the sorry pitfalls of anthropocentrism. Every member of human society is of course always subjected to sociocultural stimulation from the members of his group. Whatever a man does as a human being, and much of what he does as a mere animal, is a function of his group as well as of his organism. Any human act, even in its first expression in the person of a single individual, is a group product to begin with.[70]

Culture as "characteristic" traits. "Culture may be defined," says Boas, "as the totality of the mental and physical reactions and activities that *characterize* the behavior of the individuals composing a social group . . ."[71] (emphasis ours). Herskovits tells us that "when culture is closely analyzed, we find but a series of patterned reactions that characterize the behavior of the individuals who constitute a given group."[72] (Just what "close analysis" has to do with this conception is not clear.) Sapir: "The mass of typical reactions called culture. . . ."[73] This view has, of course, been held by others.

Two objections may be raised against this conception of culture: (1) how does one determine which traits characterize a group and which traits do not—how does one draw the line between the two classes, culture and not-culture?

---

[70] More than one hundred years ago Karl Marx wrote: "Man is in the most literal sense of the word a *zoon politikon,* not only a social animal, but an animal which can develop into an individual only in society. Production by isolated individuals outside of society . . . is as great an absurdity as the idea of the development of language without individuals living together and talking to one another," *A Contribution to the Critique of Political Economy,* Chicago: Charles H. Kerr, 1904, p. 268.

[71] Franz Boas, *The Mind of Primitive Man,* rev. ed., New York: Macmillan, 1938, p. 159.

[72] Melville J. Herskovits, *Man and His Works,* New York: Alfred A. Knopf, 1948, p. 28.

[73] Edward Sapir, "Do We Need a Superorganic?" *American Anthropologist,* 1917, Vol. 19, p. 442.

And, (2) if we call the traits that characterize a group *culture,* what are we to call those traits that do not characterize it?

It seems probable that anthropologists who hold this view are really thinking of *a* culture, or cultures, plural, rather than of culture in general, culture as a particular kind of phenomena. Thus, "French culture" might be distinguished from "English culture" by those traits which characterize each. But if, on the one hand, the French and the English may be distinguished from each other by differences of traits, they will on the other hand be found to be very similar to each other in their possession of like traits. And the traits that resemble each other are just as much a part of the "way of life" of each people as the traits that differ. Why should only one class be called culture?

These difficulties and uncertainties are done away with by our conception of culture: culture consists of all of the ways of life of each people which are dependent upon symboling and which are considered in an extrasomatic context. If one wished to distinguish the English from the French on the basis of their respective culture traits he could easily specify "those traits which characterize" the people in question. But he would not assert that nontypical traits were not culture.

In this connection we may note a very interesting distinction drawn by Sapir between the behavior of individuals and "culture."

> It is always the individual that really thinks and acts and dreams and revolts. Those of his thoughts, acts, dreams, and rebellions that somehow contribute in sensible degree to the modification or retention of the mass of typical reactions called culture we term social data; *the rest, though they do not, psychologically considered, in the least differ from these, we term individual and pass by as of no historical or social moment* [i.e., they are not culture]. It is highly important to note that the differentiation of these two types of reaction is essentially arbitrary, resting, as it does, entirely on a principle of selection. The selection depends on the adoption of a scale of values. Needless to say, the threshold of the social (or historical) [i.e., cultural] *versus* the individual shifts according to the philosophy of the evaluator or interpreter. I find it utterly inconceivable to draw a sharp and eternally valid dividing line between them [emphases ours].[74]

Sapir finds himself confronted by a plurality, or aggregation, of individuals. (He would have preferred this wording rather than "society," we believe, for he speaks of "a theoretical [fictitious?] community of human beings," adding that "the term 'society' itself is a cultural construct."[75]) These individuals do things: dream, think, act, and revolt. And "it is always the individual," not society or culture, who does these things. What Sapir finds then is: individuals and their behavior; nothing more.

---

[74] Sapir (1917), p. 442.
[75] Sapir (1932), p. 236.

Some of the behavior of individuals is culture, says Sapir. But other elements of their behavior are not-culture, although, as he says, psychologically considered they do not differ in the slightest from those elements which he calls culture. The line thus drawn between "culture" and "not-culture" is purely arbitrary, and depends upon the subjective evaluation of the one who is drawing the line.

A conception of culture could hardly be less satisfactory than this one. It says, in effect: "culture is the name that we give to some of the behavior of some individuals, the selection being arbitrary and made in accordance with subjective criteria."

In the essay from which we have been quoting, "Do We Need a Superorganic?", Sapir is opposing the culturological point of view presented by Kroeber in "The Superorganic." He (Sapir) virtually makes culture disappear; it is dissolved into the totality of the reactions of individuals. Culture becomes, as he has elsewhere called it, a "statistical fiction." If there is no significant reality that one can call culture, then there can be no science of culture. Sapir's argument was skillful and persuasive. But is was also unsound, or at least misleading.

Sapir's argument was persuasive because he bolstered it with authentic, demonstrable fact. It was unsound or misleading because he makes it appear that the only significant distinction between the behavior of individuals and culture is the one that he had made.

It is perfectly true that the elements which comprise the human behavior of individuals and the elements which comprise culture are identical classes of things and events. All are symbolates—dependent upon man's unique ability to symbol. It is true, also, that "psychologically considered," they are all alike. But Sapir overlooks, and by his argument effectively obscures, the fact that there are two fundamentally different kinds of contexts in which these "thinkings, actings, dreamings, and revolts" can be considered for purposes of scientific interpretation and explanation: the somatic and the extrasomatic. Considered in a somatic context, i.e., in terms of their relationship to the human organism, these acts dependent upon symboling constitute *human behavior*. Considered in an extrasomatic context, i.e., in terms of their relationships to one another, these acts constitute *culture*. Instead, therefore, of arbitrarily putting some in the category of culture and the rest in the category human behavior, we put all acts, thoughts, and things dependent upon symboling in either one context or the other, somatic or extrasomatic, depending upon the nature of our problem.

Summary. Among the many significant classes of things and events distinguishable by science there is one for which science has had no name. This is the class of phenomena dependent upon symboling, a faculty peculiar to the human species. We have proposed that things and events dependent upon symboling be called symbolates. The particular designation of this class is not as important, however, as that it be given a name of some kind in order that its distinction from other classes be made explicit.

Things and events dependent upon symboling comprise ideas, beliefs, attitudes, sentiments, acts, patterns of behavior, customs, codes, institutions, works and forms of art, languages, tools, implements, machines, utensils, ornaments, fetiches, charms, and so on.

Things and events dependent upon symboling may be, and traditionally have been, referred to two fundamentally different contexts for purposes of observation, analysis, and explanation. These two contexts may properly and appropriately be called somatic and extrasomatic. When an act, object, idea or attitude is considered in the somatic context it is the relationship between that thing or event and the human organism that is significant. Things and events dependent upon symboling considered in the somatic context may properly be called human behavior—at least, ideas, attitudes, and acts may; stone axes and pottery bowls are not customarily called behavior, but their significance is derived from the fact that they have been produced by human labor; they are, in fact, congelations of human behavior. When things and events are considered in the extrasomatic context they are regarded in terms of the interrelationships among themselves rather than in terms of their relationship to the human organism, individually or collectively. Culture is the name of things and events dependent upon symboling considered in an extrasomatic context.

Our analysis and distinctions have these advantages. The distinctions made are clear cut and fundamental. Culture is clearly distinguished from human behavior. Culture has been defined as all sciences must define their subject matter, namely, in terms of real things and events, observable directly or indirectly in the actual world that we live in. Our conception rescues anthropology from the incubus of intangible, imperceptible, imponderable "abstractions" that have no ontological reality.

Our definition extricates us, also, from the dilemmas in which many other conceptions place us, such as whether culture consists of ideas and whether these ideas have their locus in the minds of peoples studied or in the minds of anthropologists; whether material objects can or cannot be culture; whether a trait must be shared by two, three, or several people in order to count as culture; whether traits have to characterize a people or not in order to be culture; whether culture is a reification or not, and whether a culture can enamel its fingernails.

Our distinction between human behavior and culture, between psychology and culturology, is precisely like the one that has been in use for decades between speech and language, between the psychology of speech and the science of linguistics. If it is valid for the one it is valid for the other.

Finally, our distinction and definition is in very close accord with anthropological tradition. This is what Tylor meant by culture as a reading of *Primitive Culture* will make clear. It is the one that has actually been used by almost all nonbiological anthropologists. What is it that scientific field workers among primitive peoples have studied and described in their monographs? Answer: real observable things and events dependent upon symboling. It can hardly be said that they were studying and describing imperceptible, intangible, imponderable, ontologically unreal abstractions. To be sure, the field worker may be interested in things and events in their somatic context, in which case he would be doing psychology (as he would be if he considered words in their somatic context). And anthropology, as this term is actually used, embraces a number of different kinds of studies: anatomical, physiological, genetic, psychological, psychoanalytic, and culturological. But this does not mean that the distinction between psychology and culturology is not fundamental. It is.

The thesis presented in this paper is no novelty. It is not a radical departure from anthropological tradition. On the contrary, it is in a very real sense and to a great extent, a return to tradition, the tradition established by Tylor and followed in practice by countless anthropologists since his day. We have merely given it concise and overt verbal expression.

9 Radcliffe-Brown on Culturology

A. R. RADCLIFFE-BROWN

Professor White argues forcibly and eloquently for a separate science of culture, culturology, *based on a distinct set of phenomena: a class of things and events dependent on symboling, considered in an extrasomatic context. Is it possible to develop culturology as a separate science? What theoretical and methodological problems arise from such a development? Professor Radcliffe-Brown, a leading figure in British social anthropology, has many important comments on these and related questions. His argumentation is also spiced with interesting ethnographic illustrations.*

Source: Abridged from "White's View of a Science of Culture" by A. R. Radcliffe-Brown. Reproduced by permission of the author's estate and the American Anthropological Association from *American Anthropologist*, Vol. 51, No. 3, 1949, pp. 503–512.

1

Professor Leslie White has argued very forcefully for the view that in the study of human life and behavior we must recognize three different disciplines dealing with three different "levels" of phenomena—mind, society and culture. This view is accepted explicitly by a number of anthropologists in America and implicitly by many more.

I do not wish to quarrel with the view held by Kroeber and White that "cultural" phenomena may be studied in abstraction from society; that is, from social life as a system of relations and interactions between persons and groups. What can be done in this way is shown by linguistics, where the phenomena of language are studied in abstraction from the social relations in which speech is used for communication. Similarly it is possible to study music without reference to the societies which have produced the music.

But if there are to be two sciences, one of social phenomena and the other of cultural phenomena, both of them distinct from psychology and from history in the ordinary sense, we must be able to make clear distinction between sociological enquiries, problems, methods, theories and explanations and those of the science of culture. I do not find that these distinctions have been clearly made, but on the contrary I find a great deal of vagueness and ambiguity in the discussions of the subject.

My own preferred field of study is social anthropology. This was defined by Frazer in 1907, and again by Malinowski in 1926, as that branch of *sociology* that deals with "primitive" or preliterate societies. Just as mechanics is the study of mechanical systems, and psychology is the study of mental or psychical systems, so sociology is the science of social systems. A social system consists of individual human beings interacting with one another within certain continuing associations. Thus social anthropology is concerned with the forms of association or social integration in primitive societies, seeking to arrive at an understanding of their variations, and to enquire into the conditions of stability in social systems as systems of integration of persons.

2

Cultural anthropology, if I understand its exponents correctly, is not concerned with relations between persons but with relations between "culture traits." Yet in the literature of the subject I often find the two terms "culture" and "social system" used as if they were alternative terms for the same thing. Thus in the article by White which will be discussed later we are offered what purports to be an explanation of rules of exogamy in terms of culture, a "culturological" as distinct from a sociological theory. White, however, speaks of these rules as "institutions," "created by *social* systems." This may be a slip of the pen for "cultural systems" but the slip is significant. So is the slip of Kroeber when in one place he speaks of a person as a "member" of a culture. One is a member of an English-speaking community, but not a member of the English language.

In his paper on "The Definition and Prohibition of Incest" in the *American Anthropologist,* White has offered us a "culturological" theory. The rules prohibiting marriage or intercourse between kin are to be explained, not in terms of social integration or cohesion, which would be a sociological explanation, nor in terms of the mental characteristics of human beings, which would be a psychological explanation, but in terms of the "organization of culture traits." The fundamental proposition of the theory is that "incest was defined and exogamous rules were formulated in order to make cooperation compulsory and extensive, to the end that life be made more secure."

I do not propose to make a critical examination of this theory. I wish to take it only as an example of the way in which the science of culture deals with a particular problem, and to compare it with the way in which sociology could deal with the same problem. It will, I suppose, be admitted that law and morals are social phenomena and that therefore rules relating to marriage between relatives, and the treatment of sexual intercourse between kin as sinful, criminal or immoral, may be made the subject of sociological enquiry and of sociological theory. The rules in question would then be considered not in relation to culture but in relation to social integration, the linking together of persons in a social structure of continuing associations. It happens that I have for many years held and taught a sociological theory on this subject; and of this I propose to give, not an exposition, but a brief outline. My purpose is only to afford an opportunity of comparing the theoretical science of society with the theoretical science of culture, taking the latter as being represented by the article of Professor White.

From the point of view of comparative sociology the discussions of the prohibition of incest have been vitiated by the failure to distinguish two different but connected problems. The first of these is concerned with the rules relating to marriage between relatives, rules which vary greatly in different societies, but which no society is without. These rules are of two kinds. Certain marriages between relatives are disapproved or prohibited. On the other hand, in many societies marriage between certain kinds of relatives is approved, preferred, or even obligatory. It is quite evident that a sociological theory must deal with all these rules, with preferred or permitted marriages equally with those prohibited or disapproved. Further, the purpose of the theory must be to enable us to understand or explain the variations in this matter that are found in different social types. Any proposed theory that does not do this is not worthy of any consideration as a sociological theory. This rules out as being perfectly useless a great deal of what has been written on the subject. The test of a theory is its application to the understanding of particular instances.

The second problem is that of incest, and this refers not to marriage but to sexual intercourse outside marriage. Where such intercourse takes place between kin it may be regarded in a particular society as constituting immorality, sin, or crime of a special kind, distinct from intercourse between unrelated persons. This is what is specifically incest. Marriage, and sexual intimacy outside marriage, are from a sociological point of view quite different things. In some states of the United States first cousins are not permitted to marry, but sexual intercourse between the cousins seems to be regarded as not incest but merely fornication, a somewhat lesser, and different sin.

I will first give a very brief outline of the sociological theory of the regulation of marriage. The proof of the theory would require, of course, not an article but a book. But here the statement of the theory is merely intended as an example of a possible sociological theory. Each society has its own particular kinship system, that is, a set or system of relationships between persons connected by kinship or through marriage, including those relationships, such as those between members of a clan, which are regarded in the society as being relations of kinship, though there may be no traceable genealogical connections. These relationships are institutionalized; there are patterns or rules of conduct to which persons who stand in certain relations are expected to conform. A marriage is a rearrangement of social structure, involving the modification of certain existing relations and the formation of certain new ones.

The general theory of the regulation of marriage is that the social function of the rules is to preserve, maintain or continue the existing system of institutional relations. When in a particular system a marriage between relatives has for its effect to continue, renew, or reinforce the existing system of relations it tends to be approved or preferred or even, in some instances, made obligatory. On the contrary, where a marriage between relatives would disrupt or throw into disorder the existing system of relations, it tends to be disapproved or prohibited; and the greater and more widespread the disturbance that would be caused by a marriage, the stronger is the general resistance or disapproval with which it meets. The general theory is thus formulated, not in terms of culture, but in terms of social integration or social structure. To be understood, the rules regulating marriage in any particular society have to be examined in their relation to the kinship structure of that society as a continuing system of the arrangement of persons in institutionalized relationships.

It is perhaps necessary to point out that the formulation of a law or principle of this kind does not exclude the possibility of exceptions in particular instances. It is a law of nature that human beings have the heart on the left side and that they have three joints to their fingers; but there are exceptional individuals who have the heart on the right or who have only two joints to their fingers. The exceptions call for special explanation, whether in biology or in sociology.

The commonest forms of preferred or approved marriages between relatives are marriage with the wife's sister, the wife's brother's daughter, the wife of a deceased brother or mother's brother, and marriage between cousins. In my experience, in the study of kinship systems over forty years, it is usually easy to see how these marriages of relatives renew, or continue or reinforce existing relations between persons and groups. Thus in marriage with the daughter of the mother's brother a man has taken a wife from a certain family and in the next generation his son takes his wife from the same family. But each society has to be considered separately, and it is impossible to deal in an article with the innumerable instances in which the theory seems to receive confirmation.

Turning to prohibited marriages we may take the instance of marriage with the daughter of the father's brother. In most African societies there is a definite institutionalized relationship of a man to his father's brother and the latter's wife and children. The father's brother is a sort of "father," his wife is a "mother" and his children are brothers and sisters. There is a quite different set of relations for a man to his wife's father and mother and brothers and sisters. In such tribes marriage with the father's brother's daughter would completely disrupt the system of relationships. His "father" would become a father-in-law, and his "mother" would have to be avoided as a mother-in-law; his "brothers" would become brothers-in-law. Even his own father would have to be treated as a sort of father-in-law, since he is father's brother ("father") to the man's wife. The father would have to change his behavior to his own brother, since the latter has now become his son's father-in-law. There would have to be an extensive series of sudden changes in the way in which persons were required to behave to one another.

But there are some societies in Africa which lack these institutionalized relationships to the wife's relatives, and in these societies a man is permitted to marry the daughter of his father's brother, while in some Arab societies such marriages are preferred.

Consider such rules as the following: in the Nkundo tribe of the Congo a woman is forbidden to marry, in a second marriage, the husband's father's brother's son of her first husband's mother's brother's daughter; amongst the Hera of Mashonaland a man may not marry a woman of the lineage of his wife's brother's wife though he may marry his wife's sister or women of the lineage of his mother's brother's wife. It is difficult to see what such rules have to do with making cooperation "compulsory and extensive," but they can be readily understood by reference to the existing social structure of these tribes.

Where a definite rule exists there is usually behind it a unanimous opinion or sentiment. But we must recognize, as sociologists, that there are often differences of opinion or sentiment in a particular society. I have listened to Australian aborigines discussing at great length whether a particular marriage should or should not be permitted. In the Hehe tribe of East Africa Gordon

Brown reports that some persons approve of marriage with the mother's brother's daughter because they think it will strengthen or renew the existing solidarity between the families; but others fear that the tensions that result from the marriage relationship may, on the contrary, weaken rather than strengthen that solidarity and recommend avoidance of such marriages. In England from 1835 to 1907 there was a heated controversy over the question whether a man might be permitted to marry his deceased wife's sister, many persons arguing either for or against. In 1907 such marriages were finally legalized but many ministers of the church still disapprove of them. These differences of opinion or sentiment are just as important, as sociological facts, as are general agreements; they call for explanation in terms of general theory. In fact they provide very valuable means of testing theory.

In dealing with the regulation of marriage we are directly concerned with social structure. But in dealing with fornication, and with that special variety of it known as incest we are concerned with those moral and religious sentiments which are essential to the existence of an ordered system of social relations. The sexual relations between husband and wife are part of the institutional arrangement of marriage; and are subject to moral and religious and even legal control. Sexual relations outside marriage are, from the social point of view, something quite different. Each society has its own current sentiments about fornication, adultery, incest, homosexuality. The study of these and of their variations in different societies is a task for that branch of sociology that is concerned with moral and religious attitudes. It cannot be claimed that much progress has yet been made with studies of this kind.

What is most characteristically and strongly condemned as incest is sexual intimacy with the closest relatives—mother, daughter, sister. It is felt that such conduct is of a different and worse kind than fornication between non-relatives. Parallel to this is the feeling that to kill a father or a mother is a different and more serious offense than the killing of some unrelated person. The parallel between parricide and incest is seen clearly in the drama of ancient Greece. The first requirement for a sociological theory is the recognition that incest is normally an offense against religion. In many primitive societies incest and witchcraft are conceived as being the same kind of thing. In conversation with a native of South Africa I asked about sexual intimacy between brother and sister; his comment was, with horror in his voice, "That would be witchcraft." The identification of incest with witchcraft occurs frequently in African peoples, and an interesting development of it is the belief that a man can obtain the greatest possible power as a sorcerer by incestuous connection with his mother or his sister. Another significant fact is the high degree of sacredness that is attributed in some societies, as in Hawaii, to the offspring of a union of brother and sister. The same theme is found in mythology. In mediaeval Europe incest and witchcraft were matters to be dealt with by the Church as offenses against religion; it is only recently in England that incest is subject to the secular courts and is punished as a crime.

There is already current a theory of the basis for the moral and religious repulsion to sexual intimacy amongst members of the same family. It was briefly stated by Durkheim in 1897 in the first volume of the *Année sociologique* (page 59 and following). It is briefly formulated in the passage from Malinowski (quoted by White on page 431 of his article). It is to be found formulated or suggested by several other writers.

Briefly the theory is that human beings generally feel that there is a fundamental incompatibility between the kind of personal relation that results from or is implied in sexual intimacy and the kinds of sentiments which are regarded as appropriate and obligatory between mother and son, father and daughter, and brother and sister. There is, as Durkheim says, a feeling that if sexual intimacy between such pairs of persons were permitted or even conceived as possible, the family would be no longer the family and marriage would be no longer marriage. The family is commonly an object of religious sentiment, not only in modern Christian societies. The doctrine of the Church that incest is a direct attack on the sacred character of family life, comparable to parricide, is sound sociology.

It is in reference to intercourse with the nearest relatives that these feelings of moral and religious repulsion reach their greatest intensity. But in many societies the prohibition against sexual intercourse is extended to more distant relatives. In wide-range kinship systems such as characterize many primitive societies a man is required to think of certain relatives as though they were relatives of the same kind as mother or sister or daughter and to direct his behavior toward them on this basis. A most obvious way of socially establishing and maintaining these relationships is by the rule that not only marriage but also sexual intimacy is forbidden.

Many societies have created, as an essential part of their social structure, wide-range kinship systems whereby every person is provided with a large number of near and more distant relatives arranged in categories or groups. The extreme development of this tendency is seen in the Australian tribes in which a man stands in a definite relation of kinship to any person with whom he has any social contact. What is sometimes called "exogamy" in such a tribe as the Kariera is simply the rule that a man may only take a wife from one particular category of relatives, namely the category that includes his mother's brother's daughter. In other societies the wide-range recognition of kinship is provided by the formation of groups of unilinear descent in the form of lineages or clans. The result of this is that for a given person, all the members of his own lineage or clan are relatives of certain kinds or categories, and the members of his mother's clan or lineage are all relatives of other kinds or categories. What is called the rule of exogamy is the prohibition against marriage between persons who are kin by virtue of belonging to the same lineage or clan. In its full development the system requires that a man should treat all the members of his own lineage and clan as "brothers" and "sisters," and since not only marriage but also sexual intimacy are forbidden between brother and sister, one way of emphasizing the bond of kinship, is to forbid sexual intimacy between a man and a woman of the same lineage or clan.

In this way the prohibition against sexual intercourse may be extended to all women whom a man may not legally marry. But the extension is not always complete or enforced. In Melanesia and Africa we find instances in which sexual intimacy with a woman with whom marriage is not permitted, for example by the rule of clan exogamy, is regarded as not incestuous, not serious, but permissible or at least a peccadillo. Amongst the Nkundo, for example, a man may not marry a woman from a clan or lineage that is regarded as related to his own, since marriage would throw the structure into disorder; but he may have a liaison with a woman of that group without committing incest, and there is a special term (*lonkana*) for such affairs. As the Tallensi remarked to Fortes in connection with a similar situation, "Copulation and marriage are not the same thing."

3

Thus the problem considered by Professor White from the point of view of a science of culture can also be approached from the different point of view of comparative sociology. Whatever may or may not be included in sociology, I take it that the study of forms of social structure and of social integration are specifically sociological, neither psychological nor "culturological." Otherwise it would seem that there is no such thing as sociology at all, and this is contrary to White's main contention.

The first question that arises is: Can there be two different and valid theories in this matter, one giving a sociological and the other a "culturological" explanation? If so, can there also be a separate valid theory of a psychological kind? Are the same phenomena to be susceptible of different kinds of explanation, independent and equally valid? It seems desirable to know where we stand in this matter. My own theory is that the rules relating to the marriage of relatives, and also the rules against sexual intimacy between kin outside marriage, are to be understood by their social function as serving to maintain the stability or equilibrium of family and kinship structures; and it cannot be held that this is not sociological explanation, unless there is no such thing as sociology.

The second question is: In what sense is White's theory a cultural and not a sociological theory? The theory is that rules regulating marriage and sexual intercourse "were formulated in order to make co-operation compulsory and extensive." But co-operation, as it is usually conceived, is a social phenomenon, a matter of the integration of persons in joint or collective activities. All questions of social integration, the linking of persons in fixed social relations, are sociological. It would seem that White is smuggling a sociological theory into what is held to be the separate and independent science of culture. That he himself is vaguely aware of this is indicated by his statement that these rules are "created by *social* systems."

A third question is: How does this theory afford a means for understanding or explaining the variations in the rules in different societies? The statement of White is that "these variations are to be explained in terms of the specific circumstances under which cooperation is to take place. One set of circumstances will require one definition of incest and one form of marriage; another set will require different customs. The habitat and the technological adjustment to it, the mode of subsistence, circumstances of defense and offense, division of labor between the sexes, and degree of cultural development, are factors which condition the definition of incest and the formulation of rules to prohibit it." Has this theory been tested by reference to any specific instances? If so we should like to have them indicated. The test of a theory is its ability to explain particular instances. I have tested my own sociological theory in many different societies over many years, and am now fairly satisfied with the results. One suspects that White has hardly begun to test his theory, since in each instance it would require the consideration of a very large number of variables as factors involved in the variations in the rules as to marriage. One would like some indication, for example, of how the presence or absence of cross-cousin marriage is conditioned by "the means and circumstances of offense and defense" or "the means of communication and transportation."

The various factors mentioned by White in the passage quoted above do not vary much in Australian tribes. But the regulation of marriage does vary. Again, these factors are the same in the Nguni and the Tswana in South Africa, but the former look with horror on marriage with a father's brother's daughter which the latter permit.

In early England and Wales persons who were related "within the fifth degree" counting through both males and females, were forbidden to marry; this would apply to all second cousins. In modern England and Wales second cousins may marry and there is no legal or religious objection to the marriage of first cousins although a few persons disapprove of such unions. I do not find it possible to imagine how White would explain this difference in terms of the various factors he mentions. The sociological explanation is fairly simple, in terms of the historic change from a wide-range kinship system with its institutions of *wergild* and *galanas*, and its rules of inheritance by which sixth cousins of all kinds might have a claim, to the narrow-range system of the present day.

4

It seems desirable to draw attention to some of the obscurities in White's statement of his thesis in his article on "The Expansion of the Scope of Science." The thesis he supports here is that there are, or ought to be, three distinct sciences, psychology, sociology and the science of culture. We ought therefore to be able to distinguish clearly the fields of these distinct studies.

White's statements about sociology are as follows. Sociology is described as "being but a science of group behavior, of collective psychological determinants." With this, as a sociologist, I am in complete disagreement. "When sociology took form as a distinct discipline it was dedicated to the study of the collective aspect of behavior." I do not think this is true of Herbert Spencer, for example. "Thus sociology turns out to be social psychology, and social psychology is psychology." "Sociology became, for the most part, social psychology, and *social* psychology is of course psychology." Thus, while White maintains that sociology is a study distinct from both psychology and the science of culture, in contradiction with this he holds that sociology is, at any rate for the most part, merely psychology. And if there is some kind of sociology distinct from psychology he entirely fails to tell us what kind of study it is or what are the facts with which it deals. His real view is contained in a passage in which he objects to the existence of a separate science of sociology. "Sociology devoted itself to the interpretation of superindividual (i.e., social) psychological determinants of behavior, and in so doing became social psychology. But, with few and relatively insignificant exceptions, it failed to distinguish and to recognize superpsychological (i.e., cultural) determinants, and thus failed to complete the science of human behavior by becoming a science of culture (i.e., culturology)." Thus what White thinks is wrong with sociology is that it tries to exist as an independent discipline instead of becoming a study of culture as conceived by White himself. There is here very clearly a complete lack of logical consistency. Either sociology does or ought to exist, or it does not or ought not to exist.

The best way to distinguish different branches of science is by reference to the class of empirical systems with which each is primarily concerned, the task of any branch of science being to discover the general characteristics of a class of empirical systems. Thus mechanical science deals with mechanical systems, one branch of chemistry with molecular systems, physiology with organic systems, and so on. Psychology is correctly defined, not as the study of behavior, but as the study of psychical systems, and a system of this kind consists of the psychical events that occur in a particular human being throughout the course of his life. Sociology is also not to be defined as a study of behavior; it is the attempt to discover the general characteristics of *social* systems. The components or elements of a social system are persons, not acts of behavior or mental events. A person is, for example, an Englishman, a father, a bricklayer, a member of a trades union, a Methodist, and so on. A social system is a system of the association of persons in a social structure. The sociologist studies the forms of association found amongst human beings.

The word "culture" has many different meanings. As a psychologist I would define culture in accordance with its dictionary meaning in English, as the process by which a human individual acquires, through contact with other individuals, or from such things as books and works of art, habits, capabilities, ideas, beliefs, knowledge, skills, tastes, and sentiments; and, by an extension common in the English language, the products of that process in the individual. As an Englishman I learned Latin and French and therefore some knowledge of Latin and French are part of my culture. The culture process in this sense can be studied by the psychologist, and in fact the theory of learning is such a study.

As a sociologist the reality to which I regard the word "culture" as applying is the process of cultural tradition, the process by which in a given social group or social class language, beliefs, ideas, aesthetic tastes, knowledge, skills and usages of many kinds are handed on ("tradition" means "handing on") from person to person and from one generation to another. The sociologist is obviously obliged to study the cultural traditions of all kinds that are found in a society of which he is making a study. Cultural tradition is a social process of interaction of persons within a social structure.

White does not seem to recognize either of these concepts of culture. For him culture is essentially "suprapsychological and suprasociological." But his definition of culture as a special kind of reality does not seem to me to be altogether clear. He tells us that a domesticated horse, the concrete individual quadruped, is a "culture trait" (page 202). So is a hoe (page 203). But a clan is also a culture trait (page 193). This apparently means the actual collection of human beings who form the kind of social group that we call a clan. Is every social group to be regarded as a culture trait—a nation, the British Commonwealth, the Roman Church, a particular trades union, a regiment of an army, an international scientific congress, or an industrial corporation? If not, what is the reason for singling out such a group as a clan? Is a human being such as a king or a prime minister or the president of a republic a culture trait? If so how do we distinguish between individuals who are and those who are not culture traits? We are told to distinguish between horses, domesticated horses being culture traits but not wild horses.

Culture traits, says White, are real things, and we may readily admit this for horses and hoes. "Customs and institutions—culture traits in general—constitute a distinct class of phenomena. As such it may be treated as a closed system.

Culture is a thing *sui generis;* culture as *culture* can only be explained in terms of culture" (page 192). Not only do culture traits act on individuals (page 202) (is a kick from a mule an action of a culture trait?); culture traits causally determine one another within the closed system. I do not think it is possible for the ordinary person to understand what this means until a number of examples are given with detailed treatment. A method or a theory can only be understood by means of application to specific problems or instances.

The study of culture is at least as old as sociology or psychology. Writers concerned themselves with "civilizations," for example the civilization of ancient Greece or ancient Rome. For the English and French words "civilization" the Germans substituted "Kultur" and writing about Kultur was a favorite theme of the German romanticists of the early nineteenth century. The study of Kultur or of civilizations was treated as belonging to history or to the philosophy of history. I think that Kroeber and Toynbee may be said to be continuing this tradition each in his own distinctive way. But White does not seem to be content to follow along that path. He is not content with Kroeber's study of "formal causes" in the Aristotelian sense, but demands the recognition of culture traits as efficient causes producing effects on other traits and on individuals.

I submit that Professor White has failed not only to justify his thesis, but to present it in a logical and understandable way. Are we to recognize three sciences, psychology, sociology and science of culture, or only two, excluding sociology as being only social psychology? Some of us who are sociologists believe that sociology does exist as a science, just as distinct from psychology as psychology is from physiology, or physiology from chemistry. Its subject matter, I repeat, is the forms of association or social integration found amongst human beings. Does Professor White recognize this as an existing or possible study? If we admit the existence of a sociology, then White has not made clear the distinction between the enquiries, methods, problems and theories of comparative sociology and those of a distinct science of culture. What is the nature of the difference of studying clans as associations of persons or features of social structure, and studying them as "culture traits"? What is meant by the "behavior" of a culture trait (page 198)? If culture consists of a collection of culture traits and these are real things "which can be and are experienced as real things" what are the chief classes of culture traits? We are offered a few examples, such as a domesticated horse, a hoe, a clan, a polygynous household (one husband and three wives) but we are also told that customs and institutions are culture traits. A statement about culture traits in general cannot have any precise meaning. It can apply equally to hoes, and clans and such customs as shaking hands or sleeping in pyjamas, or drinking mint juleps. Is the science of culture able to explain, as psychology cannot, and explain in some way different from an historical explanation, why some people eat with knives and forks, and others with chopsticks (page 189)? These are some of the questions that call for answers before we can understand what Professor White really means.

10 Culture and Individuals

ANTHONY F. C. WALLACE

Radcliffe-Brown raises many important questions concerning White's view of culture, including: (1) Can we have different kinds of explanations for a given problem, and consider all such answers equally valid and independent? (2) How, following White, will sociological explanations differ from culturological explanations? (3) How does one go about testing the value of White's approach by field work? It should be noted that Radcliffe-Brown does not directly reject White's views; rather he asserts that they cannot be properly evaluated until the various problems raised by them are answered.

The questions raised by Radcliffe-Brown, when linked to those presented by Morris Opler, provide the culturologists with much food for thought. An important issue raised in Professor Opler's paper is "When cultural determinists portray the molding influences of a culture on its carriers, the culture is invariably represented as something monolithic and undeviating, and one would think . . . that people roll from the relationship like pieces of dough stamped out by a cookie cutter." Professor Wallace's paper is much concerned with this very issue. Is culture indeed something uniform for a population; or is "a culture" seen quite differently from the viewpoints of different role-players within it? If the latter be the case, as Anthony Wallace believes, how is this "cultural variety" best conceptualized? The paper that follows presents interesting ideas on these questions.

This essay questions four commonly held and logically coherent assumptions which together make up a theoretical system called "cultural determinism," and proposes a reformulation of certain current doctrines about the relationships between culture and personality which are based on the cultural determinist

SOURCE: Reprinted from "Individual Differences and Cultural Uniformities" by Anthony F. C. Wallace, *American Sociological Review,* December 1952, pp. 747–750, by permission of the author and the publisher.

system. The four assumptions are (1) that culture is an external environment uniformly perceived by and pressing upon all members of a given society, (2) that this cultural pressure determines a uniformity of behavior, including parental behavior (which largely defines the child's experience), (3) that therefore all "normal" members of a society must have the same basic personality structure ("national character"), and (4) that consequently culture can be said to mold personality. The criticism itself is not a rejection of the idea of a determinative relationship between culture and a most frequently and most closely approximated personality type, or the idea of a determinative relationship between culture and other mass social and economic phenomena. It is, however, a denial of the adequacy of general formulations and of specific research designs based on the cultural-deterministic assumption, whether explicit or implicit, that culture is a unitary, external, "super-organic" environmental force which mechanically determines and molds individual behavior and, by extension, individual personality.

The word "determine" is an ambiguous one. A class of phenomena may be regarded as being determined by certain factors directly, without intervention of other factors, as for instance in the determination of a projectile's trajectory by such variables as the angle of the tube, gravitational pull, the force of the propulsive charge, atmospheric resistance, wind deflection, and the rifling of the bore. This sort of determination approximates the classic concept of causation in specifying necessary and sufficient conditions, both for a class of phenomena and for any specific case within that class. This may be called *mechanical determination*. But the word "determine" is often also applied to correlation data, and variables significantly correlated with a phenomenon are dubbed "determinants" of it even though the relationship may be admittedly indirect, obscure, and neither necessary nor sufficient as an explanation, as when ecological zone of transition is recognized as a determinant of delinquency. What is essentially described by this sort of determinacy is a statistically significant concomitant variation of incidences, and so it may be called *probability determination*. Misunderstanding occurs, however, when the remaining problem of the "mechanical" determination of individual cases is overlooked, and a "probability" determination is interpreted as being the mechanical determination of specific events. This kind of fallacy is committed in cultural determinism, which asserts a *mechanical* determination by culture of individual event, behavior, and personality.

The Concept of Culture

The idea of uniform behavior is implicit in the concept of culture. When an ethnographer describes the culture of a society, he is describing ways of doing things which are more or less *uniformly* used. But the careful ethnographer recognizes that this uniformity of thought, speech, and action, although substantial, is not complete. Within the society there are individual differences in age, sex, geographical location, health and constitution, social class and caste, occupation, income, personality, and so on, and in many areas of behavior the cultural uniformity extends only to the boundaries of sub-groups more or less rigidly defined on the basis of one or more of the above criteria. This may lead the ethnographer to speak of sub-societies and sub-cultures; he may refer to a "youth-culture," may say that his description refers only to urban middle class, may implicitly or explicitly exclude females from consideration. In addition to these variations, which might be called the "systematic alternatives" of a culture, there are also a number of more or less "random alternatives"—particularly in societies with competitive market economies. These alternatives are the several acceptable ways of doing virtually the same thing available to any given person—taking a bus instead of a trolley, buying a "contemporary" house or keeping an apartment, and so on. In their finer expressions, these random alternatives are sometimes called cases of "marginal differentiation." Coca-Cola, Pepsi-Cola, and other colas would hardly go down in the ethnographer's notebook as separate culture traits, nor would all different women's hats, or the variations of machine-made standardized parts. And, finally, while any given culture will have recommendations ready-made for handling practically all conceivable situations, a significant quantity of human behavior does *not* accord with its proper culture at all. While this quantity is apparently very slight, in comparison with the quantity of conforming behavior, and hence is often passed off as exceptional, it cannot realistically be ignored, any more than the physicist can ignore air resistance in calculating the behavior of a falling body, even though the acceleration of falling bodies is calculated on the assumption of a vacuum. The behavior of persons suffering from neurological or emotional disorders, for instance, may be strange to their culture. Even normal people now and then do things which are not culturally predictable. People make mistakes. People do wrong or foolish things. People invent new ways of dealing with problems which are not always widely accepted. The issue, however, is not so much whether or not individual behavior approximates cultural norms —it generally does—as the recognition that it is not culture which compels, but the individual who chooses. Occasionally he chooses not to use the culturally standardized way.[1]

We may therefore say that the concept of culture itself, insofar as its implications of normality and uniformity are concerned, is a *quasi-statistical* one. A culture trait, as seen from this viewpoint, is a most frequently and most closely

---

[1] It is not necessary here to go into the philosophical question of free will. The individual's choices may indeed be determined; the point is that they are not mechanically determined by culture.

approximated type of behavior, a point on a distribution curve, and behavior can be called "conforming" to culture when it falls within the range of marginal differentiation around that point. One may speak thus of "cultural probabilities." One of these is the probability that any individual with a problem will use *some* culturally recognized technique for solving it. This probability will vary according to the problem, and presumably will be rather high —let us say, arbitrarily, on the order of 0.98. The probability of his use of a *specific* cultural trait for a specific problem will vary according to the number of systematic and random alternatives his culture affords for the solution of that problem, and the extent to which the given area of behavior is culturally standardized at all, and will usually be much less than the first probability. Even lower probabilities attach to the likelihood of an individual's associates (parents, co-workers, spouse, children) presenting any given sequence of specific culturally standardized behaviors. A repetition of exactly the same sequence of behaviors in two cases, duplicating even the varieties of marginal differentiation, is evidently so improbable as to deserve being called impossible.

This argument does not involve a denial of the reality of culture, or of its importance as a probability determinant of other mass phenomena. The quasi-statistical regularities of culture certainly do exist, and are as real as other hard facts like mortality rates and cost of living indices. When one is concerned with mass phenomena, it is even correct to speak of "cultural factors" in the sense of probability determination. Thus, the fall in the net reproduction rate in the United States is demonstrably correlated (presumably in a non-mechanical determinative relationship) with, among other things, an increasingly urban concentration of the population. But *individual* behavior and *particular* events, to greater or lesser degree, may or may not exemplify the quasi-uniformities of culture, and even within the ambit of a culture may be exceedingly variable. To explain why any urban woman (or any group of urban women) has two children instead of eight, if one wishes to describe the mechanics of the case, it is obviously not sufficient merely to remark that she lives in a city. To do so would, of course, confuse mechanical and probability determination.

National Character

It is possible to consider the general problem of personality formation, in the context of this discussion, without subscribing to any particular substantive theory. We may say very generally that a personality is formed as a product of the particular experiences of an individual organism. Presumably, not all experiences are equally weighty in influence; there is general agreement, the writer supposes, that the developing organism's interactions with people are of primary significance. Within the first six years of life (which are said by many psychiatrists to be especially important, although we need not deny significance to later years), a child experiences innumerable events involving people. General categories of events would include birth, feeding, being cleaned, being talked to, being left alone, weaning, bowel and bladder training, learning to talk, play, self-care, minor or major injuries or illness, and as many other items as one wishes to detail. People involved include various selections and combinations of father, mother, brothers, sisters, playmates, adult relatives, adult neighbors, and others. Considerable variation is to be expected, on the basis of the theoretical considerations presented above, and in fact undoubtedly occurs in any society in all categories of infantile experience. These variations are partly a matter of accidents like death and illness, partly of marginal differentiation within accepted cultural norms, partly of traumatically deviant behavior by parents and other associates. They are also built into the culture itself as "systematic alternatives," in many cases being correlated with occupational groups, class, region, etc., and as "random alternatives," several ways being equally acceptable and feasible. The infinite variability of experience continues throughout the individual's life. The probability that any new born infant chosen at random in any society will have any given sequence of formative experiences, when such considerable variation exists in possibilities of experience in each category, is relatively slim.

The culture thus never can present itself as a constant environment to all members of a society, as every ethnographer knows after working with more than one informant. While the cultural quasi-uniformities in themselves exist, like sex ratios, they are not equally perceived by every one. It is gross fallacy to suppose that a culture is a uniform environment for all of a population. No two members of a society carry in their heads the same picture of its culture (not even if they happen to be professional culturologists), because no two persons have had the same experiences or have selected or invented the same techniques for solving their problems. The point should be made explicit: *A culture, in its totality, is no more a part of any one's behaviorally significant environment than is the totality of his physical surroundings.*

The implications of the foregoing considerations for the relationship of culture and personality should now be generally apparent. Inasmuch as individual personality, described as a set of techniques of behavior (both overt and covert) characteristic of a person, is assumed to be formed by a highly complex history of particular events involving his interaction with a limited number of other persons, *the probability of any definable sequence of formative events is equal to the probability of the emergence of a given type of personality, and the total number of individuals possessing that type of personality will be the product of that probability and the size of the population.* As previously stated, the probability of a given sequence of formative experiences is relatively low even if each component is culturally standardized; consequently the frequency of occurrence of a given national character type should be low, too.

A Field Study of National Character

In the summers of 1948 and 1949 the writer collected seventy Rorschach protocols (36 male and 34 female) from adult (age 16 and over) Tuscarora Indians resident on the Tuscarora reservation in New York State.[2] There were 352 adult Tuscaroras according to the writer's census of 1948, 179 male and 173 female. The sample was very closely proportional by age and sex and contained rough quotas for such categories as chieftainship, clan-membership, membership in the lacrosse team, and the like. It was not a random sample, subjects being recruited by a process of personal contact involving a few intermediaries. The total population of the reservation was approximately 600. Although there were, of course, cliques, and persons could be ranked as of generally higher or lower social status, the population was apparently too small and homogeneous for an intra-reservation class system to have developed with systematic differences in behavior and limitations of social contact. Acculturation, furthermore, had proceeded so far that even the extreme proponents of nativism and assimilation respectively were not systematically different in language, religion, dress, occupation, or attitude toward the clan system and chief's council.

The somewhat naïve initial hypothesis was that there would be a clearly homogeneous personality type, recognizable even by superficial inspection of the records. The problem actually became one of defining any common structure at all. There was indeed one trait, high W percent,[3] held almost in common, but to describe a common structure it was not sufficient to concentrate on this one trait when fully 21 variables were under consideration. Nor was it possible simply to strike averages in all 21 categories, then interpret the pattern of the averages, and finally attribute this "type" to the whole population —a procedure which patently would have violated the fact that the subjects were *not* all alike, and would have introduced gross distortions in those variables where the distribution was asymmetrical.

The notion of a common personality structure was abandoned. In its place was put the concept of a type of personality more closely approximated by more individuals than any other type, and deducible from a knowledge of the culture, which constitutes by definition the most frequently and most closely approximated mode of experience. The term "modal personality structure" was borrowed from Cora DuBois to refer to this most frequently and most

---

[2] The following analysis of the Tuscarora and Ojibwa Rorschach data is an abbreviation of the more elaborate presentation made in a monograph now in press: Anthony F. C. Wallace, *The Modal Personality Structure of the Tuscarora Indians, as Revealed by the Rorschach Test,* Smithsonian Institution, Bureau of American Ethnology, Bulletin 150, Washington, D.C.

[3] The presence of "high W percent" (30 percent and above) in a protocol is conventionally interpreted to be evidence of a tendency to think in terms of abstractions rather than of concrete individual phenomena.

closely approximated type. For each of the 21 variables, the modal score was identified, and the standard deviation of the distribution calculated. Estimating the reliability of Rorschach test scores as 0.8, a function of the standard error of measurement was applied to set up limiting scores on either side of the mode, within which statistically significant differences, at the 0.03 level of probability, from the modal score did not exist. All 70 records were scanned, and those selected which in all 21 variables were not significantly different from the modal scores of those variables. Twenty-six individuals out of the sample of 70 were found to have produced Rorschach protocols which were not significantly different, in the above-specified terms of statistical reliability, from the modal scores in each of the 21 scoring categories. These 26 records were finally reduced to a "modal type" by calculating mean scores; the profile of means in the 21 categories of the 26 modal records was defined as the modal type, and its interpretation extended only to those 26 records (which seemed admissible, since these 26 had been operationally defined as equivalent).

While this technique manifestly did some violence to the data, in ignoring the certainty that the 26 modal records are not really equivalent, it seemed to be open to fewer objections than other techniques, and did provide a way of defining a type of personality which was demonstrably more closely approximated by more people than any other type. Obviously the decision as to the level of probability acceptable in setting up the limits of distinguishability—an arbitrary decision—affected the number of individual cases regarded as being represented by the mode, as well as the exact mean values later calculated. But using these limits (which equaled one standard deviation on either side of the mode) it was found that only 37 percent of the sample could be regarded as having a structure of personality not recognizably different from a modal type. Presumably such bias as the crude sampling procedures entailed meant that a truly random sample would have been even more disparate. This modal 37 percent was not significantly disproportional in age or sex.

A second body of 102 Rorschach protocols, collected by A. I. Hallowell from Ojibwa Indians in the Lake Winnipeg, was analyzed by the same procedures for comparative purposes. It was found that 29 (28 percent) of the 102 Ojibwa Rorschachs fell within the Ojibwa modal class. The incidence of a modal type of personality was thus of a roughly similar order of magnitude in both samples, even though there are substantial cultural differences between the two societies (the Ojibwa from whom the protocols were selected being a much less acculturated, predominantly hunting people). But there is no question that the two modal types are significantly different from one another, even though there are some common elements (which might be expected)—only 5 of 102 Ojibwa protocols fell within the Tuscarora modal class. The difference between the two most closely approximated types the writer would attribute to the cultural differences between the two populations.

11 Sex and Culture

MORRIS FREILICH

Professor Wallace's ideas about the lack of uniformity within a cultural context are nicely amplified in a recent paper by Morris Opler. He writes:

> *As one of the proofs that we are all cut to the measure of our culture, we are sometimes reminded that individuals of the same tradition learn to speak the same language. Winston Churchill spoke and wrote English, and so do hippies and the boy who fails in freshman English. The image of uniform culture is arrived at only through Procrustean thinking that inevitably presents a mutilated version of its subject.**

Clearly, "the same culture" is really not "the same" for all the people who live in it. At least two groups, living in the same culture, *have considerable differences in their respective goals, and the means they utilize to achieve them: men and women. The paper that follows attempts to highlight these differences by focusing on one aspect of social life where considerable conflict exists: sexual relations. This discussion of sex conflicts in Trinidad enables the student to view the data and the analysis somewhat objectively. A little thought will quickly bring to light that the system presented is not unique. As James Thurber has most humorously shown us in* The Thurber Carnival, *the "war of the sexes" exists as an unending battle in such peace-loving countries as the U.S.A.*

Sexual Life of Negro Peasants in Anamat, Trinidad[1]

Anamat, a relatively isolated community in Eastern Trinidad, is situated in the cocoa-coffee highlands frequently referred to as "the bush." Living "in the bush" is, for townsfolk, doing without such basic comforts as electricity,

SOURCE: Reprinted from "Sex, Secrets and Systems" by Morris Freilich from *The Family in the Caribbean:* Proceedings of the First Conference on the Family in the Caribbean, edited by Stanford N. Gerber, pp. 47–62. Reprinted by permission of the Author, Editor and The Institute of Caribbean Studies. Copyright 1968 by The Institute of Caribbean Studies, University of Puerto Rico.

* Morris E. Opler, "Culture and the Human Potential," *Human Potentialities: The Challenge and the Promise,* ed. Herbert A. Otto, St. Louis: Warren Green, 1968, pp. 21–45.

[1] The field work period was 1957–58; and the data to be presented was collected by the writer, his wife Natalie Asch Freilich, and a full time assistant (the 32-year-old daughter of a Negro peasant).

gas, running water, telephones, and good transportation facilities. For Anamatians, it represents a place where you can live "cool and quiet" with but "racial problems" to mar the otherwise idyllic environment. Negro and Indian peasants live together in neighborly enmity—rarely permitting their mutual dislike for each other to escalate into physical violence—and farm (on the average) twenty-one-acre holdings.

Anamatian Negroes have several well-liked pastimes; these include cricket, and sexual involvements with the daughters and wives of their neighbors. This latter "game" referred to hereafter as *the sex-fame game*—has consequences ranging from kinship relations to economics. The basic details of the sex-fame game follow.

Anamatian Negroes believe that everyone has a sexual appetite the satisfaction of which is natural and pleasurable. Men whose sexual needs are almost insatiable are referred to as "hot boys," "sweet men," and "wild men"; and such *real men* require sexual gratification both frequently and in great variety. Hot boys who are frequently sexually involved with many women receive the social acclaim known as "fame," and to be a "famous man" is the goal of almost every adult male. Men receive additional acclaim for their "foolin' abilities"—abilities to make convincing promises to women which they expect to break.

Sex is considered both a pleasing activity and an enjoyable subject matter for frequent discussion. Two terms that are often used in such talk are "breed" and "brush." Breed refers to a situation where a male has sexual rights over a female and the ability to exercise such rights for the production of offspring. Although breed is most often used to refer to the sexual relationship between a man and his spouse, it is extended to refer to an implied right of a man to sexual intercourse with any female living in his house, or working for him, with whom such intercourse would not constitute incest. Prestige from a breeding situation is obtained, not by high frequency sexual activities, since here a man gets only what is already his, but rather from the production of children. The siring of many children indicates the maleness of the male.

A "brush" is a sexual act involving a male and a woman over whom he has no sexual rights. To get a brush, therefore, a male must approach a woman as a suppliant and indicate his interest in her as a sexual object. The term generally used for this kind of approach is "beg." A man telling his friend of a recent sexual conquest generally describes the situation in a manner which indicates his personal charm and his begging talents. In begging for sex, almost any strategy used is "good" if it succeeds. In the words of one peasant: "There is nothing wrong in telling a girl anything to get what you want. If you can't fool a woman you are not a famous man, and the women will confuse you and get what *they* want." Begging strategies considered effective include promises to bring the lover expensive presents, making eloquent declarations of love, and making convincing promises of marriage—which often include promises to rid oneself of a wife. A strategy never used by an honorable man is *force:* a sexual conquest is, by definition, getting a woman to acquiesce when she has the free will to refuse.

Sex-games frequently follow a well understood sequence: (1) an initial move by the male indicating his sexual interest in a given woman; (2) a friendly refusal by the woman—both to permit her to receive maximum returns for her services, and to permit the male to show his begging abilities; (3) eloquent begging by the male; (4) a decision by the woman either to provide or to withhold sexual services. Should the woman consent, (5) a mutual agreement as to the time and place of the sexual rendezvous; and (6) a final "contract" with duties and responsibilities implied for both parties. To wit, the woman expects the affair to be completely secret and expects some "recompense" for "giving" sex to the male. The male—if married—expects the woman to help him keep their relationship secret from his wife and expects to provide some reciprocity for "getting" sex. He understands that although he cannot possibly keep many of his promises, a failure to provide *some* reciprocity will quickly terminate this particular relationship and negatively influence the outcome of all his future beggings in the community.

The critical factors which appear to account for *who plays* in the sex-fame game and why *some play more often than others* are (1) beliefs of males, (2) beliefs of females, and (3) a set of *operational rules*—rules developed by the community which help actors predict the *probable* outcome of given actions. For example, men believe that *all women*—single or married—may be begged for sex, and that *all men* may play the role of sexual beggar. In the words of one peasant:

> Married men and bachelors both have the same sight and the same lust, so both must have many women. Some women want to limit the man to one woman; but you don't limit the bull . . . the priest say, "Stay with one woman, you know canon law." I say, "I am no lawyer, but I know that is not common sense."

Two general exceptions exist to these beliefs: first, a given male believes that *his* sister—if single—is not approachable for sex—and if married—is only approachable by her husband. Second, a given male believes that *his* wife is approachable by none but himself for sexual favors. In sum, men believe that they and the husbands of their sisters have *monopolistic* sexual privileges with their wives, but other men have only *preferential* sexual privileges. Other husbands thus only have first call (so to speak) for their wives' sexual services; they themselves have the only call.

Women start married life holding one or two polar viewpoints. Most women believe that old love affairs must be terminated on marriage and that no new ones may be started. Others believe it permissible to accept sexual advances even after marriage. The former generally believe that their husbands, too, must give up other women on marriage. The latter believe that the husband need not give up other women on marriage; however, they generally wish he would. Women's beliefs in this area are strongly associated with a more fundamental female belief: that men and women are social equals and that therefore social rules apply equally to males and females. Since their husbands never give up the sex-fame game after marriage, and since other men continue to approach them for sex, sooner or later, most women come to believe that outside sex is permissible, as long as such affairs are kept secret.

The operational rules used by men to guide their sexual beggings are first, *community-shared information about the probability of successful begging with given women.* Men know that their chances of success are higher with women who are currently husbandless than with women currently living with a man; are higher with lower class women than with the wives of peasants; are higher with women whose husbands stray infrequently; and are higher with women who need the goods and services they receive in exchange for sexual favors, than with women for whom such goods and services are but extra luxury items. The men also know that some of the peasants' wives firmly believe that marriage puts an end to past affairs and to any possible future ones. Women with such beliefs will rarely be approached for sexual favors.

Secondly, the attractiveness of a woman will, in part, determine how much begging she receives. In general, younger women are considered more attractive than older women; and virginity is considered an attractive feature. In the words of one peasant "some men have preference for a virgin, but to achieve that is hard."

On the basis of these operational rules lower class women are begged for sex more often than women of higher classes. Such lower class women will tend to have husbands who stray frequently, usually need the goods and services that a lover brings and generally believe that outside love affairs are all right. Lower class women who do not have these beliefs are given little sympathy concerning their economic problems. For example, when one such deviant complained that her husband was a poor provider, a peasant answered her: "You have lots of ways of making money"—he eyed her up and down for about ten seconds and continued, "You don't make use of what you have!" The audience, consisting of a resident anthropologist and two other peasants, smiled their approval.

The operational rules used by women to guide their behavior in the sex-fame game include *shared information concerning* (1) the economic standing of given males, (2) the social state of men—single, married in common law, legally married, (3) men's reputations as lovers, and (4) men's reputations as keepers of secrets. Richer males are known to be better risks for keeping promises involving money expenditures than poorer males. Thus, although in his late sixties, one of the wealthiest peasants of Anamat never had begging problems—Mr. F, it is known, "is always good to his friends." Men unencumbered by legal or common-law wives are believed more often—when they promise marriage—than already married men promising to leave a wife. Men with common-law wives are believed more often—when they promise marriage—than males with legal wives. Legal wives—it is well known—are not easily disposed of.

Some men have reputations for great sexual abilities; others, like Mr. D, have the reputation of valiantly trying (in bed) but rarely succeeding. The former generally have a begging advantage over the latter. Some men are known for their abilities to keep secrets; others have the reputation of being untrustworthy. Other things being equal, the former are more often successful sexual beggars than the latter.

Irrespective of the reputation given males have for keeping secrets, men regularly—and often quite eloquently—broadcast their sexual escapades. They obviously have to, since their fame depends on (1) their sex activities, (2) their abilities to distribute personal sex information, and (3) their abilities to make such information appear credible.

Broadcasts of sexual conquests generally take place during all-male encounters and include boastings—by the broadcaster—of his great personal abilities as a sexual beggar. In one such gathering statements were made such as:

> Some of the fellows here don't know how to fool a woman. They don't know how to speak to a woman properly; they can't tell her, "I love you." After I get a woman alone for awhile and talk to her, I begin to beg for a brush. I beg and beg and she can't refuse me.

The audience generally evaluates the information of a given broadcaster rather critically. They then communicate both his message and their analysis of it through informal community channels. The siring of an outside child is proof positive of a conquest, thus one strategy used by some men to achieve greater fame is to claim paternity over children whose parentage is in doubt. Members of the community and their friends generally achieve a consensus as to who sired a given child. Males, other than the agreed-on-father, who continue to claim paternity, are referred to as "trying to give themselves fame." A more subtle strategy used by a few is to deny paternity in situations where there is general agreement that the child is theirs. The latter situation generates much talk involving the "denying father" who thereby increases his "fame."

For males there is little reason to worry about contraceptive measures. As one informant told me:

> If I had an outside child I would try to keep it. I would offer it first to my mother and then to my sister. My mother would not be vexed (in this kind of situation). The son becomes a hero, like a fellow goes to war and returns with medals. The women can't push this boy around, he pushes them around.

For the woman an outside child is a source of trouble from her family. As one woman told me, "For a girl to bring an outside child home is to disgrace the family. They will take you in but you will see much trouble." For the married woman an extra child is more work and more restrictions on her freedom of movement. In the words of one woman: "The children hold the Creole women back so they don't want many; (with many) they can't go to dances as they like, nor to wakes. Nor can they get about the way they like to."

Women, both single and married, attempt to guard against pregnancy. The contraceptive devices used most frequently include gynomin tablets, "withdrawal," Epsom salts placed inside the vagina prior to intercourse, drinking quicksilver and rum, and eating young pineapples. Since most of the adult males have sired *some* outside children—uncertainty existed on exactly how many a given male had sired—clearly these contraceptive devices are frequently ineffective.

The men frequently take the initiative in sexual relations with their wives; and many women speak of their husbands as almost forcing them into sexual relations at times. The reluctance of wives to always give into their husbands' sexual demands are due to several reasons. First, at times wives get *very angry* at their husbands' sexual escapades and use the withholding of sexual favors as a sanction. Secondly, wives are frequently concerned about getting pregnant, and when such a concern is greatest, the wife will probably refrain from sexual relations with her husband. Thirdly, sexual rebuttals are often a consequence of the male's possessiveness. That is, many of the women react negatively to their husbands' views that wives are always available to them for sex. Women generally concede to their husbands' sexual desires for two reasons: first, they do not want to cause a row over sex; secondly, they do not wish husbands to believe they are being sexually satisfied by a lover.

The sex-fame game obviously influences family life in general and a brief discussion of these links is necessary.

Conjugal Life and "Outside" Women

Marriage is postponed by the younger males of the community until such time as they realize either or both of the following facts: first, that many strategies exist to minimize a wife's interference with her husband's sex-escapades. Second, that the encumbrances of a wife vis-à-vis the sex-fame game, are more than balanced by the benefits which accrue to a male from marriage. The male is generally concerned about the sexual compatibility of himself and his future spouse, and sexual intercourse prior to marriage is common. As one peasant put it, "Me ain't buying no cat in the bag."

Most men believe that their sexual lives are best served by getting a common-law wife rather than a legal wife. On this matter the males argue as follows: First, the sexual advantages of marriage are the same whether one marries in common law or legally. In both cases a wife is thought of as supplying the husband with sexual privileges which can be exercised at any time the husband so desires. Secondly, common-law marriage has none of the disadvantages of legal marriage; an unsatisfactory wife can be easily dispatched; and, one can still promise other women legal marriage in the future in return for present sexual favors. Concerning the latter point one peasant said:

> A (legally) married man must spend more money on girls because he don't have no foolin' power. He cannot get sex by promising other girls that he will leave his (legal) wife and marry them legally.

Most of the wives of the Creole peasants of Anamat are annoyed by the sexual exploits of their husbands and would rather have a husband who does not "run all about." However, the emotional reaction is not uniform for all these women. Some are more upset than others and some express their annoyance more violently than others. Some of the women are, temperamentally, more jealous than others. They constantly "study" (think into deeply, worry about) their husband's activities. A very jealous wife will at times make embarrassing scenes and do her utmost to break up an outside affair. Generally, even the jealous wives do not initiate violent confrontations with outside women. Most of the wives of the community find such confrontations extremely distasteful. A crisis in family relations is always created when the lover initiates a confrontation with the wife and publicly proclaims that she is "the outside woman." Such a broadcast usually includes verbal attacks on the wife's ability to fulfill her sexual role. The reactions of the wife to the taunts of the lover are always extreme; she always becomes very angry and frequently either threatens the lover with bodily harm or attacks her then and there.

Wives who "do not jealous their husbands," pride themselves on the control they maintain over their feelings. Many wives describe their reactions to outside affairs as "cool, cool." Such a relaxed attitude to a husband's love life is considered to be a superior one, and one which went along with a wife's development of maturity.

No matter how little a woman "jealouses her husband" and how "cool, cool" she is, the money spent on outside women is frequently a major source of conflict between husbands and wives. The wives are always fearful that funds necessary for running the house are being squandered for fêtes and for gifts to outside women. What many wives find particularly annoying is the fact that they help their husbands economically by "working in the cocoa," and then income that they helped create is spent on other women! Women find it very upsetting when their husbands have one outside woman for a long period of time. Such an affair is seen as more threatening to the continuation of the marriage than many short-term affairs.

Other things being equal, the amount of concern a woman shows appears to be inversely related to her age: the older the wife the less the emotional reaction to her husband's exploits. Three factors account for this general tendency: a decreasing interest in sexual matters going along with the aging process; an increasing ability to cope with the sex-fame game, going along with experience; and the decrease of their husbands' sexual escapades going along with his own aging processes.

Sexual Life as a System

The sexual life of Negro peasants has systemic elements which can be presented in a variety of frameworks (models). Let us first look at these elements and then concern ourselves with the manner of interlinking them. We have—it seems to me—a situation which involves people with legitimate right to play the sex-fame game (*personnel*); their *time orientation, beliefs, goals, strategies, and sentiments;* and community information:

1. *Personnel*	Male and Female adults
2. *Time Orientation*	The Present
3. *Beliefs*	a. Sex is good b. Real men want sex often with many women c. Women *give* sex d. Men give valued objects for sex e. Clever men "fool" f. Sexual escapades are "private affairs" (1) for women, this means they are secret (2) for men, this means that broadcasts are made in little friendly settings g. Men who are successful beggars deserve prestige h. Wise women stay "cool" when husbands stray
4. *Goals of Males*	a. To be known as "hot-boys" b. To have "fame"

5. *Goals of Females*	a. To have their sexual escapades kept secret b. To avoid pregnancy c. To avoid confrontations with outside women d. To have promises made to them kept e. To have husbands who rarely take outside women; and who spend little money on the latter
6. *Community Information* (Providing the basis for the Operational Rules)	a. Most sexual affairs are secret to no member of the community b. Men know which women will probably acquiesce to their wishes c. Women know which men are likely to keep their promises
7. *Strategies*	a. Male—to frequently beg for sex; to discuss conquest often and eloquently; to claim paternity in cases of doubt b. Female—to be with men who are honorable: who will not discuss their sex life, who will keep promises
8. *Sentiments Associated with Sexual Escapades*	a. Excitement, pleasure, freedom

The system—it will soon be clear—has tendencies making both for states of balance or equilibrium and states of imbalance or disequilibrium. The former can be presented as follows.

Sexual encounters have a dualistic quality for women—sexual experiences are intrinsically pleasurable, but have a possible unfortunate consequence: pregnancy, restricting women's freedom and providing husbandless wives with some temporary shame. For men, sexual encounters are intrinsically enjoyable and are avenues to social applause. Since men and women are equals in a sexual encounter, its rewards are equalized by defining women as giving and men as taking sex. The "takers" must beg and reciprocate for favors received. Men attempt to keep their sex "expense" low to have the funds for many affairs and to receive extra fame for their fooling power. These attempts tend to cut short given affairs. Short duration affairs with one woman are congruent with (1) men's desires for variety in sexual experiences—maximizing their "excitement," (2) men's desires for fame—partly a function of the number of women with whom involvements exist, (3) minimizing threats to a given marriage—long duration affairs are most disruptive of marital relations.

The richer the peasant the more he can afford sexual affairs, the more his promises are believed and the more affairs he actually has. The poorer the woman, the more often she will accept lovers. The sex-fame game is thus a mechanism for the distribution of surplus goods; keeping the latter within the community and enhancing community integration.

Marriage is considered by the peasant as a "now-for-now" affair; and common-law unions were considered superior to legal ones. The sex-fame game helps to lead a peasant from wife to wife—that is, facilitates serial polygyny—by providing him with relationships with many women, each of which can be evaluated as a possible future wife. Common-law marriage facilitates the "divorce" process. The disruptive elements of the sex-fame game on marital relations weakens the nuclear family and by contrast strengthens the matrifocal family: a membership unit peasants consider of prime importance in their lives. The children produced by outside affairs create pseudo-kin ties between males, females, and their offspring. Community bonds are enhanced by these pseudo-kin links which also act as mechanisms for the distribution of surplus goods.

Sexual life of Anamatian Negroes has been analyzed *as if* it could be presented as one cultural system in *a general state of balance or equilibrium.* Viewed in this way the system has a major flaw: *men and women playing the sex-fame game have diametrically opposite goals.* Indeed, my label for this game, though well fitting the man's viewpoint, does little justice to the woman's. The *secret-sex game* is a more appropriate title for her game. The goals of these two types of players are better contrasted as:

Sex-fame game (Men)

1. To have sexual escapades widely known
2. To get lovers pregnant—for greater fame
3. To keep few promises
4. To have many outside women
5. To have a common-law wife

Secret-sex game (Women)

1. To have sexual escapades kept secret
2. To avoid pregnancy
3. To have all promises kept
4. To have husbands who take few outside women
5. To be a legal wife

The *sex-fame game* remains an appropriate label for the phenomena being analyzed since it is the male's goals which—by and large—are met rather than those of the female. Most community members know the "secret" sex life of most community members; women's attempts to avoid pregnancy are not always successful; promises made are rarely kept in their entirety; conjugal relations are more frequently based on common-law marriage than on legal marriage, and husbands have many—not few—outside women.

Given the contradictory goals of men and women, and given the system's "preference" for male goals, what options are available to the women? The women can elect to be non-players in the sex-fame game; they can play cautiously—selecting partners who are comparatively honorable; they can play and create crises when partners do them wrong. Non-playing means giving up the positive consequences of active involvement—companionship, pleasure, goods and services, and a presentation-of-self as an equal of the males. Playing cautiously helps little—men must fool and broadcast their conquests to achieve their goal of fame. Playing and creating crises is the only realistic option left; and it is the one generally taken. This latter option is not particularly satisfying to the women.

The angry, tearful, and upset wife loses community prestige and sees her husband rarely. The wife who accosts her husband's lover loses even more prestige and creates considerable problems for herself (see below). The lover who, because of broken promises, acts like an angry wife, quickly loses her lover. Should she accost his wife, the lover gets known as "a shameless woman" from whom married men stay away. Men are blamed as much as their shameless lovers when a wife is accosted by their "sweethearts." As one wife put it: "Every man has a girl friend and that is all right if kept secret. But many men allow the girl to give the wife words; that is unmoral. These things make the woman at home feel bad."

The Meaning of "Secrets"

Why should a woman approaching the wife of her lover be considered shameless? Why should men be responsible for keeping lovers away from wives? Why are they "unmoral" if they don't do this? If it is "all right that every man has a girl friend" why should it be kept secret? Since such "secrets" are well known in the community, why does "the woman at home" feel bad when confronted by the husband's lover? Does she assume that her husband—unlike all the others of the community—has no lover? Let us look at these questions in terms of two frameworks: *individuals* and *the system.*

The women of Anamat know that all men have outside women. However, they frequently *do not* have positive proof of the existence of a specific love affair, at a specific point in time, involving *their* husband. Though generally aware that "something is going on," the wise, "cool, cool" wife acts *as if* all at home is well. Such behavior is most rewarding for her: first, she gets prestige from the community for her mature behavior. Secondly, she gets the benefits of "the self-fulfilling prophecy."[2] By acting as if the husband has no outside woman, her conjugal relationship can improve and the husband may (if only temporarily) put off outside affairs. At worst, the "cool, cool" wife sees more of her husband, and has a better relationship with him than do angry and upset wives. The wife who acts as if all was well at home gets more

[2] Robert K. Merton, *Social Theory and Social Structure,* New York: Free Press, 1957.

than prestige from the community for such behavior; she gets practical support. People will not talk openly about her husband's affairs. These escapades become (so to speak) classified material, which can only be transmitted to close friends as "secrets." The wife then keeps her own suspicions and information secret and other community members do the same, helping her maintain *the fiction* that all is well in her house. When each Anamatian provides this service to all wives, the women of the community do not lose face by their husbands' activities; and the men can continue their sexual life with but minimal troubles from their wives. In brief, on the personal level the "secret" sex-life of Anamatians helps everyone live better in the community, with minimal loss of face and embarrassment.

On the system level of analysis, the treatment of sexual matters as classified data provides a compromise solution to the basic system conflict. The males' sex-fame game requires *maximal communications of sexual encounters;* the females' secret-sex game requires *maximal secrecy for sexual encounters.* A compromise solution is to move sexual information quietly (so to speak) through underground channels. Those who are able to tap these channels—sooner or later most of the community—must act publicly as if they really do not know.

The questions posed previously can now be easily answered. A woman approaching the wife of her lover makes the wife feel bad by providing positive proof of her husband's outside sex life. The wife's immediate reaction of angry and, at times physical, violence is a function of being made to look an unhappy truth in the face. The encounter has yet more serious consequences. The wife can no longer publicly present herself as an adequate role-player. Outside women, when confronting a wife, usually make sure that an audience is present. The wife-lover encounter thus includes a public broadcast of information considered as classified by the community. The public broadcast of classified material breaks the convention of "secrecy" for this particular affair, and community members thereafter openly talk about it. The wife (at least temporarily) is put "on stage" in the role *inadequate wife.* Since every wife in the community is vulnerable to similar "on-stage" placement, it is possible that the sexual life of all the community can be transferred out of the "classified file."

Making public the sexual life of system members shatters the compromise solution—the fiction of secrecy—that makes the system viable. Without this fiction of secrecy, the contradictory goals of the two major factions stand out in stark opposition. The system attempts to "protect itself" from structural change by providing supports for its compromise solution. Actors who break the fiction of secrecy are defined as "shameless" and "unmoral"; those who support it are called good, responsible and "cool, cool."

The system's "efforts" at maintaining a state of equilibrium frequently fall short of desired goals. Actors find it difficult to live in terms of the compromise solution. As the tensions of individuals increase, acts eroding the fiction of secrecy pile up; broadcasts to get fame are made too openly; sexual information is distributed too publicly; wives chastise lovers and lovers confront wives. At such times as these, actors accept the negative sanctions of the system for the personal rewards they receive. Open broadcasts of sexual conquests—although considered bad form by some of the listeners—have valuable feedback effects. Weakening egos are envigorated. Confrontations with wives or lovers function as problem-airing and problem-sharing devices. Tensions are temporarily reduced by a direct confrontation with an assumed cause of one's problems—a husband's lover, a wife. Sufferings of women are lessened by distributing them into the realm of men's lives—by quarrels with husbands or with lovers.

Conclusion

A systematic cultural analysis requires that (at the very least) two viewpoints are fully described: those of the males and those of the females. As male and female goals are juxtaposed it will frequently be found that the system contains a basic conflict: as men's goals are maximally met, women's goals are minimally met, and vice versa. For the people involved to be able to live relatively peaceful lives, it is necessary, therefore, to develop strategies which (1) keep the conflicts from frequently escalating into violent confrontations, and (2) pacify injured parties when confrontations do occur. Differently put, *the culture* alone cannot handle all the problems that humans face. In addition a social system needs what I call *operational rules*. The operational rules which community members follow may well be a kind of storehouse of information out of which new culture develops.

12 Culture and Freedom*

LAURA THOMPSON

A point implicit in "Sex and Culture" is that the individual, although constrained by a cultural tradition, is yet a decision-maker. Social life, that is, contains a measure of freedom. This subject is very ably developed by a well-respected cultural theorist, Laura Thompson.

The number of obligations that adults in our society must meet is rapidly increasing. Most of us feel practically no relationship to the decision-making groups who profoundly affect our behavior. Our commitments are regulated by agencies and rigid deadlines outside ourselves. Under these circumstances what has happened to our freedoms? With the increasing complexities of modern life where can we turn for release and self-fulfillment? What is the meaning of freedom in today's world?

In this paper, I discuss some angles to man's dilemma concerning freedom and commitment and I suggest that, on the basis of recent discoveries revealing new facts about mankind, scientific anthropology can bring a fresh perspective to this perennial problem. Specifically, modern anthropology affords the framework for new scientifically-grounded concepts of man, culture, and human freedom.[1] A scientific approach is suggested toward the practical problem of implementing some of these new concepts, under propitious circumstances, in the modern world.

I

Scientific anthropology teaches us how to ask relevant questions in relevant context. Applying this lesson to our problem, we may ask: Freedom from

SOURCE: Reprinted from "Freedom and Culture" by Laura Thompson. Reproduced by permission of the author and the Society for Applied Anthropology from Vol. 24, No. 2, 1965 *Human Organization*, pp. 105–110.

* This paper, in slightly changed form, was presented as part of a series on "Freedom and Commitment" at the San Francisco State College Downtown Center, San Francisco, March 25, 1963. It is based on personal experiences and field explorations in two modern dictatorships, Nazi Germany and pre-war Guam, as well as in several American Indian tribes.

[1] Franz Boas, "Liberty Among Primitive People," *Freedom, Its Meaning*, ed. R. N. Anshen, New York: Harcourt Brace, 1940, pp. 375–380; David Bidney, *Theoretical Anthropology*, New York: Columbia University Press, 1953 and *The Concept of Freedom in Anthropology*, The Hague: Mouton, 1963; B. Malinowski, *Freedom and Civilization*, New York: Roy Publishers, 1944.

what? Freedom for what? Freedom in what context? These questions confront us with a basic ingredient in our thinking and discussions about man. I refer to culture—the crucial factor which frequently is omitted from discussions about human problems, whether reference is made to international, national, and regional issues, or to problems concerning the community, the family, and the individual.

Now what do we mean by culture? Each of us has his own answer to this question and the same diversity of opinion holds for professional anthropologists. For the concept of culture is to anthropology what the concept of life is to biology. It defines the area of problem and measures our maturity as human scientists. Hence in asking the question, "What do we mean by culture?" most anthropologists are not looking for final answers. Rather, we seek adequate working concepts in line with relevant facts about mankind which have been discovered by the methods of science. Anthropologists are constantly revising their ideas of the nature of culture, re-examining them, and building them into a broader frame to encompass man's actual behavior in relation to himself and to his community and his world. We shall go deeper into this question, but for the present let us define culture as "the way of life of a human community." This includes the community's habitual way of relating its members to one another, to other groups, and to the environment, as well as the group's less apparent attitudes, values, and conception of the world.

Popular notions about culture tend to reflect a philosophy of life which emphasizes man's paucity of inventiveness while stressing the role of external contingencies in determining behavior and personality. One might say that such definitions perceive a community's way of life as superimposed from without. When external man-made contingencies are viewed as determining the forms and institutions of a culture we call this approach "cultural determinism." It emphasizes the *commitment* aspect of our view of mankind as a social species, rather than the *freedom* aspect.

There are many contemporaneous variations on the notion of cultural determinism. One might be called social determinism which, in line with Emile Durkheim[2] and others, emphasizes the determining influences of society on the behavior, thoughts, feelings, attitudes, and values of an individual from birth to death. Then there is economic determinism which, according to Marx and Engels,[3] stresses the role of historically determined economic institutions in integrating cultural systems. A closely related view is that of geographic determinism. This is well exemplified in some of Ellsworth Huntington's work.

---

[2] Emile Durkheim, *Suicide, A Study in Sociology,* trans. Spalding and Simpson, Glencoe, Ill.: The Free Press, 1951. First ed. 1897.

[3] Karl Marx, *Capital: A Critique of Political Economy,* ed. F. Engels, New York: Modern Library, 1906.

In his later years, Huntington[4] explained human behavior as largely determined by geographic environmental factors, especially climate. Unilinear evolutionists such as Lewis H. Morgan[5] also may be thought of as cultural determinists. Morgan saw all cultures as progressing from savagery through barbarism to civilization along a one-way upward path. This notion underlies the idea of "progress" common among Americans today. Leslie A. White[6] is probably the leading American anthropologist who, emphasizing the technological basis of cultural systems, espouses this school of thought, although the work of some members of the American Historical School of Anthropology such as A. L. Kroeber,[7] at least in his earlier years, also illustrates the approach.

During the last two or three decades professional anthropologists have had many opportunities to observe, at first hand, planned experiments in cultural determinism and thus to test the theories of the determinists under favorable circumstances. For example, during the 1930's I observed off and on for several years the behavior of a Lower Saxon rural community in west Germany under diverse pressures from the central government of a modern dictatorship. Many of the farmsteads of this community were classed as one-family hereditary domains called *Erbhöfe* or entailed estates. By means of the law regarding hereditary domains (May 15 and September 29, 1933), Hitler attempted to consolidate the position of the peasant class by establishing a category of stable, middle-sized peasant proprietors, bound to the soil and possessing farms as large as 125 hectares (c. 309 acres)—i.e., large enough for the maintenance of one family and not sufficient to constitute an estate of capitalist exploitation.[8] A number of *Erbhöfe* had been in the same family for many generations, some for a thousand years.[9] According to a traditional arrangement, hereditary in the male line, at least one hireling family occupied a corner of almost every *Erbhöf*. Members of the hireling family contributed a traditionally fixed number of days' labor annually to the owner in exchange for the use of a dwelling house and a few acres of *Erbhöf* land. Also, each *Erbhöf* was related to one or more *Erbhöfe* in the vicinity by a system of traditional neighbor rights. Accordingly, the owner could count on certain kinds of services during family life crises such as marriage and death. These he repaid on a reciprocal basis.

In many Lower Saxon rural communities owner families, hirelings, and

---

[4] Ellsworth Huntington, *Mainsprings of Civilization,* New York: Wiley, 1945.

[5] Lewis H. Morgan, *Ancient Society. Research in the Line of Human Progress from Savagery Through Barbarism to Civilization,* Chicago: C. Kerr, 1877.

[6] Leslie A. White, *The Science of Culture: A Study of Man and Civilization,* New York: Farrar, Straus, and Cudahy, 1949, p. 19.

[7] A. L. Kroeber, *Anthropology,* New York: Harcourt Brace, 1923.

[8] Henri Lichtenberger, *The Third Reich,* trans. and ed. K. S. Pinson, New York: Greystone Press, 1937, p. 223.

[9] Cesare Santoro, *Hitler's Germany as Seen by a Foreigner,* 3rd English ed., Berlin: Internationaler Verlag, 1939, p. 292.

farm laborers formed a social hierarchy of long standing. The peasant proprietors occupied the upper rung of the status ladder, farm laborers the lower rung, hirelings the middle. For farm owners, the class system had a caste-like rigidity in that a son who inherited a farm looked to another *Erbhöf* of comparable social status for a wife who could bring him not only an appropriate dowry but also the physical strength and the culture of his class—namely, attitudes, values, and specialized skills—needed to be a successful *Erbhöf Hausfrau.* In neighboring villages, professionals such as the veterinarian, physician, banker and school teacher outranked small business owners and shopkeepers, who themselves outranked skilled technicians and laborers such as bakers, blacksmiths and mechanics. According to the local prestige system of the rural community under observation, the village social hierarchy ranked below proprietors of *Erbhöfe* and above the hirelings. Although most Lower Saxon communities are solidly Lutheran in religious affiliation, the one under observation professed the Roman Catholic faith. Here the priesthood had its own Vatican-oriented hierarchy which was considered quite separate from the local social class system. The priesthood was highly respected by members of all social classes.

Examining the problem posed by the cultural determinists in the context of the observed behavior of this rural community, we may ask: How did members of the several classes react to various kinds and degrees of pressure from the central Nazi government? One such pressure was designed to obliterate social class distinctions and conflicts.[10] As might be expected, individuals belonging to classes at the lower end of the status scale, regardless of political affiliations, welcomed the official attempt to raise their social positions. About ten percent of these lower-class individuals became registered members of the National Socialist Party and it was from the roster of Party membership that the village mayor, a baker, and other local Party leaders were chosen. Individuals belonging to the upper classes especially peasant proprietors, on the other hand, rejected the Nazi regime to a man and ignored, so far as possible, the movement to lower their status although with a certain wry humor they complied with government regulations which they could not evade. That is, regardless of how much they altered their overt behavior temporarily under pressure to conform to official regulations, emotionally and ideologically they retained intact the culture of their class.

An example will illustrate the point. In order to increase the available food supply, the government attempted to force the peasants to market their produce at fixed prices and claimed the entire annual yield from each farm with the exception of a small portion considered necessary to meet the immediate needs of each member of the farmstead household. The household in which I lived

[10] Lichtenberger, pp. 66ff.

consisted of the proprietor, his wife, and five of his thirteen children, a young farm laborer who helped in the fields and barn, and a girl who helped with the milking and in the kitchen. In order to prevent waste and reduce home consumption the minimum annual needs of each member of the group were calculated down to the last ham. Although the owner allowed government inspectors to estimate the potential yield of his crops as they grew in the fields and also to estimate that of the domestic animals (horses, cows, pigs, and chickens) in his barn, conforming to these government orders irked and impoverished him since they reduced the available cash sorely needed to cover the substantial overhead of his farm enterprise.[11] On the other hand, these government measures, as well as a federally dictated reduction in working day obligations, tended to enrich the local hireling families who, for the first time, began to accumulate substantial cash savings.

Despite the efforts of the central regime, however, the farm owners in this rural community found a way not only to ridicule but also to circumvent government regulations designed to force them to associate socially with lower class individuals. For example, they boycotted the Farmers' Ball, held annually just before Lent, since this traditional social function was open to hirelings and laborers for the first time by government order. The point I wish to stress is that when administrative pressures were relaxed the upper classes reasserted traditional attitudes in terms of behavior patterns familiar to them as part of their traditional culture.[12]

I observed a similar cultural phenomenon in pre-war Guam, a Pacific island of 225 square miles which has been a United States' possession since the Spanish American War. Here the American naval colony, ignoring the highly developed native social-class system, superimposed itself as a ranking ruling class on the local community, and lumped all natives together into a single lower class. The Guamanians, while complying outwardly to military government regulations designed to enforce the new class structure, continued among themselves to observe their own rules of rank and of chiefly etiquette in somewhat changed form. Indeed, they preserved their traditional class system for sixty years despite the lack of its recognition by the ruling power.[13]

After centuries of practice under Spanish domination, the Guamanians had become expert at tactics of evasion long before the Americans set foot on the island. When pressured beyond their threshold of tolerance by the government, Guamanians tended to ridicule their administrators by singing humorous

---

[11] Heinrich Fraenkel, *The German People Versus Hitler,* London: Allen and Unwin, 1949, p. 169.

[12] Hans Spier et al., eds., *West German Leadership and Foreign Policy*, Evanston, Ill.: Row Peterson, 1957, p. 5.

[13] Laura Thompson, *Guam and Its People,* Englewood, N. J.: Greenwood Press, 1969, pp. 54–57.

couplets in the native Chamorro language which few Americans bothered to learn. These couplets were set to the tune of a traditional ditty called the *chamorita.*

On the other hand, when the Japanese Navy captured and occupied Guam during World War II, the Guamanians used these skills to serve the United States. For example, they hid an American radio corpsman from the occupying Japanese forces and succored him during the entire Japanese occupation of the island, almost three years. In order to keep this one American Marine alive and concealed for the duration, the loyal natives endured beatings, rape, and murder, since the Japanese feared the corpsman would use his radio skills to communicate information to the American fleet, which incidentally he did not do. Instead, it was the Guamanians themselves who, using these same skills at subterfuge, furnished the Americans with intelligence useful in retaking the island. A group of natives from Merizo village on the southwest shore took a boat out to sea and succeeded in contacting the approaching American fleet and in furnishing information regarding the enemy.[14] Thus when faced with a conflict of loyalty between two military dictatorships—that of the United States Naval Civil Government and that of the Japanese occupation forces—the Guamanians chose what might be considered the lesser of two evils.

II

To the casual observer the overt behavior of individuals in a modern dictatorship might lead to the conviction that human beings and human communities may be manipulated and controlled effectively by pressures from outside themselves, such as military regulation and government fiat. It may thus appear to validate a hypothesis of cultural determinism. Of course such pressures in their most extreme form do engender the death of the individual and the genocide of the group, as is well illustrated by the Jews of Germany during the Nazi regime and the natives of the Marquesas islands after their discovery by Europeans. But a closer look at human behavior, a look which takes into consideration not only overt aspects of behavior readily observable from without but also an understanding of the covert cultural phenomena hidden from casual observation, reveals that despite outwardly conforming to pressures backed up by force, the individual and the community may, if able to retain life, also retain values, attitudes, and a traditionally successful outlook on life. When pressures are relaxed, the traditional covert culture tends to reemerge, usually in slightly altered form. Thus, short of escape or death of the individual or migration or genocide of the community, it seems that the core value orientations of a culture tend to persist for centuries and even for millenniums.

---

[14] Thompson, p. v.

This generalization is validated by empirical findings from many research projects; for example, the Indian Education, Personality, and Administration Research. The latter was a multidiscipline project sponsored in part by the Society for Applied Anthropology, financed by the United States Office of Indian Affairs and designed to assist Indian administrators in improving the welfare of American Indian tribal communities. The results of depth psychology tests and guided interviews, administered to a representative sample of 1,000 individuals in six tribes, revealed that despite pressures from the American Government and the surrounding American industrial civilization, individuals in all tribes studied, while outwardly conforming to government-enforced American norms of behavior, tended to retain their aboriginal outlook on life and their native conception of the universe, including their belief in the principle of immanent justice.[15]

The cases mentioned above, based on first-hand observations of the behavior of individuals and groups in two modern dictatorships and several tribal dependencies, and many more that might be cited if space permitted, suggest that cultural determinists (including, of course, social and economic determinists) tend to become so involved with certain superficial aspects of a complex human event, for example the overt behavior of a community at a specific point in a historical time sequence, that they overlook the need to investigate the entire human event as a complex whole in relevant situational context, in order to understand it. A scientific anthropologist's job is to avoid such superficialities and attempt to understand the human group phenomenon under consideration in all its relevant dimensions with its components in dynamic interrelationship and set in effective environmental frame.

During the last two or three decades we have witnessed significant advances, along these lines, in theoretical approach and methodology employed by anthropologists who have attempted to understand communities as complex wholes including their individual human components. The work of anthropologically-oriented psychiatrists such as Carl Rogers,[16] of psychiatrists who are also anthropologists such as Erik H. Erikson,[17] Alexander H. Leighton,[18] and G. M. Carstairs,[19] and of anthropologists who have studied psychiatry such as Weston La Barre[20] and George Devereux,[21] has taught us to examine human

---

[15] Laura Thompson, "Attitudes and Acculturation," *American Anthropologist,* 1948, Vol. 50, pp. 200–215.

[16] Carl Rogers, *Client-Centered Therapy; Its Current Practice, Implications, and Theory,* New York: Houghton Mifflin, 1951.

[17] Erik H. Erikson, *Childhood and Society,* New York: W. W. Norton, 1950.

[18] Alexander H. Leighton, *My Name is Legion,* New York: Basic Books, 1959.

[19] G. M. Carstairs, *This Island Now,* Reith Lectures, London: *The Listener and BBC Television Review,* November 15–December 20, 1962.

[20] Weston La Barre, *They Shall Take up Serpents; Psychology of the Southern Snake-Handling Cult,* Minneapolis: Minnesota University Press, 1962.

[21] George Devereux, *Mohave Ethnopsychiatry and Suicide: The Psychiatric Knowledge and*

behavior from a deeper, more inclusive point of view. For example, they are helping us to incorporate discoveries about man's unconscious into our working hypotheses and concepts about culture.

The work of anthropologically-oriented geographers such as Carl O. Sauer,[22] of anthropologically-oriented ecologists such as Paul B. Sears,[23] Marston Bates,[24] and Alfred Emerson,[25] and of anthropologists who are geographically and ecologically oriented such as C. Daryll Forde[26] and Harold Conklin,[27] is aiding us in efforts to extend our frame to include the effective environment of the community viewed as an ecosystem of which the human group under investigation is one component, and to place the ecosystem in relevant physical context. For present purposes, an ecosystem may be defined as a balanced organization of transacting organic species in the context of that part of the environment essential to its welfare.

General semanticists such as A. Korzybski[28] and S. I. Hayakawa,[29] meta-anthropologists such as D. Bidney, [30] and linguists such as Edward Sapir,[31] B. L. Whorf,[32] and Dorothy Lee,[33] have contributed toward developing our insights regarding the nature of the human symbolizing process and its relation to the creation and development of a culture by a human community, and also to our understanding of the role of culture as the primary human device for resolving a human community's practical living problems in relation to its total life situation. And theoretical physicists such as Lancelot L. Whyte[34]

---

the Psychic Disturbances of an Indian Tribe, Smithsonian Bulletin 175, BAE, Washington, D. C.: U. S. Government Printing Office, 1961.

[22] Carl O. Sauer, *Agricultural Origins and Dispersals,* Bowman Memorial Lectures, New York: American Geographical Society, 1952.

[23] Paul B. Sears, *Charles Darwin, The Naturalist as a Cultural Force,* New York: Scribners, 1950, p. 108; *The Ecology of Man,* London Lectures, Eugene, Oregon: Oregon State System of Higher Education, 1957.

[24] Marston Bates, *The Forest and the Sea,* New York: Random House, 1960.

[25] Alfred Emerson and Roy R. Grinker, eds., *Toward a Unified Theory of Human Behavior,* New York: Basic Books, 1967, pp. 147–164.

[26] C. Daryll Forde, *Habitat, Economy and Society: A Geographical Introduction to Ethnology,* London: Methuen, 1949.

[27] Harold Conklin, *Hanunoo Agriculture in the Philippines,* Rome: FAO, 1957.

[28] Alfred Korzybski, *Science and Sanity: An Introduction to Non-Aristotelian Systems and General Semantics,* Lancaster, Pa.: International Non-Aristotelian Library, 1933.

[29] S. I. Hayakawa, *Language in Action: A Guide to Accurate Thinking, Reading and Writing,* New York: Harcourt Brace, 1942.

[30] Bidney (1953), (1963).

[31] Edward Sapir, *Culture, Language, and Personality; Selected Essays,* ed. D. Mandelbaum, Berkeley: University of California Press, 1949.

[32] Benjamin L. Whorf, *Language, Thought and Reality: Selected Writings,* ed. J. B. Carroll, New York: Wiley, 1956.

[33] Dorothy Lee, *Freedom and Culture,* Englewood Cliffs, N. J.: Prentice-Hall, 1959.

[34] Lancelot Law Whyte, *The Unitary Principle in Physics and Biology,* New York: Holt, Rinehart and Winston, 1949.

have assisted us in updating our outmoded concepts of form and natural processes and in developing toward a space-age mentality.

III

When we examine the behavior of human communities and their individual components from this deeper, more inclusive viewpoint, we come up with an entirely different concept of culture from that of the cultural determinists. A culture from this new vantage point may be defined operationally as the supremely human, symbolic creation of a community, in conjunction with its self-creation and maintenance as an organic unit through time and in relative isolation.[35] A culture as it is created, recreated, and developed anew every day and by each new generation of the group, functions primarily as the major tool forged by a local community to resolve its practical, situational living problems of maintenance, self-defense, reproduction, and rearing of the young, and completion of the life cycle through the generations. In other words, a culture is basically a complex symbolic device created by a human community in the interests of its own self-actualization as a human group in its specialized ecological niche.

The traditional culture of the town-dwelling Hopi Indian farmers of northern Arizona, for example, fits their semi-desert environment like hand to glove.[36] Each human component of the community actively builds his own version of the community's culture into his own neuromuscular system by an organic process starting with conception and birth and extending throughout the life span of the organism. The idiosyncratic nature of this life-long enculturation process within each individual human being accounts to a considerable extent for the phenomenon of ongoing cultural change. Investigation of human communities situationally through time, within this extended frame, suggests that a human community tends toward the creation and re-creation of its own culture. In other words, the local community is the cradle of culture.[37]

Culture-building and culture-changing processes are probably unconscious to a considerable extent, although they may be consciously purposive, institutionalized, and brought under community control.[38] Until the last few decades,

---

[35] L. K. Frank, *Cultural Determination and Free Will,* Cincinnati: Hebrew Union College, Jewish Institute of Religion, 1951, p. 36; B. Malinowski, *The Dynamics of Culture Change,* New Haven: Yale University Press, 1945, p. 42; Thompson, *Toward A Science of Mankind,* New York: McGraw-Hill, 1961, chap. 10.

[36] Laura Thompson and Alice Joseph, *The Hopi Way,* New York: Russell and Russell, 1965, chap. 1.

[37] Thompson (1961), pp. 160–161.

[38] See, for example, C. M. Arensberg and A. H. Niehoff, *Technical Cooperation and Cultural Reality,* Washington, D. C.: Agency for International Development, Department of State, 1963, pp. 49–94 and W. H. Goodenough, *Cooperation in Change,* New York: Russell Sage Foundation, 1963, chap. 13.

for example, the Papago Indian farmers of the southern Arizona desert met nightly in each village community. All the adult males of the village attended these local assemblies where the practical problems of community living were discussed and decisions based on unanimity of the group were reached.[39]

IV

We have come a long way from the viewpoint of the cultural determinists. However, a closer look at some of the findings of laboratory and field research in the life sciences reveals that our new position is well supported. According to distinguished neurologists such as C. Judson Herrick[40] and G. Ellett Coghill,[41] man along with all forms of organic life, is an active, self-developing and self-actualizing phenomenon. Activity which is self-directed toward maintenance, reproduction, self-perpetuation, and completion of the life cycle through the ongoing generations, is the primary characteristic of organisms according to leading biologists, such as E. S. Russell.[42]

Even the older generation of physical anthropologists reinforced this position, as for example with the hypothesis regarding the evolution of man that bipedal locomotion in hominids preceded the development of the brain. According to this view, propounded in detail by Earnest Hooton,[43] erect bipedal locomotion on the ground freed the forelimbs to use tools and to produce tools, a change of activity associated in man with the development of the human hand, the enlargement and increasing complexity of the human brain, especially the forebrain, and other compensatory changes.[44] Also, let us note with Washburn, Lasker, Dobzhansky,[45] and other modern biological anthropologists and human geneticists that a situational approach to community behavior accounts to a considerable extent for the tendency of local breeding populations to develop into microraces (or subraces) by processes of ongoing human evolution.

To understand the meaning of recently discovered facts concerning human

---

[39] Ruth Underhill, *Social Organization of the Papago Indians,* Columbia University Contributions in Anthropology No. 30, New York: Columbia University Press, 1939, p. 12.

[40] C. Judson Herrick, *The Evolution of Human Nature,* Austin: University of Texas, 1956.

[41] C. Judson Herrick, *George Ellett Coghill, Naturalist and Philosopher,* Chicago: University of Chicago Press, 1949.

[42] E. S. Russell, *The Directiveness of Organic Activities,* New York: Cambridge University Press, 1945.

[43] Earnest A. Hooton, *Up from the Ape,* New York: Macmillan, 1931, p. 131.

[44] A. L. Bryan, "The Essentials for Human Culture," *Current Anthropology,* 1963, Vol. 4, pp. 297–301.

[45] Sherwood Washburn, "The Study of Race," *American Anthropologist,* 1963, Vol. 65, pp. 521–531; Gabriel Lasker, ed., *The Processes of Ongoing Human Evolution,* Detroit: Wayne State University, 1960; Theodosius Dobzhansky, *Mankind Evolving: The Evolution of the Human Species,* New Haven: Yale University, 1962.

group phenomena and the hypotheses explaining them which are emerging in our time, we should consider some limitations to the self-creating process of the human community regarding its culture and microrace. Already in 1913 the anthropologist Alexander Goldenweiser called attention to the operation of what he termed

> the principle of limited possibilities in the development of culture.[46]

Since that time many discerning students of man, community and society, including Boas, Tönnies, Brownell, Murdock, Leighton, Honigmann, Lins, Thompson, and Washburn[47] have contributed facts and insights which help to clarify our thinking along these lines.

It is becoming increasingly clear that, as with all organic community processes, the local human community's self-directed processes of culture and microrace creation and revision operate within definite and describable structural limitations related to the kinds of genetically determined forms transacting with the kinds of culture and personality forms characteristic of the human species and the effective ecosystem in its local habitat. Man is a social organism, a part of the phenomenological world, and subject to the natural laws and processes which govern that world. As V. Gordon Childe[48] has noted, "Man makes himself," but the point being stressed here is that man makes himself into a self-actualizing community only within the limitations and potentialities of his cultural and genetic heritage and his environmental situation. Man as an individual definitely does not make himself except in relation to his group and community, his region and world.

V

Here we are reaching toward the core of our dilemma concerning the problems of human freedom and commitment from the viewpoint of the new science of mankind. At the beginning of this paper we asked the following questions: Freedom from what? Freedom for what? Freedom in what context?

---

[46] Alexander Goldenweiser, "The Principle of Limited Possibilities in the Development of Culture," *Journal of American Folklore,* 1913, Vol. 26, pp. 261–290.

[47] Franz Boas in Ruth Benedict, *Patterns of Culture,* New York: Houghton Mifflin, 1934, p. XII; Ferdinand Tönnies, *Fundamental Concepts of Sociology,* trans. C. Loomis, New York: American Book Co., 1940, pp. 172–173, 200; Baker Brownell, *The Human Community,* New York: Harper and Bros., 1950, p. 41; G. P. Murdock, *Social Structure,* New York: Macmillan, 1949, pp. 115–116; A. H. Leighton, *Human Relations in a Changing World; Observations on the Use of the Social Sciences,* New York: Dutton, 1949, p. 102; John Honigman, *Culture and Personality,* New York: Harper, 1954, p. 80; Mario Lins, *Foundations of Social Determinism,* Rio de Janeiro, 1959, p. 7; Thompson (1961), pp. 210–212; and Sherwood Washburn, p. 525.

[48] V. Gordon Childe, *Man Makes Himself,* London: Watts, 1956.

We are now in a position to venture a tentative answer to these questions from the viewpoint of a modern anthropologist.

Freedom in terms of the human individual may be viewed appropriately, from the standpoint of the new scientific anthropology, only in the context of his species heritage. In other words, human freedom is a function of *humanness* which includes the human species' propensity to form local communities united in the direction of a common goal of self-actualization as a human organic group by means of the creation and evolution of human culture, personality, and microrace. As an evolving organic species inhabiting a specific locus in the changing, existential world, we are committed to a process of self-actualization of ourselves as a group phenomenon within the limitations and potentials of our situation. This situation may be community-wide, regional, world-wide, or even in time interplanetary in scope. Regardless of how our community may be expanding, this is a commitment which we must accept, examine, and understand if we would be free and self-fulfilled.

From this perspective, perhaps what we need is a revised Bill of Human Rights based on the findings of modern science. From the viewpoint here expressed, top priority of such a revised Bill of Rights would be the right of every human being to exist and develop as a whole human organism. This would mean accepting his right to belong to a community which is part of a local ecosystem in relevant physical context as part of our planet earth. On one hand, it would mean understanding and accepting man's organic heritage and those aspects of his nature which relate him as a member of an evolving species to the rest of the animal kingdom and the evolving organic world. On the other hand, it would mean understanding and accepting man's essentially *human* heritage and those aspects of his nature which differentiate him, as a human being, from the rest of the universe. This understanding and acceptance would include man's propensity, as a member of an earth-rooted group, to create, re-create, design, and develop a culture tailored to afford him maximum freedom for self-fulfillment within the limitations and potentialities of his own genetic heritage and those of his community, his region and his world.

In sum mankind, through its propensity to create and evolve cultures and microraces, is unique as earth's only organic species endowed with the power to develop its own potentials for freedom. This may be accomplished by means of community processes whereby each human group so builds its culture, within the limitations of its organic heritage and its existential situation, into institutions, behavior patterns, attitudes and values, to afford its members opportunities for optimum self-fulfillment as human organisms. Freedom is a function of group and individual commitment to the limited possibilities and potentials of the distinctively human organic group process in situational context.

Thus phrased, the dilemma of human freedom and commitment is not a vague, abstract or philosophical issue. It is a practical problem involving culture creation and culture revision in line with human potentialities within specific environmental limitations. So formulated it may be faced squarely by each community and each individual and perhaps, under propitious circumstances, it may be resolved according to the methods of science.

13 From Warfare to Structural Steel: Adapting Culture to Environmental Changes

MORRIS FREILICH

The dilemma of human freedom and commitment is not a vague, abstract or philosophical issue. It is a practical problem involving culture creation and culture revision in line with human potentialities within specific environmental limitations.

(*Laura Thompson, 1965*)

The paper which follows is one long example illustrating the wisdom of Dr. Thompson's conclusion.

Introduction

In 1886 the Dominion Bridge Company hired some Mohawks[1] to work as unskilled laborers on the Victoria Tubelar Bridge. The bridge which abutted on reservation land brought about the first contact Mohawks had with the structural steel industry. As of today, the great majority of Mohawk males between the ages of 18 and 60 are skilled structural steel workers. These facts suggest the following problems: firstly, why did the Mohawks as a tribe take up steel work? Secondly, why have they remained in this occupation for seventy years? I will attempt to show, and substantiate with field work information, that given certain historical accidents, specific cultural factors made it, as it

SOURCE: Reprinted from "Cultural Persistence Among the Modern Iroquois" by Morris Freilich, *Anthropos*, Vol. 53, 1958, pp. 473–483, by permission of the publisher.

[1] Before 1721, the term Iroquois is used to refer to the Five Nations: Mohawk, Oneida, Onandaga, Cayuga and Seneca. After 1721 the Tuscarora became a member of the League of the Iroquois and the confederacy was often referred to as the Six Nations.

were, necessary for the Mohawks to go into structural steel. Further, that once in structural steel, specific cultural factors kept them there.

Analytically, we have to deal with two major variables: culture and environment. We hypothesize a connection between general environmental change and cultural change. The exact nature of such a connection we hope to discover after an analysis of the following:

1. Mohawk males prior to their "continuous first hand contact" with the white man.
2. The changes in their environment during the intermittent period.
3. The way of life of Mohawk males today.

Historical Mohawk

From sources which deal with the Mohawks historically (Morgan, Colden, Fenton, Jenness), we get the following information:

Mohawks, aboriginally, lived in palisaded villages. Each village contained several Long Houses. Within the Long House lived several matrilocally extended families and "the longhouse took the name and insignia of the clan of its dominant family."[2] The society was matrilineal, and women were mainly responsible for subsistence activities.

The men hunted to provide the extra delicacies of meat and fish, but they were mainly concerned with politics and war. They lived in a world of men, where prestige was obtained by the great warrior, and where women were considered inferior. As Morgan tells us: "The warrior despised the toil of husbandry and held all labor beneath him."[3]

Warfare most frequently took place on a small group level. A renowned warrior would suggest a particular enterprise and then try to interest others in it. At this time a war dance was held and past exploits were recounted to arouse the interest of the males. Colden describes war party formation as follows:

> When any of the young men of these Nations have a mind to . . . gain a reputation among their countrymen, by some notable enterprise against their enemy, they first communicate their design to two or three of their most intimate friends; and if they come into it an invitation is made in their names to all the young men in the castle . . . , the promoters of the enterprise set forth the undertaking in the best colours they can; they boast of what they intend to do and incite others to join from the glory there is to be obtained.[4]

---

[2] B. H. Quain, "The Iroquois," *Cooperation and Competition Among Primitive Peoples*, ed. Margaret Mead, New York: McGraw-Hill, 1937, p. 256.

[3] Lewis H. Morgan, *League of the Ho-De-No-Sau-Nee, or Iroquois*, 1901. Reprinted, New Haven: Human Relations Area Files, 1954, p. 320.

[4] Cadwallader Colden, *The History of the Five Indian Nations of Canada*, 2 vols., 1904, Vol. 1, pp. 22–23. Reprinted, Ithaca: Cornell University Press, 1958.

No one had the authority to order another to go on the warpath. Authority was not of the lineal type, as in the European tradition, but rather similar to the pattern among the Fox Indians, where acceptance of directives by executants in collective action, was considered a matter of choice. Colden states "The Five Nations have such absolute notions of Liberty that they allow no kind of superiority of one over another."[5]

When the warriors returned from the warpath, they received definite social applause.

> They had the opportunity to recite deeds of valor publicly at the victory dance . . . , each [war leader] had a war post on which he made pictographs to commemorate his deeds . . . , and success . . . is said to have influenced the possibilities of winning a beautiful wife.[6]

From around 1640 to the end of the eighteenth century, the men spent increasingly more time at warfare and less in subsistence activities. Fenton divided this part of Iroquois history into two warring periods:

1. The period of Iroquoian wars for the fur trade;
2. The period of colonial wars.[7]

The fact that the women took care both of subsistence activities and the home made it possible for the men to keep going off to war. It was the women who stored the grain, so that when a man returned from war there was always food to eat, be it in his wife's house or his mother's.[8] Should the men drift into any Iroquois village, the principle of hospitality required that they be fed. Fenton suggests that "hospitality may have helped solve the problems of a military economy."[9]

If we examine Mohawk society, a model can be constructed which has the following characteristics:

A matrilineal society composed of matrilocally extended families with women supplying the community with essential foods, having fixed residence, and taking care of home and family. Their relationships with each other are relatively constant for long periods of time.

The men lived in a world of men where women[10] were useful appendages

---

[5] Colden (1904), Vol. 1, p. 28.

[6] Quain (1937), pp. 268–269.

[7] William N. Fenton, "Problems Arising From the Historic Northeastern Position of the Iroquois," *Smithsonian Misc. Collection*, 1940, No. 100, pp. 159–251.

[8] Snyderman tells us that women were frequently instrumental in starting war parties. He states "there were many instances where the matron solicited, cajoled, bullied or paid with wampum, individual warriors to take to the war path in order that prisoners be brought back for adoption" (1948) p. 19. We would differentiate the matrons (clan mothers) from non-matron women. The former had considerable status in the tribe; they elected and disposed of *sachems* (civil chiefs); initiated some war parties and disposed of prisoners.

[9] Quain (1937), p. 254, footnote 2.

[10] I refer here to the non-matron women.

who looked after the mundane parts of life, provided food and shelter, cared for the children and were available for men's sexual pleasures. Men had brittle, intermittent relationships with each other. These were formed around different warrior chiefs and created strong bonds only for the duration of a particular war party. Here in the world of men, one could fight, boast, talk men's talk and be a warrior. To a great extent men were their own masters; no one could order them to do anything (except in retribution for criminal offenses). The men chose whether they would join a war party, and could leave it any time they so desired, suffering only the loss of public esteem. The great prestige of the warrior status made for frequent war parties. Colloquially speaking the warrior returned to the tune of "Home the Conquering Hero Comes," and to hear it again and again, he necessarily had to keep leaving for war.

Environmental Changes

The environment (the total milieu) had been slowly changing ever since contact with the white men, but the drastic changes took but a comparatively short time.

> At the time of the French defeat at Quebec . . . the basic configurations of Six Nation society were still maintained . . . ; before the end of the eighteenth century, the Nations of the Confederacy were already located on reservations.[11]

The Iroquois' alliance with the British, and Washington's decision to lay waste to the Indians' fields and lands were important factors which led to the rapid changes.

The problem for the Mohawk male was simply one of adjustment to a reservation situation. The hunter now had little opportunity to hunt—the warrior was forbidden the warpath.

> Let us examine what the Mohawks actually did. They "became voyageurs for the fur companies. Their expeditions took them in quest of furs to the country beyond Red River, and soon after 1798, a Mohawk party had skirmished with the Blackfoot. . . . Meanwhile on the St. Lawrence . . . [others] furnished raftsmen and lumberjacks to the timber industry."[12]

As canoe men, guides and carriers, they accompanied Franklin and Richardson to the Polar Seas. That the male still yearned for the role of warrior can be deduced from the following:

> On September 23, 1812, Granger, [the Indian agent at Buffalo Creek] reported that the young men of the Nation [the Iroquois] could not be restrained from

[11] John A. Noon, *Law and Government of the Grand River Iroquois*, New York: Viking Fund Publications in Anthropology, 1949, No. 12.
[12] Fenton (1940), p. 212.

fighting—that if the United States declined their services they would fight under the British Flag.[13]

It is important to note that it is not loyalty to a cause, which led the Iroquois into battle, but rather *the desire to fight.* And fight they did at every opportunity.

> Along with the Canadians they defeated the American invaders at the Battle of Chateaugay in 1813, and in 1838 they defeated Nelson's partisans who were marching on Montreal.[14]

In the last half of the nineteenth century, the Mohawks were engaged in timber rafting, river boating, dock work and circus work. In 1886, they took to structural steel work and soon this became the occupation par excellence for Mohawk males.

How is it, we ask, that the great majority of Mohawk men found their niche in structural steel? Our answer is simply that participation in the structural steel industry enabled the Mohawks to closely duplicate their pre-reservation period social structure. Let us then examine the way of life of modern Mohawks to demonstrate the similarities with the past.

Modern Mohawk

The Caughnawaga Mohawks live in several small communities in Eastern Canada and the United States. The Caughnawaga reservation is about 10 miles south of Montreal and is considered by one and all as home. For seventy years now, the men have been leaving Caughnawaga to do structural steel work in Canada, Alaska and the United States. Until recently women remained on the reservation taking care of home and children and awaiting the return of their menfolk.

Two decades ago (1938 in Brooklyn) small Mohawk communities were formed in a few American cities, New York (Brooklyn), Detroit, and Buffalo.

On the reservation mothers and their married daughters tend to live near each other, frequently owning adjacent houses. In Brooklyn, the matrilaterally extended family is often found either in the same apartment house or in adjacent apartment houses. Practically all the Mohawks in Brooklyn live within short walking distance of each other.

The Mohawk male remains in school just long enough to fulfill minimum requirements. He is usually intelligent and shows leadership abilities in sports. He can rarely be interested in continuing his schooling; he wishes to become a steel worker.[15]

---

[13] Louis Babcock, *The War of 1812 on the Niagara Frontier*, Buffalo, N.Y., 1927, p. 27.
[14] David Cory, *Within Two Worlds*, New York, 1955, p. 61.
[15] This information was received from teachers of the schools that Mohawk children attended

Structural steel work requires little formal training. A boy reaching the age of 17 or so is brought into a gang by his father, uncle, cousin or brother who happens to be the foreman or a close relative or friend of the latter. The initiate is "broken in" or "shown the ropes." For a short time he earns apprentice wages; however, as soon as he can do a full man's job, he demands and gets full pay ($150.00 per week). Construction work entails remaining at a job in a given area for a relatively short time. When the job is finished, another is found somewhere else. Not to be frequently out of work necessitates keeping in close touch with the rest of the Mohawk steel workers any one of whom may learn of a job.

In the early days of steel, this meant that the reservation at Caughnawaga was the central information center. After the completion of one or more jobs, the men would go home, see their families and get together with the boys to swap stories of narrow escapes off the "ledges," of the women they "had" in different towns, and to find out about future work opportunities. Usually "pushers" (foremen) would have jobs lined up and be looking for gangs. Soon it would be time for the men who fearlessly worked up high to leave for another job so that they could later return victorious.

They left with their gang, consisting of age mates, and a "pusher," an older, more experienced steel worker. As in the case of the warriors, there was the chance that some of them would not return alive, for this was dangerous men's work. Men worked, played, lived and died with men. The women tried (and still try) to get as much of the money the men brought home as possible. They still keep up the home and take care of the children. In essence they still "store the grain." The men, left alone, would drink away their earnings.

Comparing the models of Mohawk society, past and present, we find the following characteristics common to both:

A. Women

1. Maintaining a fixed residence.
2. Looking after the home and children.
3. Storing the "grain" (be it maize or money).
4. Living in close contact with the matrilineal family.
5. Having constant relationships with other Mohawk women.
6. Providing hospitality for their males and gang.

B. Men

1. Leaving a home base to be able to return as conquering heroes.
2. Bringing of booty home as a sign of a successful expedition (slaves or

---

in Brooklyn, New York. It was confirmed by informal interviews of many Mohawk boys between the ages of 8 and 16.

goods by the warrior; a new car or a large "wad" of money by the steel worker).

3. Achieving certain observable accomplishments, which can be spoken of at length and greatly exaggerated ("We laid low the Erie lands" or "We built the Empire State Building").
4. Working in an all-male group under the leadership of a more experienced tribesman.
5. Being subject to the minimum of lineal authority, under a leader that one picked; for short periods of time (length of the war party or job assignment—in both cases the Mohawk leaves any time he wants to).
6. Becoming a full member of the group without having to undergo a long, formal learning period.
7. Having chances to display daring and courage and thereby gain personal prestige both from the whole community and from the group one fought or worked with.
8. Having excitement as an ever present ingredient.
9. Leaving the maintenance of home and family to the women.
10. Forming short and brittle bonds around a leader (war chief or "pusher").

It is of interest to note that all the occupations the Mohawk took up prior to steel work, to wit, river navigation, lumberjacking, railroading, dock-working, and circus work, necessitated leaving home for lengthy periods of time. Further, that there was in each case little or no directive authority. The Mohawk of today, like his forebears, does not like being told what to do. If the "pusher" gives too many orders, the Mohawk leaves the gang.

I have explained above why the Mohawk stayed in steel by showing a continuity in Mohawk social structure from aboriginal times until today.

The question remains how did the Mohawk get into steel? In part, at least, this requires a historical explanation.

In 1886, an accident (from the point of view of the Mohawk), the building of the Victoria Tubelar Bridge brought the Mohawk and structural steel together. Then, as now (with the St. Lawrence Seaway), local labor was needed to supplement the imported labor force, and Mohawks went to work as unskilled laborers. The bravado and excitement-seeking aspects of the warrior role led Mohawks to climb girders even when they did not have to. This is the kind of daredevil activity in which Mohawk males still participate. Some examples from my field work include driving 90 miles per hour on a winding road at night in the mountains of New York State in an old car while inebriated; accepting a dare to go faster than the speedometer could register; and two men having sexual intercourse with a girl while her fiancé was asleep beside her.

But, back to the past. Seeing the Mohawks' *apparent* lack of fear of heights, some of the foremen on the job decided to teach a few of them riveting, firing, welding, etc. As soon as a few Mohawks were proficient structural steel workers, they taught their sons, brothers, cousins and friends construction work. Here was a means by which the status of warrior and most of the complex attached to it could be well duplicated, in the absence of warfare.

The Mohawk steel worker had no difficulty getting his tribe into steel. For to be a man—if you could not be a warrior, steel work was a close second best. To get someone into steel was similar to getting him into his first war party. Frequently, Mohawks have boasted to me: "I got Angus his first job," or "Didn't I break in Bob," or "I taught Joe steel work," etc. As more and more males got into steel, it was progressively easier to get other Indians in. The "In group" was the steel workers. This, just as being a warrior, was a way of life; it meant living in a male world. That the formula "*to be a man = to be a warrior*" changed in a relatively short time period to "*to be a man = to be a steel worker*" was due to the similarities in the essence of the two ways of life.

Mohawk "Warriors" Today

Before giving a short account of what the Indians themselves think of steel, let me present the environment in which my field work was done.

A large percentage of my time was spent in the Longhouse[16] bar in Brooklyn, New York. This is a club room, recreation hall, central information center and home to the Indian steel workers and their friends. Periodically, the Indians tear the place apart; they feel it their right, since it is their home. If outsiders give any sign of attempting to make it their clubroom too, blood flows fast and furious.

The Longhouse is perhaps the Brooklyn symbol of the fusion of warrior and steelworker. As one enters, "Custer's Last Stand" is prominently displayed, and around the room drawings of Iroquois warriors are intermingled with helmets of structural steel workers. It is at the Longhouse too, that the Indians meet every Friday night during the summer to leave for the reservation. Why they spent 25 hours in a car (round trip to Caughnawaga) nearly every week, to be on the reservation for a day was something that puzzled me greatly. The answer came in the theme of "home the conquering hero."

My position in the Longhouse came to be that of a guy who liked to drink and hang around with the Indians and who spent week-ends with them on the reservation. Several other non-Indians have similar status around the bar, so once I got to know a few Mohawks, there was a place for me in Longhouse society.

As to the Mohawks' feelings about steel work, one Indian (Joe Smith) told me: "For steel you need guts—you gotta be strong—you have to have it here"

[16] The names used are fictitious but refer to actual places and people.

(pointing to his brain). He went on: "I'm a big chief, you know. I have an Oldsmobile, money in the bank, two homes, a yacht (not true), and a farm (not true). I'm a real red Indian. Feel my face—I don't have to shave. I have red skin but I'm a foreman."

Foreman or "pusher" is equated with big chief by Joe Smith and many other middle-aged Indian pushers. The equation "foreman = big chief" is derived from the fact that both lead a party of young Indians to an assignment where booty and prestige are to be acquired.

Another Indian, Sam Johnson, said with pride: "Caughnawaga Indians are the best steel workers in the world. It's in their blood." The statement, "Steel is in our blood," is perhaps the closest the Indians come to understanding the role continuity in steel, of the strong, daring, home-leaving warrior. The statement is frequently made and always with tones of pride and superiority over other peoples.

Joe Redson speaking to John Bull about steel work, said, for example: "It's in your blood, ain't it? You want your freedom, outside in the fresh air, don't you?" That freedom, meaning lack of the lineal authority which directs, is here important and not fresh air, can be deduced from the fact that the Indians never appear to be bothered by the scarcity of fresh air in the Longhouse bar, where they often sit for hours on end.

John Bull spoke of the little money Indians had in the bank because of "bumming around and drinking"; and how he had often considered getting another job where he would make less but live on a budget and save money. Joe Redson replied, "No, you'll stay in steel. No one tells you to, but you do . . . I did not tell my son to go into construction work, but that's what he is doing."

As to the men not in steel work, direct questions about them lead to answers such as: "That's their business," or "They like something else." But indirect questioning led to comments such as "Jack was no good, he was scared to be on the bars," or quoting Mrs. Peters, "Some Indians are not in steel work—*they couldn't make it.*"

Their definition of a real man is in terms of the warrior transplanted into the steel situation. "Now Bob" said Russel, "was a real man. He was a pusher and did not call up and say, 'Do so-and-so'—he came up and showed you. He would often swing around just hanging by his feet and when he pushed a pin in, it went. He could push them in with his bare hands."

Like most fearless, daredevil warriors, "pusher" Bob died with his boots on, and his glory is still frequently recounted. He fell off a girder.

As to whether the Mohawks lack a fear of heights (a belief held by many people both anthropologists and laymen), I was fortunate enough to be around when a few Indians in the Longhouse were discussing this very subject. Russel said, "I pray every morning that I'll come back alive." The others agreed that when you are up there on the outside of a building, you are afraid. Joe

Ringer said, "I've yet to meet the man who's not afraid up there . . . if you were not afraid, you would not be a good steel worker as you would not be careful." The group were fairly inebriated during this discussion. Usually, it is impossible to get them to admit fear of heights for two reasons. Firstly, the Indian has completely accepted the white man's stereotype of him as "the surefooted Indian." Secondly, *a warrior is not afraid.* A frequent statement of the Mohawks is, "Indians are afraid of nothing." Their fear of heights is the normal one of men who know that work on the girders is dangerous; however, just as the possibility of death did not deter the warrior from the warpath, it does not deter his descendant from structural steel work. In both cases, participating in dangerous activities is the sign of being a man.

If the role of warrior persisted (though modified), we would expect it to show up at other times as well as at work. This expectation is justified, as the following examples will show.

The preferred service for the Mohawks was the United States Marines. A number volunteered, not only for this "toughest of outfits," but also for direct assignment for overseas combat duty.

Over and over again, I have been told by the Mohawks, "An Indian never backs away in a fight," or while discussing cowardly actions, "You'd never see an Indian do that."

Jack (an informant) proudly related to my wife and me how he and his friend had "beaten up a couple of guys" in Canada. He was completely unconcerned that one of the fellows that he stabbed was in the hospital on the critical list. He expressed his real concern as follows: "I can't go back to Canada as the cops are looking for me." In reply to my question as to why he got involved in such a mess, he replied, "I like to fight . . . that's how I have fun." Jack is not unique; most of the younger men like to fight, and they relate with great pride how they got rid of many Puerto Ricans and Negroes who started to frequent their bar. On a number of occasions, Mohawks have attempted to pick a fight with me, and only a great deal of pride-swallowing prevented me from being beaten up. The evidence which could be multiplied, shows at every turn the structural continuity between the way of life of the warrior and that of the Mohawk steel worker.

Summary and Conclusions

I have attempted to show why the Mohawks went into and stayed in structural steel work. That a bridge was built which partly rested on reservation land was a historical accident; however, for the Mohawks to show off their fearlessness by running around on rafters was not an accident. This was a new variation of a culturally accepted manner of achieving prestige, to wit, through acts of daring. Because of this behavior, a few Mohawks were taught construction work, which, being group or gang work, allowed the trained Mohawks to form gangs of their own. The ability to form gangs, to work well together on a group assignment, to learn the work in a gang situation, all came from the already culturally patterned behavior of the warriors going off together on the warpath. Thus it was that the Mohawks got into steel and once in, the similarity of roles, authority patterns, etc., in short, the ability to maintain a similar way of life to that of the warrior, has kept the Mohawk in steel.

14 Ecology and Culture

MORRIS FREILICH

Mohawk males believed in the heroic nature of life. A male had to be a glory-loving hero. When environmental changes made one kind of heroic role (i.e. the warrior) impossible, Mohawks found another (i.e. the structural steel worker). For the Mohawk males freedom meant being allowed to be what a man must be. Maintaining this freedom meant grabbing a lucky break (the bridge being built near the reservation) and utilizing it for one's freedom strivings. These creative efforts by Mohawks were triggered, so to speak, by the problems created for them when the "White Men" took over their lands. In brief, environmental changes led to creative decision-making, which led to a measure of cultural persistence. Clearly the environment here, and in most social situations, is an important factor, to be well understood, before the socio-cultural situation can "make sense."

What precisely does "the environment" mean? How is it best conceptualized? Is there some general relationship which exists between environment and culture? These and related questions are discussed in Julian Steward's important work, Theory of Culture Change *(University of Illinois Press, 1955). And the following paper subjects Steward's environmental model to critical analysis.*

Introduction

Alfred North Whitehead has described modern science as an interest in relating stubborn facts to general principles; a "union of passionate interest in

SOURCE: Reprinted from "The Natural Experiment, Ecology and Culture" by Morris Freilich, *Southwestern Journal of Anthropology,* Vol. 19, No. 1, 1963, by permission of the publisher.

the detailed facts with equal devotion to abstract generalization."[1] Modern anthropology has a passion, indeed, for the detailed facts, but couples this with a nebulous attachment to abstract generalization. It has therefore a wealth of facts but a paucity of principles.

A problem that must concern us as scientists is: How can our ethnographic facts be used more efficiently to increase our stock of general principles? Or, differently put, how can anthropology be made more scientific in terms of modern scientific goals?

Modern science, it is generally acknowledged, dates from the introduction of the experimental method.[2] In the sister social sciences of sociology and anthropology, and particularly in anthropology, minimal use has been made of this method. Explanations usually given for the minimal use of the experiment include: the complexity of the data, the related problems of vested interests and maintaining objectivity, the problem of sampling, the problem of control and the problems—both moral and methodological—of manipulating humans.[3] Experimentation as a regular part of anthropological methodology would lead, I submit, to a sharpening of concepts, a sophistication of measuring devices and finally to an increase in empirically based principles. It is therefore most urgent that this method be carefully re-examined for its possible incorporation into the study of culture.

The essence of the experiment lies in the close observation of phenomena where the critical variables are controlled.[4] Two points here are worth noting. First, variables considered "critical" are needed for an experiment. Second, control over such critical variables is a relative matter; we can speak only of experiments with superior or inferior controls. As Festinger has remarked about recent laboratory studies in the social studies: "we must include under the term 'laboratory experiment' a wide range of studies with varying degrees of control and precision."[5]

In *Research Methods in the Behavioral Sciences* three major types of experiments are discussed: the laboratory experiment, the field experiment and the

---

[1] Alfred North Whitehead, *Science and the Modern World,* New York: The New American Library, 1959, p. 10.

[2] W. I. B. Beveridge, *The Art of Scientific Investigation,* New York: Random House (Modern Library), 1957.

[3] Oscar Lewis, "Controls and Experiments in Field Work," *Anthropology Today*, ed. A. L. Kroeber, Chicago: University of Chicago Press, 1955; R. Freedman, Amos H. Hawley, et al., eds., *Principles of Sociology: A Text with Readings,* New York: Henry Holt, 1956; Francis E. Merrill, *Society and Culture: An Introduction to Sociology,* Englewood Cliffs: Prentice-Hall, 1958.

[4] Beveridge.

[5] Leon Festinger, "Laboratory Experiments," *Research Methods in the Behavioral Sciences,* eds. Leon Festinger and Daniel Katz, New York: Dryden Press, 1953, p. 137.

natural experiment.[6] Let us examine these forms further and see to what extent all, or some of them, can be usefully incorporated into general anthropological methodology. The laboratory experiment is "one in which the investigator creates a situation with the exact conditions he wants to have and in which he controls some, and manipulates other, variables."[7] The field experiment is "a theoretically oriented research project in which the experimenter manipulates an independent variable in some real social setting in order to test some hypothesis."[8] And the natural experiment is "a change of major importance engineered by policy makers and practitioners and not by social scientists. It is experimental from the point of view of the scientist . . . (since) it can afford opportunities for measuring the effect of the change on the assumption that the change is so clear and drastic in nature that there is no question of identifying it as the independent variable."[9]

It is undeniable that human animals living in society and behaving according to the dictates of historically derived cultures represent extremely complex phenomena for study in a laboratory. However, some scholars have shown that complex phenomena can be reduced to a minimal number of critical variables and these can be studied in laboratory situations. For example, Guy Swanson has provided evidence that the behavior of crowds of all sizes can be expressed in the behavior of three people acting under controlled conditions.[10] Rose and Felton have shown the possibility of creating culture in laboratory conditions.[11] By the careful selection of critical elements in society and culture, Rose and Felton were able to construct models of socio-cultural systems which enabled them to study, under laboratory experimental conditions, such concepts as: closed and open societies, invention of culture and diffusion of culture.

Anthropologists of diverse theoretical orientations appear to share a common commitment to the natural history approach;[12] it is doubtful therefore that the laboratory experiment would be used by many of them, even as an additional methodological tool. However, in the field and natural experiments man is studied in his natural environment; and such studies would therefore be more

---

[6] Leon Festinger and Daniel Katz, eds., *Research Methods in the Behavioral Sciences,* New York: Dryden Press, 1953, pp. 78–170.

[7] Festinger and Katz, p. 137.

[8] Festinger and Katz, p. 101.

[9] Festinger and Katz, p. 78.

[10] Guy E. Swanson, "A Preliminary Laboratory Study of the Acting Crowd," *American Sociological Review,* 1953, Vol. 18, pp. 522–533.

[11] Edward Rose and William Felton, "Experimental Histories of Culture," *American Sociological Review,* 1955, Vol. 20, pp. 383–392.

[12] Laura Thompson, *Toward a Science of Mankind,* New York: McGraw-Hill, 1961.

congruent with existing practices of, and ideas about, anthropological field work.

The field experiment has been used to good advantage by many highly reputable anthropologists.[13] Researchers such as Allan Holmberg and associates have combined planned change endeavors and experimental work and have both assisted communities to become independent and provided important theoretical statements.[14] Although the work of many applied anthropologists has been sophisticated both in design and general methodology,[15] applied anthropology is treated by many social scientists as an illegitimate sibling of "theoretical" anthropology. A common charge that has been made against applied anthropology is that it is unscientific.[16] Apparently, for many non-applied anthropologists, field experiments and similar work done by the applied anthropologist represent too radical a change from the natural history approach to be acceptable. For many, particularly those whose training or identification is "Boasian," it is "the exhaustive collection of data" which is the typical province of anthropology and not the manipulation of such data.[17]

The most conservative of anthropologists, however, can find little argument with the natural experiment, for such studies differ minimally from traditional anthropological field work. The importance of the natural experiment for anthropology warrants some further discussion of the tactics and methodology here involved.

The Natural Experiment

Following the discussion in Festinger and Katz's important book, I have described the natural experiment as one where the researcher selects a situation for study where *change of a clear and dramatic nature* has occurred. In essence the argument of the natural experimenter is that this type of change can be treated as an independent variable in an experimental setting, and its effects can be observed and recorded. Or, differently put, the socio-cultural system in which a clear and dramatic change has occurred is, for a given time,

---

[13] See, for example, Donn V. Hart and Paul Meadows, *Selected Abstracts in Developments Administration: Field Reports of Directed Social Change,* Syracuse: Syracuse University, Maxwell Graduate School of Citizenship and Public Affairs, Publication 3, 1962.

[14] Allan R. Holmberg, "Participant Intervention in the Field," *Human Organization,* 1955, Vol. 14, pp. 23–26; "The Research and Development Approach to the Study of Change," *Human Organization,* 1958, Vol. 17, pp. 12–16; "Land Tenure and Planned Social Change," Human Organization, 1959, Vol. 18, pp. 7–10.

[15] R. N. Adams and J. J. Preiss, eds., *Human Organization Research,* Homewood, Ill.: The Dorsey Press, 1960.

[16] Oscar Lewis (1955).

[17] Marian W. Smith, "Boas' Natural History Approach to Field Method," *The Anthropology of Franz Boas,* ed. Walter Goldschmidt, American Anthropological Association Memoir No. 89, 1959, p. 54.

a natural laboratory, where given variables are in a state of control so that the effects of an independent variable (the change) can be studied. Thus, the argument would here continue that it hardly matters how control is achieved; what is important is that it is there and can be used for experimental purposes. The role of the researcher using the natural experiment is then to opportunistically capitalize on situations which exist.[18] Following French, the opportunism of the researcher lies in searching for situations where change of a clear and dramatic nature has occurred and using such situations as "natural" laboratories.

It should be noted that change of a clear and dramatic nature can be represented by a whole series of phenomena: cultural, social, ecological, demographic and so forth. Further, such changes become most useful for experimental purposes when they are related to a theoretical framework. For example, the work of Steward and associates in Puerto Rico (which I would call a natural experiment) is important theoretically not only because this was an experimentally oriented study with a number of controls built into it,[19] but also because the study was directly related to a theoretical framework—cultural ecology.[20] Similarly, Goldschmidt's recently completed study in East Africa is important for theoretical anthropology both for its experimental design and its relationship to a theoretical framework.[21] Studies such as these add to our library of detailed facts and increase our ability to make abstract generalizations.

To summarize, the anthropologist can do various kinds of natural experiments using a change in culture, ecology, demography, as his independent variable. The factors that all natural experiments would have in common irrespective of the particular problem under investigation are (1) a natural history orientation, (2) a socio-cultural system where an independent variable is in a state of natural isolation, (3) the possibility of studying the effects of the independent variable on the dependent variables, since other factors which may influence the dependent variables are in a state of natural control, and (4) a problem investigation related to a theoretical framework.

To stay within the naturalistic and non-manipulating tradition, anthropologists engaged in natural experiments would give up some of the control available to those doing laboratory experiments. However, in doing so, they would not be simply giving up some control to maintain the tradition of their discipline. Indeed, as Katz has shown, natural experiments have certain

---

18 John R. French, Jr., "Experiments in Field Settings," *Research Methods in the Behavioral Sciences,* eds. Leon Festinger and Daniel Katz, New York: Dryden Press, 1953, p. 99.

19 Julian Steward, et al., *The People of Puerto Rico,* Urbana, Ill.: University of Illinois Press, 1956.

20 Julian Steward, *Theory of Culture Change,* Urbana, Ill.: University of Illinois Press, 1955.

21 Walter Goldschmidt, "Socio-Cultural Concomitants of Ecological Change," Ms., n.d.

inherent advantages. Their major advantage is "that the manipulation of variables is much more powerful. The real world can and does produce role reversals, drastic changes in group norms, institutional revolutions, and group conflicts in a fashion impossible in the laboratory."[22] In addition, natural and field experiments have certain advantages over laboratory experiments. First, these studies can continue over longer periods of time. Thus, if a process (p) is isolated in system (s) at time (t) the validity of this finding can be checked by studying system (s) at time (t + 1); other things being equal (p) should still be part of the system. Second, direct observation of phenomena is possible and there is less need to make inferences from limited data. Third, these studies permit the experimenter to use multiple measures for the study of given phenomena. In the laboratory it is frequently necessary to use a single measuring instrument, and correlations obtained from a single instrument may be influenced by various side effects.[23]

The natural experiment, although differing minimally from traditional anthropological field studies, thus parallels in structure the laboratory experiments done in the physical and biological sciences. Although some control is lost by going outside of man-made laboratories, compensations are to be had in (1) the powerful manipulation of variables that is possible, (2) the checks available on the validity of the findings and (3) the possibility of observing man in his natural habitat so that real problems, rather than manufactured ones, can be solved. As suggested above, anthropologists, although rarely referring to their work as "experiments," have done what is here being called "natural experiments." Apart from the natural experiments done by Steward and associates, and Goldschmidt and associates, there is Linton's famous study of the effects on Tanala social organization of a change in food production.[24] These and other similar studies have shown that it is possible to arrive at empirically based generalizations by conducting natural experiments.[25] However, the natural experiment has, as yet, not become a formal aspect of anthropological methodology; and the minimal use of an experimental approach remains a basic defect in the study of man. As Stouffer has put it: "One of the greatest weaknesses of social science has been the infrequency of its use of deliberately designed controlled experiments, which are the only sure method of determining whether a change in one variable actually will be followed by a change in another."[26]

---

[22] Daniel Katz, "Field Studies," *Research Methods in the Behavioral Sciences,* eds. Leon Festinger and Daniel Katz, New York: Dryden Press, 1953, p. 79.

[23] Katz (1953), pp. 81–82.

[24] Ralph Linton, "Tanala of Madagascar," *The Individual and His Society,* ed. Abram Kardiner, New York: Columbia University Press, 1939, p. 251–290.

[25] Julian Steward and Robert Manners, "The Cultural Study of Contemporary Societies: Puerto Rico," *American Journal of Sociology,* 1953, Vol. 59, pp. 123–130.

[26] Samuel A. Stouffer, "A Study of Attitudes," *The Scientific American,* 1949, Vol. 180, pp. 11–15.

The study which follows attempts to illustrate further the scientific possibilities inherent in the use of the natural experiment. The paper as a whole is an attempt to stimulate greater interest in experimental work, so that anthropology can share in the benefits which accrue to experimentally oriented sciences.

Theory, Hypotheses, Procedures, and Methods

In conducting a natural experiment anthropologists, like their colleagues in the physical and biological sciences, can begin with a theoretical framework, and derive a hypothesis therefrom for testing. In the natural experiment the next step is to *find a situation* where the critical variables of the hypothesis are in a state of "natural" control and where it is possible to study the effects of the independent variable.

The theoretical framework used in the study which follows is *cultural ecology,* as described by Julia Steward. Steward defines cultural ecology as the *interaction between technology and the culturally defined manner of exploiting the environment.* According to cultural ecological theory, such interaction is a "creative process," an important determinant of culture change. As Steward puts it, "over the millenia cultures in different environments have changed tremendously, and *these changes are basically traceable to new adaptations required by changing technology and productive arrangements.*" (Italics inserted.)[27]

Working within this framework, I derived the following hypothesis: *If two groups which differ considerably in cultural traditions make the same cultural ecological adaptation, then there should be a core of culture shared by both groups which is related to the common mode of adoption.* The hypothesis was tested in the village of Anamat, in Eastern Trinidad, where East Indians and Negroes live together in neighborly enmity and do peasant farming in terms of common "folk science" technology.

To test this cultural ecological hypothesis it was necessary to collect certain kinds of data, to analyze such data into comparable categories and to accept or reject the hypothesis on the basis of the data collected. The data collection procedures followed the usual anthropological field techniques. The writer and his wife spent approximately eleven months in the village of Anamat and became accepted members of the Anamatian community. Observation of and participation in community activities was for the first month of field work the major method used. In the months that followed, although the observation and participation method was continued, it was used as a subsidiary method to the following: informal and formal questionnaires, life histories, group seminars

[27] Julian Steward, *Theory of Culture Change,* Urbana, Ill.: University of Illinois Press, 1955, p. 37.

with East Indians and Negroes on their cultural practices, special informants and analysis of records kept by the Anamatian peasants relating to their land holdings.[28] In addition local field assistants were hired to obtain certain kinds of confidential data which I had difficulty in obtaining. It was also possible for me to get the part-time assistance of a clerk in the office of Registrar General of Trinidad. The latter was able to provide historical data on land holdings for Anamat and land in the immediate vicinity of this village.

Two major types of data were collected from both the East Indians and the Negroes—ecological and cultural. The ecological data were collected to verify that the adaptations of East Indian and Negro peasants were indeed similar. The cultural data were collected in order to observe to what extent similarities in ecological adaptations had led to similar cultural practices in areas of social life not directly connected with subsistence activities.

To verify that the cultural ecological adaptations of both groups were the same, I obtained data on the size of the land holdings, the relative fertility of the land of each group (East Indians and Negroes), the nature of the land holdings (free-hold title, rent, lease, etc.), the cash and subsistence crops grown, the personnel who worked the land, the time spent working the land, the technology used, the crop yields and the incomes obtained. The data collected led to the conclusion that the East Indians and the Negroes had the same general environmental conditions and made specific ecological adaptations which were similar enough to be considered "the same" for the purposes of this natural experiment.

General environmental conditions were the same because East Indians and Negroes worked land all of which was situated in the same small village of Anamat. They both therefore shared common climatic conditions, such as rainfall, temperature, humidity, hours of daylight; they had common transportation facilities to and from their land holding and to and from market areas.

Specific ecological adaptations were considered the same for the following reasons: First, both groups worked similar sized land holdings (see Table 1). The average East Indian peasant worked a holding of 20.6 acres; the average Negro peasant worked a holding of 21.9 acres.

Second, the land of East Indians and Negroes was dispersed throughout

---

[28] All the peasants of Anamat did not keep written records of crop yields, sales and other matters pertaining to their land. Nor did all the peasants who had such records permit me to see them. However, I was able to work with a number of the actual records that were kept. Part of the problem in getting to see the records kept by the Anamatian peasants was that I arrived in the village shortly after an income tax law had been passed in Trinidad. Further, I occupied the only vacant house in the village, which happened to be an ex-school house owned by the Trinidadian government. It took considerable time and energy to convince all of the peasants in Anamat that I was an anthropologist and not a government spy looking into income tax matters.

Anamat. No part of the village could be considered "East Indian" or "Negro." Since the land of both groups was scattered throughout the community, it is possible to assume that the fertility of the soil was essentially the same for both groups.

Third, nearly all of the land worked by both groups was owned by freehold title by those who worked it. The East Indians owned 96.7 percent of the land they worked; the Negroes owned 92.9 percent of the land they worked. Both groups rented the balance of the land they worked.

TABLE 1. Land Holdings of Negro and East Indian Peasants in Anamat, Trinidad

	10 acres or less	*11–19 acres*	*20–30 acres*	*Over 30 acres*	*Total no. of holdings**
Negroes	6	11	8	6	31
East Indians	7	8	13	3	31
Totals	13	19	21	9	62

* In order to have an equal number of Negro and East Indian peasants, 4 Negro peasants who live in Anamat were not included in this study. The exclusion of these peasants, however, in no way changes the basic data or conclusions of this study. Ethnographic data collected from these peasants substantiates the conclusions reached.

Fourth, the major cash crop for both groups was cocoa and for both an additional cash crop was coffee. For a small minority of peasants, both East Indian and Negro, extra income was obtained from the sale of bananas and dasheen (*Araceae*).

Fifth, crops grown for home consumption were mainly such root crops as the following: yams (*Dioscoreaceae*), sweet potatoes (*Convolvulaceae*), cassava (*Euphorbiaceae*), tannia (*Marantaceae*) and dasheen (*Araceae*).

Sixth, although both groups had strong attachments to consanguineal families (see below), they both mainly lived in nuclear family households, and the land was mainly worked by the members of such a household. The head of the house (usually a male for both groups) did most of the work on the land. He was assisted by his wife and children, particularly during the crop time when the cocoa and coffee had to be picked.

Seventh, the time spent working the land was extremely similar for both groups. For both, the working week was generally Monday through Friday with a half day of work on Saturday. Both groups of peasants found it difficult to tell me exactly how much time they spent working on the land each day. Both stated that it all depended on what had to be done at a certain time of the year. When I urged them to provide me with an estimate of how long they believed they worked on an average day, I received data which averaged 7.5 hours a day for the East Indians and 7.6 hours a day for the

Negroes. For most of the peasants, both East Indian and Negro, the working day started around 7:30 to 8:00 in the morning and ended about 4:00 to 4:30 in the afternoon. All the peasants told me that when they had a lot of work that had to be finished at a given time they worked until it got dark, and at such times work on Sundays was not uncommon. Such long working weeks occurred mainly during the heavy cocoa crop seasons—November through December, parts of January and April. The Negroes spent more time away from the land than the East Indians during such fête seasons as Christmas and Carnival. This time, however, was approximately balanced by East Indians participating in family *pujas* (prayer meetings) and other Hindu religious observances.

Eighth, both groups used a technology which in terms of recognized practices of working cocoa estates could be considered as unscientific.[29] They both practiced what could be called a folk-science of agriculture. This was mostly based on information which was passed down orally from their peasant farming parents and which was shared by the whole community. In addition "MacDonald's Farmer's Almanac"[30] was used by some of the farmers as an extra guide. This almanac was considered by a number of East Indian and Negro peasants as an important source of farming information. The nature of the information contained in this almanac can be deduced from its cover, which states in bold type: "Tells When to Plant and Harvest by the Moon . . . (makes) Predictions about Crops, The Weather, Sickness and Lucky Days."

Finally, the crop yields and the income for both groups were extremely similar. Although it might be possible to deduce that peasants working similar sized holdings in similar unscientific ways would have similar crop yields and income, I attempted to obtain information in this area directly. On the basis of a limited number of records I was allowed to examine, together with the answers I received on questionnaires about crop yields and income, I was able to come to the following conclusions. The average yield per cocoa tree per year was 0.76 lbs. for East Indians and 0.70 lbs. for Negroes—this, when it is possible with scientific methods to average 2.73 lbs! Further, the average income per acre was $86.18 for the East Indians and $81.35 for the Negroes.

Statements made by the Anamatian peasants on the farming abilities of East Indians and Negroes further supported the conclusion that the two groups had similar average incomes. To the question: "Who are better farmers, Negroes or East Indians?" the general answer first received was related to the cultural affiliation of the person being questioned—Negroes stated "Negroes" and East Indians stated "Indians." After a short discussion, however, when the

---

[29] C. Y. Shephard, *The Cocoa Industry in Trinidad,* Port-of-Spain, Trinidad: Government Printing Office, 1937.

[30] J. MacDonald, *MacDonald's Farmer's Almanac,* Binghamton, N.Y.: The Atlas Printing Co., 1956.

questioned person was asked to name "good" and "poor" farmers in Anamat, it was usually concluded by the informant that both groups had a fairly equal share of good and poor farmers. Put differently, it was agreed by most of my informants that East Indians and Negroes farmed about equally well.

To summarize, both groups were considered as making the same cultural ecological adaption since both:

1. shared the same climatic conditions,
2. worked land of similar acreage,
3. worked with similar biotic and edaphic (soils, relief and drainage) features,
4. spent similar amounts of time working the land,
5. used the same folk-science technology,
6. used the same kind and number of personnel (head of the house) to do most of the farming,
7. worked to produce the same cash crops: cocoa and coffee,
8. worked to produce the same crops for home consumption (root crops),
9. shared the same market and transportation facilities,
10. obtained similar incomes from their subsistence activities.

Cultural Data

In collecting cultural data from East Indians and Negroes in Anamat, special care was taken to spend approximately equal time with both groups so as not to bias the data. This balance was maintained by careful planning and record-keeping of interactions with Anamatians. Initially each group tried to monopolize my time, each respectively trying to demonstrate that only they had a culture which could interest an anthropologist. Within a short time, however, it became generally known and accepted that I was a strange kind of individual who liked East Indians and Negroes equally well.

Cultural data was obtained from both groups on economic practices, marriage, the family, extended kinship ties, authority patterns, leisure activities, expressive symbols, religious practices, involvement in community affairs—both social and political—and on the various roles in their respective systems. The cultural data collected showed that although East Indians and Negroes made a similar ecological adaptation and earned similar incomes, their cultural practices, in areas of social life not directly connected to subsistence activities, were extremely different.

Money was spent differently by East Indians and Negroes. Although the average Negro household contained only one child and the average East Indian household had 3–4 children, both groups spent similar amounts for food and clothing. Thus, per family member, the East Indians spent far less on food and clothing than the Negroes. The East Indians, however, spent more money on housing than the Negroes. Fourteen of the East Indian peasants (45%) lived in brick houses as against eight of the Negro peasants (26%) who lived in brick houses. The balance of the peasants of both groups lived in galvanized-roofed houses (14 East Indians and 20 Negroes) and karat huts (3 East Indians and 3 Negroes).

The East Indians also spent more money on education than the Negroes. At the time of this study two sons of East Indian peasants were studying in universities in England and one other East Indian youth was planning to go to England. None of the Negro peasants had sons studying in a university, nor did any of the Negro youths plan on going to a university.

The Negroes spent more money than the East Indians on pleasure or what they called *fête*. A fête, for the Negro, was a situation which contained at least two of the following: people, talk, rum, music, dance and sexual play. If all or most of these phenomena were present in a given party, the Negro would consider himself to be in a "big fête" or "real fête."[31] The East Indians spent more money than the Negroes on religious matters. These usually took the form of the *puja*, the family prayer meeting, which was held in the house or the yard of the person "making a *puja*."

In short, Indians spent more money on capital items which would affect their future (housing, education, religion), while Negroes spent more money on non-capital items which were fairly quickly consumed and which related to a present rather than future time orientation. Going along with a different use of money by East Indians and Negroes was a different use of time. The *pujas* of the East Indians brought them into frequent contacts with members of their extended families; the fêting of the Negroes was usually done with friends rather than family and frequently took the Negro male away from his nuclear family.[32] Thus East Indians spent more time with the members of their family than did the Negroes. To the extent that the use of time may represent an operational measure of values, it could be said that "the family" was far more valued by East Indians than by Negroes. Such a conclusion would be congruent with the following facts: (1) East Indians bringing religious services into the home, the place which houses the family; and (2) East Indians building more expensive and permanent housing than the Negroes.

The East Indians lived in a joint family setting: a life-long household economy of three generations, with patrilineal inheritance, patriarchal authority

---

[31] Morris Freilich, "Serial Polygyny, Negro Peasants and Model Analysis," *American Anthropologist,* 1961, Vol. 63, pp. 955–975.

[32] Morris Freilich, "Cultural Diversity among Trinidadian Peasants," unpublished doctoral dissertation, New York: Columbia University, 1960; "Cultural Models and Land Holdings," *Anthropological Quarterly,* 1960, Vol. 33, pp. 188–197.

and patrilocal residence rules. Although the joint family household frequently split into nuclear households, the latter were usually placed within close proximity of each other and close contacts were had between the members of a joint family. While a given Indian might be living in his own house and be relatively independent economically, the directives of a father or an elder brother were still orders and not suggestions.

The Negroes lived in nuclear households but had strong affectionate ties to a matrifocal family: a three generation consanguineal unit with a minimal membership of a mother, her brother, her son and daughter and her daughter's children. Authority patterns were here equalitarian. Directives were given by elder members of the family in the form of "advice" rather than orders.

The marriages of the East Indians were arranged by their elders; and the father of a young Indian girl would attempt to get a youth for his daughter who was of "good family" (i.e. of a caste which was, at least, of equal status with his own) and who lived in a village other than his own. The marriage was supposed to last for life. The Negroes selected their own mates and understood that a given marriage was only supposed to last for as long as man and wife "cooperated"; when one or both parties thought that the proper "cooperation" no longer existed, it was time for them to separate. As the Anamatian Negro put it, a marriage was a "now-for-now" affair.

In terms of associational patterns the East Indians maintained a sharp separation of the sexes in all social activities. Be it at a family *puja* with fifty or more people congregating in and around one house or during a friendly visit of a man and his wife, the Indian women would rarely interact with any of the males present. The Indian women understood and accepted the fact that their place was with the other women who were present. The Indian men would similarly consider it improper to have social intercourse with the women on these occasions. Social intercourse across sex lines was greatly limited in Indian culture and occurred mostly between a man and his wife when they were alone.

For the Negro a get-together without members of the opposite sex being present would represent a very dull party. The associational activities of the Negro peasants in Anamat thus usually included interactions between members of both sexes. At such times some of the men would have opportunities to talk to some of the women present, in private. Part of the content of these conversations frequently included the male "beggin' for a brush" (proposing that the woman and he meet later for sexual play). If a given woman agreed, it was understood by both parties that the man was to be the recipient of a favor which must be later repaid in terms of some goods or services. Thus sex was for the Negroes of Anamat a medium of exchange along with money (British West Indian dollar). The use of sex as a medium of exchange fitted in well with the cultural system of the Negroes: it facilitated the serial polygyny which was practiced; it led to a more equalitarian distribution of goods and services and was congruent with the fête complex which was a major goal of this system.[33]

In summary, the East Indian and Negro peasants in Anamat were part of two extremely different cultural systems, the former having a way of life which in many important areas was similar to the cultural practices of the Hindu peasants in India,[34] the latter maintaining cultural practices developed in the slavery plantation system of the New World.[35] It is outside the scope of this paper to describe more completely the cultural practices of East Indian and Negro peasants in Anamat; most of such information has been presented by the writer elsewhere.[36] It is possible, however, to summarize the data I collected in Anamat in terms of two systems, presented as mechanical models.[37] The models were constructed by using the following points of reference as structural categories: *time, space, people, authority, exchanges, sanctions* and *goals*.[38] In terms of these categories, questions were asked and answered on the basis of the ethnographic data collected in Anamat. For example, in reference to the category *time* the question asked was: "What is the basic time orientation of the group: is it past, present or future?" Similar questions were posed for each of the categories of the models (see Table 2). The mechanical models used here were, in actuality, the sum of all the content (i.e., answers to questions posed) of all the structural categories.

In terms of these categories East Indians in Anamat can be described as: (1) being future-oriented in time, (2) using village space for most of their interactions, but extending such space to include the villages of the members of their extended family, (3) being members of a joint family, (4) possessing a hierarchical authority system, (5) exchanging goods and services by using money as a medium of exchange, (6) exchanging women (indirectly) with joint families of other villages, (7) exchanging information by the use of the English language, (8) having supernatural, polytheistic sanctions and (9) having "family improvement" as a major goal.

The Negroes, in terms of the same categories, can be described as: (1) being present-oriented in time, (2) using the village space for most of their interac-

---

[33] Freilich (1961).

[34] West Bengal Government, ed., *India's Villages,* West Bengal Government Press, 1955; McKim Marriott, *Village India: Studies in the Little Community,* American Anthropological Association Memoir 83, 1955.

[35] Freilich (1961).

[36] Freilich (1960, 1961).

[37] Claude Levi-Strauss, "Social Structure," *Anthropology Today,* ed. A. L. Kroeber, Chicago: University of Chicago Press, 1955.

[38] Morris Freilich, "Cultural Persistence Among the Modern Iroquois," *Anthropos,* 1958, Vol. 53, pp. 473–483.

TABLE 2. Points of Reference for Two Cultural Models

Time	What is the basic time orientation of the group; is it the present, the past or the future?
Space	In what area is most living done, and under what circumstances is there an extension of this area?
People	What is the basic kinship unit of the group, and what is the nature of associational activities?
Authority Structure	What is the nature of order-giving and order-receiving in the group?
Exchange System	What kinds of exchanges occur with respect to (a) goods and services, (b) women, (c) symbols?
Sanctions	What sanctions effectively control behavior in the group?
Goals	What kinds of behavior receive most prestige per unit of time, energy and expense incurred?

tions, but extending this space, mainly, by traveling to fêtes in other communities where they interacted with friends, (3) being members of a matrifocal-consanguineal family, (4) possessing a loose, equalitarian authority system, (5) exchanging goods and services by using money and the sexual services of women as media of exchange, (6) exchanging women (indirectly) with other matrifocal families on a temporary basis, (7) exchanging information by the use of the English language, (8) having social sanctions and fatalism as major forms of sanctions and (9) considering "being in a big fête" as a major goal.

A comparison of the cultural systems of East Indians and Negroes in Anamat will show that they are extremely different (see Table 3). The content elements which are similar—use of the village for most interactions, use of money as a medium of exchange and use of English as a means of exchanging information—cannot be related to the shared mode of cultural ecological adaptation. The use of the village for the majority of the interactions of the Anamatians is very similar to village life in most cultures; it cannot therefore be related to the common adaptations of the East Indian and Negro peasants. The use of money as a medium of exchange and the use of the English language are also unrelated causally to cocoa and coffee peasant farming. The money (British West Indian dollar) and language used in Anamat is the same as that used all over Trinidad and is directly related to the fact that till recently this was a British colony.

Since the independent variable—a common form of cultural ecological adaptation—did not lead to a common core of culture shared by East Indians and Negroes, and since the cultural elements similar in the two groups cannot

TABLE 3. Models of East Indian and Negro Cultural Systems

Points of Reference	*Cultural Systems*	
	East Indian	Negro
Time	The future	The "now"
Space	Village; extended by permanent villages of kin	Village; extended by temporary fête centers
People		
Kinship Unit	Joint family	Consanguineal-matrifocal
Associational Patterns	With family	With friends freely chosen
Authority	Patripotestal, rigid, hierarchical	Loose, equalitarian
Exchange		
Goods and Services	Money medium of exchange	Money and sexual services media of exchange
Women	Indirect, permanent, between joint families	Indirect, temporary between matrifocal families
Symbols	English	English
Sanctions	Supernatural, polytheistic	Social (natural) plus fatalism
Goals	Family improvement	Fête

be related to the independent variable, the hypothesis proposed had to be rejected.

Summary and Conclusions

A type of cultural ecological adaptation was considered in this study as an independent variable of change, and two cultural traditions treated as dependent variables. A situation was selected with natural controls to test the hypothesis that a shared mode of cultural ecological adaptation would lead East Indians and Negroes to show cultural similarities related to the shared mode of adaptation. The data collected necessitated the rejection of the hypothesis. It must be concluded then that the type of cultural ecological adaptation here considered is not a causal factor of change.

Julian Steward acknowledges that cultural ecological adaptations may at times not be deterministic, that they may at times allow considerable latitude or potential variation in socio-cultural types. "Where latitude is possible," writes Steward, "*historic factors* may determine the nature of the society."

(Italics inserted.) That such historic factors are of minor importance for Steward may be deduced from his generalization about cultural ecology as a determinant of change, and from the minimal treatment, in Steward's works, given to situations where environment allows latitude.

I would submit that what Steward calls "historical factors" are of far greater import and deserve far more attention than he would allow. Such historic factors are in part the cultural traditions of groups. The importance of culture as a persisting element in human life is both implicit in general anthropological usage and attested by various empirical studies.

Steward's model of change stipulates that (1) the cultural ecological adaptation is *the* independent variable and (2) at times the influence of this independent variable approaches zero (the environment *allows* latitude). A slight modification of the model would explain better the results obtained in Anamat. The fact that East Indians and Negroes do not share similar cultural forms may be more a factor of the *cultures* considered than the form of the ecological adaptation. That is, perhaps we are dealing with two cultural traditions which are highly resistant to change, two cultures that would tend towards nonchange in any kind of environment.

For a more predictive model of change, cultural tradition must be given a less passive role to play. In a previous work which more completely described this study,[39] I proposed a model of change utilizing four polar concepts, two cultural and two ecological. The concepts suggested were: *generalized* and *specialized cultures,* and *permissive* and *deterministic ecologies.* It was suggested that the cultural concepts be used in a fashion analogous to their usage in evolutionary biology. A specialized culture would be one whose cultural forms are functionally related to one and only one type of ecology. A generalized culture would be one whose cultural forms show no specific functional relationships to any type of ecology.

A *specialized culture* which changes its environment would tend to react in terms of either culture change or cultural extinction. A *generalized culture* which changes its environment may well survive with minimal cultural changes. In terms of these concepts the hypothesis here discussed may have been rejected because of (1) permissive ecology, (2) generalized cultural systems, or (3) a combination of both. For clear-cut generalizations using these concepts, many additional studies relating culture and cultural ecology are required.

That limited conclusions are available from this experiment should not greatly concern us; rarely does an experiment in any science produce much

---

39 Morris Freilich, "Cultural Diversity among Trinidadian Peasants," unpublished doctoral dissertation, New York: Columbia University, 1960.

more. Further, as Freedman, Hawley and associates have stated,[40] the findings of a single experiment are much less likely to be conclusive in the social sciences than in physics and chemistry, and therefore "more man hours of work will probably be required in the development of theory in the former fields." What should be noted is that this kind of experimentation used the process that is today considered "science." As James Conant writes: "Science emerges from the other progressive activities of man to the extent that new concepts arise from experiments and observations, and the new concepts in turn lead to further experiments and observations."[41]

One final point: it was stated above that the data collected necessitated the rejection of the hypothesis tested. More accurately it should have been said that *within the limits of the experimental design, data collection and data analyzing techniques and the conceptual scheme used for this study, the hypothesis had to be rejected.* To make these limits minimally limiting we must attempt to improve the general methodology of our studies. A side effect of doing natural experiments, of no small importance to the science of man, is that of being forced by this technique to improve our models, to operationalize our concepts and to develop more accurate measuring devices.

15 The Importance of History

GILBERT SHAPIRO

A historical approach toward social life is fundamental for cultural anthropology, because "culture" is itself a historical concept. However, several trends in anthropological theory have attempted to relegate history to a realm of secondary importance by raising other factors above it. Thus, for example, the functionalism of Malinowski placed a strong emphasis on "the now" by emphasizing man's biological requirements. A similar approach which also underemphasizes the importance of history, is Steward's "cultural-ecology."

[40] R. Freedman, Amos H. Hawley, et al., eds., *Principles of Sociology: A Text with Readings,* New York: Henry Holt, 1956, p. 31.
[41] James B. Conant, *On Understanding Science,* New Haven: Yale University Press, 1947, p. 24.

Source: Reprinted from "The Necessity For Historical Trajectories: A Prose Argument" by Gilbert Shapiro. Delivered at the annual meeting of the Midwest Sociological Society, April 13, 1962. Reprinted by permission of the author.

Here, adaptive problems and their current solutions are made the focus of research, and history becomes "historical factors" which also play some kind of secondary, explanatory role.

The Mohawk paper illustrated the complex interconnections which exist between historical forces and present adaptive problems. The modern Mohawk in structural steel becomes an enigma, without a knowledge of Mohawk history. Similarly, the Anamat situation makes no sense if Anamatian peasants are viewed simply as peasants, currently attempting to survive through a given type of adaptation to the land. History, it would appear, must remain a major variable for the social scientist, irrespective of his sub-discipline, and irrespective of the particular problem he is studying. This broad conclusion receives ingenious support—indeed, I am tempted to say, it is fully demonstrated—by the next paper, written by a historical sociologist with strong theoretical interests, Gilbert Shapiro.

Is it possible to achieve the purposes of a scientific theory of social structure given observations at only one point in time?

This, of course, is a very old problem of sociological method. Our excuse for raising it anew is our belief that "cybernetics," particularly in the form developed by Ross Ashby as a general logic for the study of change in all kinds of systems, when critically revised and suitably adapted, offers some powerful and novel relevant ideas. The question would have no interest unless some important schools of social science took the opposing view. We suspect that all those who would build a structural-functional theory prior to, and distinct from, a theory of change, or who contrast "functional" types with "historical" or "causal" types of study are denying the necessity which is being urged here of theories and observations at two points in time. Similarly, those "field theorists" in social psychology who claim that since the future state of any system is fully determined by its present, we must interpret all behavior as an outcome of concurrent situational structures, ignoring all life-history data, are working, at another level of integration, in the opposing camp.

Perhaps the most explicit rejection of the necessity for history in the social sciences come from Malinowski in a book paradoxically entitled *The Dynamics of Culture Change.*[1] He argues that the anthropologist is properly concerned with "tradition, alive and at work, not history, dead and buried." In short, the social scientist deals only with current patterns, including the current ideas people have about their past, whether these be true or false. Gluckman, in a profound critique of this book, states:

[1] Bronislaw Malinowski, *The Dynamics of Culture Change,* New Haven: Yale University Press, 1945.

> Malinowski's theoretical denial of the value of historical reconstruction is thus contradicted by his use of it, wherever he makes a good analysis. We see here not only the necessity to study history in order to observe processes of social change, but also the need to record historical developments *in order to understand the latent drives in existing organization,* as well as its *present form.* Historians, over centuries, have been aware of this. . . .[2]

It is critical that we appreciate the full force of Gluckman's claim; not that a study of a contemporary society is given added interest, depth, moral or aesthetic value by having appended to it a chapter (usually Chapter Two!) on the historical context, but that the study of history is *necessary* in order to understand the *present* structure.

But how is this possible? We get a hint from a telling point made by Gluckman, which gains added cogency in the light of recent events:

> For example, in discussing African warfare, Malinowski states, "European occupation has obliterated the old tribal hostilities." The facts we have show that these old tribal hostilities are by no means obliterated, but are largely denied military expression. Any historian would have expected this.[3]

Almost any recent newspaper provides sufficient documentation to adjudicate this particular dispute!

The interesting point that Gluckman raises is a *methodological* one. While the field theorist may be correct in his claim that only the forces of the present can influence the future, Gluckman suggests that *we can only know those present forces* by means of historical study. Certain "latent" elements essential to that knowledge of the present which is required for prediction are unavailable to current observation. History, then, has an *indicative* function.

This situation is not unique to the social sciences. The physician frequently quizzes us about our past complaints and our family's medical history and not because of idle antiquarian or genealogical curiosity. Historical data with all their inferior reliability are often indispensible indications of the current state of the body, its probable reaction to various forms of treatment, and the very significance of laboratory tests.

A major contribution of cybernetics may be to provide a vocabulary which permits us to discuss such everyday observations with rigor, minimizing ambiguity, and consequently avoiding paradoxes. We begin with a distinction between the "machine" and the "system" which, alone, would have served Malinowski very well indeed; the "machine" is our object of investigation which, we assume, behaves in a regular, patterned, "determinate" or predictable

---

[2] Max Gluckman, *Malinowski's Sociological Theories,* London: Oxford University Press, 1949, p. 5.

[3] Gluckman (1949), p. 3.

fashion. Not every determinate or predictable object of investigation is *determined* or *predicted*, however. In the definition of a machine we assume that it would be *possible* to know its future from its present, if only we were armed with understanding of its workings. Some such assumption (the "uniformity of nature" of John Stuart Mill) is a necessary preliminary to any scientific enterprise.

Our success in determining the behavior of the machine depends not only upon its determinateness but also upon the selection of variables which we choose to measure, or the qualities we choose to classify. Every machine, as Ashby rightly points out,[4] contains no less than an infinite number of variables. One of the major difficulties (we are tempted to say the *trick*) of theory construction is to select *a set of variables whose behavior will be sufficiently regular and predictable for scientific use. This set of variables incompletely describing the machine,* and only this, is what the cybernetician calls a *"system."*

In this view, *the ideal of a science is to discover a system that is "state-determined."* This means that *from the values of its variables at any given time, it is possible to predict their values at any future moment.* (In the more technical language of cybernetics, there is no point in the phase-space through which runs more than one line of behavior.) Note that a *machine may be determinate while we have not discovered any state-determined system characterizing it.* In the state-determined system, there is no need for history; without reference to the past, we are able to predict the future from the present.

But a system may be "regular," in Ashby's terminology, without being "state-determined." The *regular* system shares with the state-determined system the admirable quality that if the system is released at any chosen initial state, it will always reproduce the same line of behavior. But some of those lines of behavior, or "trajectories," pass through the same point as others, which is to say that there are some system states which are common to more than one sequence of events. Such a system, a "regular" system, is not as attractive for scientific use as the state-determined system, for with it, it is decidedly *not* possible to predict future states from any given description of the present.

Since we have excluded mathematics as well as poetry from this prose argument, our discussion now threatens to attain intolerable levels of obscurity. To return us to the concrete, your attention is invited to the illustration borrowed from Ashby's *Design for a Brain,* which depicts a simple undulating table surface. We can do no better than to quote Ashby's lucid account at length:

> Looking down on it from above, we can mark across it a grid of lines to act as co-ordinates. If we place a ball at any point and then release it, the ball will

[4] Ross Ashby, *Design for a Brain,* New York: Wiley, 1960, p. 248.

> roll, and by marking its position at, say, every one-tenth second we can determine the lines of behavior of the two-variable system provided by the two co-ordinates.
>
> If the table is well made, the lines of behavior will be accurately reproducible and the system will be regular. Yet the experimenter, if he knew nothing of forces, gravity, or momenta, would find this two-variable system unsatisfactory. He would establish that the ball, started at A, always went to A′; and started at B it always went to B′. He would find its behaviour at C difficult to explain. And if he tried to clarify the situation by starting the ball at C itself, he would find it went to D![5]

Such is a regular, non-state-determined system. The trajectories are reproducible, but there exist some system-states, such as C from which predictions of future states are impossible. The direction of the ball's movement from C *depends upon where it has been.* Given the location of the ball at C and the fact that it started its roll at A, we have no doubt of its future locations! *Historical data are necessary for prediction within regular systems that are not state-determined!*

Undulating Table Surface*

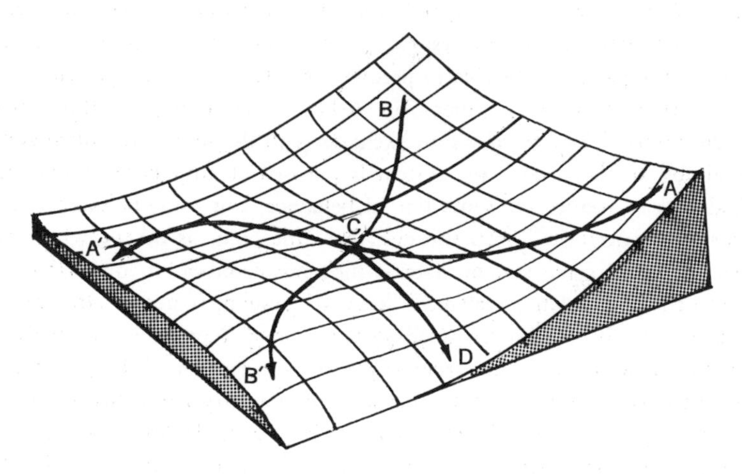

Ashby is thoroughly dissatisfied with the regular system, and seeks always the state-determined system. "In my theory I insist on the systems being state-determined because I agree with the experimenter who, in his practical work, is similarly insistent." But here, he evidently has in mind the experimenter in physics or chemistry, or those branches of biology most closely allied with those

[5] Ashby (1960), p. 249.

* From W. Ross Ashby, *Design for a Brain,* New York: Wiley, 1960, p. 248.

fields of advanced scientific development. Our old friend the physician, facing the practical task of diagnosis, reveals his use of regular systems by his continuous use of historical information, which would be simply irrelevant in a state-determined system. Similarly, I would suggest that the regular system is about the highest order of determinacy to which the theory of social structure today might reasonably aspire.

16 Culture and the History of Man

A. IRVING HALLOWELL

Once it is accepted that historical understandings must be incorporated in all aspects of anthropology, then it is logical to inquire: What of the history of modern man, Homo sapiens? *How have processes buried deep in man's evolutionary history influenced the development of man's unique achievement, culture? How, indeed, is it possible for our non-human ancestors (themselves without culture) to produce a human animal with culture? These and related questions are now discussed in a very important paper by the distinguished anthropologist, Professor A. Irving Hallowell.*

The use of behavioral or functional criteria such as speech or tools represents, of course, a piecemeal approximation to a categorical distinction which has been current in general anthropology for a long time. It is that man is unique among the Primates, and stands apart from all other animals as well, in possessing culture. In fact, the concept of culture and the identification of a human level of existence with a cultural mode of adaptation seems to have become a commonplace not only among cultural anthropologists but among archeologists and physical anthropologists, to say nothing of sociologists and others.

There are some indications, however, that it is not quite so easy to apply the generic concept of culture as the differential criterion of a human status, as was once thought to be the case. Carpenter, whose field researches among infra-human primate groups remain unparalleled, is not convinced that culture

SOURCE: Abridged and adapted from "The Structural and Functional Dimensions of a Human Existence" by A. Irving Hallowell, *Quarterly Review of Biology,* Vol. 31, 1956, pp. 88–101, by permission of the author and the publisher.

is a unique human phenomenon. Where, then, do we stand with respect to "culture" as the primary differential between man and other Primates? Rather than seek a formal definition directly, I prefer to phrase the question as, What can be said about the necessary and sufficient conditions that distinguish a human level of existence?

In the first place, I would note that culture as dealt with by cultural anthropologists has been observed, analyzed, conceptualized, and defined exclusively on the basis of data derived from ethnography and history. In the second place, direct observations and historical records apply to only one species of man—*Homo sapiens*. For other members of the genus *Homo,* behavior must be inferred from the archeological material. In other words, culture, in its richest and, to the cultural anthropologist, most typical forms is associated with *Homo sapiens* alone, so far as reliable observations go. Our concept of culture, it seems to me, must now take account of differential behavioral plateaus which, in turn, are related to structural changes.

Are we to assume that the early Pleistocene hominids Coon has labeled "half-brained men"[1] possessed culture in the same sense as *Homo sapiens?* Is a fully developed human brain structure irrelevant as a pre-requisite for a fully developed cultural mode of adaptation? Is a "half brain" as good an instrument as a whole brain for the development and functioning of human speech, music, the graphic and plastic arts, abstract thinking, and religion?

Anthropologists in the twentieth century, while giving lip service to morphological evolution, have, by the special emphasis laid upon culture as the prime human differential, implied what is, in effect, an unbridged behavioral gap between ourselves and our closest relatives. This possession of culture has tended to become an all-or-none proposition.

The principal theory which exemplifies this point of view in American anthropology is the one advanced by Wissler in *Man and Culture.*[2] Wissler projected a "universal pattern" of culture full-fledged from properties he conceived the human germ plasm to possess. He said, "The pattern for culture is just as deeply buried in the germ plasm of man as the bee pattern in the bee, . . . [thus] man builds cultures because he cannot help it, there is a *drive* in his protoplasm that carries him forward even against his will." This is psychobiological determinism with a vengeance. Actually, the content categories of Wissler's universal pattern paralleled very closely the chapter headings of any standard ethnographic monograph: technology, social organization, myths and tales, religion, and so on. But Wissler did not elaborate his hypothesis for the different genera and species of fossil Hominidae. He did not say whether the

---

[1] C. S. Coon, *The Story of Man: From the First Human to Primitive Culture and Beyond,* New York: Alfred A. Knopf, 1954.

[2] C. Wissler, *Man and Culture,* New York: Thomas Y. Crowell, 1923.

universal pattern for culture was embedded in the germ plasm of *Pithecanthropus* as well as *Homo,* and *Australopithecus* had not yet been discovered. Even later writers, like Murdock,[3] who, following Wissler, have made use of the idea of a "universal pattern" which "links all human cultures, simple and complex, ancient and modern" and whose origin must therefore be sought "in the fundamental biological and psychological nature of man and in the universal conditions of human existence," do not specify what "human" refers to in a biological frame of reference. As a matter of fact, it has always remained an open question whether the generalizations that have been made about "man" apply only to the genus *Homo* or more widely; but the lack of empirical data, linguistic as well as cultural, has left the answer moldering in limbo.

Speech was one of the major items in Wissler's universal culture pattern, but can we now assert with any confidence that speech was characteristic of all the Hominidae? If the Australopithecines are included in this family, the unequivocal answer would be No! And even if we don't, there is now no unanimity of opinion.

Once we have adopted an evolutionary frame of reference, how is it possible to draw an arbitrary line between morphological evolution and behavioral evolution, between structure and function? On the functional side, even though not open to direct observation, we must assume a social and psychological dimension. The infra-human primates maintain a social existence, and the later level of adaptation we have called cultural cannot be considered apart from a psychological dimension in evolution except by *deliberately* excluding it. As a matter of fact, comparative psychology has made it its business to deal with the psychological dimension of evolution, starting far below the primate level. And learning theory as applied to man has been developed to a considerable degree through experimental observations on rats!

I believe it can be shown that among the necessary, but not sufficient, conditions prerequisite for the development of a cultural mode of adaptation are those which must have linked the early Hominidae with their precursors and with other primate forms as well. Furthermore, I think we need a term to characterize an intermediate phase or plateau of behavioral evolution which carries some, but not all, of the connotations with which the concept of culture has been invested. The term I suggest is *protocultural.*

Data on infra-human primates observed in their natural habitat or under laboratory conditions suggest some lineaments of this phrase. For deductions from comparative behavior are as methodologically legitimate as those from comparative anatomy. It seems to me, too, that the concept of protoculture may prove useful in resolving the question: Do the infra-human primates

[3] G. P. Murdock, "The Common Denominator of Cultures," *The Science of Man in the World Crisis,* ed. R. Linton, New York: Columbia University Press, 1945, pp. 123–142.

have culture? The answer to this question too often has depended upon a formal definition of culture that takes no account of the evolutionary process. At the same time the concept of protoculture should lend support to the traditional view that culture in its fully developed form *came to be* a unique "human" attribute, if human is not identified with hominid. Yet it does not leave this characteristic feature of human adaptation rootless when viewed in the perspective of behavioral evolution.

Let us now consider some of the key points involved in the differentiation I am proposing between a protocultural and a cultural level of adaptation.

1. The term culture, however defined, cannot be dissociated from the learning process. From the time of Tylor—who used the word "acquired"—culture has always been conceived as referring to learned behavior or the products of learned behavior.

2. While culture could only have emerged in a species capable of learning, the latter mode of adaptation is, of course, not a unique human phenomenon. It can be assumed as a capacity of most animals, whether primate or not. The more important question turns upon the role which learning plays, both quantitatively and qualitatively, in the total life history of the organism. In the evolution of the Hominidae in particular, there is the basic question, What is the relation between learning in the most advanced type of *Homo* and the expansion of the cerebral cortex?

3. Culture always has a locus in social groups—communities, societies—that are organized or strucured units. The functioning of these groups is dependent upon social learning, i.e., upon influences mediated in social interaction. The individual has to be groomed to become an integral unit in an on-going social system.

Infra-human primates live in structured social groups and learning is likewise one of the conditions relevant to the operation of these at a protocultural level. Bartholomew and Birdsell[4] make the point that "even on the non-human level, population density may be controlled by behavioral factors, either genetic or learned," and that "territoriality and dominance relations, which are dependent on learned behavior, contribute to the determination of group relations and population density." Carpenter[5] has explicitly stressed the necessity of socialization as a condition for the integrative functioning of such groups: "A given number of monkeys and apes does not make or equal what I have been calling a group. . . . Suppose we try this experiment. Raise in isolation animals of the species, but of the right sex and age to compose a group which meets the requirements of the formula for the average group characteristic of

[4] G. A. Bartholomew, Jr. and J. B. Birdsell, "Ecology and the Protohominids," *American Anthropologist,* 1953, Vol. 55, pp. 481–498.

[5] C. R. Carpenter, "Characteristics of Social Behavior in Non-Human Primates," New York Academy of Science, 1942, Ser. II, Vol. 4, pp. 256–257.

a species. These individuals will then be released together. What will happen? Some may so fear others that they flee. Some will be antagonistic and fight. Others will form into groups and remain together, as had been hoped or predicted, into a single organization. Why? Even though social drives are operative and social incentives are present, the monkeys have not been conditioned to each other. They have not been socialized—i.e. they have not learned to make fitting responses to each other as complexes of stimuli. What is lacking is what I have called *integration.*

"Social integration is conceived to begin with birth and to involve definable processes of social learning and adjustment. These processes are organic and involve the expressions and satisfactions of physiological drives. From one viewpoint, effective social integration of an individual conditions it in a manner to make it responsive to the communicative acts, motor expressions, including gestures, and vocalizations. These communicative acts, involving specific stimuli patterns and fitting responses, constitute the core of group coordination. Let it be remembered that the stimulus aspects of communicative acts cannot be operative except on a background of social integrations—i.e. animals which are conditioned to each other."

Tylor in 1871 defined culture as the "capabilities and habits acquired by man as a member of society." Hart[6] has expressed the opinion that this definition "more than any other single sentence [is] responsible for the present gap between the biological and social studies. . . . Is there any real evidence [he asks] that man is the only species which can possibly profit by living in a society and thus acquiring capabilities and habits which aid his survival as a species? That methods of behavior learned after birth from the fellow members of the same species do not exist at all at any other level of culture, except the human level? If such evidence did exist, it would destroy entirely the view of nature as one continuous chain; the gap between organic and superorganic evolution would be as great as that between inorganic and organic, and astronomy would be as relevant to anthropological studies as biology." Hart goes on to say that in his opinion observations such as those reported by Zuckerman (1932) in *The Social Life of Monkeys and Apes* are "strongly indicative of the fact that in social life, as in morphology, the gap between the higher apes and man is small if not smaller than Huxley[7] suspected and as few writers since Huxley have been willing to admit." The absence of references in the anthropological literature to Hart's article is itself indicative of a failure to come to grips with evolutionary theory in socio-cultural and psychological, as well as morphological, terms. Today we can say that at the infra-human level the monkey or ape

[6] C. W. M. Hart, "Social Evolution and Modern Anthropology," *Essays in Political Economy in Honour of E. J. Urwick,* ed. H. A. Innes, Toronto: University of Toronto Press, 1938, pp. 99–116.

[7] J. Huxley, *Evolution in Action,* New York: Harper and Bros., 1953.

also acquires habits as a member of society. Besides this, the functioning of these subhuman societies as integral units appears to be dependent to a large degree upon learning.

This relation between learning and social structure is continuously operative from a protocultural level up through a cultural level of adaptation. Besides sharing a gregarious existence with the infra-human primates, man also shares one of the basic mechanisms through which social life is structured at a lower level no less than at a higher one. Thus one of the basic conditions necessary for the expansion and elaboration of social behavior and group organization at a cultural level was established prior to the morphological changes that led to both erect posture and the expansion of the cortex. We can generalize even further and say that among the higher primates, even in the absence of speech, various habits may become socialized and transmitted as group attributes. For example, when the primate colony at Orange Park was established "the pioneer chimpanzees were shown how to work the drinking fountain, and through the years ape has aped ape and no further instruction of new generations has been necessary."[8] Another example would be nest-building among chimpanzees. Nissen[9] has pointed out that there is good evidence that nest-building is not instinctive like grooming, "but is rather transmitted by imitation or tuition from one generation to the next: it is, therefore, one of the very few items of behavior seen in these animals which may be classified as cultural." It might better be called *protocultural*. Culture involves much more than the social transmission through imitative learning of acquired habits (that is, the "social heredity" concept). Together with learning, however, and in the absence of speech, it may be considered one of the prerequisites of culture, perhaps the most important earmark of a protocultural level and a necessary condition for a cultural mode of life.

Eiseley[10] has called our attention to a most important fact in the course of man's development: so far as organic inheritance is concerned, man's gut is not that of a true meat-eater, nevertheless at a very early stage he became carnivorous. In other words, as a bipedal ground-dweller of the grasslands he underwent "a transition in food habits which is unique on the planet."[11] Linked with the discovery and the use of fire, the development of these new

---

[8] W. W. Howells, *Back of History: The Story of Our Own Origins,* Garden City, N. Y.: Doubleday, 1954.

[9] H. W. Nissen, "Problems of Mental Evolution in the Primate," *The Non-Human Primates and Human Evolution,* ed. J. A. Gavan, Detroit: Wayne University Press, 1955, pp. 99–109.

[10] L. C. Eiseley, "Fossil Man and Human Evolution," *Yearbook of Anthropology,* ed. W. L. Thomas, Jr., New York: Wenner Gren Foundation for Anthropological Research, 1955, pp. 61–78; "The Paleo Indians: Their Survival and Diffusion," *New Interpretations of Aboriginal American Culture History,* Washington, D. C.: Anthropological Society of Washington, 1955.

[11] Eiseley, "Fossil Man."

food habits in the Hominidae could only have become socialized and perpetuated through learning. If it be assumed that this occurred because these dietary habits had a high adaptive value and that in the beginning they were acquired and socially transmitted without speech, this would be an example of one of the earliest stages in man's protocultural development.

4. Beach[12] has stressed the fact that the new feature of mating behavior in the primates is the "emancipation" of the female from the cyclic control of the oestrous hormones. "In no other mammalian group does such continuous mating provocation occur, for all other combinations of reproductive features lead to the limitation of mating behavior to certain physiologically defined periods, even when the animals come together in groups."[13] This suggests one of the underlying conditions that has led to the widespread occurrence of the biparental family among the infra-human primates, as contrasted with uniparental family groups among the lower mammals. Males, that is, became permanent members of a social unit consisting of the females with which they mate and their offspring. This over-all pattern of association seems to remain constant irrespective of variant forms (monogamous, polygynous, or sexually communistic as among the howlers).

In addition, infra-human primate societies are relatively small in numbers; only two generations are associated. Furthermore, individuals of the younger generation may leave at puberty and form other groups. This very limited temporal association between generations, combined with the absence of symbolic communication, imposes an inherent limitation upon the possibility that the transmission and accumulation of whatever learned behavior may exist—even the simplest habits—can affect the behavior of subsequent generations in any but very limited ways. Furthermore, two of the tentative generalizations which Carpenter[14] has formulated on grouping behavior among non-human primates emphasize (a) that such groups "tend strongly to be autonomous, self-maintaining and regulating" and "express resistance and hostility to other organized groups of the same . . . species"; and (b) that "organized groups of a population of the same species in a limited region do not have super-group social mechanisms." There is thus nothing comparable with communities or tribes on the human level, and Carpenter adds, "Kinship relations are not operative, and inbreeding is the rule rather than the exception. . . ." Biparental family patterns are, then, another identifiable trait of a protocultural level which link the Hominidae with lower primate forms.

A cultural level is reached only when the biparental unit is *transcended* as

[12] F. A. Beach, "Evolutionary Changes in the Physiological Control of Mating Behavior in Mammals," *Psychological Review*, 1947, Vol. 54, pp. 297–315.

[13] M. R. A. Chance and A. P. Mead, "Social Behavior and Primate Evolution," Symposium on Social and Experimental Biology, 7 (Evolution), 1953, pp. 395–439.

[14] C. R. Carpenter, "Tentative Generalizations on the Grouping Behavior of Non-Human Primates," *Human Biology*, 1954, Vol. 26, pp. 269–276.

the sole matrix of the social relations of individuals, and when the expanding dimensions of the social order to which individuals must adjust functions as a *moral order* as well. This development, in turn, is contingent upon the emergence of a novel psychological structure. Sexual behavior now is evaluated in relation to traditionally recognized norms of conduct in a non-familial as well as a familial context. Social sanctions reinforce culturally constituted values and standards of conduct. The introception of moral values, unconsciously as well as consciously, has become a major determinant in the behavior of individuals with a *human* psyche.

5. Although so complex a topic is beyond the scope of this paper, it is necessary to say something about the study of communication in animals compared to man. As Hebb and Thompson[15] observe, "One essential key to social organization is the means of communication, in the broad sense of the way in which the behavior of one animal induces cooperative behavior in another." These writers believe that "too much attention . . . has been given to man's special vocal behavior." In their broadly gauged conception of communication they include "reflexive" or nonpurposive communication as contrasted with phenomena of a psychologically higher order. In a recent bibliographical survey, Schneirla[16] concludes, "An adequately comparative program of study of such phenomena is long overdue, particularly to clarify the relationships of concepts such as 'sign,' 'signal,' and 'symbol,' as well as the criteria of 'language,' all of which appear to suffer from a heavy load of speculation and a minimum of systematic research. Research on questions concerning levels of phenotypic relationships through successive generations of lower animal groups, certainly basic to a needed re-evaluation of the broad problem of 'culture,' should enlist the active attention of social psychologists, sociologists and anthropologists alike." Since we do not have the results of such a program available, it is necessary to get along as best we can.

In the first place, I would assume that in all social animals some kind of communication takes place, although the sensory modalities involved may differ greatly. I would also assume that communication has a common generic function whether in animals or man: it is one means by which the coordination of behavior may be facilitated.

We know, of course, that infra-human primates lack speech, although they live in structured societies. We also know that a system of orally produced signs or signals is important in one group of New World monkeys that has been closely observed and in the Old World gibbons. Are the dozen distin-

---

[15] D. O. Hebb and W. R. Thompson, "The Social Significance of Animal Studies," *Handbook of Social Psychology,* ed. G. Lindzey, Cambridge: Addison-Wesley, 1954, Vol. 1, pp. 532–561.

[16] T. C. Schneirla, "A Consideration of Some Conceptual Trends in Comparative Psychology," *Psychology Bulletin,* 1952, Vol. 49, pp. 559–597.

guishable sounds produced by the howlers and almost as many produced by the gibbons identical throughout the species and innately determined? Or is learning involved?

If, in any non-human primate species, oral *signals* were learned and transmitted, and showed intraspecific variability, this would be a protocultural fact of great significance. As against this possibility, in the case of the howlers on Barro Colorado Island, Carpenter stresses group autonomy and hostility, but a common series of oral signals. This suggests that learning is not involved. In any event, these particular sounds seem to be clearly in the category of signals. Their utterance calls for action in some particular situation. They have no representative functions. They are not vehicles for the conception of objects or events.[17] Even the chimpanzee who has been tested in the laboratory has not convinced observers that he has much capacity for symbolization, to say nothing of symbolic communication.[18] And the observations on the homebred Viki[19] make it more evident than ever before that a chimpanzee, whatever its other accomplishments, cannot be taught to speak even with maximum encouragement. On the other hand, the Hayes seemed to experience no difficulty in communicating with Viki at a sublinguistic level. This was essential to the mutual social adjustment of Dr. and Mrs. Hayes and Viki, whose role was that of a child in their home. While Viki made relatively "little use of gestures with the hand alone, without contacting an object or person," she often pointed to things she wanted, and sometimes she made use of what the Hayes called "iconic signs." An example of the latter is when "she moved her empty hand back and forth above the ironing board, apparently to show what she wanted." Personally I should call this a gestural symbol, but this only shows the terminological difficulty *we* sometimes experience in communicating about communication. The Hayes go on to report that Viki could convert such signs into "symbols" (in the narrow sense), that is, could convey a meaning through a representative act that bore an essentially arbitrary relationship to its physical character. "When Viki was very young, we never took her for a ride in the car without taking some spare diapers along. As a result, she invented the device of asking for a ride by bringing us a handful of diapers from the bathroom. Later, she no longer wore diapers, but there were still some in the bathroom, and she still brought them out when she wanted a ride. When we eventually disposed of the non-functional diaper supply, Viki asked for a ride by running into the bathroom and coming out with a handful of Kleenex tissues—which only bore a faint resemblance to diapers. These tissues had

[17] Susanne K. Langer, *Philosophy in a New Key,* Cambridge: Harvard University Press, 1942.

[18] R. M. Yerkes, *Chimpanzees: A Laboratory Colony,* New Haven: Yale University Press, 1943.

[19] Catherine Hayes, *The Ape in Our House,* New York: Harper and Bros., 1951.

never had any direct connection with rides, and by this time Viki had quite likely forgotten how the whole thing started. Except for its history, this would now appear to be communication by means of an arbitrary convention developed by the chimpanzee."

I mention this case because, in principle, this kind of symbolization developed further is exactly what we find in human speech where there is no ostensible connection between the sounds used and the object, concept, or event represented. If a mode of *gestural* communication based on such a principle had been observed functioning in a chimpanzee social group I would call it protocultural. But the only observation we have is on a single home-bred animal. Yet it is worth noting that we have here the *invention* of an arbitrary symbol motivated by the need to communicate. To become socially useful any non-iconic or arbitrary representation, whether vocal or not, must be learned by a series of individuals. This is one of the peculiar and distinctive features of human speech.

So far as communication in man is concerned, we know that the possession of speech presumes the capacity to invent and make use of extrinsic symbolic systems, that is, representation of objects and events that can be responded to not only by the organism itself but by other organisms to whom the socially significant symbol is communicated and is the vehicle of meanings. Thus skill in the manipulation of symbols is directly involved with the development of man's rational capacities. But symbolization is likewise involved with all other psychic functions—attention, perception, memory, dreams, imagination, and so on. Representative processes, both intrinsic and extrinsic, are at the root of man's ability to deal with the abstract qualities of objects and events, the ideal as well as the actual, the intangible along with the tangible, the absent as well as the present object or event, with fantasy and with reality. A negative feature of the protocultural phase is the absence of any evidence that suggests the transformation of individual experience into any kind of socially significant symbols.

6. Finally, a word about man as the tool-maker and the status of tools at archeological horizons as an index to "culture." In recent years, with the emphasis given to the priority of erect posture over cortical expansion in human evolution, the use and making of tools in the Hominidae have been put in a new perspective. Bartholomew and Birdsell[20] have gone so far as to suggest that "protohominids were dependent on the use of tools for survival." If this be true, then of course *tool-using* would long antedate speech, to say nothing of a cultural level of adaptation. But at a subcultural level quite a few animals use tools. This has been observed in birds (Darwin's finch); in infra-human primates, in particular, various species have shown considerable

[20] Bartholomew and Birdsell (1953).

facility in implementation. The Pongidae do not appear to be especially superior.

Animal psychologists, however, have not found it easy to say exactly what constitutes tool-using. Liberally interpreted, it might well include the piling up of boxes in order to secure food, the use of sticks to achieve the same end, or pole vaulting. Nissen[21] says, "Perhaps it should refer to performances such as the breaking off of a branch of a tree or the freeing of an iron bar, as described by Köhler for chimpanzees, in order to obtain an instrument for further purposes. The nearest thing to the manufacture of tools in the ordinary sense seen in primates, is the observation by Köhler of a chimpanzee fitting together two short sticks in order to make a long one." But this observation has not been repeated.

We may assume, then, that the chimpanzee and other infra-human primates have innate capacities that enable them to make occasional use of tools, and perhaps when highly motivated even to make them. But there is no evidence that would suggest more than this. We can, therefore, scarcely deny an equivalent capacity to the Hominidae. Possibly adaptation in a new environmental corridor made tool-using and fire, along with the acquisition of new food habits, of special survival value. However this may be, it seems possible that a protocultural stage in tool-using might have been reached rather early, even before the development of speech. This is suggested by the evidence of nest-building in chimpanzees. Thus, in greatly lengthening the perspective in which tool-using should be viewed, Bartholomew and Birdsell[22] may be right: ". . . in contrast to all other mammals, the larger arboreal primates are, in a sense, tool-users in their locomotion. As they move through the maze of the tree tops, their use of branches anticipates the use of tools in that they routinely employ levers and angular momentum. The grasping hands on which the locomotion and feeding of primates depends are, of course, obviously preadapted for tool use. Rather than to say that man is unique in being the 'tool-using' animal, it is more accurate to say that *man is the only mammal which is continuously dependent on tools for survival* [my italics]. This dependence on the learned use of tools indicates a movement into a previously unexplored dimension of behavior, and this movement accompanied the advent of bipedalism. With the assumption of erect posture, regular use of tools became obligatory; the ability occasionally to use tools must have preceded this in time." Oakley's statement[23] that "though man's Pliocene ancestors were not tool-makers, they were tool-users," appears to support this view. As empirical

---

[21] H. W. Nissen, "Primate Psychology," *Encyclopedia of Psychology*, ed. P. L. Harriman, New York: Citadel Press, 1946, pp. 546–570.

[22] Bartholomew and Birdsell (1953).

[23] K. P. Oakley, "Skill as a Human Possession," *History of Technology*, eds. C. J. Singer et al., Oxford: Oxford University Press, 1954, Vol. 1, pp. 1–37.

evidence Oakley refers to the baboon skulls at Taung, which presumably were pierced by artifacts in the hands of the Australopithecines.

Oakley goes on to say, "What is in doubt is when and why in their evolutionary career the Hominidae became tool-makers." Reflecting on this problem, he opens several interesting lines of speculation. He does not think it necessary to assume that the earliest hominid tool-users, or even tool-makers, possessed speech: "There are indications that speech, as we know it, though not necessarily language, was invented only at a comparatively late stage of cultural development." (The use of the term "cultural" in this statement is an example of the need for a more discriminating terminology and the recognition of developmental levels.) Oakley speculates further that "man's earliest means of communicating ideas was by gestures with the hands . . . [and that perhaps] an increasing preoccupation of the hands with the making and using of tools could have led to the change of manual to oral gesturing as a means of communication." I am not concerned here with the plausibility of this theory; but since speech has always been considered an integral part of culture, any gestural stage in the development of communication in the Hominidae would clearly be at the level I have called protocultural.

On the basis of the empirical evidence now available, Oakley, in the same paper, presented a tabulation of six stages in the development of tool-using and tool-making in the Hominidae. The first stage is labeled "occasional use of improvised tools and weapons," and refers specifically to *Australopithecus* and Pliocene hominids. The second stage is that of "occasional tool-making" and the "dawn of Early or Lower Paleolithic." (It should be recalled here that it may be no accident of discovery that the remains of *Pithecanthropus* with which tools have been found associated [Peking Man] are of Middle Pleistocene dating.) "Regular tool-making with marked standardization" does not appear until the fourth stage, at which point the precursors of *Homo sapiens* are definitely involved. The tabulation is captioned: "Six Levels of Culture on the Basis of the Use and Making of Tools." Now it is interesting to observe that although Oakley has defined man as the tool-maker, yet he does not identify man with the Hominidae and denies to the early Hominidae the capacity for speech; nevertheless he converts "culture" into an umbrella term which, when fully expanded, he uses to cover every manifestation of tool-using and tool-making throughout the family *Hominidae*. It seems to me that without drawing too fine a line, the first two stages of Oakley's scheme would be clarified by calling them *protocultural* stages.

That some such line needs to be drawn is clearly indicated in the earlier part of his article by Oakley himself. There he stresses the wide psychological gap between *tool-using* by primates and *tool-making* by man. Referring to the chimpanzee Sultan who *made* a tool, Oakley points out that this feat was accomplished with a visible reward as incentive: "There is no indication that apes can conceive the usefulness of shaping an object for use in an imagined eventuality." He then goes on to cite a famous passage in Köhler's *Mentality of Apes* in which Köhler stresses the temporal limits, past and future, of the world of the chimpanzee. It seems to me also necessary to stress the enormous difference between the unique events in the life of Sultan that led him to make the famous tool and the human situation in which the material used for making tools, the forms they take, and the techniques of manufacture, are all part of a tool-making tradition which, in turn, is part of a more inclusive cultural whole. Sultan's feat, though remarkable, is at a subcultural level because he could not learn either tool-using or tool-making from his fellow-apes. On the other hand, so far as the early Hominidae are concerned, it seems possible, as I have said, that a tradition of *tool-using* for limited purposes and on certain occasions could have arisen before the development of speech. However, if the tools found associated with some of the early *Hominidae* are interpreted in this way, the level would be protocultural rather than cultural. I would assume that one of the criteria of this protocultural level might be the absence of standardization or functional differentiation in tool forms and little, if any, evidence of inventiveness and technological progress. The opposite would be the case where a full-blown cultural level had been reached.

A number of years ago Leslie White published a paper, "On the Use of Tools by Primates."[24] The point he made has been overlooked in recent discussions of man as the tool-*maker*. His conclusion was that "on the material and mechanical side, as well as upon the intellectual and social, culture is dependent upon the use of symbols." Tool-making at the human level implies an act performed in the present which cannot be dissociated from a purposeful use of the object at some future time. In the absence, then, of some traditional means of symbolically mediated temporal orientation, how would such behavior be possible for an ape (or perhaps an early hominid)? Tool-making is *psychologically* much more complicated than tool-using. Among other things, we would have to assume that the ape possessed a capacity for "self-awareness," and that he could somehow represent himself in some future time to himself. Thus, even though Sultan made a tool, the psychological field in which he acted was qualitatively different from that in which man acts in his tool-making. The goal toward which Sultan's needs were directed was in his immediate perceptual field, and the reward he claimed was not long delayed. But a far more important point of difference is that a man does not just make a tool: quite apart from any technological knowledge involved, he *shapes* it, and for this he must have some image in mind which necessitates intrinsic

---

[24] Leslie A. White, "On the Use of Tools by Primates," *Journal of Comparative Psychology,* 1942, Vol. 34, pp. 369–374.

representative processes. Besides, the shape image he has is not usually idiosyncratic: it is related to the shape of the tools in his cultural tradition in the same way that the material used and the technological knowledge involved are related. It is difficult to see, then, how these factors could be integrated or transmitted without speech. Yet in Pumphrey's discussion of the relation of speech to tools he remarks that there is "no valid reason for assigning intellect to a maker of implements."[25]

Thirty years ago Grace A. de Laguna[26] argued that tool-making is integral with man's capacity for dealing indirectly with things through the functioning of analytical discrimination of their objective properties not only in relation to himself, but to other things. The tool-maker must be able to distinguish clearly among properties relative to the ends he has in view. This kind of perception transcends the infra-human primate level: it necessitates conceptual thought. Thus, "it is scarcely credible, even aside from the more theoretical psychological considerations, that the art of chipping stone implements could have been developed by men who had not yet learned to speak." Furthermore, to have undergone any great development, since "the evolution of tools is essentially a social evolution"—or as we would now say, cultural—a primary condition was "the permanent organization of the social group, bound together by language." In a later, unpublished manuscript de Laguna has succinctly expressed her thought by saying, *"Homer faber* is *Homo cogitans."*

Pumphrey seems to think that the spider's web and tools actually belong to the same category. If "man" be defined as a tool maker rather than a tool-user, and artifacts in archeological horizons be interpreted as evidence of a "human" status, this characterization remains restricted, if not arbitrary, in significance unless the socio-psychological implications of tool making as an integral part of the problem are fully clarified. A scientific definition of man, to be really inclusive in scope, is contingent upon the integration of all relevant data and upon an analysis that gives full weight to all the socio-psychological factors involved in a human existence.

My purpose in suggesting that we need to discriminate between different levels of adaptation in the behavioral evolution of man is based on the fact that structural criteria alone do not seem sufficient to define a human level of existence. The recognition of a protocultural stage takes cognizance of behavior linkages between the Hominidae and other primates which, although they may be difficult to deal with, are of no less theoretical importance than the more precisely determinable morphological facts.

---

[25] R. J. Pumphrey, "The Origin of Language," *Acta Psychologica,* 1953, Vol. 9, pp. 219–239.
[26] Grace A. de Laguna, *Speech: Its Function and Development,* New Haven: Yale University Press, 1927.

Summary

1. Many definitions of Man have been proposed, but due to limited knowledge or a unilateral disciplinary approach they have been restricted in scope and have not met with unqualified acceptance.

2. The problem has persisted even into a period when reliable knowledge about the chronological aspects of man's development has been accumulating at an unprecedented rate in archaeology and physical anthropology; when novel behavioral observations on infra-human primates have become available; when the data of cultural anthropology have increased immensely, and psychologists have gained new insights into the determinants and mechanisms of behavior.

3. A human level of existence needs definition in more than structural terms, and the behavioral levels of adaptation observed in living primates are as legitimate a basis for reconstructing behavioral evolution as are deductions from comparative anatomy.

4. The term *protoculture* is introduced as a convenient term for conceptualizing a behavioral plateau that links the Hominidae with other primates. At this stage we have in rudimentary and unintegrated form many of the indispensable conditions for the development of culture in its unique form at the human level: learned behavior, biparental families, structured social groups, some form of communication, tool-using if not tool-making.

5. A further exploration of the distinction between a protocultural and cultural level of adaptation, giving full weight to the socio-psychological factors involved in a human existence, should make possible a more adequate and scientific definition of man.

17 Changing Views of Man and Culture

FRED W. VOGET

A summary article seems in order. Professor Fred Voget, in a masterful paper, shows the history of the culture concept as an evolutionary process going through several stages. Through Voget's analytical eyes we see "culture" going

SOURCE: Abridged and adapted from "Man and Culture: An Essay in Changing Anthropological Interpretation" by Fred W. Voget. Reproduced by permission of the author and the American Anthropological Association from *American Anthropologist*, Vol. 62, No. 5, 1960, pp. 943–965.

from psychogenic evolutionism *to* historical interactionism *to a* holistic cultural functionalism *and finally toward a* synthetic interactionism. *The nonitalicized words, clearly, are shorthand descriptions of complex processes, fully described in the following paper.*

Introduction

This paper is an attempt at defining the shifting interpretations of man and culture from 19th century evolutionists to the present. I have not tried to explain why anthropological views of man and culture have shifted, but have confined myself largely to exposition, content to show that when the interpretation of culture has changed, the explanation of man's relation to culture also has moved into line, and vice versa. Finally, I have endeavored to point out some of the significant implications which more recent developments hold for the future of anthropology and for an integrated science of man.

Since anthropology in its scientific aim has been committed to a cumulative unfolding of the human reality, it would be strange indeed if it did not demonstrate periodic shifts in its theoretical conceptions of that reality, defined traditionally as man and his cultural milieu. We might expect, too, that changes in the interpretation of culture would result in shifts in the view of how man relates to culture, and in the very nature of man himself. Anthropologists admittedly have avoided controversy in their own ranks over "man's fundamental nature" and they certainly have never tried to spell it out in detail. Yet, the issue of man's nature—how this primary datum may influence his cultural behavior and how in turn learned social behavior may modify basic nature—hovers in the background and intrudes upon every explanation of culture patterns and how culture changes.

Psychogenic Evolutionism (1860 to 1900)

The so-called cultural evolutionists of the 19th century must be credited with the first conceptualization of man and culture that can be called anthropological. Their basic ideas stemmed from the philosophical rationalism of the 18th century *philosophes* and the scientific positivism of the early 19th century. The political theories of Locke, Rousseau, and Condorcet carry basic assumptions that were to influence the later cultural evolutionists, including the idea that all men are alike essentially, that in their better natures men are reasoning beings and strive naturally to improve themselves and their conditions by acts of intellect and moral will.[1]

---

[1] John Locke, *Two Treatises of Government,* Hafner Library of Classics, No. 2, New York:

The approach of the evolutionists to man and his culture rested on four basic assumptions. First, they assumed that mankind was a part of nature, operating according to the laws of the universe. Second, they assumed that the natural laws governing development were unchanging through time as exemplified in the geological principle of uniformitarianism. Third, evolutionists accepted the idea that natural processes tended to move progressively from a simplicity to a complexity, from the unorganized to the organized, from something that was lesser to something that was better. Fourth, in the evolutionist view, men throughout the world held similar potentials but differed basically from each other in a quantitative development of intelligence and experience.

When applied to mankind the principle of uniformitarianism committed the evolutionists to the idea that whatever governed man's cultural development in the past governs this development equally today. Further, since man's intelligence accounted for his distinctive quality in relation to the animal world and allowed him to create social institutions and culture, it followed that mankind everywhere shared a common psychic unity. If man in the primitive world differed from his civilized confreres, it was not because of any qualitative differences in his mind, but because in the civilized world man's mental potential, his intelligence, was cultivated and developed in greater degree. In any society a man's intelligence was a product of his experiences, exemplifying the degree to which his intellective faculty could emerge and thrive in that cultural milieu. Yet, as the evolutionists saw it, phylogenetically man's rationality followed an inevitable development, as if it were driven by some inner evolutionary and cosmic force. Men in primordial days, as contemporary savages were witness, began with a limited intelligence, and as mankind moved into the cultural stages of Barbarism and Civilization, the forces of passion and of appetite gave way in progressive steps to the force of reason. Everywhere the natural history of mankind could be described as the inevitable progression from Savagery through Barbarism to Civilization. The dynamic quality of mankind, the fundamental link with universal processes, must be sought in the processes of the human mind, which was never static, but which, ever emergent, moved progressively upward in competition with baser instincts.[2]

From their writings it is clear that the evolution to which the 19th century theorists of man and culture committed themselves was basically *psychogenic*

Hafner Publishing Co., 1956; Jean J. Rousseau, *The Social Contract and Discourses,* London: J. M. Dent and Sons, 1913; Marie J. Condorcet, *Sketch for a Historical Picture of the Progress of the Human Mind,* trans. Jane Barraclough, London: Weidenfeld and Nicholson, 1955.

[2] Edward B. Tylor, *Anthropology,* London: Watts and Co., 1937; E. Sidney Hartland, *Primitive Paternity,* 2 vols., London: D. Nutt, 1909–10.

rather than cultural.[3] Yet cultural forms were vital to the evolutionist position since they held the key to interpreting man's psychic development. From qualitative differences in their cultures it was evident that peoples throughout the world had to be viewed in different stages of mechanical, intellectual, and moral progress. By arranging the institutions of mankind along a mental coordinate—from the least to the most reasoned—a chronological chart of man's intellectual history could be plotted and "index" institutions could be assigned to natural stages, quite like the geological and life charts used by students of the earth and of life forms. Once this intellectual-historical chart was completed, an institution could be readily assigned to it and the intellectual and historical stage of a particular people could be marked accurately and their future progress plotted within predictable limits.

The assumption that illogical and reasonless customs belong to an earlier time, whereas customs in agreement with a measure of reason must be later, allowed the evolutionists to breathe historicity into customs which lay beyond written documents or the dated chronologies unearthed by archeologists. The "doctrine of survivals," as this conceptualization came to be called, was a necessary corollary to the basic assumptions of psychogenic evolution and psychic uniformitarianism.[4] Now, with the use of analogues from cultures around the world, it would be possible to peel back layer after layer of the psycho-historic strata in man's progress until the very bedrock of man's intellectual beginnings had been reached. With the "doctrine of survivals" the evolutionists apparently were able to clinch their case for a psycho-cultural prehistory and to place their natural history of the mind on a firm scientific footing.

The commitment to a mind emergent also colored the entire evolutionist effort to describe and explain man in relation to his culture. The emphasis on reason did not deprive man of his feeling states. Affect, indeed, was a part of man's being, but it played a far more effective role in his past than in his present civilized state.[5] Contemporary savages were more passionate and childlike, and the passage from childhood to adolescence and to adulthood provided an appropriate analogue for the stages of Savagery, Barbarism, and Civilization, each of which rested on a more comprehensive and logically arranged experience than the stage which preceded it. Savage and Civilized men were rational in essence and operated psychologically by laws of association, but in their savage experience primitive men were wont to mis-associate

---

[3] Edward B. Tylor, *Primitive Culture,* 2 vols., Boston: Easter and Lauriat, 1874, Vol. 1, p. 68.

[4] Tylor (1874), Vol. 1, chaps. 3 and 4; Margaret T. Hodgen, "The Doctrine of Survival," *American Anthropologist,* 1931, Vol. 33, pp. 307–324; John F. McLennan, *Studies in Ancient History,* London: Macmillan, 1896.

[5] Hartland (1909), pp. 255–256; Tylor (1874), pp. 30–31.

ideas and lacked the exacting technique of critical thinking which could free them from their erroneous associations. For all that, primitive man had achieved some signal triumphs through speculative reason both in technology and in the explanation of the world. In magic he even had attained a conception of causal determinism which was analogous to the determinism of scientific explanation.[6] In the final analysis, man's progressive advances in the early stages, as they are now, derived from the speculative reasoning of "primitive philosophers" who lighted the way for the others. It followed that men, at least the intellective elite, were able to transcend the limitations of their cultural experiences and to advance the accumulation of knowledge which would lead to change and progress.

Since evolutionists had defined the essential process of reality in terms of thought, with man moving from unconscious to conscious processes, their natural history of man found little place for documented chronological history. For evolutionists the history of the events was submerged in the universal process, and while diffusion of forms and ideas was admitted, and also special adaptations to local environments, particulars such as these did not alter the general trend in independent institutional development. Historic events could be—and in practice tended to be—ignored in the interests of the broad comparative effort. So, too, the momentary historic regressions illustrated by the fall of empires were of secondary importance to the march along the road to progress and civilization.[7]

Historical "Interactionism" (1900–1925)

The second view of man and culture appears at the century mark when Boas called for repudiation of "metaphysical" presuppositions that "prejudiced" the study of man and culture alike. In place of the psychogenic "history" of the evolutionists he demanded a verified "scientific history." The grand scheme of comparative reconstruction should be abandoned and attention directed to particulars, with the express purpose of seeing how unique events actually were connected in time and space.[8]

In the new scientific view, the proper study of mankind should focus on specific cultures and their mutual interconnections and unique environmental adaptations in place of the philosophic study of culture-in-general. Obviously, anthropological data seldom presents the investigator with historically documented materials, but in the absence of precise documentation culture forms

---

[6] James G. Frazer, *The Golden Bough, A Study in Magic and Religion,* 3 vols., London: Macmillan, 1900, Vol. 1, p. 61.

[7] Lewis H. Morgan, *Ancient Society,* New York: Holt & Co., 1877.

[8] Franz Boas, "The Occurrence of Similar Inventions in Areas Widely Apart," *Science,* 1887, Vol. 9, pp. 485–486; *Race, Language and Culture,* New York: Macmillan, 1940.

could be carefully plotted and analyzed to disclose probable connections—then, and only then, could culture forms be explained as independent inventions. Even independent inventions might not yield identical psychic processes which the evolutionists require. Before any form in one area could be equated in all respects with another form in another area and thus be accepted as a parallel form, rigorous analysis must prove that both products are not the result of independent yet convergent psychological processes, or that either or both have diffused from the same or different sources.

The new historical-interactionist approach obviously introduced a new conceptualization of the man and culture reality. Causation was not immanent to a structure as the evolutionists had argued but lay outside the structure. A culture, for example, was not the product of internal processes so much as it was a consequence of interactive processes which involved one culture with another. The processes of culture growth were best described by terms like diffusion, adaptation, and interaction rather than by independent origin and parallelism, although these latter could not be wholly ruled out.[9] As cultures came to be viewed in terms of the history of their forms they were considered to be complicated accumulations of traits and complexes rather than organized systems.

By very definition of the man and culture problem the historical approach to culture could not find much place for the study of cultures as systems nor for the individual as a structured personality. The individual, like the culture to which he belonged, was a product of a complex growth, varying from others (as his culture) by virtue of his unique biology and special (historical) experiences in society. Though subject to the conditions of his cultural environment, which imposed severe limitations on the range of individual choice and action, the person nevertheless interacted with his cultural environment, adapted it selectively, influenced it at times, and even transcended it in deviant ways.[10]

In the new historical view the individual was considered subject to habit in much of his daily behavior. Habituation made for slow change and "cultural inertia was more evident in the change process than active efforts to move in new directions. Habit and feeling were as much a part of man's behavior in civilized as in primitive communities."[11] The historicists were wont to point out analogies between primitive and civilized behaviors. Modern men had totemistic inclinations in naming fraternities and athletic clubs after animals, and, if primitives made use of talismans to protect themselves, civilized men had their "good luck" charms to tide themselves over dangerous situations. "There

[9] Boas (1940), p. 297; Robert H. Lowie, "On the Principle of Convergence in Ethnology," *Journal of American Folklore,* 1912, Vol. 25, pp. 24–43.
[10] Paul Radin, *Primitive Man as a Philosopher,* New York: Dover Publications, 1957.
[11] Franz Boas, *The Mind of Primitive Man,* New York: Macmillan, 1924.

is a streak of logic as well as much irrationality in the make-up of the primitive mind; the same holds of the modern mind."[12]

The historicists, like the evolutionists, seemed to enunciate, "man is one," but they followed it quickly with "civilizations are many," since each culture is a product of a unique concatenation of historic events. The historicists in a sense were the harbingers of functionalism, but they did not understand it well, and, besides, they were too involved in the historic "accidental" processes to accept the structural (immanent) determinism which full-bodied functionalism implied.

The new scientific view of the man-in-culture process led empirical historicists to reject all efforts to define qualitative differences that would separate primitive from civilized men. There could be no "pre-logical" primitive mentality.[13]

Since men and their cultures were largely the result of "accidental" historic events and interactive adjustments, "scientific" historicism did not admit any kind of determinism. Man's behavior in any time and clime could not be viewed as biologically-determined, geographically-determined, nor culturally-determined.

Culturalism—Functionalism—Holism (1925–1940)

As American historical interactionists came to grips with the man-in-culture process some of them moved to a redefinition of culture and of the individual's relation to his "superorganic" milieu.[14] Culture was held to be an order of distinct reality, a "superorganic" in every way, "explainable only in terms of itself."

The raising of culture from its complex interrelations with other dimensions of the human context to a special and distinct reality operating according to laws of its own being initiated the third view of culture and of the man-in-culture process. Now the individual had no real part in the cultural process and the anthropologist had as little need for psychological processes for explanation as Watsonian Behaviorism had for mind and consciousness. The new interpretation made the members of any society an effect of culture—a veritable image and distinct impression of the cultural process. There was no marked effort to treat cultures as systems, and efforts of Kulturkreislehre to define "historic" culture-systems that diffused as units were roundly criticized. As Lowie put it:

---

12 Alexander A. Goldenweiser, *History, Psychology and Culture,* New York: A. A. Knopf, 1933, p. 185.

13 Goldenweiser (1933), pp. 179–188; Robert H. Lowie, *The History of Ethnological Theory,* New York: Farar and Rinehart, 1937.

14 A. L. Kroeber, "The Superorganic," *American Anthropologist,* 1917, Vol. 19, pp. 163–213.

> . . . I prefer to practice the historical method by tracing the distribution in time and space of traits with sharply defined individuality and to establish sequences where the distribution is spatially continuous or rendered plausible by documentary evidence or at least by known ethnographic principles; and the establishment of more ambitious schemes strikes me as distinctly premature.

The new cultural-historical determinists relied on Behaviorism to supply the psychological underpinning of man-in-culture processes. The evidences of conditioning presented by Pavlov were accepted casually as quite congruent with the cultural process, whereas Freudian interpretations that called attention to the reactions of individuals to cultural processes generally were vigorously opposed or ignored.

Functionalism, as interpreted by Malinowski and Radcliffe-Brown broke the historic barrier imposed by the historicists.[15] In the functionalist view, cultures were structured systems and their basic processes were largely maintenance operations. The systemic qualities of cultures and their processes then were more vital to anthropology than the tracing of historic connections and developments. Therefore, the basic processes of culture were not historic, but processes of internal and reciprocating connections. As it developed, functionalism divided into two major streams, with Malinowski stressing the relation between common biological needs and culture, while Radcliffe-Brown emphasized the structured interconnections and maintenance processes of the social system.

Both the "biological" and "institutional" branches of functionalism renewed the question of human nature and the nature of human adjustment to the cultural milieu. For Malinowski, man's universal biological needs constituted the basic reality with which anthropologists should begin their study of man-in-culture. In the final analysis culture was no more than a very complicated instrument for the fulfillment of essential survival needs. However, in developing instrumental cultural behaviors in reference to basic needs, men in different societies built up secondary need-motivations connected to these instrumental cultural behaviors.

Malinowski's need-oriented functionalism challenged the unique and accidental reality of the historicists and seated the basic human reality in man's psychological processes—right where the evolutionists had sought it in the first place. Man, in effect, was a culture-building creature because of the necessities of his inner structure.

---

[15] Bronislaw Malinowski, "Culture," *Encyclopedia of the Social Sciences,* New York: Macmillan, 1931, Vol. 4, pp. 621–645; *A Scientific Theory of Culture and Other Essays,* Chapel Hill: University of North Carolina Press, 1944; A. R. Radcliffe-Brown, "On the Concept of Function in Social Science," *American Anthropologist,* 1935, Vol. 37, pp. 394–402; *Structure and Function in Primitive Society,* Glencoe, Ill.: The Free Press, 1952.

Radcliffe-Brown, in developing institutional functionalism, also engaged in psychological problems and processes. However, within the theoretical context of social structure the important psychological operations both for the individual and for the group were derived from social interaction and role expectancies.

Whatever differences Malinowski and Radcliffe-Brown may have had over the "ultimate" sources of the human cultural reality, they were in agreement on one thing—it was grounded in *sentiment.* All cultural behavior is charged and sustained by an emotional configuration.

It is apparent that functionalists turned the anthropological stream in the direction of system and integration and laid the groundwork for describing and analyzing cultures as unified structures. Their focus on basic social and psychological processes contributed heavily to the climate of thinking that led to culture and personality studies.

The systemic study of cultures, in terms of their institutional structurings and functions, implied and indeed asserted a tightness of fit between the individual and his culture. His sociopsychological processes were grounded in emotional configurations which were largely learned, habituated and automatic if not wholly conditioned and unconscious in their operations. Functionalists, holistic configurationists, and cultural-historical determinists alike were in agreement on this datum of the man-in-culture reality, although they each arrived at this conclusion by different routes. The need-oriented functionalism of Malinowski alone provided a base for individual escape from the culture-press, since these needs were found to be in opposition to most normative specifications. Reactive behaviors based on shared need-structurings thus would allow in theory considerable numbers of individuals to initiate deviant behaviors that might transcend the pattern requirements. However, after defining this position in his early works, Malinowski left it fallow and pursued his man and culture analyses through the study of "institutions."

Synthetic Interactionism and Complexity (1940 to Present)

The period beginning with the mid-thirties and enduring to the present is marked by the appearance of outstanding trends and reappraisals in man-in-culture relationships. Developments in new fields, such as acculturation and applied anthropology, and the gradual penetration and acceptance of a tempered Freudian interpretation of personality processes, not only traced new ground but also brought accepted interpretations of man and culture under challenge. The new appraisal generally stressed the complexities of the human situation and of the need for exploring in depth the different dimensions of the human reality. There was also a growing realization that the concepts and techniques of any single social science were inadequate to the task, and that to be successful the attack on understanding and explaining human behavior must be a concerted and cooperative venture by all the social disciplines.

The social and psychological cut which functionalism brought to anthropology seated process and reality in role expectancies and in sentiments (sociopsychological processes). At best functionalists admitted a selected aspect of culture to their reality. Chapple and Coon demonstrated that social interactionism did not need the concept of culture at all to describe and explain role interaction among members of a society. Wherever individual people were studied in the interactive field situation, the concept of culture was found either too vague as an heuristic device or too indeterminant in explaining individual variations in a relatively homogeneous milieu.[16]

Part of the controversy during reappraisal involved the definition and redefinition of the concept of culture itself. For some, culture still remained "That complex whole [of] . . . knowledge, belief, art, morals, law, custom, and any other capabilities and habits acquired by man as a member of a society."[17] On the other hand, some prominent anthropologists were asserting that culture was best described as a system of "conventionalized understandings" that lay behind the manifest act.[18] In this latter view, culture would not include the products of man's organized efforts, the tools and furniture of his dwellings, for example, but would apply to man's ideas about what form they should take and how they should be valued and used.

Indeed, culture, like personality, had gone processual and psychological. However, the psychology of culture as Linton and Kluckhohn defined it in the early forties still rested on habit-conditioning. For example, Linton observed that cultures usually are perpetuated "unconsciously and as a part of the normal processes of individual training and socialization.[19]

Nevertheless, there was a growing consensus that the fit between the individuals of any society and their culture was far looser than formerly assumed. Individuals were not conditioned automatons and neither were they simple reactive products of special childhood experiences, such as breast-feeding, swaddling, and toilet discipline. Individuals in any society were partly this and something more: they were involved in reactive responses to the sociocultural milieu in which they found themselves and moved also to act out of

---

[16] Elliot D. Chapple and Carleton S. Coon, *Principles of Anthropology,* New York: Henry Holt & Co., 1942. See also John W. Bennett, "Interdisciplinary Research and the Concept of Culture," *American Anthropologist,* 1954, Vol. 56, pp. 169–179.

[17] Edward B. Tylor (1874), Vol. 1, p. 1.

[18] Robert Redfield, *The Folk Culture of Yucatan,* Chicago: University of Chicago Press, 1941, p. 132.

[19] Ralph Linton, "Nativistic Movements," *American Anthropologist,* 1943, Vol. 45, pp. 230–240; Clyde Kluckhohn, "Covert Culture and Administrative Problems," *American Anthropologist,* 1943, Vol. 45, pp. 213–229.

inculcated feeling-states; but they also acted out of deliberation and made thoughtful as well as thought-provoking choices.

In these new assessments of the man-in-culture reality it is apparent that human nature was held to have universal qualities. Part of these qualities were rooted in the biological processes and part in psychic potentialities associated with the ego processes of mastery or defense. While mankind shared the cognitive process, the basic axes of human response were grounded in emotional and largely unconscious operations. Man acted from bases which were better described by anxiety, hostility, compensation, and the like.[20]

In the view that human action was moved largely by affect-states to which the individual was habituated, a thread of continuity was maintained with prior anthropological assessments that man was not predominantly a deliberative actor. Thoughtful action more often followed than preceded the act, as myth rationalized and gave meaning to ritual. However, in giving primacy to affect-states, and especially in the place accorded to reactive constellations, contemporary anthropologists carried themselves beyond the traditional anthropological view.

Changes in the conceptualization of how any culture was organized and integrated moved in step with the view that the individual could not be conceived as a tightly integrated mirror for culture. Cultures might in some instances be configurated by a special ethos, but more often they were unified by interacting "themes" which demonstrated recurrent consistencies and inconsistencies. Opler, who first summarized this conceptualization, defined a theme as a postulate, expressed or implied, about the nature of the world and of man, of man's relation to man, and of the desirable and the undesirable. Individuals within a society operated with culture patterns that usually embodied these basic assumptions.[21] Studies in the values-base of various cultures also supported the conclusion that cultures were more or less consistently organized and oriented, but not tightly integrated wholes. Moreover, if a value, as Kluckhohn defined it, represented a conceptualization, "explicit, or implicit, distinctive of an individual or characteristic of a group, of the desirable which influences the selection from available modes, means, and ends of action,"[22] it is apparent that judgment in human action is admitted and the individual no longer is conceived to be a habituated social unit or subject wholly to unconscious feeling-states. The trend moved cautiously in the direction [of the view that] man is a complex of rational-irrational processes.

---

[20] Clyde Kluckhohn, Henry A. Murray, and David Schneider, *Personality in Nature, Society, and Culture,* New York: A. A. Knopf, 1953.

[21] Morris E. Opler, "Themes as Dynamic Forces in Culture," *American Journal of Sociology,* 1945, Vol. 51, pp. 198–206.

[22] Clyde Kluckhohn, "Values and Value-Orientations," *Toward a General Theory of Action,* ed. Talcott Parsons and E. A. Shils, Cambridge: Harvard University Press, 1951.

The period of reappraisal also witnessed some advance in the analysis of the nature and structure of culture patterns. The convergent effects of these new developments added up to a loosening of the tightly-knit unity of cultures as previously conceived and limited the impact of culture on the individuals of the society. As Linton observed, some patterns are applicable to all, hence "universals," whereas others are "specialties," and still others no more than "alternatives."[23] Greater cognizance was taken of the fact that culture patterns were phrased in two modes, the ideal and the real, and in any society the behavior of individuals might or might not show a close approximation to the ideal specifications. In final analysis, culture patterns were seen to represent a consensus in the case of the ideal pattern and a statistical (modal) construct in the case of the real or behavioral pattern.

Studies of cultures in change likewise brought fresh support to efforts at redefining the man-and-culture reality. The contact of peoples of different cultures had always been given a front rank position in the historical interpretation of culture growth and spread. When the problem shifted from plotted culture-traits to specific cultures undergoing firsthand contact, the complexity of the process began to surface. Acculturative situations (defined as persistent and pervasive contact events) underscored the fact that the human reality is a complex of interacting processes. Cultural homogeneity gave way in the change process and personal conflicts indicated the importance of subjective factors for understanding what was happening. A state of normlessness (anomie) was described for certain individuals, as in the case of "detribalized" Africans and "mixed blood" Indians. Thus, under conditions of disorganizing contact, individuals were described as virtually stripped of their sociocultural learnings and spurred to the fulfillment of ego-needs. At the same time it became evident that in breaking away from the traditional way of life, people were not at ease in an unpredictable milieu and strove to standardize their behaviors and so to stabilize their expectancies. But, in place of the mirror modification of traditional complexes, as commonly interpreted by the historicists, it was now recognized that far-reaching changes and reinterpretations of culture forms occurred in the acculturative process.

Summary and Reflections

In our brief historical review, anthropological conceptualizations of the man and culture reality are suggested to be four: (1) psychogenic evolutionism, (2) historical interactionism, (3) culturalism-functionalism-holism, and (4) synthetic interactionism. Devastating criticisms can and have been leveled at each

---

[23] Ralph Linton, *The Study of Man,* New York: Appleton-Century, 1936.

of these approaches, but in the overview, it is possible to see that each has contributed to the enrichment of anthropological awareness in problem, method, and reality. The anthropological reality-universe has been gradually broadened and deepened by the experiences derived from investigations within the narrower confines of evolutionism, historical interactionism, and culturalism, functionalism, and holism. At the moment it does not appear as if anthropologists are out of the woods by any means—they still have much exploring to do, but they now appear to have a firmer grasp on the *complexities of the human reality* and are in a much better position to define problems and to program their explanations. The emergence of "interactionism" as constituting the basic process of the human reality, and as comprising reality itself, is a signal event in the development of anthropology.

The commitment to interactionism also is notable since it seeks to describe live situations in terms of their actional processes. There is a shift from the static description of special forms (e.g., cultural traits and complexes) to the processes that have given rise to these forms, their persistencies and changes.

Through process, explanation of the *human* event rather than a cultural, "social," "geographical," or "historical," event turns out to be the essential problem. Realization of this fact explains why some anthropologists gradually have concluded that the concept of culture is inadequate to explain the human reality.

Clarification of the scientific problem in terms of human events and associated processes means that reality is no longer fragmented, and indeed cannot be organized for purposes of explanation into variant hierarchies of autonomous realities. Reality for man is not in one instance biological, in another, geographical, or social, psychological, cultural, historical, functional, or evolutionary. Each event in the human reality rather is an interacting configuration of these several analytical components of reality.

Acceptance of this basic datum (a unified interacting reality linked through time) is an achievement of no mean merit. With a unified reality-universe fully in mind there is no longer any need to discover a special autonomous reality particular to anthropology nor to debate whether it is cultural, historico-cultural, sociopsychological, functional, or evolutionary.

For some a denial of the autonomy of culture as the unique and distinctive anthropological reality may prove a difficult adjustment since it would appear to be a denial of anthropology itself. However, in its very development anthropology demonstrates the necessity for a complex and interrelated interpretation oriented to a unified human universe rather than one based on a narrow and separate dimension. By holding to culture as the sole reality in the human universe, and by asserting its independence and primacy over the other dimensions, anthropologists actually may have denied themselves what they have held to be the goals of their science—namely, to view man and his environment as a whole and to "search for a set of principles which governs man's physical and cultural development."[24]

18 Interdisciplinary Research and the Concept of Culture

JOHN W. BENNETT

Professor Voget concludes that culture is neither an autonomous phenomenon, nor one which has primacy over other dimensions—social, psychological, or historical. This argument is developed in an interesting manner by Professor Bennett whose concern is with the utility of "culture" for research purposes. Professor Bennett, whose own research career has spanned several continents over more than two decades, has been a leading figure in an intellectual struggle which has concerned many anthropologists. Namely, to what extent is the anthropologist a member of but one *"community" all of whose members consider themselves "anthropologists"? And, to what extent must the anthropologist attach himself to a larger group called "social scientists"? Professor Bennett's ideas, as of 1954, are here supplemented by his views as of November 1969, which appear at the end of the article.*

Interdisciplinary Research

In recent years the most striking characteristic of the arena of sciences dealing with human phenomena has been the tendency toward interdisciplinary attack on problems of common interest. The basic scientific objective is *explanation* rather than description, and an explanatory approach can yield interpretations with a high proportion of consensus among the participant scholars. Such consensus, and such interpretations, are made possible by the adoption of a *common conceptual scheme*, or some approximation thereof. This type of sci-

[24] Ralph Beals and Harry Hoijer, *An Introduction to Anthropology*, 2nd ed., New York: Macmillan, 1959, p. 6.

SOURCE: Abridged and adapted from "Interdisciplinary Research and the Concept of Culture" by John W. Bennett. Reproduced by permission of the author and the American Anthropological Association from *American Anthropologist*, Vol. 56, No. 1, 1954, pp. 169–179.

entific activity, and the emerging conceptual scheme,[1] is referred to variously as "the multidimensional approach," "structural-functional analysis," "problem-oriented social science," "behavior science," "action theory," and the like, the choice of term depending upon which aspect of the general activity one wishes to utilize for the name, or which particular sciences—biology, psychology, sociology, etc.—are included in the scheme.

Anthropologists have engaged in this movement in varying ways. Culture and personality studies represent one of the earlier manifestations of the trend, and, while these have recently been in process of merging into the broader approach of which they were a forerunner, they continue to attract large numbers of young anthropologists. The "applied anthropology" movement has developed interdisciplinary tendencies of a diverse and often constructive variety. Other anthropologists, frequently isolated in small institutions or in "combined" departments with other social scientists, have undertaken joint research programs with representatives from other fields. Still other anthropologists are involved in new educational experiments, like the Harvard Department of Social Relations, where the avowed intent is to establish the behavior sciences on an integrated footing.[2]

The approach is in part based on the need emerging during World War II for highly integrated information covering a large number of relevant variables. Cultural data alone, no more than sociological, psychological, political, or economic, were sufficient to answer the needs for information and prediction that accompanied highly organized psychological, economic, political, and military warfare. Anthropology as traditionally developed could supply, for example, detailed comparative and descriptive data on exotic world areas or measurements for physiological reactions of pilots, but the extent to which anthropology contributed more depended, not on anthropology itself, but on *the affiliation of anthropologists with members of other disciplines, where teamwork was the rule.* If answers to questions which demand a careful explanatory accounting of the functions of a large assortment of variables are to be given, some sort of "uni-operational" conceptual scheme (term used in *Human Organization* 1952), which permits the several sciences to equate

[1] Lest there be some misunderstanding concerning the relationship of research to common conceptual schemes, the following may be said: The intention or desire to do interdisciplinary research is not sufficient in itself to insure success. Success, measured by the ability of the research team to transform its problems and its data into mutually comprehensible categories requires some type of conceptual scheme, or body of concepts, which transcend the phenomenological boundaries of the special disciplines involved. The conduct of the research therefore simultaneously becomes a search for a scheme, and the progressive evolution of such a scheme. In some cases existing schemes may be taken over more or less intact—but in such instances they usually become revised in the process of research. Consequently it becomes possible to speak of "common conceptual schemes" both as desiderata of true interdisciplinary research, and, at one and the same time, as products of that research.

[2] Defunct in 1970 [ed.].

observations and operations, must be utilized. And, in turn, a conceptual scheme of this kind visualizes the component sciences not as independent areas of knowledge but rather as *groups of experts* on specific sets of variables, e.g., cultural anthropologists on values, sociologists on roles and interaction, biologists on genes, psychologists on personality mechanisms, economists on a special institutional phase of cultural and social behavior, and so on.

Now, a research design of this type places certain demands upon those who participate within it. In the first place, it requires a "multidimensional" perspective toward problems of man—a perspective which automatically rejects reified and/or "single variable" explanations of human phenomena. Second, it is methodologically eclectic as regards the collection of data on any variable, e.g., data on group regularities or "culture" might be collected as well in laboratory situations or by attitude survey methods as in the fieldwork approach. Third, it requires very considerable methodological rigor, and more, transformability of the data of one variable into the others (leading again to a rejection of explanatory reification of any descriptive of phenomenological variable). Fourth, it is contemptuous of any discipline which makes heavy claims for its own uniqueness or completeness.

If these features of interdisciplinary research are given some thought, it may become apparent that they clash with some features of the professional discipline of anthropology. Insistence on "culture" as the master concept with both descriptive and explanatory power, rather large claims for anthropology's expertness and destiny, the insulation of many anthropologists from current methodologically complex aspects of social science, and certain other aspects of our contemporary science are all somewhat awkward from the point of view of the interdisciplinary scientist. This might conceivably place the anthropologist working in these interdisciplinary projects in a peculiar position. On the one hand, he is called upon to adopt certain rules of the game (see above) and to perform as a particular technical expert—as an expert on the patterned aspects of group behavior, for example (note we did not say "culture"!)—and in this role he is known as an "anthropologist." But on the other hand, his very participation, and presumed acceptance of the rules concerning research on multiple variables, requires that he often discard or revise some of the more common notions of the field of anthropology. This is perhaps an experience of some importance, since many of these ideas are precisely those which have become expressive symbols of the solidarity of the company of anthropologists.

We will attempt to illustrate some of these points by a consideration of the concept of culture and its relation to interdisciplinary research.

The Concept of Culture

In the development of the concept of culture in anthropology two tendencies stand out as important. First, the concept clearly had the status of a "felt need," in that the great range of human variation emerging from research could not be understood by available biological and environmental concepts alone. Nor were purely individual behavioral traits adequate for group analysis and description. "Culture" emerged as a needed tool, and consequently it became of considerable convenience to regard any sector of human experience and its phenomena not readily explainable in other terms as a part of "culture." This has led to a tendency to permit the culture concept to assume sponge-like qualities, soaking up whole batteries of analytically distinguishable factors—a process which often slips into reification.

The second major tendency in the emergence of a culture concept appeared in the interests of anthropologists in small, face-to-face communal groups. It was observed at an early date that such groups possessed a high quotient of shared norms of conduct, and this corpus of "integrated" and "homogeneous" learned behavior traits came to be designated as the "culture" of the group. Culture thus was identified with a holistic, tribal unity, and finally this unity was assumed to be present in every human grouping, in all societies. The possibility that different types of social groups and institutional systems—for example, a nation or a corporation—might not possess such a homogeneous collection of learned traits, for the reason that face-to-face relationships were not the predominant mode, was ignored or underplayed. Culture was culture —it was the same for all human groupings and it became a "level of reality," thus much more than a useful analytical abstraction.[3]

The discovery that small, face-to-face groups possessed remarkably homogeneous sets of learned behaviors dominated anthropology until the middle 1930's. The research on nonliterate groups had served to build up an image of culture which stressed homogeneity and integration, and had resulted in a relatively static concept. Since cultures were integrated, change came with difficulty, and then largely from outside forces which disturbed the integrity of the logically coherent structures. Hence the popularity of such concepts as "diffusion," "acculturation," and "borrowing"—these terms and many others all referring primarily to stimuli originating outside of the system under investigation. Deviant trends within the culture were studied, but often it was found these deviations could be subsumed under more complex statements of the holistic pattern itself, and thus they were minimized as an agent of change. Moreover, little attention was paid to such analytical dimensions as factional conflicts, economic relationships and goals, demographic pressures, and the like.

---

[3] See Steward (1951) for additional comment on these issues. Note also Redfield's earlier decision to confine "culture" to the homogeneous folk society and exclude it from the urban (Redfield 1941). Related comments have been made by Hart (1951). Julian H. Steward, "Levels of Sociocultural Integration: An Operational Concept," *Southwestern Journal of Anthropology,* 1951, Vol. 7, pp. 37–90; Robert Redfield, *The Folk Culture of Yucatan,* Chicago: University of Chicago Press, 1941; C. W. M. Hart, "Review of: Sociologie et Anthropologie by Marcel Mauss," *American Sociological Review,* 1951, Vol. 16, pp. 405–406.

What this approach did was to restrain inquiries into subjects and problems which demanded analytical distinctions beyond the cultural. Yet, as suggested earlier, such inquiries inevitably appeared, and a series of compromise positions were worked out, appearing under the headings of functional theory, culture and personality studies, "applied anthropology," British social anthropology, and the like—all becoming prominent in the late 1930's. Although these fields attempted analyses of social relationships, functional aspects of social life, institutional variation, and the importance of the personality variable or dimension, most of them continued to work with an implicit notion of "one tribe–one culture." Many of the theoretical difficulties of these fields may be traced to the fact that in solving problems of dynamics, they attempted to use descriptive-holistic concepts of culture, instead of the needed tools of greater analytical precision.

The "culture variable" for the majority of anthropologists thus retained its status of an integrated whole characteristic of a society or group, and anthropological research, by and large, consisted of a search for the locus and changes of this tribal culture. This anthropological enterprise reached an extreme phase in the "national character" studies of World War II, when anthropologists actually attempted to isolate the ethos—the holistic face-to-face tribal culture—of great modern nations.[4]

---

[4] Some thoughtful evaluations of the attempts at constructing national character have recently appeared (see Mead 1950 and Benedict 1946), but in both of these papers the concept of whole cultures and its status as the goal of research is not questioned, though modified to some extent. All of these wartime studies were designed with practical ends: by knowing the enemy's culture one is better able to devise weapons of psychological warfare. Thus Gorer (e.g., see his comment in Mead 1950) recommended that the Japanese "way of life" and the Emperor not be attacked in propaganda, this recommendation being "based on an understanding of the *whole* Japanese culture." Gorer really means the particular expressive-symbolic aspects of Japanese culture that he studied. If he had literally studied the "whole" culture, he would have discovered the existence of liberal, universalistic, democratic elements of considerable historical depth which were crying for a change in the whole Japanese system. Politically, it might have been more expedient to strengthen the hand of these elements; because by maintaining the policy of "revere the Emperor" and the Japanese "way of life" the Allies preserved the value orientations and social relationship system which in Japan and elsewhere tends to be defeative of democratic change. Of course, the mistake lay in maintaining the policy into the Occupation—yet, the initial choice of the policy made this continuity inevitable. Gorer might have considered the Japanese *political* institutional culture—the attempt to deal with the "whole culture" simply meant an inability to discriminate betweer the differing functional significance of various institutional segments and analytical variables In a like manner, the defects and distortions of Japanese social life in Benedict's brilliant monograph, *Chrysanthemum and the Sword* (1946), are due precisely to the lack of critical discrimination among the profoundly varying status groupings, roles, and institutional patterns in Japanese society.

Margaret Mead, "The Comparative Study of Cultures and the Purposive Cultivation of Democratic Values," *Perspectives on a Troubled Decade, 1939–1949*, Conference on Science, Philosophy and Religion, 10th Symposium, New York: Harper, 1950; Ruth Benedict, "The Study of Culture Patterns in European Nations," *Transactions of the New York Academy of Sciences,* 1946, Vol. 8, Ser. 2, pp. 274–279; also, *Chrysanthemum and the Sword,* Boston: Houghton Mifflin, 1946.

Now this general conception of culture does not do particular violence to the data of descriptive historical inquiries. If the problem is one of tracing the movement, in space and time, of abstracted items of behavior, whether they be sounds, potsherds, kinship terms, or religious beliefs, it is convenient to label these items as "belonging" to a particular "culture." The archeologist who works with discrete sites or in "culture areas" demarcated by pottery styles, like the ethnologist who traces kinship customs from one tribe to another, can afford a phenomenological definition. It is actually the most convenient concept for his operations. He may push his theoretical considerations of this concept to extreme limits, but in the last analysis it remains a useful descriptive construction limited in explanatory power, and whatever connections or relatedness one observes between the patterns must remain purely *logical*—the logic of similarity and difference. Culture in this sense cannot "function," since function requires and introduces an entirely different set of analytical concepts. These are unnecessary in historical-descriptive inquiries as such.

The anthropologist who participates in any way in the new interdisciplinary movement described previously, is likely to reject this descriptive-holistic or "phenomenological" version of the culture variable. In the first place, he cannot afford to see all scientific social problems as problems of culture because he discovers that a whole range of problems require finer discriminations. If he studies social relationships in modern society and its institutions, as he is likely to do currently, he soon discovers that he cannot assume that his subjects are simply bearers of culture who are learning and interacting in the face-to-face group atmosphere. The more differentiated and impersonal structure of institutional systems of complex societies cannot be analyzed *initially* with the concept of culture pattern of learned behavior traits—other than in the most generalized and impressionistic manner. The anthropologist instead discovers a need for refined versions of certain familiar tools: studies must be made of the *roles* typical of a *system of social relationships,* the *values* and *norms* associated with these roles, the *expectations* of behavior brought to the situation by the individual actors, their *needs* and *motivations,* and finally, the varying dimensions of the "situation" itself. Anthropologists are not unfamiliar with these analytical variables, but in the great body of cultural anthropological research, they often have been obscured by the emphasis on culture.[5]

In the second place, the interdisciplinary cultural anthropologist observes that culture *as such* is a purely descriptive concept, and that in order to be included as a variable in any investigation of interaction or social relationships

[5] The assortment of analytical variables noted in this paragraph consists, of course, of those most suitable for the analysis of institutional variation and change at the social level. A problem which required a multidimensional approach to say, personality development would be structured differently and contain certain additional or different variables. See Tolman, "A Model for the Personality System," *Toward a General Theory of Action,* ed. Talcott Parsons and E. A. Shils, Cambridge: Harvard University Press, 1951.

it must be translated into terms which are meaningful as factors in behavior, or in social action. It *is not enough to say that "culture" is at work; one must specify exactly how and in what locus.* The "culture" becomes transformed into concepts such as "value orientation," "norms," "expectations," "means" and "ends," "group atmosphere." These terms represent differing functions of systems of patterned regularities in behavior, they play definite and differing roles in the response of individual to individual, and they fulfill varying missions in the total analytical process. Thus "culture" can "explain" human phenomena only when it is seen as part of a system of relationships between people. It is their *response to* and *use of* the "patterns" that is of moment.

This leads to a third consideration. In dynamic interdisciplinary research the cultural anthropologist not only breaks "culture" down into a series of analytical variables, or operational concepts (and also stresses new variables which are not "cultural," e.g., "social relationship"), but *he also becomes critical of the holistic notion of "one tribe–one culture."* He substitutes—if he uses "culture" at all—what might be called a systemic or institutionally varying definition of the cultural variable. He simply observes that in the process of interaction in any concrete system of social relationships, certain traits come to be patterned, or regularized. These systems of patterns, or institutions, must be isolated as the meaningful factors or sets of factors in their concrete, *and varying,* situations. There is no commitment to the size or duration of the human group with the "culture"; it is simply the pattern-construct aspect of any interactive process; in most cases, values or norms.

If the anthropologist understands these procedures—and he must in order to be a fully cooperative team member—he will likely reject, in whole or part, certain aspects of the approach to culture. In particular, he is likely to be skeptical of tendencies toward explanatory reification, mechanical-historical (processual) "culture theory," and tribal holistic concepts. His "skepticism" does not necessarily mean "disbelief," for he recognizes the legitimate roles these concepts may play at their own levels.[6] *But he becomes, through his experience, a different kind of anthropologist*—one who often finds little in common with the historical school; and *vice versa.*

The Emergence of an Analytical Scheme

The foregoing remarks have summarized consequences for the concept of culture deriving from certain contemporary movements in the social sciences.

[6] This point should be emphasized, lest it be thought that the matters discussed in this paper constitute an argument against the use of "culture" in any and all contexts. The importance and value of the concept in historical descriptive studies is not questioned. But the concept in that form is felt to be inadequate for studies of human interaction or institutional variation.

The same process may be viewed also as the culmination of certain long-range trends in cultural anthropology itself—this was anticipated in previous paragraphs where developments in cultural anthropology demanding analytical distinctions beyond the simpler "cultural" ones available were cited. Further discussion of this matter will conclude this paper.

It was remarked previously that in some sense the stress on "culture" in anthropology has often operated to obscure or rub out analytical distinctions which permit finer discrimination between the variables and phenomena of human social life. A convenient example is probably found in the temporary submergence in the early years of the century of inquiries into kinship—a study which demands fine *systematic* distinctions between status position, role, norms of conduct, and the like—after Morgan's and Rivers' pioneer efforts. This temporary subsidence followed the rise to popularity of the culture concept, and for at least a decade or more, interest in large and voluminous concepts like "universal pattern" and "diffusion" obscured the analytical efforts of scholars like Radcliffe-Brown, who have been concerned with people in interaction rather than with holistic abstractions.

It is the conviction of the writer that cultural anthropologists have been insufficiently aware of the tendencies in their own ranks toward the emergence of an analytical scheme which is potentially equipped to supplement the abstractive scheme of culture constructs. Malinowski's work in retrospect would appear to mark some sort of turning point in cultural anthropological studies, in that the concept of "function," because it poses a dynamic rather than a descriptive static question, requires an analytical scheme above and beyond "culture." This is utterly apparent in Malinowski's works, particularly the earlier pieces, yet Malinowski himself never seemed fully aware of the implications of his own doubts concerning the standard cultural interpretations of the period. The generally superorganicist article on "Culture" in the *Encyclopedia of the Social Sciences* is sufficient evidence of this.

One of the clearest expositions of an analytical scheme in Malinowski's writings appears in the closing pages of "Baloma."[7] He begins his concluding discussion by requiring that the "social dimension" of a belief be explored, over and above the mere recording of the versions of the belief current in the group. That is, he is saying that the belief has several dimensions of variation in addition to the standard-group-typical-descriptive pattern version, which the anthropologist of those days was likely to collect to the exclusion of anything else. In the subsequent pages this "social dimension" emerges: (1) the belief will vary in terms of the various *social institutions* in which it plays a role; (2) it will vary according to the way it is involved in the *emotional behavior of*

[7] B. Malinowski, "Baloma: the Spirits of the Dead in the Trobriand Islands," *Magic, Science and Religion,* ed. R. Redfield, Glencoe, Ill.: Free Press, 1948, pp. 213–216.

individuals; (3) it will vary according to *individual cognitive* and *imaginative manipulation;* (4) it will vary according to the different *statuses* and *roles* of individuals who use it as a *means to an end* in social action. The terms underlined are the writer's; Malinowski was not constructing an analytical conceptual scheme but simply describing the "social dimension" of supernatural belief. Yet these are the terms applied today to the variables he perceived.[8]

In later years contributions like Bateson's *Naven*[9] and, still later, Kluckhohn's *Navaho Witchcraft*[10] were accorded just accolades for their exploration of the needed analytical variables, while the purely descriptive cultural studies gradually became the gentle pedestrian background of the science of cultural anthropology. The Bateson contribution was principally in the direction of an exploration of the significance of social role as a channelizer and selector of behavior, and the Kluckhohn offering stressed the ways men redirect hostile behavior and assuage anxiety. It is true that both researchers utilized cultural concepts and showed general concern with the configurated aspects of behavior. However, the important contributions were not to culture *qua* culture, but to other analytical dimensions of social behavior. Or, saying it another way, phenomena which had often been grouped, by other anthropologists, into an undifferentiated culture construct, were factored out, so to speak, into relevant and manipulable variables. And, by doing so, an explanatory dimension to "cultural" research was added.

Thus there has been a strong tendency in cultural anthropology, for at least three decades, to recognize and develop an analytical scheme which would rise beyond the boundaries of the culture concept and would permit explanatory solutions to the problems of social behavior and interaction among humans. However, while this has been underway, the purely culturological approach has reached a certain peak of development in the national character studies cited previously. The tendency is in general opposed to that which seeks the development and use of an analytical scheme, even though for the solution of subsidiary problems the whole-culture approach often finds it necessary to use the appropriate variables, with or without acknowledgement of the significance of such use.

---

[8] Among numerous examples of contemporary schemes, see Talcott Parsons and E. A. Shils, eds., *Toward a General Theory of Action,* Cambridge: Harvard University Press, 1951, Pt. I; J. W. Bennett and M. Tumin, *Social Life: Structure and Function,* New York: Knopf, 1948, Pt. II; Kingsley Davis, *Human Society,* New York: Macmillan, 1949, Pt. I. A related scheme is presented by S. F. Nadel, *The Foundations of Social Anthropology,* Glencoe, Ill.: Free Press, 1951, which is interesting in that it is offered as social anthropological theory, but is acknowledgeably based on structural functional sociology and interdisciplinary behavior science formulations. Linton's *Study of Man* (1936) has probably enjoyed its long and deserved popularity primarily because of its analytical contributions, like the distinction between ascribed and achieved status, and status and role.

[9] Gregory Bateson, *Naven,* Cambridge, England: Cambridge University Press, 1936.

[10] Clyde Kluckhohn, *Navaho Witchcraft,* Cambridge, Mass.: Peabody Museum, Harvard University, 1944.

Thus, as Kluckhohn and others have suggested, analytical schemes are required whether the ultimate goal of analysis is some sort of picture of a whole culture, or whether more segmental objectives are present. The culture concept and its descriptive subsidiaries—"pattern," "trait," and the like—are simply insufficient in themselves, or in elaboration at their own level, to provide the discriminatory power needed in the analysis of human interaction. An approach which gets down to the "sense data," as it were, of human relationships is required, and anthropology, along with other social sciences, has been in the process of developing concepts needed in such an approach.[11]

However this may be, cultural anthropologists should be willing to recognize that sociology and social psychology have probably accomplished much more along these lines, and that anthropology must be ready, in the coming decade, to learn a great deal from these sister sciences. The anthropological demonstration of the variability of human customs, and its total historical perspective on man's accomplishments, are fundamental in the social sciences and constitute anthropology's major and signal contributions, but they are a lesson and a body of knowledge which by themselves are not sufficient to solve problems of finer grain. To do this, anthropology must be willing to borrow concepts from neighboring fields (see Beals).[12]

As such borrowing—which is really coexperimentation with other sciences on the utility of concepts and factorable expressions of human social life—takes place, one will see the gradual emergence of an interdisciplinary conceptual scheme and research program in which cultural anthropology will have a role to play. Precisely what that role may consist of is not entirely clear at present, although Parsons' suggestion of anthropology's responsibility for the further clarification of culture concepts and their relation to analytical concepts is an interesting one.[13] Along with this may go some reasoned tempering of anthropology's rather grandiloquent claim that it represents the only self-contained science of man. This claim may be coming to sound slightly hollow

---

[11] One important implication of this concerns the theoretical poverty of the well-known anthropological "schools," like functionalism. From the point of view developed in this paper, these schools are not theoretical positions, but rather *aspects* from which one approaches empirical data (i.e., from the standpoint of time series; in terms of unique qualities; with respect to inter-connectedness of elements, etc.). What these schools have lacked is a theory of social behavior which can provide chains of testable hypotheses. Note how an exception to the rule provides such hypotheses: *Navaho Witchcraft.* Since its publication a whole series of coordinated researches have been set in motion. The point is that a theory of social behavior requires an analytical scheme; an analytical scheme requires a precise, not a vague, definition or rather denotation of the status of the culture construct. It is the writer's feeling that sooner or later, this question of the denotation of culture is going to have to be answered by anthropology, if it is to survive as a field of study. (See Barnett's *Innovation* for one suggestive answer.)

[12] Ralph L. Beals, "Urbanism, Urbanization, and Acculturation," *American Anthropologist,* 1951, Vol. 52, pp. 1–10.

[13] Talcott Parsons, "The Present Position and Prospects of Systematic Theory in Sociology," *Essays in Sociological Theory, Pure and Applied,* Glencoe, Ill.: Free Press, 1949, p. 40.

in the ears of those persons who have been sold a large package only to find that, while it contains brilliant oddments, it is somewhat lacking in the precision and conceptual equipment necessary for the solution of contemporary problems of importance in the social sciences.

Comments added by J. W. Bennett in November 1969

A lot of water has gone under the bridge since this paper was written; I feel it desirable to supply some comments bringing my own ideas up to date.

1. In the original, unedited version, there was a section entitled "Federation vs. Integration," omitted from this reprinted version. While commenting on a nonexistent passage may be a dubious procedure, the issue is important. In this section of the original paper, it was pointed out that true interdisciplinary research in the sense of attempts to develop causal relationships between diverse phenomena did not exist. However, so far as the human-science disciplines are concerned, some progress has been made since then: examples are coordinated investigations in the "policy sciences"; various types of research combining economics and behavioral sciences. So far as anthropology itself is concerned, progress has been made toward causal linkages between levels of phenomena in the spheres of: human adaptability to natural and cultural environments; evolutionary studies of cultural and biological change; and ethnosemantic research suggesting linkages between cognitive processes and cultural behavior. Still, the relative modesty of these various efforts outside of and within anthropology testifies to the enormous methodological and sociocommunicative difficulties of true multidisciplinary research.
2. The paper appears to make a case for "structural-functional" research of a generalized Parsonian type, involving "interdisciplinary" investigation of several variables, culture perhaps being one of these. While I would continue to support the general recommendation for multidisciplinary study, I am much less inclined to support a structural-functional approach. The structural-functional approach is being replaced or modified by a more dynamic, problem-solving approach emphasizing patterns of adaptation to changing reality. That is, more emphasis is currently thrown on problem-solving, decision-making, time-binding—and much less on abstract concepts like "role," "value," "social system." Examples of the new approach are social exchange theory in sociology, and Barth's ecological transactionism in anthropology. I myself now adhere to this approach. I believe that it furthers the general objectives formulated in the paper, but in a way not visualized at the time of writing. Moreover, it avoids the nonhistorical bias of functionalism and provides for a systematic approach to change. There is a focus on relevant, ongoing, consequential behavior and its milieu, and less emphasis on idealized concepts and

patterns, devoid of milieu considerations. Thus, my assertion in the last section of the paper that a new analytical scheme will emerge in anthropology, seems to have come true, at least in part. And the role of "culture" has certainly diminished. But the precise form of this scheme is not the one I envisaged, although it shares some common elements.

3. The treatment of the concept of culture in the paper is in need of revision. While I would not go back on my sketch of the development of the concept in anthropology and my criticism of its extension to societal entities actually lacking its relevant dimensions, I would now be willing to make a special case for a concept of culture on the grounds of the adaptational approach noted previously. That is, a category of data susceptible of definition as culture emerges when patterns of coping or adaptation are reinforced in some fashion, so as to become consistent adaptive strategies, available for use in concrete situations. This conception of culture is close to the notion of tradition, or rather, "tradition" is relevant as a concept describing the perseveration of particular adaptational behaviors. Thus, while I go along with the plea in the paper to de-reify culture and make it a goal of analysis rather than an existential assumption, or explanation, I would now "look" for "culture" in a behavioral process: as a particular property of certain temporal action patterns expressed by the actors in the form of reasons and rationalizations; i.e., a cognitive category.

4. I still adhere to the dictum of the paper to the effect that while anthropology has provided many brilliant and sharply-etched fragments of human experience, it nevertheless lacks conceptual refinements suited to the solution of important contemporary problems. However, I would now distinguish between what I regard as the reluctance of sociocultural anthropology (and applied anthropology) to engage in research on major social issues and the increasingly important social macrocosms of our time; and, on the other hand, the quite evident progress and success of paleoanthropology to produce significant basic scientific knowledge on the emergence of man. Indeed, I would say now that the chief failing of sociocultural anthropology has been its slow progress toward a viable means of making microsocial phenomena significant for larger entities, or of finding ways of studying these larger entities and their processes. This particular methodological problem is not present in paleoanthropology, with its larger entities of populations and regions, its long historical sweep, and its ability to ignore distracting minutiae.

5. Footnote 4 provides some comments on the "whole culture" concept using the wartime and early postwar analyses of Japanese cultural character as examples. On the whole the writer stands with the critical approach taken there so far as the basic theoretical issue is concerned. That is, "whole culture" should include the widest possible frame of reference, and not draw conclusions of broad relevance on the basis of the study of a single sector, in this case

certain personality tendencies produced in socialization. However, the footnote needs correction in two areas: (1) in recent years investigations by William Caudill, George De Vos, and others seem to have established pervasive influences of early socialization on Japanese adult personality in the sphere of achievement motivation—although class differences are also noticeable. That is, new meanings and significance of the cultural-character approach in the study of national cultural entities are beginning to emerge, especially for the case of Japan. (2) The political question involved—the advisability of preserving the Emperor—seems to me at this date to have been less of an error than I implied in the footnote. I feel now that the peculiar combination of scarce natural resources, strong achievement-oriented behavior, and vulnerable geopolitical location makes centralization and unity unusually important in the case of Japan—the problem is simply one of how much "democracy," in the sense of tolerance for intrasocietal conflict, can Japan tolerate and still retain the high level of production she requires in order to survive?

6. When this paper was originally published, A. L. Kroeber wrote me, in effect, that I appeared to speak for a small anthropology within a larger general social science, while he advocated a large, separate science of anthropology, coordinate with other social sciences. In a subsequent interchange, it became clear that Kroeber's position was based on his selection of descriptive and historical themes as the central focus of anthropology, whereas I was following the then current behavior-science position with its fusion tendencies. I believe I made it clear to him, however, that in no sense was I opposed to descriptive-historical studies, only the exclusive identification of anthropology with them. I suppose that to be consistent, I should have to admit that I have no right to identify anthropology with behavior science. Somehow I no longer feel that profitable discussions can be held on the question, "what is the real nature of anthropology?" Anthropology is an eclectic field—eclectic in both subject matter and methodology—and its nature will change as its several components achieve their various successes and failures. It is, and remains, as George Stocking has pointed out, a "pre-paradigmatic" field, in which controversy will continue to rage over the true nucleus of the field, and oversimplified explanations will continually emerge, in the search for some atomic core of theory and explanation.

19 Studying Social Change

FREDRIK BARTH

In essence, we are told by Professor Bennett that the traditional anthropological approach to culture must be modified for the needs of modern research. Culture, that is, cannot by itself explain all the complexities of social interaction, social structure, historical continuities, and change. A complete explanation, for Bennett, requires the combined efforts of cultural anthropologists, sociologists, biologists, psychologists, and others interested in human existence. Bennett also reminds us that adequate explanations of socio-cultural phenomena must be able to explain change, not as something unusual and strange, but rather as an intrinsic aspect of human life.

The problems inherent in studying change, let alone mastering the principles underlying it, are well described in the paper that follows. Its author, Professor Fredrik Barth, has done research in many different socio-cultural situations. He is, therefore, highly qualified to discuss the complex problems inherent in change. Again, as in John Bennett's paper, we are told of the futility of following traditional methods; and again, "culture" is taken off the pedestal, as the all-powerful, "all-knowing" concept.

Traditional anthropological description in terms of pattern and custom, convenient as it is for certain purposes, results essentially in accounts that do not adequately portray change. Change is more easily handled if one looks at social behavior as allocations of time and resources. Analyses of ongoing process that the latter view makes possible seem more productive of insight into the nature of social change than has been the case with typological and comparative approaches.

The analytical contribution of modern anthropology to the understanding of social change has been limited, despite the fact that our material is becoming increasingly rich with most dramatic cases of change. I shall use the opportunity that a brief and general discussion of the wide theme of social change offers to make a preliminary diagnosis of why this should be so, and to suggest certain requirements and reorientations that I feel are necessary if we wish to

Source: Reprinted from "On the Study of Social Change" by Fredrik Barth. Reproduced by permission of the author and the American Anthropological Association from *American Anthropologist*, Vol. 69, No. 6, 1967, pp. 661–669.

remedy this situation. I shall argue in favor of (a) a greater attention to the empirical study of the events of change, and a need for concepts that facilitate this; (b) the necessity for specification of the nature of the continuity in a sequence of change, and the processual analyses that this entails; and (c) the importance of the study of institutionalization as an ongoing process.

We should not underestimate the effects on our discipline that giving first priority to the understanding of change may have. There has been a comfortable convention in social anthropology till now of treating "social change" as if it were a topic of anthropological investigation like "religion" or "domestic organization," something that may be discussed in addition to, and preferably subsequent to, other substantive fields in the description of social systems. But if we couch our description of these aspects of society as if we were dealing with forms that do not entail and reflect processes, we cannot expect that the terms and concepts we develop in this description will serve us with equal facility in the description of changing forms.

To understand social change, what we need to do as social anthropologists is to describe all of society in such terms that we see how it persists, maintains itself, and changes through time. This may mean recasting many of our terms for the description of social systems, not merely adding a chapter of additional data. To do the job of analyzing change adequately may mean that we will do some of the odd jobs less adequately, or at least less simply, than we have been doing. To someone who does not share this priority, the efforts may look unnecessarily complicated and relatively fruitless. But for those who give the understanding of change high priority, it is wishful thinking to expect that we can build indiscriminately on all the concepts that our discipline has developed for other purposes.

Because of our general unwillingness to abandon well-established routines, studies explicitly addressed to the investigation of change have been prone to contain descriptions of a social system at two points in time—or even at one point in time!—and then to rely on *extrapolation* between these two states, or from the one state, to indicate the course of change. I feel that if we want to understand social change, we need concepts that allow us to observe and describe the *events* of change. Our contribution as social anthropologists must lie in providing such primary materials for understanding the processes; it lies in our powers of observation out there where change is happening today, and not in producing secondary data by deduction and extrapolation. If this means that we must recast our very description of social systems in order to accommodate these data about the events of change, that makes our task more difficult but also more interesting.

The reason for the social anthropologist's impasse when he tries to add change to his traditional description of social systems is found in the basic characteristics of the descriptive concepts we habitually use. We wish to characterize groups, societies, or cultures, and to do this we have to aggregate individual observations. We generally think of the procedure as one where we aggregate individual cases of behavior to *patterns* of behavior, specifying the common features of the individual cases. Such patterns we think of as customs: stereotyped forms of behavior that are required and correct. Some of us may choose to emphasize the *moral* character of customs (and thus the possibility of eliciting them directly from informants) rather than their *stereotyped* character, but in either case we feel that the two are connected. We then construct a system composed of such formal features, and characterize the whole system as one "with" dowry, or "with" cross-cousin marriage, or "with" ambilocal residence.

This kind of morphological concept of custom as the minimal element of form has been fundamental to our thinking because it serves such a useful purpose. It allows us to aggregate individual cases into a macrosystem and to maintain the connection between the two levels. We avoid the difficulties of some of the other social sciences of using different kinds of concepts for the description of microunit and the macroaggregate: a man "gives" a dowry and a society "has" dowry. A custom has morphological characteristics that are like those of an individual item of behavior, and on both levels we can use the same descriptive and characterizing terms. And so we can observe people practicing the very culture that we abstract, whereas nobody practices socio-economic class or gross national income.

But such a concept of custom makes the pattern as a whole unobservable, except as exemplified in the stereotyped aspects of each individual case—the aggregate pattern can never be observed by measurement. A custom is revealed only in a series of more or less representative exemplifications. And change in a pattern, or change from one pattern to another, is even less observable; there is no way to observe and describe an event of change, except perhaps in the field of legislation.

A statistical view of the practice of customs does not provide a way out. We may observe breaches of custom—but is a breach of custom an event of change? We may even summarize a frequency, a rate of breaches of custom; we will still know nothing about the probability or imminence of a change in the custom, or about the direction of change that frequent breaches signal.

I feel that we need rather to use concepts that enable us to depict the pattern itself as a statistical thing, as a set of frequencies or alternatives. If we, for example, look at social behavior as an allocation of time and resources, we can depict the pattern whereby people allocate their time and resources. Changes in the proportions of these allocations are observable in the sense that they are measurable. New allocations are observable as concrete events that may have systematic effects and thus generate important change. And this view does not entail that we limit ourselves to the description of an economic sector of activities only; it can be applied to the whole field of social organization, to describe how people in fact manage to arrange their lives.

Sharp's classic description of the introduction of the steel axe among the Yir Yoront of Australia stands out as an illuminating case-study of social change precisely because it adopts this perspective.[1] It provides an understanding of change by explaining the changing bases from which people make their allocations. We see how Yir Yoront women no longer need to offer as much submission to their husbands because they no longer need to go to them to obtain an axe; we understand why people no longer allocate time and resources to intertribal festivals because they are no longer dependent on them to obtain their tools.

This way of isolating the underlying determinants of social forms, so as to see how changes in them generate social systems, implies a view of behavior and society that is rather different from what has frequently been adopted in anthropology. What we see as a social form is, concretely, a pattern of distribution of behavior by different persons and on different occasions. I would argue that it is not useful to assume that this empirical pattern is a sought-for condition, which all members of the community equally value and willfully maintain. Rather, it must be regarded as an epiphenomenon of a great variety of processes in combination, and our problem as social anthropologists is to show how it is generated. The determinants of the form must be of a variety of kinds. On the one hand, what persons wish to achieve, the multifarious ends they are pursuing, will channel their behavior. On the other hand, technical and ecologic restrictions doom some kinds of behavior to failure and reward others, while the presence of other actors imposes strategic constraints and opportunities that modify the allocations people can make and will benefit from making.

I would therefore argue that it is unfruitful to explain a social form, a pattern, directly by hypothesizing a purpose for it. Individual actors and individual management units have purposes and make allocations accordingly; but a social form, in the sense of an over-all pattern of statistical behavior, is the aggregate pattern produced by the process of social life through which ecologic and strategic constraints channel, defeat, and reward various activities on the part of such management units.

This analytic perspective stands in marked contrast to the anthropological predilection for going from a generalized type construct of a social form to a list of "prerequisites" for this general type. Though these two exercises are so close in many formal respects, their objectives are strikingly different. In one case, a social form, or a whole society, is seen as a morphological creature within

[1] Lauriston Sharp, "Steel Axes for Stone-Age Australians," *Human Problems in Technological Change,* ed. E. H. Spicer, New York: Russell Sage Foundation, 1952.

certain requirements that need to be ascertained, in the functionalist tradition, the better to understand how it is put together. In the other case, a social form is seen as the epiphenomenon of a number of processes, and the analysis concentrates on showing how the form is generated. Only the latter view develops concepts that directly promote the understanding of change.

I have been concerned recently to analyze the institution of the beer party in the society of the Fur, a village-dwelling population in Darfur province of Sudan that subsists mainly by the hoe cultivation of millet.[2]

One may describe the norms or customs governing this institution and show how it organizes a group of persons around a joint task. Beer is supplied by a host, and guests arrive to drink, sing, and work for the host. Some of the guests are there by invitation; many arrive unasked and unannounced, to share in the work and the beer and the company. In all these respects, one beer party is like another beer party, and this brief description summarizes the gross customary features of the institution. As far as changes in the institution go, all that the informants, or an anthropologist with longer field work in the area than myself, might be able to say is that beer parties are becoming fewer or more rowdy.

If one wishes to describe an institution as a pattern of the allocation of time and resources, one needs to specify the set of alternatives. In a beer party you can be *guest* or *host*, or you may choose to allocate your own labor directly to your own millet field. Different frequencies of these allocations entail different kinds of community life; although they may be looked at as behavioral outputs, their frequencies have structural implications for the society.

Thus, where there is a predominance of allocation of own labor to own fields, this entails a limited circulation of labor services in the community as a whole and a low level of neighborliness and community life. Differences in wealth are constrained by the range of the labor capacity of each cultivator-householder.

Where on the other hand there is much beer party activity and reciprocity in the host-guest relationship, this maintains an egalitarian, communal peasant community through the constant circulation and redistribution of labor services and rewards.

But the actual extent of reciprocity also needs to be measured. If some consistently act more as hosts than as guests, they are transforming some millet into labor. An increased rate of nonreciprocal allocations of this kind leads to an increased social differentiation, where some simultaneously obtain both wealth and leisure; that is, it leads to change in the direction of increased social stratification.

---

[2] F. Barth, "Economic Spheres in Darfur," *Themes in Economic Anthropology,* ed. R. Firth, London: Tavistock Publications, 1967.

One may therefore argue that these behavioral outputs feed back on the structure of the community itself. The ubiquitous beer party guest, who is exchanging labor directly for beer, does not ask himself: How will this allocation affect our system of social stratification? Yet his allocations, made on the basis of limited considerations, do in fact create directions and constraints on possible change. It is only through attention to the frequencies of allocations, by describing the pattern itself as a set of certain frequencies, that it becomes possible to observe and describe such quite simple events of social change.

Because of an interest in observing events of change, a group of us in Bergen decided to turn our attention to the study of entrepreneurs.[3] The choice was rather obvious in that entrepreneurs are clearly agents of change: they make innovations that affect the community in which they are active. Entrepreneurs are also much more common and active in some communities and societies than in others, and the dynamic character of some societies has sometimes been explained by the prevalence of entrepreneurs in them.

The anthropological study of entrepreneurs and entrepreneurship has characteristically sought to show the common characteristics of entrepreneurs, and thus the prerequisites for the emergence of entrepreneurship. What we did was to ask, not what makes the entrepreneur, but what does the entrepreneur make: what can one say about his enterprise, is it possible to characterize it as an event of change?

Now in retrospect, one might see several alternative ways of pursuing this question and simpler ways of handling it than the ones we adopted in that particular study. But what proved stimulating to us then and later was the way this question directed us to look for ways of characterizing and describing change itself, rather than the prerequisites for change. We attempted to characterize particular cases of entrepreneurial activity as new kinds of allocation. But since our major interest was not in an individual or a category of individuals, but in a social system, we had to go on to characterize this social system and show how the entrepreneurial activity in question was changing it. We therefore had to try to show the system of allocations in the entrepreneur's community and to place his new allocations in relation to these others. In this material and elsewhere one finds that entrepreneurs effect new conversions between forms of goods that were previously not directly convertible.[4] They thereby create new paths for the circulation of goods, often crossing barriers between formerly discrete spheres of circulation.

This activity cannot be without effect on the culture of the members of an entrepreneur's community. If we look for the bases on which people make

[3] F. Barth, *The Role of the Entrepreneur in Social Change in Northern Norway,* Bergen-Oslo: Norwegian Universities Press, 1963.
[4] Barth (1967).

their allocations in primary cultural facts such as people's categorization of different kinds of goods and their preference criteria for evaluating different outcomes of their allocations, then we are relating their choices to the cultural values or value orientations to which they subscribe. The entrepreneurial coup, where one makes one's big profits, is where one discovers a path by which something of little value can be transformed into something of great value. But looked at this way, entrepreneurial successes produce new information on the interrelations of different categories of valued goods. The information produced by such activity will render false the idea that people have held till then about the relative value of goods, and can reasonably be expected to precipitate reevaluations and modifications both of categorizations and of value orientations. In other words, it changes the cultural bases that determine people's behavior, and in this way entrepreneurial activity becomes a major wellspring of cultural and social change.[5]

However, the main point in the preceding discussion is the most general one: I feel that it is important for social anthropologists to realize that we further our understanding of social change best by using concepts that make the concrete events of change available to observation and systematic description.

There is also a requirement of another order that needs to be observed in such studies. To speak about change, one needs to be able to specify the nature of the continuity between the situations discussed under the rubric of change. Change implies a difference of a very particular kind: one that results from an alteration through time and is determined by the constraints of what has been, or continues, in a situation. Let me use a very simple illustration: Imagine a situation where you stand looking into an aquarium, and you observe a fish. A moment later you find yourself looking at a crab in the same place where the fish was. If you ask yourself how it got claws instead of fins, you are implying a certain kind of continuity: this is the same body, and it has changed its shape. If, on the other hand, you say to yourself that this is the same aquarium, you are specifying another kind of continuity, implying a set of constraints that leads you to formulate other hypotheses about the dynamics of change in this instance. Different specifications of the nature of the continuity that ties two situations together in a sequence of change gives rise to very different hypotheses about the mechanisms and processes of change. For every analysis, it is therefore necessary for us to make explicit our assertions about the nature of the continuity.

In physical anthropology, the principle of noninheritance of acquired characteristics represents a step toward such a specification of the nature of continuity. And the increasingly rigorous study of change has only been made possible

[5] F. Barth, *Models of Social Organization,* Royal Anthropological Institute Occasional Paper No. 23, London, 1966, esp. pp. 16–20.

through the explicit assertion that what continues through time may be described as a gene pool, and that changes in form reflect changes in the frequencies of genes in the gene pool of the population.

In archeology, a hand-axe does not breed a hand-axe, and the typological vocabulary that seemed to imply this kind of continuity has largely been dropped in favor of an explicit recognition that the continuity is found in (a) the cultural tradition of the tool-makers. However the constraints on the processes of change implied by this axe are very poorly understood. Perhaps for that reason, archeology seems so far to have been more successful when specifying other kinds of continuity, such as (b) the constancy of materials, implying constraints that help us understand the courses of change in techniques and art styles, or (c) the continuity or slow change of environment, enabling archeologists to see successive cultures as changing adaptations to the environment.

In social anthropology, the specification of continuity is highly problematical. To formulate hypotheses about change, we must be able to specify the connection, that is, the processes that maintain a social form, an institution, or an organization. An item of behavior does not breed an item of behavior. What then is it that creates continuity of society from one day to the next?

Obviously, one can say that society is in the minds of men—as experiences and expectations. If forms of behavior can be described as allocations with reference to evaluated ends, then what persists in the minds of men can be understood as items of credit and debt, as prestations outstanding that make the actors pick up where they last left off. In more general terms, one can see a continuity of agreement between people about the distribution of assets—that is, about the location of rights in statuses distributed in the population. Underlying these one might expect to find shared cultural schemes of classification and evaluation.

But the aggregate pattern of behavior, the structure of society, is not determined by this alone, so this does not exhaust the factors of continuity. What people do is also significantly constrained by circumstance: a whole range of facts of life, mainly ecological, enters as components because people's allocations are adjusted and adapted in terms of what they experience as the observed outcomes of their behavior. The strategic constraints of social life also enter and affect behavior: people's activities are canalized by the fact of competition and cooperation for valued goods with other persons and thus by the problems of adapting one's behavior to that of others, themselves predictive and adaptable.

I would argue that since these various components are all involved as determinants of the forms of aggregate social behavior, consequently they must all enter into our specifications of the continuity connecting situations in a sequence of change; and any hypothesis about social change is inadequate unless it takes all these constraints of continuity into account. It may be a convenient shorthand for structural comparison to say that a matrilineal kinship system changes into a bilateral one, or that a linear organization develops into a segmentary state. But such a formulation is *not* a convenient shorthand for the series of events of change that have taken place, since it begs the whole analysis by implying a naive and mechanical kind of continuity between the two forms, like that between the fish and the crab in the aquarium.

Let me illustrate what I mean by a simple example, again based on material from the Fur.[6] Fur household organization is one where each adult individual is an economic unit for himself; each man or woman produces essentially what he or she needs for food and cash, and has a separate purse. Husband and wife have certain customary obligations toward each other: among other services, a wife must cook and brew for her husband, and he must provide her with clothes for herself and their children. But each of the two cultivates separate fields and keeps provisions in separate grain stores.

This arrangement can be depicted as a system of allocations (Figure 1). A

FIGURE 1

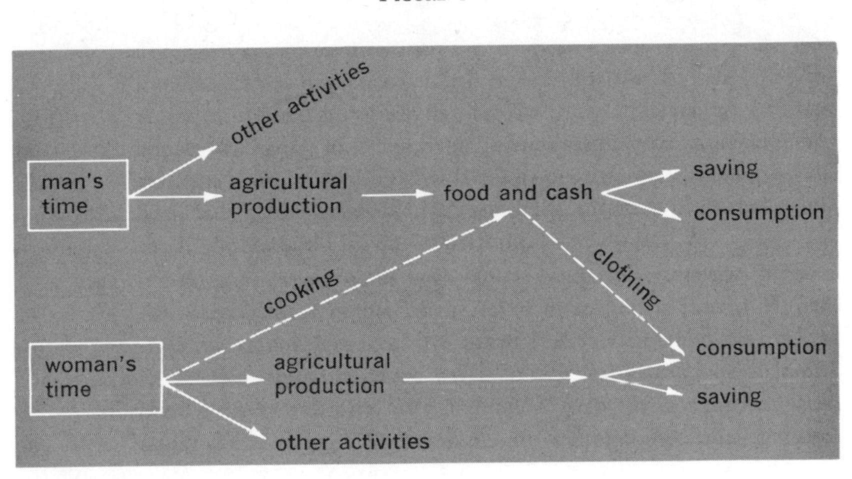

woman must allocate a considerable amount of her time, varying with the season, to agricultural production. By virtue of the marriage contract, she is also constrained to allocate time to cooking and brewing beer for her husband. The husband, on his side, owes it to his wife to allocate some of his cash to consumption goods for her. Such patterns of allocation are thus one way of describing the structure of Fur family and household.

[6] This material derives from Gunnar Haland as well as my own field material. Gunnar Haland, "Ervervform og etnisk tilhorighet. En studie av nomadieseringprosesser blant fastboende hakkebrukere i det vestlige Darfur," unpublished thesis, University of Bergen, 1967.

Some of these Fur couples change their mode of life and become pastoralists like the surrounding Baggara Arabs.[7] Together with this change in subsistence patterns one finds a change in family and household form, in that such couples establish a joint household. Their allocations change, as compared to those of normal Fur villagers (Figure 2). The husband specializes in the activities that

FIGURE 2

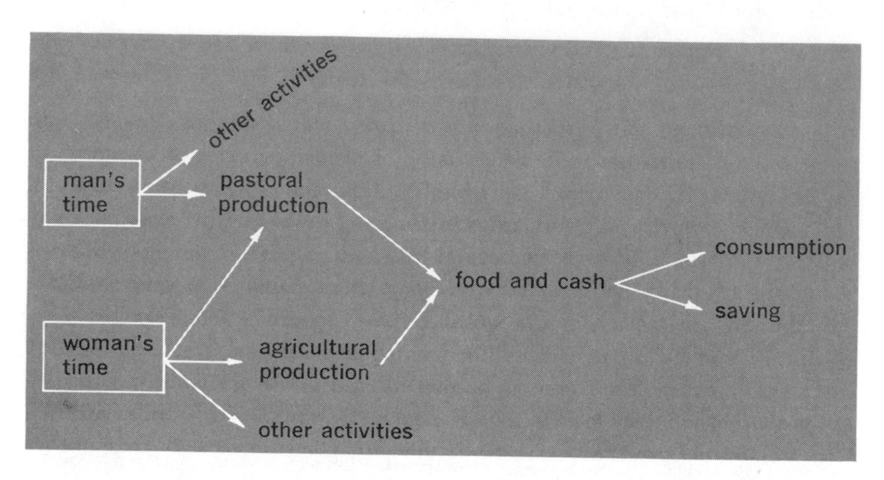

have to do with herding and husbandry, while the woman cultivates some millet, churns butter and markets it, and cooks food. They have a joint grain store and a joint purse and make up a unit for consumption.

In the anthropological tradition, one might reasonably formulate the hypothesis that what we observe here is a case of acculturation: as part of the change to a Baggara Arab way of life they also adopt the Arab household form. This manner of describing the course of change implies a very concrete view of household organization as one of the *parts* of Arab culture, a set of customs that people can take over.

Fortunately, the ethnographic material provides us with a test case for the acculturation hypothesis: some Fur cultivators, in villages where they have no contact with Arab horticultural populations, have recently taken up fruit-growing in irrigated orchards as a specialized form of cash-crop production. Among such Fur too, one finds joint households, but with a slightly different pattern of allocation (Figure 3). Here the conjugal pair make up a unit both for production and consumption, jointly cultivating the orchard and sharing the returns.

To maintain the force of the acculturation explanation of the form of the

[7] Haland (1967).

FIGURE 3

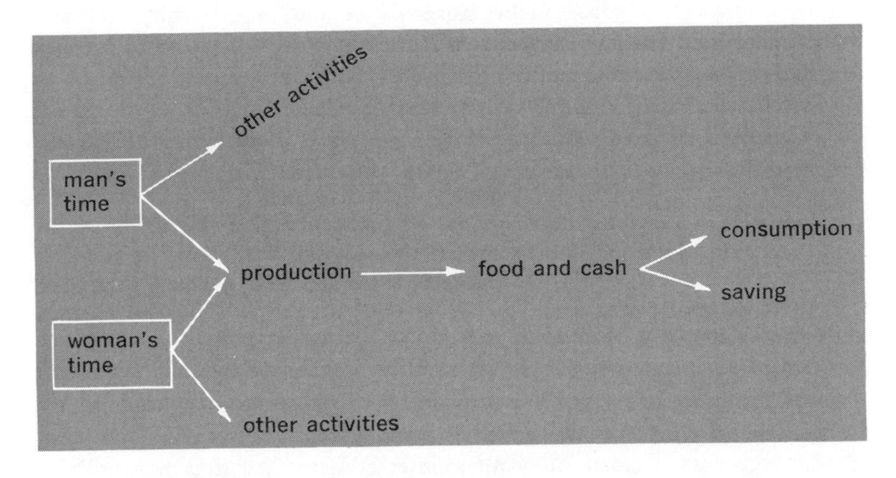

nomad households, one would have to look for similar factors in the case of orchard cultivators and hypothesize a change in values and acculturation to modern life among them. But it is difficult to see the sources of influence for such acculturation; more importantly, a restatement of the nature of the continuity provides opportunities for other kinds of hypotheses. If we agree that behavior in households is determined by several kinds of constraints, that all behavior is "new" in that it constitutes allocations of time and resources made or renewed in the moment of action, and that households persist because their forms are recreated by behavior each day, then we need to ask what the other determinants of these allocations are. To explain a changing pattern of activities, we need not hypothesize changed categorizations and values: we can also look at the changed circumstances that may well make other allocations optional when evaluated by the *same* standards.

Indeed, the traditional range of behavior and allocations in a Fur village indicates that the Fur do not subscribe to any kind of prohibition in joint conjugal households—such arrangements are just not very convenient. A fair autonomy of husband and wife is regarded as a good thing, and joint economic pursuits are a potential field for conflict. Moreover, the techniques of millet cultivation are such that persons work individually in any case; and where a person desires help during peak seasons, he or she can mobilize labor in bulk through a beer work party. In the case of irrigated cash crops, on the other hand, the horticultural techniques are such that it may be convenient to cooperate. Persons with neighboring plots often do so; occasionally, a husband and wife will also decide to cultivate a joint field—because they "like" to work together and because they can partly take turns at irrigation, etc., partly cooperate.

The advantages of this jointness in cultivation are rather limited, only slightly reducing the labor input required for the same result, and few spouses choose to work jointly. But in a situation where one of the spouses can specialize in herding, the other in cultivation and dairying, cooperation offers great advantages. Similarly, where a pooling of labor in specialized arboricultures and fruit-picking gives far greater returns than millet cultivation, it is also clearly to the advantage of both spouses to go together over production and share the product jointly.

One may hypothesize a persistence of values in all these different situations: (a) a preference for husband-wife autonomy, and (b) a preference for the minimization of effort in production. How can spouses further these interests in different situations where environmental constraints change? Where effective production can be pursued individually, persons will be able simultaneously to maximize both interests. Where pooling of labor in orchards gives great returns with limited effort, this allocation on the balance gives the greatest advantage to both spouses. Where they thus have a joint share in the product, it is difficult and meaningless to divide it up when the mutual obligations of cooking and clothing tie the spouses together anyway for certain aspects of consumption—so joint households are generated. Finally, where complementarity and cooperation are not only advantageous but necessary, as in a nomadic setting, the necessary allocations will similarly create a joint household, organized on a slightly different pattern from that of the orchard owners. It is by considering *all* the factors of continuity in the situation of change—in this case both valuational and technical-economic—that we are in a position to formulate, and choose among, the full range of relevant hypotheses.

In this example, then, we find that change in household form is generated by changes in one variable: the relative advantage of joint production over separate production. This is hardly a surprising conclusion. But if we attack the problem in terms of a typology of household forms, we might be led to classify household type I (individual households for each person) and household type II (joint conjugal households) as very different forms and to worry about how type I changes into type II, which is like worrying about how the fish changes into the crab. Yet the situation is clearly not one where one household body changes into another household body: it is one where husband-wife sets, under different circumstances, choose to arrange their life differently. By being forced to specify the nature of the continuity we are forced to specify the processes that generate a household form. We see the same two people making allocations and judging results in two different situations, or we see a population of spouses performing allocations in a pattern that generates predominantly individual households in one opportunity situation, joint households in another. We are led to seek the explanations for change in the determinants of form, and the mechanisms of change in the processes that generate form.

In our efforts to understand social change, this general viewpoint shifts our attention from *innovation* to *institutionalization* as the critical phase of change. People make allocations in terms of pay-offs that they hope to obtain, and their most adequate bases for predicting these pay-offs are found in their previous experience or in that of others in their community. The kinds of new ideas that occur can no more determine the direction of social change than mutation rates can determine the direction of physical change. Whatever ideas people may have, only those that constitute a practicable allocation in a concrete situation will be effected. And if you have a system of allocations going—as you always must where you can speak of change—it will be the rates and kinds of pay-offs of alternative allocations *within that system* that determine whether they will be adopted, that is, institutionalized. The main constraints of change will thus be found in the system, not in the range of ideas for innovation, and these constraints are effective in the phase of institutionalization.

The comparative rates of pay-off of alternative allocations, which determine the course of institutionalization, must be seen from the point of view of actors or of other concrete units of management that dispose over resources and make allocations. Individual actors will naturally make frequent misjudgments of what the pay-offs of their allocations will be; but as the outcomes become apparent through experience, they can be realistically evaluated. If the pay-offs are great, one can expect the behavior to be emulated by others; if, on the other hand, the results are not desirable for the actor, he will not be emulated, and he will also himself attempt to revert to older allocations.

But the process of institutionalization is not simply one of duplication; the allocations of one unit can also have direct implications for other units. They may find their opportunity situation changed, not only through the possibility of emulation, but also through a new need for countermeasures or through new opportunities for activity. The aggregate patterns that can emerge in the population will thus be shaped by the fact of competition and the constraints of strategy. To depict these constraints on actors and the way they will determine the aggregate pattern of choices in a population, we need models in the tradition of game theory.

I do not wish to minimize the complexity of the dynamics of such change and adjustment. My main point is that most of the salient constraints on the course of change will be found to be sociological and interactional, and not simply cognitive. They will derive from the existing social and ecological system within which change is taking place. And finally, they can most usefully be analyzed with reference to the opportunity situation of social persons or other units of management capable of decision-making and action; the mechanisms of change must be found in the world of efficient causes. It should follow from this that though it may be a convenient and illuminating shorthand of culture history to differentiate between "emergent" and "recurrent" change, the mechanisms involved seem to be essentially the same: we must use the same tools to understand the continuities that constitute society in each case.

In summary, I should like to submit that this general line of analysis—which is being pursued in various ways by numerous colleagues in the United States and elsewhere—makes it possible for us to improve our analytic and predictive understanding of social change. I have had to harness it in this presentation to be specific, incomplete and doubtless in many ways inadequate exemplifications. But its essentials are a concentration on the observation of *events* of change and a specification of the nature of *continuity:* the constraints of the whole system that is changing.

Conversely, I would suggest that approaches that rely on typologies of overt social forms, or seek to characterize and compare different courses of change, will not provide as ready insights into the nature of social change.

20 The Science of Culture

GEORGE P. MURDOCK

Temporary confusion is an important stage in the development of scholarly understandings. The critical word here is temporary; *for prolonged confusion leads either to disinterest or madness. The student at this point has probably reached the confusion stage. Where are all these arguments concerning culture leading to? Who is the wise scholar to follow? How is it possible to link all these papers into something comprehensible? Professor Murdock, a leading anthropological theoretician, and editor of the journal* Ethnology, *comes to our aid in the next essay by attempting to integrate the previous discussions.*

Professor Murdock argues that the differences anthropologists debate are really quite superficial. In actuality they all agree as to what the essence of culture is all about.

Social anthropology and sociology are not two distinct sciences. They form together but a single discipline, or at the most two approaches to the same subject matter—the cultural behavior of man. This identity has been all too frequently overlooked—by the general sociologists in their mad pursuit of

SOURCE: Reproduced by permission of the author and the American Anthropological Association from *American Anthropologist*, Vol. 34, No. 1, 1932, pp. 200–215.

the alluring mirages of social philosophy, methodology, and utopianism, and by the anthropologists in their eagerness to unearth before it is too late the facts of ethnography from which alone a general science of culture can be developed. If the anthropologists in many cases have failed to see the forest for the trees, the majority of the sociologists have yet to learn that such a thing as a tree exists. Nevertheless, the leaders in the various branches of these two allied fields, working independently, have succeeded in accumulating a respectable body of general conclusions based on inductive research. It is no longer admissible to spin out new theories of society and culture from the cozy depths of an armchair. We must start from the facts, of which an imposing mass has been assembled, and from the existing body of conclusions derived from the facts and verifiable by them. When this is done, and the deductions of armchair theorists are treated with the neglect they deserve, the apparent inconsistencies in the results of the reliable investigators in the several fields seem to fade away, and the broad outlines of an actual science of culture stand revealed.

That culture, a uniquely human phenomenon independent of the laws of biology and psychology, constitutes the proper subject of the social sciences, is a proposition accepted with practical unanimity by social anthropologists today. A large and increasing proportion of sociologists hold substantially the same position, and agree with Willey that

> the study of culture—the processes of its origin and its growth, its spread and its perpetuation—constitutes the study of sociology.[1]

As regards the exact definition of culture, however, and its precise relation to the data of the biological sciences, certain vagueness still prevails. Even the brilliant analysis of Kroeber[2] has left the concept hanging in a rather mystical though splendid isolation. Recent studies in various fields, however, have shed new light on the subject, and there seems to be no longer any basis for the criticism that the concept of culture is baseless or "supernatural." The differences in interpretation that exist are more apparent than real. They are for the most part differences in emphasis only, resulting from the fact that some authorities have stressed one factor and others another. It is the thesis of this paper that the various approaches are, actually, not contradictory, but supplementary; that there adherents [to "culture"] err, not in what they assert, but in what they deny; that, in short, a true conception of culture will flow, not from the rejection of divergent points of view, but from their acceptance and reconciliation. After all, culture is a complex subject, and over-simple,

---

[1] M. M. Willey, "The Validity of the Culture Concept," *American Journal of Sociology,* 1929, Vol. 35, p. 208.

[2] A. L. Kroeber, "The Superorganic," *American Anthropologist,* 1917, Vol. 19.

particularistic explanations have gone out of fashion in the social sciences. It is here maintained, then, not that the students of culture should unite on some new concept, but that they are already in substantial harmony and need only to recognize that an adequate picture of culture emerges from a mere synthesis of their conclusions.

There is, in the first place, universal agreement—if we except the extreme racialists, eugenists, and instinctivists—that cultural behavior is socially rather than biologically determined; that it is acquired, not innate; habitual in character rather than instinctive. Culture rests, in short, not on man's specific germinal inheritance, but on his capacity to form habits under the influences of his social environment.

> Instinct and the capacity to form habits, while related functions, are present in any animal in inverse ratio.[3]

Habitual behavior, being more susceptible to modification as the result of experience, possesses a certain "survival value" which has led to selection in its favor during the course of organic evolution. Hence, in general, as we rise in the organic scale the proportion of specific instinctive reactions declines while adaptive behavior becomes correspondingly more prominent.[4] The higher the animal, the fewer its instincts and the greater its ability to profit by experience. Man stands in this respect at the head of the animal world; he is the habit-forming creature *par excellence.*

> If we neglect the vegetative . . . and the direct life conserving functions, such as attack and defense, there are few complete and perfect instincts in man yet observed.[5]

Briffault,[6] following Fiske, has sought to explain the adaptability of man's behavior, its comparative freedom from fixation by heredity, by the immaturity of the human child at birth and the prolongation of infancy; the network of association fibers in the brain, he maintains, is organized under the influence of environmental factors before heredity, as it were, can complete its work. Be this as it may, however, no doubt exists of man's supreme habit-forming capacity and of its basic role in culture. The endeavor, fashionable among psychologists not long ago, to interpret cultural phenomena as the manifestations of an equipment of assorted instincts, is now completely outmoded, its *coup de grâce* having been dealt by Bernard.[7] Man's habit-forming capacity,

---

[3] J. B. Watson, *Psychology from the Standpoint of a Behaviorist,* Philadelphia: J. B. Lippincott, 1919, p. 254.
[4] R. Briffault, *The Mothers,* 3 vols., New York: Humanities Press, Inc., 1927, Vol. 1, p. 45.
[5] Watson, p. 254.
[6] Briffault, Vol. 1, pp. 96–110.
[7] L. L. Bernard, *Instinct,* New York: H. Holt and Co., 1924.

of course, has an instinctive or hereditary basis. The individual comes into the world equipped with a vast number of unorganized responses, which he gradually organizes into habits as the result of experience. It is through this "conditioning process" that cultural activities, like all other habits, are acquired. As Tozzer points out:

> from the point of view of human culture we can eliminate everything but those characteristics of man which he learns from his fellow man.[8]

The student of culture by no means denies the existence or importance of heredity. He accepts fully, and cordially welcomes, the immense strides being made by the science of genetics. He neither asserts nor denies that the laws of heredity, well established for anatomical and physiological traits, apply also to mental traits. This question, he believes, it is the province of psychology to decide. But he does deny that the laws of heredity can contribute to his understanding of cultural phenomena—phenomena which are in no respect hereditary but are characteristically and without exception acquired. The student of culture assumes heredity as a starting point, as a mere condition perhaps comparable to the geographic environment, and that is all.

Heredity merely underlies culture. It gives man the unorganized responses which are organized through the conditioning process into habits. It also furnishes him with the mechanism—the sensory, nervous, and motor apparatus—through which all behavior, acquired as well as instinctive, individual as well as social, finds expression. And finally, it probably provides him with certain basic impulses which urge him toward behavior that will satisfy them. The nature and number of these impulses, indeed their very existence, still need to be established by careful objective research. Nevertheless, the student of culture is probably justified in assuming them on the strength of their almost universal acceptance, although it is not his province to weigh the respective merits of the "wishes" of Thomas, the "dispositions" of Williams, the "drives" of Woodworth, the "socializing forces" of Sumner, the "residues" of Pareto, and the countless similar concepts of other writers. He assumes them, but he recognizes that neither they nor any of the other contributions of heredity determine or explain cultural phenomena. At best they merely direct human activities into certain main channels. Thus a sex impulse drives men to seek sexual gratification, and presumably underlies the marriage relation, while other impulses may similarly lie at the root of language, economic organization, religion, etc. The complexes of habit patterns which, in human society, surround the various impulses and their satisfaction are known as "institutions," which Allport correctly regards as clusters of "similar and reciprocal responses of a large number of individuals"[9] rather than as entities in themselves capable

[8] A. M. Tozzer, *Social Origins and Social Continuities,* New York: Macmillan, 1925, p. 56.
[9] F. H. Allport, "The Nature of Institutions," *Social Forces,* 1927, Vol. 6.

of acting upon and controlling individuals. The institutions of economic organization, marriage, religion, etc., which recur in all civilizations because they presumably have their roots in hereditary impulses or drives, constitute in their ensemble what Wissler has aptly termed the "universal culture pattern."[10]

It is of the utmost importance to note, however, that although heredity probably establishes the broad outlines of the universal culture pattern, it in no way determines the content of the latter. Heredity may enable man to speak, but it does not prescribe the particular language he shall employ. It may drive him to some form of sexual association, but the impulse may find adequate satisfaction in a wide variety of polygynous, polyandrous, and monogamous relationships. In short, culture owes to heredity only the number and general character of its institutions, not their form or content. Here, where environmental influences alone are at work, almost infinite diversity prevails. If we compare human behavior to a fabric in which heredity furnishes the warp and habit forms the woof, the warp remains everywhere much the same, for the student of culture is forced to recognize the essential

> equality and identity of all human races and strains as carriers of civilization.[11]

The woof, however, varies with the number and variety of cultural influences. Since the warp remains comparatively constant, cultural diversities are due solely to diversities in the woof. To continue the figure, in the lower animals, whose behavior consists in the main of instinctive responses, the woof of habit is so thin and scanty that it scarcely ever conceals the strands of the warp. To this is due the unfortunate but natural tendency of biological scientists, familiar with the overwhelmingly important role of heredity in animal behavior and cognizant of man's animal ancestry, to assume that human behavior is necessarily similarly determined and to seek explanations of cultural phenomena in terms of race or instincts or other organic factors. They overlook the fundamental fact that, in man, habits, especially those of cultural origin, overlie the hereditary warp so thickly that it is extremely difficult to perceive the latter at all, as is evidenced by the endlessly conflicting attempts to reconstruct man's "original nature." The students of culture, on the other hand, agree that explanations in terms of heredity are inadmissible, and that an adequate analysis of culture must start with a recognition of the unique role of habit in human behavior.

Habit alone, however, is far from explaining culture. Many cultureless animals possess a considerable habit-forming capacity, and some of the mammals are in this respect not radically inferior to man. Social scientists agree, therefore, that culture depends on life in societies as well as on habit. Individual

---

[10] C. Wissler, *Man and Culture,* New York: Thomas Y. Crowell, 1923, pp. 73–97.
[11] A. L. Kroeber, "Eighteen Professions," *American Anthropologist,* 1915, Vol. 17, p. 285.

habits die with their owners, but it is a characteristic of culture that it persists though its individual bearers are mortal. Culture consists of habits, to be sure, but they differ from individual habits by the fact that they are shared or possessed in common by the various members of a society, thus acquiring a certain independence and a measure of immortality. Habits of the cultural order have been called "group habits." To the average man they are known as "customs," and anthropologists sometimes speak of the "science of custom."

> The process of custom forming is similar to that of habit forming and the same psychological laws are involved. When activities dictated by habit are performed by a large number of individuals in company and simultaneously, the individual habit is converted into mass phenomenon or custom.[12]

To the anthropologist, group habits or customs are commonly known as "culture traits," defined by Willey as "basically, habits carried in the individual nervous systems."[13] The sociologists, on the other hand, almost universally speak of them as "folkways." General agreement prevails, therefore, that the constituent elements of culture, the proper data of the science of culture, are group habits. Only the terms employed are at variance.

Of the several terms, "folkway" possesses certain manifest advantages. "Custom" lacks precision. Moreover, though it represents adequately enough such explicit group habits as words, forms of salutation, and burial practices, it scarcely suffices for implicit common responses, mental habits, or ideas, such as religious and magical concepts, which are equally a part of culture. The term "culture trait," though it covers both of these types of group behavior, is also used to include material objects or artifacts, which are not group habits, indeed not habits at all but facts of a totally different order. Artifacts are not themselves primary data of culture, as is shown by the recognized distinction between their dissemination by trade and the process of cultural diffusion proper.

> Material objects are considered as the outgrowths of habits; the material culture is transmitted, in the long run, in terms of knowledge of how to make material objects.[14]

"Culture trait" thus suffers from a basic inconsistency which renders its use frequently misleading and conducive to confusion of thought. The inadequacy of the term is tacitly recognized by anthropologists when they point out the danger of considering artifacts apart from their cultural setting.

---

[12] F. S. Chapin, *An Introduction to the Study of Social Evolution,* rev. ed., New York: The Century Co., 1915, p. 178.
[13] Willey, p. 207.
[14] Willey, p. 207.

> Articles of everyday use, which might seem identical to the museum worker, may be utilized for vastly different purposes by each of the several tribes which employ them and with entirely different emotional reactions.[15]

The substitution of "folkway" for "culture trait" would obviate all these difficulties. The term has never been employed for artifacts themselves but only for the group habits which surround them—the processes of their manufacture, the styles of decorating them, the methods of using them, the current ideas about them, etc. The folkways, in short, supply the social setting. The acceptance of "folkway" by the science of culture would have the great advantage of reducing the data of the science to a single class of strictly comparable phenomena. These phenomena, moreover, are objective behavioristic facts susceptible of repeated verification—an absolute prerequisite for a scientific study. The attempt in certain quarters to build a sound scientific structure on the quicksand of unverifiable subjective facts, such as "attitudes," has proved singularly sterile.

> A study of the behavior of man shows that actions are on the whole more stable than thoughts.[16]

What differentiates the folkway from the individual habit is primarily the intervention of society. Non-gregarious animals, whatever their habit-forming capacity, could not possibly possess culture. From this it results that culture is superindividual. Individuals, to be sure, are the carriers of culture; a culture has no real existence save as it is embodied as habits in the nervous organization of the individuals who compose the group.

> A culture is a system of interrelated and interdependent habit patterns or responses.[17]

Nevertheless, culture does not depend on individuals. An ordinary habit dies with its possessor, but a group habit lives on in the survivors, and is transmitted from generation to generation. Moreover, the individual is not a free agent with respect to culture. He is born and reared in a certain cultural environment, which impinges upon him at every moment of his life. From earliest childhood his behavior is conditioned by the habits of those about him. He has no choice but to conform to the folkways current in his group. Culture is superindividual, also, in the fact that its constituent folkways have in every case a history of their own, a history of their origin and diffusion which is quite independent of the lives and qualities of individuals. Even in the case of invention—the formation of a new habit which becomes a folkway when

---

[15] M. J. Herskovits, "The Cattle Complex in East Africa," *American Anthropologist,* 1926, Vol. 28, p. 241.

[16] Franz Boas, *Anthropology and Modern Life,* New York: W. W. Norton, 1928, p. 148.

[17] Willey, p. 207.

adopted by others—the individual is little more than the agent of social and historical forces. The study of parallel inventions shows that cultural innovations spring, not full-fledged from the brains of their reputed inventors, but from the cultural background or "cultural base," in each case as a synthesis of many previous inventions.

> While each step in an invention is made by a specific individual, no step can be taken until necessary antecedents have been established, no matter what the abilities of the inventor. Because the inventor utilizes the transmitted culture and is limited by it, . . . it may be said that invention is superindividual.[18]

This view does not deny or minimize genius, but simply maintains that it is irrelevant to culture. Even more clearly is the history of folkways superindividual. An innovation may spread or stagnate, have its rise and fall, undergo countless historical fluctuations and vicissitudes. But in any case, once launched into the stream of culture, it is beyond the power of any individual to control. Evolution in the folkways, as Keller[19] has so overwhelmingly demonstrated, is governed by massive impersonal forces. Hence it is both possible and permissible to study the history of a folkway, or the evolution of culture in general, without reference to individuals or their organic and mental characteristics.

The fact that culture is superindividual lifts it beyond the sphere of psychology. As Lowie has expressed it:

> the principles of psychology are as incapable of accounting for the phenomena of culture as is gravitation to account for architectural styles.[20]

Psychology deals only with the individual. It can and does study his hereditary traits. It can also study the genesis of an individual habit, or of a group habit in the individual. As social psychology it can concern itself with the responses of the individual to his social and cultural environment. But it is powerless to explain the development of culture. No psychological laws can possibly account for the evolution of the radio, or the diffusion of the use of tobacco, or the spread of the commission form of municipal government. It is a matter of indifference to psychology that two persons, instead of one, possess a given habit, but it is precisely this fact that becomes the starting point of the science of culture.

Cultural phenomena, from their independence of the laws of biology and psychology, may be said to operate in a distinct realm—the "superorganic." The concept of the superorganic, though named by Spencer,[21] was first

---

[18] Willey, p. 210.
[19] A. G. Keller, *Societal Evolution,* New York: Macmillan, 1915.
[20] R. H. Lowie, *Culture and Ethnology,* New York: Boni and Liveright, 1917, pp. 25–26.
[21] H. Spencer, *Principles of Sociology,* 3 vols., New York and London: D. Appleton and Co., 1923 (first pub. 1882–1896), Vol. 1, pp. 3–15.

consistently adhered to by Lippert,[22] and first clearly formulated and analyzed by Kroeber.[23] According to this concept, the phenomena of nature fall into three great realms: (1) the inorganic, where the chemical and physical sciences study the phenomena of matter and energy; (2) the organic, where the sciences of biology and psychology study living organisms and their organic behavior; and (3) the superorganic, where the social sciences study cultural and historical phenomena. The superorganic, to be sure, rests upon the organic, precisely as the latter rests upon the inorganic. But the science of culture is just as distinct, as to subject matter, laws, and principles, from biology and psychology as the biological sciences are from those of the inorganic realm. This point of view does not deny the fundamental unity of all nature, nor the legitimacy in each realm of utilizing to the utmost the knowledge acquired in the realm immediately below it, nor the possibility or even probability that the superorganic may be ultimately resolvable into the organic, and both into the inorganic. It merely maintains that natural phenomena are divided into three realms of ascending complexity, and that the data of each may be most profitably studied by its own students with their own methods and instrumentalities.

Although it is society which intervenes between, and in large measure distinguishes, the organic from the superorganic, society alone, even in conjunction with habit, is insufficient to explain the existence of culture. As Kroeber points out:

> something more than gregariousness is needed to produce culture; otherwise cattle would possess it.[24]

Society alone does not raise behavior to the superorganic plane, for, although many lower animals live in societies, none of them possesses culture.

> In this respect a tremendous gulf separates man and the lower forms of life, the anthropoid apes and social insects not excepted.[25]

The uniqueness of human culture is revealed by a comparison between man and the social but cultureless insects. A justly famous passage by Kroeber will lose none of its luster by another repetition.

> Take a couple of ant eggs of the right sex—unhatched eggs, freshly laid. Blot out every individual and every other egg of the species. Give the pair a little attention as regards warmth, moisture, protection, and food. The whole of ant

---

22 J. Lippert, *Kulturgeschichte der Menschheit in ihrem organischen Aufbau,* 2 vols., Stuttgart, 1886–1887.

23 Kroeber (1917).

24 A. L. Kroeber, "Sub-human Culture Beginnings," *Quarterly Review of Biology,* 1928, Vol. 3, p. 330.

25 C. M. Case, *Outlines of Introductory Sociology,* New York: Harcourt Brace, 1924, p. xxix.

> "society," every one of the abilities, powers, accomplishments, and activities of the species, . . . will be reproduced, and reproduced without diminution, in one generation. But place on a desert island or in a circumvallation two or three hundred human infants of the best stock from the highest class of the most civilized nation; furnish them the necessary incubation and nourishment; leave them in total isolation from their kind; and what shall we have? The civilization from which they were torn? One tenth of it? No, not any fraction; nor a fraction of the civilizational attainments of the rudest savage tribe. Only a pair or a troop of mutes, without arts, knowledge, fire, without order or religion. Civilization would be blotted out within these confines—not disintegrated, not cut to the quick, but obliterated in one sweep. Heredity saves for the ant all that she has, from generation to generation. But heredity does not maintain, and has not maintained, because it cannot maintain, one particle of the civilization which is the one specifically human thing.[26]

The social phenomena of the ants are instinctive rather than acquired, transmitted through the germ plasm rather than through tradition, in short, biologically rather than culturally determined. All analogies drawn by enthusiastic biologists between human and insect or other animal societies, fall to the ground on this point. However striking the similarities may appear, they are never more than superficial.

The oft-cited parallel between human marriage and forms of permanent mating among certain lower animals, especially the birds, furnishes an excellent illustration of this fallacy. When a male and a female bird associate in a seemingly monogamous relationship, they do so because they are impelled by a specific mating instinct. It is an organic rather than a superorganic fact. Man, on the other hand, marries because in the course of his cultural evolution he has developed around his sexual impulse certain conventional taboos and restraints which leave marriage as the proper and socially sanctioned form of sexual association. The only organic fact involved is the sexual impulse or drive; a specific mating instinct is lacking. The impulse urges man only to seek sexual gratification; it does not even predispose him to contract a permanent union; the form of expression it takes is determined by cultural factors alone. The almost infinite variety of marriage forms precludes the possibility of a specific mating, much less a monogamous, instinct in man. As Lippert so aptly phrases it:

> the institution of human marriage is not a subject of a natural history but of culture history.[27]

Nevertheless, the majority of writers on this subject have confused the organic

[26] Kroeber (1917), pp. 177–178.
[27] J. Lippert, *The Evolution of Culture,* New York: Macmillan, 1931, p. 69.

and superorganic, perhaps none so persistently as Westermarck, who thus states his major premise:

> The marriage of mankind is not an isolated phenomenon, but has its counterpart in many animal species and is probably an inheritance from some pre-human ancestor.[28]

From such a premise he can only reach, for all his wealth of data and his serious scholarship, conclusions of the utmost unreliability. Yet many students of culture, with an amazing inconsistency, have accepted uncritically the results of a work which violates their every canon.

The analysis of social phenomena among the lower animals demonstrates that society, however essential, is insufficient in itself to explain culture. This fact needs to be stressed, for the danger is, not that the role of society may be overlooked, but that it may be overemphasized. Indeed, the tendency among sociologists in particular has been to single out society, not as an outstanding factor in culture, but as their very subject of study itself. Thus they commonly define their field, not as the science of culture, but as the "science of society." They ignore the fundamental distinction between the social and the cultural, which Stern[29] has so clearly pointed out. Allport, too, though with a different object in mind, has repeatedly attacked what he calls the "group fallacy."[30] Not society, but culture is the distinctively human phenomenon. Those sociologists who have overlooked this fundamental fact have spent their time seeking "social processes" common to ants, cattle, and men alike, and they have found little save abstractions distressingly suggestive of the "conation" and "cognition" which an outmoded psychology once accepted as realities. The sterility of their work, as reflected in the contempt for sociology manifested by scholars in other fields, shows that they have been on the wrong track. As a consequence, the social anthropologists, whose results have encountered anything but a contemptuous reception from historians and others, now find themselves joined by a rapidly increasing school of "cultural sociologists," who realize that the proper study of sociology is culture.

If society does not suffice to explain culture, just what is it which, when added to social life, has made possible the development of culture in the human race? Numerous writers have suggested human intelligence as the answer to this question. It has frequently been pointed out that man's typical manner of adapting himself to his environment differs significantly from that of the lower

[28] E. Westermarck, *The History of Human Marriage,* 3 vols., 5th ed., New York: Allerton Book Co., 1922, Vol. 1, p. 72.

[29] B. J. Stern, "Concerning the Distinction between the Social and the Cultural," *Social Forces,* 1929, Vol. 8.

[30] F. H. Allport, "The Group Fallacy in Relation to Social Science," *Journal of Abnormal and Social Psychology,* 1924, Vol. 19.

animals. His characteristic mode of adaptation, it is suggested, is mental; that of the animals, physical. The development of one great physical adaptation, the human brain, has rendered unnecessary any further important physical specialization, since it enables man, for example, to invent fur clothing in the Arctic instead of developing a fur coat of his own, or to invent an airplane instead of growing wings. On the basis of this distinction Keller defines culture as the "sum of synthesis of mental adaptations."[31] Biological scientists go even further in stressing the importance of the human brain and human intelligence. But important as this factor unquestionably is, it by no means suffices to explain culture, and it has probably, like society, been considerably overemphasized.

> The distinction between animal and man which counts is not that of the physical and mental, which is one of relative degree, but that of the organic and social, which is one of kind.[32]

Recent studies[33] have clearly demonstrated that the anthropoid apes possess intelligence, "insight," or "ideation," of an order comparable to that of man, inferior only in degree; that both apes and men, for example, solve problems by intelligent behavior as opposed to the mere trial-and-error learning characteristic of the rest of the animal world. Yet, in spite of their intelligence, the apes lack culture.

A realistic view of human culture indicates that the role of intelligence is smaller than many have assumed. It is a truism of psychology and almost a matter of general knowledge that the chief use of the human mind is the invention of reasons or justifications for our beliefs and actions. The science of culture has suffered much in the past from rationalization or wishful thinking, and it should be among the first to minimize the importance of intelligence in human affairs. Comparatively little intelligence is needed to acquire a habit or folkway, none to preserve it.

> Most habitual responses occur on a relatively low level of consciousness.[34]

Intelligence probably plays a more prominent part in the life of the individual than in that of society. At any rate, practically the only social process in which it demonstrably plays a significant role is invention. Yet it is a fact that apes also invent.

> With the ape inventive but cultureless, the question arises whether we have not perhaps hitherto exaggerated the importance of invention in human culture. We

[31] Keller, p. 21.

[32] Kroeber (1917), p. 169.

[33] W. Kohler, *The Mentality of Apes,* New York, 1925 (rev. ed., London: Routledge, 1956); R. M. and A. W. Yerkes, *The Great Apes,* New Haven: Yale University Press, 1929.

[34] L. L. Bernard, *An Introduction to Social Psychology,* New York: H. Holt & Co., 1926, p. 34.

> are wont to think of it as the creative or productive element in civilization. We tend to view the other processes in culture as essentially those of transmission, preservation, or decay. The idea of progress, which has so powerful a hold on the unconscious as well as the conscious thought of our day, may have led us to overemphasize the role of invention. Perhaps the thing which essentially makes culture is precisely those transmissive and preservative elements. . . .[35]

While it would be absurd to deny intelligence any importance in culture, the evidence clearly suggests the need of a search for other factors.

"That which distinguishes man from animals," says Anatole France, "is lying and literature." This aphorism expresses, with a characteristic twist, a widely if not universally recognized truth. The underlying idea, in more prosaic terms, is that man differs from the animals in the possession of language, which undoubtedly goes far to explain his possession of culture as well as his propensity for both forms of story-telling. Kroeber has shown that the lower animals completely lack true language. Their cries, unlike human speech, are instinctive rather than acquired, organic rather than social. They convey to other animals, not objective ideas such as most human words represent, but merely subjective emotional states, such as suffering or sexual excitement. Thus they are comparable only to such words as the "ouch" uttered by a man unexpectedly pricked with a pin.[36]

Since culture is not innate, it must be acquired anew by each individual and transmitted from generation to generation. It is this transmission of folkways which insures the continuity of culture in spite of the impermanence of the individual. The folkways thus transmitted constitute what is called the "social heritage" of the group. But culture is not only continuous; it is also cumulative.[37] New inventions and acculturations from without are added to the stream of culture in each generation, and in most cases the new does not displace the old. Thus we still retain wine in spite of the later invention of distilled spirits, and both in spite of Prohibition. The stream of culture, the social heritage, thus shows a definite tendency to grow richer and fuller with the passage of time. This does not mean that cultural acquisitions are never lost, but the "lost arts" of antiquity are few by comparison with the arts which have survived alongside newer inventions.

Both the transmission and diffusion of culture require some means of communication. Imitation alone seems insufficient. To be sure, certain songbirds, when reared in the nests of another species, are said to acquire and transmit the songs of their foster-parents. But except for such crude germs, nothing resembling a social heritage exists among the lower animals. What gives lan-

---

[35] Kroeber (1928), p. 340.

[36] A. L. Kroeber, *Anthropology,* New York: Harcourt Brace, 1923, pp. 106–107.

[37] Tozzer, p. 9.

guage its importance in human culture is the fact that it alone, with its derivatives such as writing, seems to provide an adequate means of communication. It alone makes possible the transmission of folkways, the continuity and accumulation of culture, the very existence of a social heritage. Without language, man would be little better off than the animals, as is proved by studies of deaf-mutes and other speechless persons.[38] In a society without language, each individual would have to begin exactly where his parents began; he could possess only individual habits, not group habits; his behavior, in short, would be confined to the organic level.

Many authorities have recognized this fundamental role of language in culture.

> The cultural life of man as distinguished from the social life of sub-human groups is dependent on articulate language. . . . The most important influence of language on social life is derived through its making possible the accumulation and transmission of culture. Recent studies in sub-human animals, especially of anthropoid apes, reveal the presence of many factors upon which culture depends, learning, inventiveness, memory, even the beginnings of symbolic abstraction. But the absence of an articulate language prevents cultural life in the sense possessed by men.[39]

If the transmissive and preservative elements in culture are basic, says Kroeber,

> then the indispensability of speech to the very existence of culture becomes understandable. It is the communications, perhaps, more than the thing communicated, that count. At any rate the fact that speech, to the best of our knowledge, is as thoroughly wanting among the anthropoids as is culture, tends to confirm this conception.[40]

Four factors, as we have now seen, have been advanced by various writers, and have received wide recognition, as explanations of the fact that man alone of all living creatures possesses culture—namely, habit-forming capacity, social life, intelligence, and language. These factors may be likened to the four legs of a stool, raising human behavior from the floor, the organic level or hereditary basis of all behavior, to the superorganic level, represented by the seat of the stool. No other animal is securely seated on such a four-legged stool. Many live in societies. Some manifest no mean intelligence and habit-forming capacity. None, however, possesses language. Just as no one or two of these factors alone can suffice to explain culture, so no animal can maintain an equilibrium on a stool with but one or two legs. All four legs seem necessary to attain the level of the superorganic, and man alone possesses all.

---

[38] Briffault, Vol. 1, pp. 23–40.
[39] Stern, p. 267.
[40] Kroeber (1928), p. 341.

The case of the anthropoid apes is particularly instructive. They possess three comparatively well-developed legs of the cultural stool, lacking only language. And they appear to hover on the very verge of culture. Köhler has described the fads which occur with great frequency in groups of chimpanzees. From time to time one of these restless and curious animals makes an invention or discovery, e.g., sucking water through a straw, painting objects with white clay, catching ants on a twig moistened with saliva, teasing chickens by offering bread in one hand and jabbing with a sharp stick held in the other, or climbing rapidly to the top of a pole planted vertically on the ground and jumping off before it falls. The rest of the group then takes up the innovation by imitation, and for days or weeks the new practice rages with all the vigor of a recent fashion among humans, only to disappear after its novelty has worn off. While the fad lasts, it is certainly a group habit, an incipient element of culture. Only the absence of language, apparently, prevents the retention and accumulation of such acquisitions and their transmission to succeeding generations as a social heritage. Chimpanzee fads, in short, differ from human folkways only in their impermanency.[41] Kroeber would therefore seem to be wrong when he states that they possess no "residuum of unmitigatedly cultural material."[42] Little more than a time element differentiates the chimpanzee use of straws from the modern American folkway observable in soft-drink parlors, or the ape's use of the "jumping stick" from human pole vaulting. The chimpanzee seems to be in the position of a man insecurely perched on a four-legged stool of which one of the legs is wanting. He can preserve a precarious balance only for a short time before the stool overturns and plunges him and his incipient culture once more to the organic floor.

The well-informed reader will find little that is new in the foregoing, little indeed that is not already widely accepted among students of culture. But this is precisely the purpose of the article, namely, to demonstrate that an adequate conception of the nature and basis of culture already exists and needs only to be recognized. The various partial interpretations of culture, stressing some of the basic factors and neglecting or even denying others, turn out upon examination to be not mutually exclusive but complementary. The general recognition of this fact should go far toward clearing the air of dogmatism and laying the foundation for constructive cooperative effort in solving the manifold problems of the science of culture.

---

41 Kohler (1925).

42 Kroeber (1928), p. 326.

21 Manufacturing Culture: Man the Scientist

MORRIS FREILICH

The answer to our persistent question "what is culture really?" *has been brought to the point of Murdock's synthesis of 1932:*

> *[Students of culture] are already in substantial harmony and need only to recognize that an adequate picture of culture emerges from a mere synthesis of their conclusions.*

But what of the present? The Western world has undeniably changed since the 1930s, and an integrational, mediating model of culture is needed to fill that forty-year gap of rapid change and adaptation to change.

The following paper synthesizes and acts as arbitrator for cultural theory from Tylor's beginnings in "psychic unity" to Lévi-Strauss's structuralism and the final model of "V-R Guidance Systems." And by the end of the process we find that man, in a uniquely twentieth-century phrasing, is Scientist, information-hungry, but unavoidably human. No longer torn by theorists between being creator of his culture and acting as a messenger-boy for cultural traditions, he emerges as "a decision-maker, not a puppet . . . , not a machine . . . ."

What Does "Culture" Mean?

What does "culture" mean? Is it a superorganic phenomenon? Is man in control of his own culture, or is he but a puppet playing a part in a play he did not write? How did culture develop? Is cultural evolution a fact of human existence? Does the environment determine culture? These and related questions have been discussed in depth by a number of scholars, including several who rank among the leaders of anthropological thought. The reader who has carefully studied these writings will yet feel that *the* meaning of culture has *not* been presented. The best approach to culture is therefore a matter of individual choice: it requires selecting the meaning that a given theorist has discovered. By selecting the views of one scholar, one must necessarily reject the views of others. How is this to be done, scientifically? Few objective guidelines exist to help us in deciding who is right and who is wrong.

A better strategy is to assume that all the views herein presented are correct. That, like blind men standing around an elephant, everyone has grabbed a piece of the truth; and that the final answer (the whole elephant) is discovered by adding together all the bits of information presented. Essentially, that is the goal of this essay: to develop an "integrational" model of culture.[1] To do this I must start with one theorist, state his view of culture, and slowly graft on the ideas of others. A good place to begin is with the seminal work of E. B. Tylor.

Cementing Theories

Tylor, considered by many the father of cultural anthropology, deserves considerable applause for handling a dilemma which could cripple a lesser brain. The question at issue was magnificent and awe-inspiring: *What is the meaning of human existence?* And, standing in opposing corners, were two powerful protagonists: "Science" and "the Church." Science (the left "horn" of Tylor's dilemma) proclaimed the truth of Darwinian evolutionary theory. Man was an animal among animals, bereft of a special creation and an idyllic youth in the Garden of Eden. This ego-deflating picture of *Homo sapiens* was challenged by the church (Tylor's right "horn"). Traditional theology declared: God created man in his own image, and gave man dominion over all living things. Man's kinship to animals was a heretical idea, concocted by atheists and other rogues. These traditional views, however, were contradicted by considerable data which suggested that evolution really did occur; so back to the left horn. But this too seemed improbable from a common sense viewpoint. Man had a soul, a great intellect, delicate manners; and his creativity often bordered on the divine.[2] What in animal life could be compared to the magnificence of Gothic architecture, to the aesthetic purity of a Bach fugue, to the mechanical perfection of Newtonian physics? How could a creature with apish ancestry create an empire over which the sun never set?

Evolution appeared to be "true," however, and its acceptance involved more than a readiness to accept animal ancestry in the far distant past. If man everywhere had a common ancestor, then "mankind" represented a biological and psychic unity. How could this bio-psychic unity be explained in the light of ethnographic writings on "primitive" societies? Tribes were currently in existence whose customs, at best, seemed like the behavior of children, and at worst, were more like animal than human living.[3]

---

[1] The approach being used owes a great debt to George Peter Murdock, who long ago suggested that the answer to the question "What does culture mean?" may be discovered by piecing together the views of many scholars. See his essay in this volume.

[2] This theme is picked up in a very interesting manner by Roger Wescott in *The Divine Animal,* New York: Funk and Wagnalls, 1969.

[3] For example, Tylor wrote, "the trite comparison of savages to 'grown-up children,' is in the main a sound one, though not to be carried out too strictly. In the uncivilized American or Polynesian, the strength of body or force of character of a grown man are combined with a mental development in many respects not beyond that of a young child of a civilized race." Edward B. Tylor, *Researches into the Early History of Mankind and the Development of Civilization,* London: John Murray, 1865, p. 108.

Slipping artfully in between the left and right horns of his dilemma, Tylor provided an answer that was (1) consistent with the scientific findings of his times, (2) flattering to man wherever he existed, and (3) most flattering to the Victorian audience with whom Tylor was communicating. Man, although belonging to the animal kingdom, was distinct from other animals. Man had culture; other animals did not. The unbridgeable chasm which existed between human and animal life was completely explainable by this gem which animal society lacked. Animals behaved instinctively, humans culturally; animal life, therefore, was *qualitatively* different from human, cultural, existence. Hence, while the physiology of a Bach or a Newton was comparable limb-by-limb to the physiology of other primates, the works of the former were creative additions to a cultural complex, and the behavior of the latter was biologically determined.

The "psychic unity of man" as used by Tylor further helped to explain the vast difference between animal and human living. The mind of man, in all its essentials, was everywhere similar; and everywhere, this mind was capable of fashioning a culture. Man's psychic unity provided him with a common creative ability, which man everywhere used for many purposes, including the manufacture of culture. The cultures produced by man were everywhere quite similar, in all their basic traits. Given man's bio-psychic unity it was still unclear, however, why the cultures of the world should have many basic similarities. Tylor had an answer: Man's common environment provided him with similar challenges. Similar problems attacked by similar minds must lead to similar, cultural solutions. As Opler tells us:

> . . . Tylor saw in man's natural environment a reasonably uniform background of challenge and opportunity. In spite of climatic differences and variations in resources, life could be maintained in most regions into which man penetrated. Everywhere there was need for protection against the elements and foes, human and nonhuman. Throughout most of the world, nature provided materials to be utilized for shelter, dress, and artifacts, and in nearly all regions, sufficient animal and vegetable food existed to support human groups. The world and its people appeared to Tylor to be a vast laboratory in which uniform causes operating in similar settings might be expected to yield comparable results.[4]

It is instructive to note that when Tylor explained the vast gap which exists between human and animal society, he placed strong emphasis on human creativity and human similarity. Human creativity (shared by all humanity because of the bio-psychic unity of man) is universally linked to culture: a product of human existence. Human creativity, when linked with a basically similar environment, leads to similar cultures everywhere. From within this

[4] Morris E. Opler, "Cause, Process and Dynamics in the Evolutionism of E. B. Tylor," *Southwestern Journal of Anthropology,* 1964, Vol. 20, pp. 123–144.

creativity focus, culture itself must be seen as a problem-solving tool. Man's first need, Tylor tells us, is "to get his daily food." Thus wherever man lives, he creates economic institutions to help solve sustenance needs. Tylor's *creativity focus* included three propositions: (1) man is actively involved in the creation of culture, (2) culture is a problem-solving tool, and (3) culture is essentially the same wherever it is found.

Thus far Tylor had dealt nicely with the problems of man and his animal ancestry; but what of "civilized" versus "primitive" man? For these problems too, Tylor had an acceptable answer. While some of the essentials pertaining to social living were everywhere similar *structurally,* various societies differed greatly in cultural *content.* In truth, man's first need everywhere is to get his daily food, and everywhere such needs are satisfied by economic institutions which define *what is food, how it is best obtained, and when and with whom one eats.* However, some people live precariously in a hunting and gathering economy, while others have a secure food supply based on agriculture. Given man's psychic unity and the basically similar challenges provided by his environment, how are such (and other) cultural differences explained? Tylor's simple and effective answer was *evolution:*

> In successive evolutionary stages family life becomes more secure, thinking more logical, knowledge more detailed, artifacts more efficient, religion more firmly wedded to morality, and abundance more general. Tylor applied this conception of evolutionary progress through stages of Savagery, Barbarism, and Civilization. . . .[5]

Culture, like man, evolves; and cultural evolution, like biological evolution, is progressive; inferior forms regularly give way to superior forms. Just as man is superior to non-human animals, so barbaric culture is superior to savage culture, and civilization is superior to both. Within this evolutionary framework, in which culture invariably travels along a road whose end is civilization, what does psychic unity of mankind mean? Irrespective of what individuals do or do not do, culture will follow its predestined path. The individual rides a cultural elevator whose program reads: Only up. Questions concerning human creativity are here meaningless. The question now becomes: Can man adapt to the ever more rarified cultural "air" into which he is elevated? The answer, again linked to the "psychic unity of mankind," is Yes! "Psychic unity of man," when tied to unilineal evolution, has a changed meaning; for man is now seen as a "rider" who everywhere can accept progress. And, progress, for Tylor, included radical changes of the human mind. For example, the beliefs and practices subsumed under "magic" came from "a condition of mind which we of the advanced races have almost outgrown, and in doing so have under-

[5] Opler, p. 130.

gone one of the most notable changes which we can trace as having happened to mankind."[6] In a low stage of culture, man operates with a primitive mentality. Very commonly he "believes that between the object and the image of it there is a real connection, which does not arise from a mere process in the mind of the observer, and that it is accordingly possible to communicate an impression of the original through the copy."[7] The inevitable cultural advances that evolution brings about, slowly uplift man: agriculture raises him into the stage of barbarism and writing lifts man higher yet, up into the rationalities of civilization.

It is instructive to note that when the problem is "Why does cultural variation exist?" the answer "cultural evolution" implies a passivity of mankind. The mysterious inevitability of cultural progress makes man but a receptacle into which culture is poured. This *passivity focus* includes three propositions about man and culture: (1) man is a passive, puppet-like creature, completely moldable by culture, (2) culture is a mysterious phenomenon, programmed for progress, and (3) given societies are currently at different stages of cultural evolution.

Tylor's writings provided many examples of these two contradictory ways of looking at man: (1) the creativity focus, with man the creator of a cultural world distinctly different from animal *society,* and (2) the passivity focus, with man as the mold into which ever more progressive cultural traits are poured. While Tylor was unable to resolve this dualistic view of man, his definition of culture clearly broadcast a partiality toward "passivity." Differently put, Tylor's classic definition emphasized man's role as *an acquirer* of culture (man the mold); it said nothing of man as *a creator* of culture (man the manufacturer). This point is more obvious if Tylor's definition of culture is translated into modern language: *Culture is a system of information acquired by man as a member of society.*[8]

Boas disagreed with this view of man and culture. In his words:

> It is hardly necessary to consider culture a mystic entity that exists outside the society and of its individual carriers, and that moves mysteriously by its own force. The life of society is carried on by individuals who act singly and jointly under the stress of their own activities and those of their forebears.[9]

Tylor, the armchair theoretician, provided a scheme which attempts to explain all human activities at all times. Boas the scientist wanted solid,

---

[6] Tylor (1865), p. 3.
[7] Tylor (1865), p. 120.
[8] The writings of such scholars as Kroeber and White thus represent a continuation and refinement of Tylor's passivity focus; while the works of such scholars as Boas, Sapir, and Morris Opler represent a continuation and refinement of Tylor's creativity focus.
[9] Franz Boas, *Anthropology and Modern Life,* New York: W. W. Norton, 1928, pp. 235–236.

empirical proof that universalistic, progressive, cultural evolution occurred. Since such proof was not forthcoming, Boas set his sights on the more manageable goals that Professor Wax discusses in "The Limitations of Boas' Anthropology" (Chapter 2).

Boas found anthropology replete with generalizations that were so speculative that the facts to support them were unobtainable. Understandably then he became hyper-critical of all generalizations. Boas found anthropology with little valid data; therefore it is not surprising that "Boas preached empiricism to his students almost as a crusade." In truth, "Science seeks the general statement, the universal proposition," but the universalistic generalizations that Boas inherited created no obviously productive research paths for him to follow.

Anthropology, as Boas found it, provided two possible work strategies: (1) to continue in the Tylorian school of speculative generalizations based on "rubber-data,"[10] or (2) to develop a solid, empirically-based science of man. By choosing empiricism, Boas laid the foundations for a science of man. Understandably then he "was intensely loyal to the individual phenomenon"; in the individual as a decision-maker, in individual creations, and in life-history materials. Given these interests it becomes difficult to type Boas as either scientist or historian; at different times and for different purposes he was either one or both. Looking at Boas from the framework of "The Superorganic," Kroeber saw him as contributing "little to Tylor's attempt to isolate and clarify the concept of culture." In actuality, Boas emphasized variables missing in Tylor's formulation of culture: man the manufacturer, man in control accepting, rejecting, modifying, and adding to his tradition. The culture that man acquires in one generation, and the culture that he manufactures, is transmitted to the generation that follows. Better put, the older generation *attempts to transmit* to its offspring what it considered proper behavior and thought. For various reasons these attempts never achieve complete success: enculturation agencies (peer groups, for example) help the individual to reject *some* traditions; the individual's personality, interests, talents, etc., lead him to reject given aspects of his culture; and so forth. The culture which is acquired by a new generation is therefore different from the culture which the parent generation acquired. Moreover, every generation attempts to mold the tradition it acquires to better suit its own environment, and, in every generation, some people are better molders than others. From within this Boasian framework it is important to study the exceptional individual, the person who manufactures more culture than the less creative members of his society.

---

[10] Data collected and presented in ways which enable any "theorist" to stretch it in various directions to fit his own pre-conceived scheme. See Morris Freilich, ed., *Marginal Natives: Anthropologists at Work*, New York: Harper and Row, 1970, p. 7.

FIGURE 1: Information Flows in Human Society

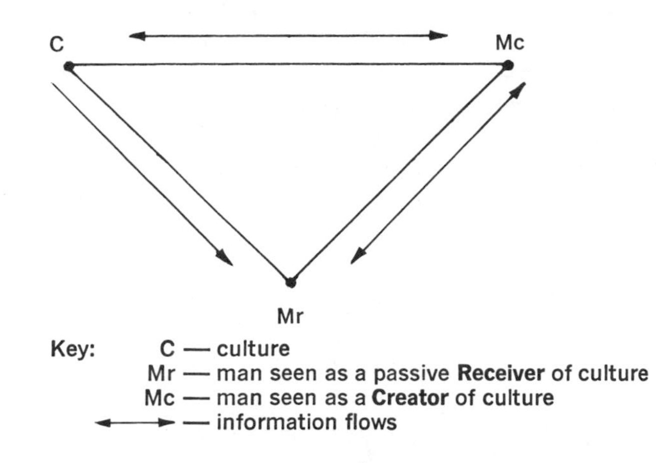

Tylor's definition of culture omits "the products of human social life," because his emphasis was on man's passivity, not his productivity. No such omission is present in Boas' formulation: "Culture embraces all the manifestations of social habits of a community, the reactions of the individual as affected by the habits of the group in which he lives, and the *products of human activities* as determined by the habits."[11] The individual is *affected* by the habits of his group, not determined by them, and human activities have outputs—products.

With Boas we get an attempt to link the three critical variables which are basic to all human existence: *information from the past* (culture); *humans acquiring such information* (socialization or enculturation); *and humans adding, deleting, and modifying such information* (human decision-making). When culture is linked both to socialization or enculturation on the one hand (the passivity focus) and to human decision-making on the other (the creativity focus), we have the beginnings of an anthropology which can function as a full partner in modern social science programs.[12]

The triadic model within which Boas struggled is also the framework within which Sapir worked. For both these scholars man's relationship to culture was dualistic: in my terms, man was both "Mr"—a passive *receiver* of culture—and "Mc"—an inventive *creator* of culture (see Figure 1). For Sapir this meant that anthropology had a rather special goal: to develop a true "psychiatric science of man." Culture can only be discovered within the individual, for it starts "from the needs of a common humanity." Culture is the "experience

---

[11] Franz Boas, "Anthropology," *Encyclopedia of the Social Sciences,* New York, 1930, Vol. 2, pp. 73–110 (Italics mine).

[12] See John Bennett's essay in this volume.

that the individual values or perceives as significant" and it is maintained by a group of culture-carriers who (often unconsciously) select such valued experiences. Sapir's emphasis on human decision-making helps culture to lose some of its mystery. Humans perceive, humans select, and that which is valued somehow gets transformed into culture: information from the past that can influence action in the present, and perhaps the future. For Sapir, the only conceivable stuff of human experience is "personalistic meanings." Hence it is impossible to separate culture from man. Kroeber, in his classic work "The Superorganic," disagrees.

Kroeber's paper reverts back to a topic dear to Tylor, evolution. By 1917, "evolution" had completely captured the imagination of the scientific community. As Kroeber tells us, human civilization or progress "which exists only in and through living members of the species is so unmistakingly similar to the evolution of plants and animals, that it has been inevitable that there should have been sweeping applications of the principles of organic development to the facts of cultural growth."[13] In "The Superorganic" Kroeber is concerned that this great fascination with evolution does not blind scholars to the differences which exist between physical (organic) evolution, and cultural (superorganic) evolution. With organic phenomena, heredity is "the indispensable means of transmission." With culture (superorganic phenomena), however, transmission of information occurs in a social context where the participants need not have biological links to each other. Animal life is based on organic processes (e.g. a dog raised with a family of cats will bark, not mew); human life has its bases in social or superorganic processes ("the content, at least, of our own minds comes to us through tradition"). And it is at this point that Kroeber begins to develop what I call the passivity focus.[14] Tradition or culture, we are told, is a message; and it is the message that is important, not man, who is but an insignificant carrier and conveyer of information. The message is written on paper (humans) who may be of all types (just as paper varies in fibre); but the character of the paper is unimportant, since any paper (any human) can have any message (any culture) inscribed on it. In the language of model analysis, Kroeber says: Let us construct an informational model of human life. We can act *as if* man is *only* a receiver and transmitter of information and see what pay-offs such a model provides.

Morris Opler finds this superorganic model lacking in a critical variable—human creativity:

> . . . this doctrine of a cultural realm, separate or separable from man, where invisible strings are pulled to make the human puppets dance, is embraced mainly by materialists who, because they hesitate to grant man too much in the

13 A. L. Kroeber, "The Superorganic," *American Anthropologist,* 1917, Vol. 19, pp. 163–213, especially p. 164.
14 Kroeber (1917), p. 178.

> way of will, creativity, and control, are sure they constitute a bulwark against mysticism and supernaturalism. But they have managed to develop their own updated brand of vision experience and have been permitted to gaze on a shadow in which cultural ideas and artifacts jostle each other, breed, take direction, and determine man's course. . . . [In actuality] culture is the work of humanity; we have the impression that it is autonomous only because it is anonymous.[15]

To separate man from culture is, for Opler, the height of nonsense; for Leslie White, it is the only way to develop a true science of culture. In "The Concept of Culture," White does more than restate the position of the superorganicists; in addition he attempts to answer the arguments of the humanists—those, like Opler, whose cultural framework includes the *creativity focus*. Culture, for White, is a thing *sui generis,* a phenomenon that operates on its own distinct level. To explain culture, it is quite unnecessary to bring in man; culture causes culture, a cultural trait stands in a particular relationship to other cultural traits. For example, "The steam engine and textile machinery were introduced into Japan during the closing decades of the nineteenth century and certain changes in social structure followed; we add nothing to our explanation of these events by remarking that human beings were involved. Of course they were. And they were not irrelevant to the events that took place, but they are irrelevant to an explanation of these events."[16]

The argument here is that the changes in the social structure of Japan (in family organization, kinship roles, role relationships in general, etc.) which followed the introduction of the steam engine and textile machinery, *had to follow;* that the introduction of steam engines and textile machinery anywhere, at any time, will inevitably lead to changes in social relations. Why should this be so? White does not tell us directly but the answer is implied. Culture is a system, and a system is a set of elements (here cultural traits) that relate to each other in such a way that if one element changes so do all the others. A system, then, has some kind of order which must be maintained. When something new comes into the system (e.g. the steam engine) the old orderliness is thrown out of gear. A new type of order must now be developed, one that can include the presence of the new cultural traits. The notion that culture is but *one* system; that cultural explanations are sufficient (tell us *enough* of what we want to know about something); that cultural systems are most often in states of equilibrium (that order is the rule); that a state of disequilibrium (something new is added or something old disappears) will be followed immediately and inevitably by one type of adjustment—these and related ideas are built into the culturological approach.

---

[15] Morris E. Opler, "The Human Being in Culture Theory," *American Anthropologist,* 1964, Vol. 66, pp. 507–528.

[16] Leslie A. White, *The Science of Culture,* New York: Grove Press, 1959, p. 240.

Radcliffe-Brown critically analyzes some of these propositions.[17] He asks White to explain (1) precisely how culturological theory is useful ("The test of a theory is its application to the understanding of particular instances"), (2) how to distinguish between sociological phenomena and cultural phenomena, and (3) what to do with sociological explanations (such as his own explanation of incest taboos). If culturological explanations are sufficient, then theories like Radcliffe-Brown's must be scrapped. However, sociological theories pertaining to the integration of groups and to the maintenance of social structure appear to be just as valid as White's culturological statements!

With little injustice to White's views it is possible to present a modified culturological position which is more consistent with other views of culture:

(1) Culture is an emergent form whose essence lies in the symbol.

(2) Man, the symbol creator, user, and manipulator, can be studied from a variety of frameworks, including those provided by cultural anthropology, sociology, and psychology.

(3) Cultural anthropology is primarily concerned with cultural phenomena: phenomena dependent on symboling, considered in an extra-somatic sense.

(4) It is usually useful for the cultural anthropologist to *begin* his conceptualizations by thinking of culture *as if* it were a completely independent system: a set of phenomena which exists independent of its human creators and carriers. From the viewpoint of modified or neoculturology the triadic model of culture (mapped in Figure 1) must be changed to indicate the "ability" of culture to function as a system *sui generis*.

The modified model (mapped in Figure 2) shows how we can treat culture as if it were purely a superorganic phenomenon (S-level), and also shows that information flows from culture to man in his two roles: Mc and Mr (cultural manufacturer and cultural consumer). This more complex model of a sociocultural system is yet too simplistic to handle all the significant events and processes that occur in a society. My final model of culture must somehow answer Radcliffe-Brown's critique of culturological anthropology. In particular it must be able to handle his statement: "there are often differences of opinion or sentiment in a particular society . . . (these) are just as important, as sociological facts, as are general agreements: they call for explanation in terms of general theory," Radcliffe-Brown suggests that culture is not uniformly perceived by all the members of a society: a view congruent with those presented in "Individual Differences and Cultural Uniformities" and in "Sex and Culture" (Chapters 10 and 11). Differences of opinion among members of one society are indicative of some freedom of action enjoyed by man in spite of his cultural tradition. Man's freedom and his freedom strivings are stressed in

[17] See his essay in this volume.

FIGURE 2: A Model for Man and Culture

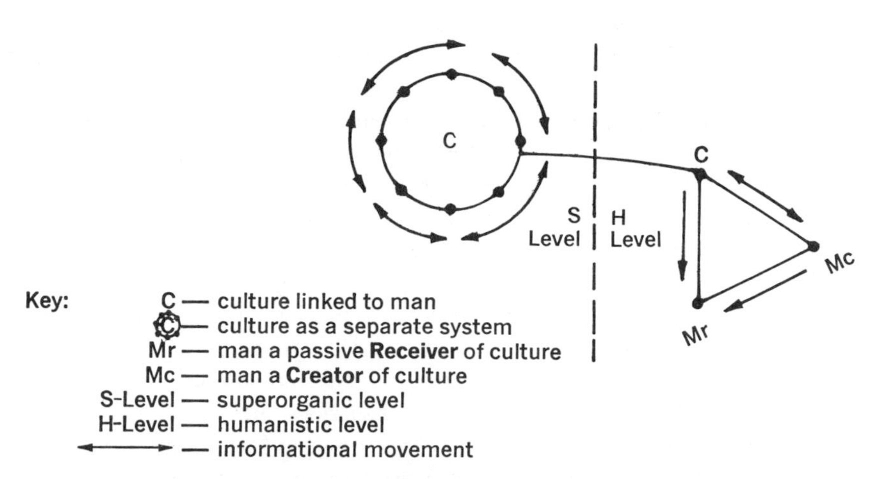

Laura Thompson's important paper, "Freedom and Culture" (Chapter 12). Here we are told of scientific findings which allow us to speak of man's propensity "to create, recreate, design, and develop a culture tailored to afford him maximum freedom of self-fulfillment." Now the fact that basic themes continue in a cultural tradition for hundreds of years in no way denies man's creativity and his attempts at self-fulfillment. For example, the Mohawk steel-workers discussed in "Cultural Persistence Among the Modern Iroquois" (Chapter 13) were attached to the notion that a real man is *brave, fearless, and danger-loving*. For them a job befitting the dignity of a man had to include these "manly" ingredients. It took considerable creativity on their part, first, to discover the suitability of structural steel work for their purposes, and second, to plan, organize, and manipulate people and situations so that Mohawks as a group could gain easy entry into the steel-work industry. Differently put, the Mohawks found maximal self-fulfillment in the warrior role; their creative adaptation to a greatly changed environment allowed them to keep the essential ingredients of this role.

The Mohawk discussion indicates (1) that man—a creative actor who adapts his culture to better fit changes in his environment—must be central to any theory of culture,[18] and (2) that history must somehow be brought into a final model of culture. Professor Shapiro's paper (Chapter 15) demonstrates this latter point: social and cultural life can, at present, only be described by *regular*

---

[18] Essentially this is Bidney's position: "The interdependence of the levels of natural phenomena implies that no level is in fact completely intelligible apart from reference to the levels below it. . . . Similarly it is to be expected with psychological, cultural and biological phenomena." David Bidney, *Theoretical Anthropology*, New York: Columbia University Press, 1953, pp. 48–49.

systems and these, unlike *state-determined systems,* do not allow us to predicate future states from any present state. To get better understanding of future states we need to discover how the present state came to be. We need to study history.

A notion underlying Shapiro's paper, one which I applaud, is that social life is very complex. At this juncture in our development of a science of man we cannot hope to develop state-controlled systems describing this complexity. The best we can do now is to develop regular systems. Given the complexity of our subject matter and our professional naiveté, it would seem best to do our research cooperatively, working closely with professionals from related social science disciplines. This, precisely, is Bennett's point in "Interdisciplinary Research and the Concept of Culture" (Chapter 18). Culture, for Bennett, must be considered within an enlarged framework that permits us (1) to isolate more precisely the critical factors of given situations, and (2) to work with interdisciplinary teams. Put differently, Bennett tells us that culture is but one, and not always the most important, influence on human behavior and that we need to study such factors as roles, norms, expectations, needs, motivations, and the varying dimensions of the "situation itself."

A factor long considered *important* (for some a major cause, for others an influence) in human action is the natural environment. My own research supports the position that Melville Herskovits long ago presented; namely, that the environment *influences* cultural formation, often setting limitations on the kind of institutions which could be developed.[19] This too appears to be Barth's position in his valuable paper on social change (Chapter 19). Like Bennett, Barth finds "culture" too simplistic a concept to handle all the complexity involved in change. To understand change Barth wants to look at agents of change, types of people whose decisions to act in particular ways affect many others. For Barth the role "entrepreneur" is critical to the change process, since this change agent, when successful, produces

> new information on the interrelations of different categories of valued goods . . . [which] will render false the idea that people have held till then about the relative value of goods, and can reasonably be expected to precipitate reevaluations and modifications both of categorizations and of value orientations. In other words, it changes the cultural bases that determine people's behavior, and in this way entrepreneurial activity becomes a major wellspring of cultural and social change. (Chapter 19, p. 245)

What Barth is telling us concerning social and cultural change is very important for our quest. The vague category "values" is given concreteness with

[19] Melville J. Herskovits, *Cultural Anthropology,* New York: Knopf, 1960.

a linkage to "goods." The value of various goods (and indeed, services) is based on information about them. Information, for Barth, lies at the base of values; therefore, when entrepreneurs change the informational banks of a community, their activity becomes a "major wellspring of cultural and social change." For Leslie White the essence of culture lies in the symbol; for Barth it seems to lie in "information." Both these positions can be integrated by answering the question: What is it that makes the symbol such a powerful force? The answer appears to be "The symbol is powerful because it is a highly effective carrier of information." In other words, we can agree with White that the symbol does indeed lie at the core of culture; but we must focus on its purpose—*to store and transmit information.*

The integration of the culturological approach (where culture is analyzed apart from those who utilize it) and the humanistic approach (where culture and man are intimately connected) is greatly facilitated when culture is considered as an informational system. Informational systems (as the linguists have well demonstrated) must, at times, be analyzed separately (S-level, Figure 2); at other times, questions concerning the utilization, storing, and retrieval of information necessitate the focus on man the information-creator, the information-carrier, and the information-user. This analysis indicates that the question "Should we use a culturological frame or a humanistic one?" cannot *a priori,* be answered. Clearly, it depends on the problem being researched. In sum, Leslie White and Morris Opler are both right in general; and each is right only for certain types of problems.

The integrative conclusion reached thus far is not novel, but it appears useful: *Culture is an informational system.*[20] Thinking of culture as information opens a door into a world full of fascinating questions. First, what type of information is culture? If I hit the reader's knee at a specific point, a kick must follow. Information of a type has been presented and the response is automatic—a kick! Is culture this kind of information? The answer is a very definite No! It is common knowledge that man does not always behave in the way his culture considers proper. Deviations from cultural norms are at times large, and we speak of crime and criminals; at times they are small, and we speak of nonconformity and deviants. Often the nonconformity lies in areas considered relatively unimportant, in which case we consider it as an example of a breach in etiquette. Sometimes the "wrong" acts are in areas lying at the heart of the culture, in which case we use phrases such as "immoral behavior" and "irreligious acts." However, irrespective of the size of the deviation or its position (close to or far from the core of the culture) the fact that deviations

[20] John M. Roberts, "The Self-Management of Cultures," *Explorations in Cultural Anthropology,* ed. W. H. Goodenough, New York: McGraw-Hill, 1964.

occur is conclusive proof that cultural information is not automatically followed by "proper" behavior. To comprehend the type of information that "culture" includes necessitates that we take a roundabout route to understanding.

Culture and Behavior

A consensus is slowly developing among scholars that in order to understand *anything* (say X) we must look to the purpose of X. That is, phenomena of all types must be handled as if they had a purpose or goal. Norbert Weiner, for example, recently concluded that criminal law worked badly because of its uncybernetic nature; i.e. because its goals were unclear.[21] Similarly the great anthropological theorist, S. F. Nadel, in one of the last sentences he ever wrote, said: To understand social structure we must keep in mind that structures are part of human life, and that human life is purposeful.[22] Since culture, like social structure, is closely linked to human living, it too must be considered as if it had a purpose. In short, to understand the concept "culture" we must assume that *culture has a purpose.*

Given that culture has a purpose, what, precisely, is it? It is well accepted that culture is man's major advance in the area of problem-solving; it enables him to utilize the problem-solving strategies of countless generations. Culture, in brief, is a problem-solving mechanism; its purpose is to help humans solve their life problems.

Now, as Arthur Koestler has recently shown, no problem-solving mechanism can be created (in either biological or sociocultural systems) which is programmed to deal separately and uniquely with every possible problem that may arise. This is so for various reasons including, first, the information such a mechanism would need is astronomically large, since it would have to include specific answers to every specific problem that may ever arise. How could such a phenomenally large amount of information be stored? How could it be retrieved fast enough to make it useful? That is, how could the right bits of information be found quickly when needed? Second, no system can possibly contain all the information necessary to solve every problem, because no sys-

---

[21] See John A. Robertson, "The Cost of Overcriminalization," *Psychiatry and Social Science,* 1969, Vol. 3, p. 3.

[22] S. F. Nadel, *A Theory of Social Structure,* Glencoe, Ill.: The Free Press, 1957. Similar notations are found in modern systems theory and related works. See, for example, Walter Buckley, ed., *Modern Systems Research for the Behavioral Scientist,* Chicago: Aldine, 1966; Ludwig von Bertalanffy, *General Systems Theory,* New York: George Braziller, 1968; and Arthur Koestler, *The Ghost in the Machine,* New York: Macmillan, 1967. It now seems strange to realize that at one time "goal" and "purpose" were almost dirty words for the tough-minded scientist. Purpose in particular presupposes a mind, a mystical thing whose existence was denied by behaviorists. The breakthrough was achieved, I suspect, when it was possible to translate a soft, sentimental word like "mind" into a tough, no-nonsense word like "black box." See W. Ross Ashby, *Design for a Brain,* New York: Wiley, 1960.

tem can predict every possible future contingency.[23] If culture, as a problem-solving mechanism, cannot treat every problem uniquely and individually, it must treat problems as types. Culture, therefore, provides *general answers* (types of solutions) to general problems (types of queries). Differently put, culture has no one-to-one relationship with *behavior* (specific answers); rather it consists of *rules* (prescribed guides for conduct) and other *guides* (general answers). In simple language, and to summarize, since culture is a problem-solving mechanism, and since it cannot provide man with specific behaviors to solve all his problems, it must therefore provide him with guides. Culture is thus *a guidance system* for solving human problems.

In presenting culture as a system with a purpose, I remain in the mainstream of anthropological thought. Although various scholars differ as to what the purpose of culture is, underlying their disagreement is the shared notion that a purpose exists. Tylor, for example, believed that the purpose of culture is to raise man from the lowly life of a savage to the heights of rational, civilized living: progress is culture's purpose.[24] This evolutionary position with its historical emphasis, can be contrasted with Malinowskian functionalism with its utilitarian emphasis. But Malinowski too believed that culture has a purpose: to solve man's biological and social problems.[25]

In emphasizing the *guidance* aspect of culture I stand in very respectable anthropological company. Sapir, for example, describes man as reacting in an individualistic way to the guides that culture presents. "Culture, following Sapir, can be regarded as a complex of demands to which the individual responds in his own personal way; in doing so, he defines, or at least expresses, his personality structure and at the same time extends his personality by responding to demands in a way that he had not done before."[26] And, my distinction between culture (as guides for action) and action itself, parallels Ford's distinction between culture as a body of beliefs and rules and behavior itself (what man does).[27]

---

[23] The latter point seems obvious, and can be proven in various ways not suitably discussed at length here. One way relates to the paper by Gilbert Shapiro. In brief, two types of systems exist in the language of cybernetics: *state-determined* (where knowledge of the system at time T allows prediction of all future states of the systems) and *regular* (where all future states cannot be predicted). Human sociocultural systems are not *state-determined;* they may not even be *regular!* All future states of these systems cannot be known at a given time, therefore no informational system (such as culture) can develop answers to all possible problems of the future.

[24] Edward B. Tylor, *Primitive Culture: Researches into the Development of Mythology, Philosophy, Religion, Language, Art and Custom,* 2 vols., London: John Murray, 1871.

[25] See his essay in this volume.

[26] See Chapter 3.

[27] Clellan S. Ford, "Society, Culture and Human Organism," *Journal of General Psychology,* 1939, Vol. 20, pp. 135–179. For the present I am using "rules" and "guides" interchangeably; a formal distinction is made, however, in later portions of this essay. In presenting culture as "guides," man becomes best viewed as "a decision-maker," a frequently used

The distinction between culture—as some kind of rule system—and behavior, has much value for anthropology. Among many other utilities (see below), it helps to rid anthropology of a problem which too many scholars have spent too much time discussing: the ontological reality of culture (see Leslie White's essay). Worries about the "existence" of culture can now be shown to be interesting games, but from a scientific viewpoint, time-wasting activities comparable to the classical attempts to calculate the number of angels who can stand on the head of a needle. Guides and rules exist, as anyone who has received a speeding-ticket will acknowledge. Their use, non-use, and misuse is quite easy to demonstrate; given behaviors are either consistent with the guides which pertain to them, or not so.

The separation of culture as rules from behavior, parallels a separation that many modern linguists have found extremely useful: between *competence* (the knowledge a speaker has of his language) and *performance* (the actual usage of language).[28] Competence, for me, represents *a knowledge of rules* and such knowledge, as Mrs. Durbin has pointed out, "enables [a native speaker] to distinguish between a sentence and a nonsentence, to generate an infinite number of sentences, some of them completely novel, to impose an appropriate semantic interpretation on each sentence, however novel it might be, to impose meaning even upon grammatically deviant sentences. . . ."[29] In utilizing the competence versus performance distinction and the larger model of which this is a part (the transformational model of linguistics) Mrs. Durbin has presented a novel and exciting description of Jainism.[30] I am suggesting that the distinction *cultural rules versus behavior,* when systematically utilized, will have similar valuable contributions in areas outside of religion.

Many anthropologists share my belief that culture should be defined as rules or guides.[31] And such a view of culture is congruent with, although not equivalent to, Kroeber's superorganic notions. Culture considered as a guidance system is clearly a superorganic phenomenon, as Kroeber long ago argued.[32] Guides can be treated as if they had a life of their own, and such an analytical frame will generate important understandings about the nature of human life. *By itself,* however, this superorganic frame is insufficient: it tells us little about

---

frame in recent writings. See, for example, Ward H. Goodenough, "Frontiers of Cultural Anthropology," *Frontiers of Cultural Anthropology,* Philadelphia: Proceedings of the American Philosophical Society, 1969, Vol. 113, No. 5.

[28] Noam Chomsky, *Aspects of the Theory of Syntax,* Cambridge, Mass.: M. I. T. Press, 1965.

[29] Mridula A. Durbin, "The Transformational Model of Linguistics and Its Implications for an Ethnology of Religion: A Case Study of Jainism," *American Anthropologist,* 1970, Vol. 72, p. 336.

[30] Durbin, pp. 334–342. Jainism has today less than one million adherents. It arose in the sixth century B.C. in Benares, India and spread westward and northward.

[31] See Morris Opler, "Some Implications of Culture Theory for Anthropology and Psychology," *The American Journal of Orthopsychiatry,* 1948, Vol. 18, pp. 611–621.

[32] See his essay in this volume.

large chunks of reality exemplified by situations where man does not heed cultural rules; and it tells us nothing about the creator of culture—man. Differently put, although culture is a superorganic phenomenon, it is much more than that. Therefore, in order to understand the "much more," we need a model for culture which includes information as to how man creates culture and how culture (in classical feedback fashion) creates man. The notion of culture as guides sets us on the right road for developing the required model. Moreover, this notion frees man from the undignified image implicit in some superorganicist formulations: culture's slave. Man creates guides for his own life, and from this point of view, the guides belong to him. Man is, in part, shaped and molded by the guides he has created, and from this latter viewpoint, he belongs to them. Man and culture are locked together in a reality called human life and no analytical key can keep them separate. In sum, culture is a guidance system created by man, for man. The interrelationships which develop between man and culture are therefore basic to an understanding of man. The fact that man does not automatically follow cultural guides—the fact that man is quite often a cultural sinner—necessitates the maintenance of a distinction between culture (as guides) and behavior. Completely independently, Clifford Geertz sends Anthropology the same message in *New Views of Man:*

> Culture is best seen not as complexes of concrete behaviour patterns—customs, usages, traditions, habit clusters—as has, by and large, been the case up until now, but as *a set of control mechanisms—plans, recipes, rules, instructions (what computer engineers call "programs")—for the governing of behaviour.* . . . When seen as a set of symbolic devices for controlling behaviour, extra-somatic sources of information, culture provides the link between what men are intrinsically capable of becoming and what they actually, one by one, in fact become. Becoming human is becoming individual, and *we become individual under the guidance of cultural patterns,* historically created systems of meaning in terms of which we give form, order, point, and direction to our lives.[33]

Why is it that man at times rejects cultural guides? Clearly this is a complex question which brings to mind such profound problems as: Does man have free will? On a general level, however, a rather simple answer exists. Man is subject to many pressures, each of which can influence his behavior: the natural environment, human biology, personality, and body type, to name but a few. Culture has no monopoly on human guidance; therefore man at times follows other guides.

Once said it appears quite obvious: culture is *one guide* among many which "compete" for man's attention. Using a multi-guide approach to human

---

[33] Clifford Geertz, "The Impact of the Concept of Culture on the Concept of Man," *New Views of Man,* ed. John R. Platt, Chicago: University of Chicago Press, 1965 (Italics mine).

behavior permits us to rephrase some old questions in superior form. For example, the argument between anthropologists and geographers (among others): Does culture determine behavior or is geography the cause of human action? is now restatable in ways more conducive to enlightening research. Now we can say: Both culture and the environment respectively are guides to action and thought. Let us therefore attempt to discover (1) under what conditions cultural guides take precedence over environmental ones; (2) under what conditions environmental guides take precedence over cultural guides; (3) under what conditions environmental guides are transformed into cultural guides (the essence of the cultural-ecological approach in anthropology);[34] and (4) under what conditions man follows neither cultural nor environmental guides.

By considering culture as but one guide among many, I remain within a framework supported by George Peter Murdock and Emlyn Merritt. Opler summarizes Murdock's views as follows.[35]

> As Murdock sees it, then, a prime characteristic of culture is that it is ideational. The basic element of culture is not the behavior of an individual or individuals. It is, rather, the idea held by the members of the group that certain behavior is *appropriate*. But, according to Murdock, there is no assurance that the individual will perform the culturally defined act. A strong biological drive may cause him to do the inappropriate deed. Special circumstances may prevent him from realizing the cultural norm. Thus culture and behavior part company, *for culture becomes one of the determinants of behavior,* the biological drives, the individual personality, and the countless factors of the particular situation being others.

Very similar views have, more recently, been presented by Merritt, who believes that "culture" takes on too much importance in anthropology because of the continued use of a false dichotomy in discussions on determinism: instinct versus learning. Professor Merritt believes that a closer study of the findings of modern biology would place "culture" into a more modest position as a determinant of human action.[36]

Culture in Evolutionary Perspective

Culture, according to Murdock, is but "one of the determinants of behaviour." Put another way, culture belongs to a *family of concepts* and each "family member" is *an influence* on behavior. For me, culture belongs to the

---

[34] See Julian Steward, *A Theory of Culture Change,* Urbana: University of Illinois Press, 1955.

[35] Opler (1948), p. 615 (Italics mine).

[36] Emlyn J. Merritt, "Natural Selection and Human Behavior," *Journal of Theoretical Biology,* 1966, Vol. 21, p. 410; "On the Importance of Cultural and Biological Determinants in Human Behavior," *American Anthropologist,* 1967, Vol. 69, pp. 513–514.

family of "guidance systems" and membership in such a family makes it possible to define "culture" correctly. That is, following well-accepted scientific procedures, a definition of X must first state the family to which X belongs (technically, the *genus* or class that includes the thing defined). Then the definition must proceed to list the *differentia,* the items that set the subject apart from other things in the general class. The *genus* is here guidance systems, and it includes phenomena such as *biology, personality, numbers* (the size of group in interaction), and *habitat.*[37]

The *differentia*—the characteristics which distinguish culture from other guidance systems—have yet to be spelled out. Working towards these ends, it is useful to return to Dr. Hallowell's question: Given that our ancestors were animals without culture, where did culture come from? Colloquially, how can something come out of nothing? Culture as used here really means "cultural information": information humans "own" collectively by working and playing together. Is there anything animals own collectively for similar reasons? Yes, animals belong to communities, and some of their behavior is based on shared information, which is developed and learned out of "living together." Differently put, animals who live in communities own *social information.*[38] Our pre-human ancestors lived in communities, therefore they owned social information. Clearly then, culture, or cultural information, did not "come out of nothing": it came out of social information. Using ($\equiv$) to mean "own" or "owned," and ($>$) to mean "became" allows us to present the following equations and deductions.

1. Animal communities $\equiv$ social information;
2. Human communities $\equiv$ cultural information;
3. Some animal communities $>$ human communities when social information $>$ cultural information.

Actually, depending on the focus of the discussion, the conclusion (No. 3) can be presented in two related ways. First, *some animal communities became human communities, when social information became cultural information.* Second, animals became human *because* social information became cultural information.

This second wording is actually an exciting postulate concerning the birth of

[37] The importance of the non-cultural guides to action listed here has been described in many works. The reader can find vast bibliographical reference and useful information in George Simmel, *The Sociology of George Simmel,* trans. and ed. Kurt Wolff, Glencoe, Ill.: The Free Press, 1950; Eliot D. Chapple, *Culture and the Biological Man,* New York: Holt, Rinehart and Winston, 1970; M. Freilich, "Ecology and Culture: Environmental Determinism and the Ecological Approach in Anthropology," *Anthropological Quarterly,* 1967, Vol. 40, pp. 26–43.

[38] See Chapple and, among many other interesting works in this area, Harald Esch, "The Evolution of Bee Language," *Scientific American,* 1967, Vol. 217, pp. 96–104.

both modern man and culture: *Modern man was born out of an informational transformation. The "operation" consisted of changing social information into cultural information.* This postulate, like all postulates, is not provable; however it is reasonable in accordance with known facts, and pregnant with research possibilities. Let us begin with the following question. If man's ancestors transformed social information into cultural information (analogous to transforming flour into cake) they must have had reason to *give up* social information to "make" culture (i.e. one gets "rid of" flour by making a cake). Why did they do so? Strangely enough, it appears that our ancestors were able to give up social information and keep it at the same time (i.e. they were able to have their cake and their flour); for it is clear that we, too, continually transform social information into cultural information, with no obvious loss. To understand the above we must ask first, "What precisely is cultural information?" Second, precisely how does it differ from social information? And, third, what is the nature of this transformational (baking) process?

Following Ruth Benedict, culture defines normality, and the normal is "a variant of the concept good."[39] Similarly, Evans-Pritchard tells us that culture belongs in the category "moral systems."[40] Cultural information seems to be *information pertaining to the good.* Or, better, culture is *information which defines the proper.*

What then is social information? Social information is community data which summarizes that which is considered "the smart." As Tylor long ago recognized, man's first problem is to get his daily food—survival is the king of problems. To survive really means to adapt successfully to one's habitat. Successful adaptation is a matter of smartness, not goodness. The problems nature poses for man must be tackled with smartness not propriety, with ingenuity not piety, and with resourcefulness not righteousness. If man's prehuman ancestors survived and came to a natural end, they, of necessity, led "smart" lives: they followed social rules, which in essence represent a "record" of the smart responses of group members. With the appearance of *Homo sapiens,* evolution reached a critical phase; there now existed an animal blessed and plagued with a big brain which permitted a strange new process: *self-awareness.*

Self-awareness is a two-edged sword, providing pleasures and problems. On the one hand (the sharp edge), increasing satisfactions are created by the knowledge of an internal existence. On the other hand (the dull edge), knowledge of an internal existence creates a new need—*the need to be proper.* Since

[39] Ruth Benedict, "Anthropology and the Abnormal," *Journal of General Psychology,* 1934, Vol. 10, pp. 59–80.

[40] E. E. Evans-Pritchard, *Social Anthropology and Other Essays,* New York: The Free Press, 1964.

culture is, by definition, a mechanism for human problem-solving and since a major problem of human existence is, by postulation, *how to be proper,* culture, of necessity, includes processes for creating properness.

From within this viewpoint culture has two rather contradictory jobs to do: (1) to solve *external,* adaptive, problems that demand smart solutions; and (2) to solve *internal,* self-awareness problems which demand the creation of a new phenomenon—properness or goodness. The basic human dilemma—to be smart and survive, or to be proper and feel good—was solved by modern man (*Homo sapiens*) quite ingeniously: *The smart was transformed into the proper.* Behaviors defined as "smart" became "good" when they had "proved" their adaptability, effectiveness, and efficiency to the satisfaction of community members. This process, invented by man's first human ancestors, continues to exist. Today the smart still gets transformed into the proper and this manufacturing process is often referred to as *institutionalization.*[41]

It should be noted that a model of human social and cultural life is here being proposed which includes the following ideas: (1) man must adapt smartly to his external environment in order to survive; (2) man observes and evaluates his own behavior and that of his community, and categorizes some activities with labels roughly equivalent to "the smart"; (3) some activities previously defined as "the smart" are later put through a manufacturing process called "institutionalization." After institutionalization, smart information is dubbed by some term equivalent to "the proper" or "the good"; and (4) man transforms the smart into the good because he has to—he has a need to be proper.

The notion that man creates culture—here "properness"—because he has to, is hardly a novel idea; it is implicit in the evolutionary positions of many nineteenth-century scholars (see Chapter 17) and is more explicitly presented in the writings of such anthropological "greats" as Bronislaw Malinowski and Clark Wissler. In summarizing Malinowski's contribution to anthropological theory, Voget included the following important insight: Malinowski's need-oriented functionalism "seated the basic human reality in man's psychological processes—right where the evolutionists had sought it in the first place. Man, in effect, was a culture-building creature *because of the necessities of his inner structure.*"[42]

Wissler's presentation of his own, very similar, insights was unfortunate; his choice of words made his ideas appear mystical.

---

[41] See Harold E. Smith, "Toward a Clarification of the Concept of Social Institution," *Sociology and Social Research,* 1964, Vol. 48, No. 2.

[42] Fred W. Voget, "Man and Culture: An Essay in Changing Anthropological Interpretation," *American Anthropologist,* 1960, Vol. 62, p. 951 (Italics mine).

> The pattern of culture is just as deeply buried in the germ plasm of man as the bee pattern in the bee . . . man builds culture because he cannot help it, there is a *drive* in his protoplasm that carries him forward even against his will.[43]

Understandably then, Wissler's ideas were attacked, and at times quite satirically.

> This is psycho-biological determinism with a vengeance. . . . Wissler did not say whether the universal pattern for culture was embedded in the germ plasm of *Pithecanthropus* as well as *Homo*. . . .[44]

The beliefs of Malinowski and Wissler (among others) that man must create culture, are important insights which anthropology has used too infrequently and too sparingly. These valuable contributions to the understanding of man can be maximally utilized by defining culture as *guides for the proper*. We can now represent the cement which binds man and culture together by a simple postulate: *Man needs to be proper*. To be human, man must consider himself worthwhile, worthy, proper—his sanity depends on it.

The postulate, *man needs to be proper,* cannot here be fully developed and support for it must be somewhat limited. However, it is necessary to indicate the kinds of supporting ideas and concepts which (1) make this postulate appear very reasonable, and (2) hold promise for useful research done in terms of it. First, a well-accepted universal in man's social life is religion. Among the central goals of any religious system is to tell man how to live properly. For man to be certain that what he considers "the proper" really is just that, most religions provide supernatural support for their properness rules. In short, "being proper" is so central to man's life that almost everywhere we find man, there we also find a supernatural system certifying the properness of a given way of life.[45]

Second, many psychotherapists appear to base their whole therapeutic enterprise on the notion that man needs to be proper. Differently put, a central goal in the labors of many therapists is to make their patients *like themselves,* to consider their everyday life as good and proper.[46]

Third, it is generally accepted that one attribute of *Homo sapiens* is *rationalization;* man makes what he does (i.e. what he has considered smart) appear reasonable, good, noble, and proper. Man's frequent rationalizations are de-

---

[43] C. Wissler, *Man and Culture,* New York: Thomas Y. Crowell, 1923.

[44] A. Irving Hallowell, "The Structural and Functional Dimensions of a Human Existence," *Quarterly Review of Biology,* 1956, Vol. 31, pp. 88–101.

[45] See Melford Spiro and Roy D'Andrade, "A Cross-Cultural Study of Some Supernatural Beliefs," *American Anthropologist,* 1958, Vol. 60, pp. 456–466; Anthony F. C. Wallace, *Religion: An Anthropological View,* New York: Random House, 1966.

[46] See, for example, Albert Ellis, *The Theory and Practice of Rational-Emotive Psychotherapy,* New York: Lyle Stuart, 1964.

ducible from the postulate "Man needs to be proper." Fourth, according to psychoanalytic theory, man has an inborn sense of shame. Shame too is deducible from man's need to be proper; for without a properness need, what is the meaning of shame? Fifth, it is well understood that man is an evaluative animal. Wherever we find him we find that he has ranked all phenomena around him. Now, it is reasonable to argue that when the *Homo sapiens* brain made introspection possible (and indeed inevitable), one of man's activities was to attempt to evaluate himself. Following *social rules* he could ask himself "Am I smart?" or "Am I not smart?" and such questions could rarely be answered immediately with any degree of certainty. Whether an activity is smart or not is only known after all of its consequences are known; and that takes much time. *Homo sapiens* the evaluator wanted to know immediately; he therefore had to change the question "Am I smart?" to "Am I proper?" The properness question is immediately answerable. Sixth, from the point of view of the community (the larger system) it is important that individuals act smartly; that they adapt effectively to environmental challenges, particularly in "primitive" societies. Yet it is not possible to supervise all individual members all the time, to see that they indeed behave in smart ways. By transforming the smart into the proper, community leaders put a "policeman" into every human system. Theologians call such a policeman "the soul," the psychoanalysts call it "the super-ego." Finally, Edmond Cahn in a book that won wide acclaim (*The Sense of Injustice*), has postulated the existence of a sense of injustice. A sense of injustice, like the sense of shame, is deducible from the need to be proper. Cahn's own words may make his postulate more meaningful.

> The sense of injustice may now be described as a general phenomenon operative in the law. Among its facets are the demands for equality, desert and *human dignity* . . . the sense of injustice is the implement by which assault is discerned and defense prepared. . . . In fine, the human animal is predisposed to fight injustice.[47]

---

[47] Edmund Cahn, *The Sense of Injustice,* Bloomington: University of Indiana Press, 1949 (Italics mine). A more complete documentation of the proposition that man has a need to be proper (or man has a need for culture and therefore creates it) must await a longer text currently in preparation (*Man: An Anthropological View*). It might however be in order to add the supporting views of a scholar who is rapidly becoming a major spokesman for what might be called "The New Anthropology," Clifford Geertz.

> As our nervous system—and most particularly its crowning curse and glory, the neocortex—grew up in great part in interaction with culture, it is incapable of directing our behavior or organizing our experience without the guidance provided by systems of significant symbols. . . .We are, in sum, incomplete or unfinished animals who complete or finish ourselves through culture. . . .

In short, Geertz tells us that culture is a guidance system, and that man, as we now know him, cannot exist without it. In my language, man has a need for culture, for guides toward "the proper." For without a knowledge of what is proper, man's "crowning curse and glory"—his neocortex—would create for him instant insanity. See Geertz (1965).

Manufacturing Culture

Homo sapiens appears to have pulled off a fantastic *coup* by inventing culture; and particularly by manufacturing culture out of social (smart) rules. Modern man seems to be able to satisfy his psychological needs to be proper at the same time he is solving his survival problems. Unfortunately, this idyllic picture of human living misses a large chunk of truth—the smart does not get transformed into the proper quickly; *the manufacture of culture takes much time!* By the time a bit of smart behavior becomes proper it may no longer be smart, for the general environment has probably changed. For example, at one time (in the United States) it was smart, but not proper, for young ladies to smoke in public. Today it is proper for them to smoke almost anywhere; however, it is no longer smart. The general environment now includes information which seems to indicate that smoking is a suicidal activity.

The conclusions appear obvious: all that is proper is not smart, and all that is smart is not proper. Therefore *man cannot live by properness alone.* To live effectively anywhere (in simple "primitive" societies, or in modern complex systems), man requires the aid of at least *two* guidance systems: culture and social information. Culture, the guides that come from the past, satisfies man's needs for propriety. Continuities with the past give stability to social life, allowing the old and the young to have enough in common to understand each other if they want to. And with some continuities the society can develop and maintain a social structure.[48] Social information, the guides that are currently considered smart, help man in solving his immediate environmental problems—how to get into college, how get a job, how to stay out of an unjust war, how fast to drive, how to get elected to public office, etc. Social information assists man in living more creatively by providing alternatives to culture; social information provides the "raw material" out of which future culture will be manufactured. With culture and social information operating as twin guides for human living, human society becomes a marriage between continuity and propriety (the bride?), and adaptive change and creativity.

It is beyond the confines of this work to analyze the precise ways in which social information becomes transformed into cultural information. The data for this type of analysis are currently quite sparse. However, the logical possibilities can be stated in very general terms. Transformations from the smart into the proper follow "routes" describable as (1) S>P, the smart can be transformed into the proper; (2) NS>P, the non-smart can be transformed into the proper; (3) S>NP, the smart can be transformed into the non-proper; and (4) NS>NP, the non-smart can be transformed into the non-proper (see

[48] See M. Freilich, "Towards a Model of Social Structure," *Journal of the Royal Anthropological Institute,* 1964, Vol. 94, pp. 183–200.

FIGURE 3: Manufacturing Culture: Transforming the Smart (and Non-smart) into the Proper (and Non-proper)

Non-Cultural Information	Cultural Information	
	P	NP
S	S>P	S>NP
SN	NS>P	NS>NP

Direction of the Manufacturing Process →

Key:
S — smart
P — proper
NS — non-smart
NP — non-proper
S>P — the smart gets transformed into the proper
S>NP — the smart gets transformed into the non-proper
NS>P — the non-smart gets transformed into the proper
NS>NP — the non-smart gets transformed into the non-proper

Figure 3). It is logical to assume that viable societies regularly use the S>P, and the NS>NP transformations; *the smart* is regularly transformed into *the proper,* and *the non-smart* is regularly transformed into *the non-proper.* However, some indications do exist that current American society often uses the *NS>P transformation:* that which is *non-smart* is made into the *proper.*[49]

The model for culture and society thus far developed has one major proposition: Any group with a history utilizes two or more guidance systems. Such guides to action systems include *culture*—guides for the proper—and *social information*—guides for the smart. The rest of this essay will attempt to marshall some support for this proposition. It will conclude with the description and evaluation of a model—V-R Guidance Systems—which indicates the complete dimensions of the dichotomy *smart versus proper.*[50]

The Human Dilemma: Propriety or Smartness

Now what proof exists for my proposition that at least two guidance systems exist for every society: culture (guides for the proper) and social information (guides for the smart). Let me begin with a profound quotation from Evans-

[49] See Jules Henry, *Culture Against Man,* New York: Random House, 1963.

[50] This model was originally developed as an aid for the anthropological field worker. See Freilich (1970), especially pp. 506–519.

Pritchard. In discussing his belief that anthropology can never be a science Evans-Pritchard yet found it useful to consider social life as "a system." In his words,

> Human societies are to be understood as social systems only because social life must have a pattern of some kind, in as much as man, being a reasonable creature, has to live in a world in which his relations with those around him are ordered and intelligible.[51]

In brief, man needs order in his life; he cannot live without order. Order is so important to man that, almost invariably, man has asked and answered questions in his cosmologies concerning the creation of original order in the world. In the various descriptions which exist concerning the creation of *original* order, some supernatural agent is presented as the order-maker. Who makes order, *now,* when it comes to man's mundane social life? Clearly, man does himself! Traditional anthropology would have us believe otherwise. Namely, while it is true that man needs order to live in a meaningful (i.e. predictable) world, he does very little today to create order. Order is there because all humans are born into a culture. The great order-maker today is culture, not man. The inadequacies of this explanation are clarified by the following argument: first, if modern man requires order in his life, it is reasonable to assume that pre-human man also had such requirements. Since the latter had no culture to create order for him, this pre-cultural animal must have created order for himself. If a pre-cultural animal with a brain capacity smaller than that of *Homo sapiens* can create order, then surely *Homo sapiens* is capable of order-creation. Second, given that *Homo sapiens can* create order, and given that he needs order in his life, it is *unreasonable* to assume that he is currently too lazy or too disinterested in his own welfare to continue order-creation. Third, if culture and only culture creates order, where does order come from in currently thriving animal communities? Fourth, if man's order came only from culture, and given that he needs order, man would never break cultural rules. Such deviations would prove too costly for an animal who craves order for such deviations would take away the *only* orderliness that man has in life. In point of fact, man does break cultural prescriptions; he even seems to enjoy doing the "culturally wrong." It is reasonable to assume that part of this enjoyment is due to experiencing a novel order, an order intrinsic to behaviors which are "culturally wrong."

My assumption that order—of a non-cultural type—exists at times when

---

[51] Evans-Pritchard. In Oswalt's words, "To single out a particular concept and label it as the most basic of empirical truths would be presumptive, and yet in a search for fundamentals one principle stands out. It is that there is order and coherence in all aspects of life." Wendell H. Oswalt, *Understanding Our Culture,* New York: Holt, Rinehart and Winston, 1970, p. 2.

cultural rules are not followed is more than reasonable: it is well documented by empirical evidence. Anthropologists and sociologists, among others, have shown that culturally wrong behaviors are patterned; they make up a system. They have an order of their own! From the many anthropologists who have found this to be the case I will list only the better known works: (1) Raymond Firth's documentation of how Polynesians use "established modes" for circumventing mourning taboos;[52] (2) Bronislaw Malinowski's descriptions of how Trobriand Islanders developed *patterns* of avoiding exogamy rules;[53] (3) Morris Opler's work on how avoidance rules, when violated, are broken in predictable ways;[54] and (4) James Slotkin's material on "customary ways of not conforming to custom."[55]

Strangely enough, this and related data have not been systematically incorporated into cultural theory. My question—Why not?—can be answered as follows: It is not easy to give up well-accepted notions concerning a concept which lies at the core of one's field! Culture, anthropology's central concept, is still for many anthropologists *the idea* which explains everything that people do.[56] If culture or custom is everything, then, it is nonsensical to say "customary ways of not conforming to custom." Differently put, for those who belong to the culture-is-everything school, data concerning man the nonconformist are embarrassing data. And embarrassing data are best forgotten.

The average man in the street knows well that customary ways do exist for avoiding cultural rules and he generally uses such knowledge when he drives his car, when he fills out income tax forms, when he tries to get his candidate elected for office, and in similar situations. Anthropologists, too, seem to have this information while enacting the roles "driver" and "citizen." Strangely enough this information is forgotten in most cultural analyses.

The fact that anthropologists "forget" that (1) nonconformity is a system, and (2) the nonconformity system is distinct and separate from culture, is understandable from a knowledge of traditional cultural theory. As mentioned above, man is here frozen into the image of culture's slave, and this freezing process was aided by an analytical distinction that many anthropologists accept as part of their bible. I refer to Ralph Linton's unfortunate dichotomy, "ideal

---

[52] Raymond Firth, *Primitive Polynesian Economy,* London: Routledge, 1939.

[53] Bronislaw Malinowski, *Crime and Custom in Savage Society,* New York: Humanities Press, 1926, pp. 71–84.

[54] Morris Opler, "Rule and Practice in Jicarilla Apache Affinal Relatives," *American Anthropologist,* 1947, Vol. 49, pp. 453–462.

[55] James S. Slotkin, *Social Anthropology,* New York: Macmillan, 1950.

[56] For example, a theoretical anthropologist recently described the whole of human society as a "subsystem, or part of culture." Strangely enough some anthropologists still cling to these views! The death of conceptual models, like that of operatic heroines, appears to be a slow and painful process. See David Kaplan, "The Superorganic: Science or Metaphysics?" *American Anthropologist,* 1965, Vol. 67, pp. 958–976.

culture" (that which people should do) and "real culture" (that which people really do). In an otherwise valuable book (*The Study of Man*), Linton attempted to handle important anthropological understandings analytically and systematically.[57] Linton tried to show (1) that man does not always follow the cultural prescriptions of his society; and (2) that in his nonconformity man behaves in predictable ways. Stuck with Tylor's "passivity focus" (man, the puppet of culture) Linton's solution for both nonconformity and predictability was logical but false. For Linton, when man was rebelling against his culture, man was still acting culturally: he was following "real" culture. When man was not rebellious, he was floating in the midst of his cultural stream: he was following "ideal" culture. Culture, like God, was "in charge" of all things, the proper and the improper, the good and the evil.

Linton's model of reality—where culture replaces God—caused theologians little concern; however its repercussions on cultural theory were serious. First, it re-enforces the image of man as a mechanical appendage of culture, a depressing picture which mangles rather than mirrors human reality. Second, Linton greatly oversimplifies reality by presenting two concepts ("ideal culture" and "real culture"), when he needs several. Let me explain. If we start with a small piece of ideal culture, say a driving rule called S, *two* sets of behaviors must be distinguished: behaviors consistent with S ("proper" driving) and behaviors inconsistent with S ("improper" driving). The importance of making these distinctions is clarified if S is made "concrete." Let us consider S as a road sign commonly seen on North American highways which tells us "Speed limit—60." Proper behavior is here a host of driving speeds (generally between 40 and 60 m.p.h.) utilized by a variety of types of drivers (from little old ladies to scared middle-aged men). Since most of my readers are more interested in "improper" behavior than in "proper" behavior, and since the former has more to teach us than the latter, let us concentrate our analysis on *the improper.*

The observant reader who is also a driver will have noticed that when he (or she) drives faster than the sign "says," the speed utilized is approximately the same speed which most drivers nearby are using. That is, the "improper" driving speeds that most of us use are *patterned:* generally we do not drive *uniquely*. Similarly when we behave improperly in situations other than driving—completing income tax forms, developing budgets, and dealing with subordinates (see below)—we also act in roughly the same improper manner as most of our associates. Indeed it is only when we try to be improper uniquely that we get into trouble—then (in North America) we get labelled "kook," "nut," and "criminal." Not only do we escape negative social sanction when

[57] Ralph Linton, *The Study of Man,* New York: Appleton-Century, 1936.

doing the patterned improper but, strangely enough, we receive some positive reaction from our community: they consider us "regular," "with-it" people who know the "score." The patterned improper is often considered to be "the smart" way of doing things.

Beginning with Linton's "ideal culture"—the rule—and going to what people do, "real culture" is therefore no simple dichotomy. Real culture must itself be subdivided into *four types*. First we must distinguish between proper "real culture" (behavior that is consistent with "ideal culture"), and improper

FIGURE 4: Linton's "Ideal Culture" versus "Real Culture" Modified

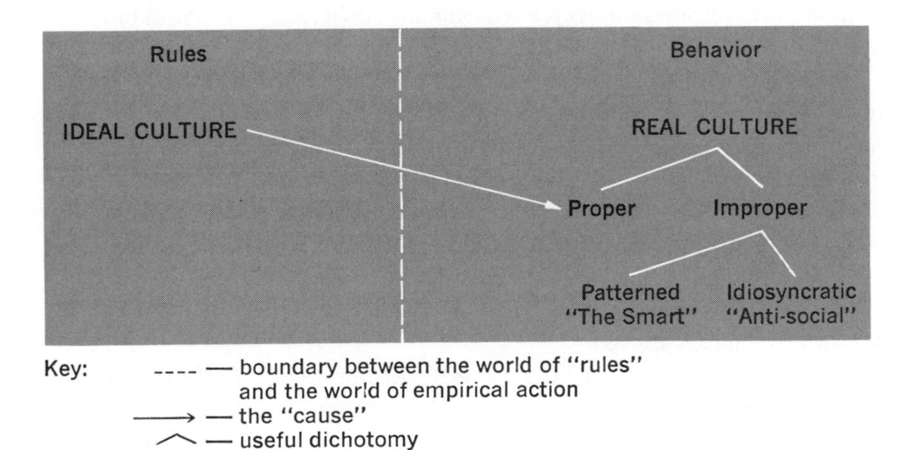

"real culture" (behavior that is inconsistent with real culture). Second we must take improper real culture and subdivide it: into the *patterned improper*—henceforth called "the smart"—and the *idiosyncratic improper*—henceforth called the "anti-social."

Contrary to first impressions all this dichotomizing (see Figure 4) is not just intellectual juggling for purposes of amusement. No, the focus here is on a rather strange phenomenon: behavior which is improper, but which receives a certain degree of social applause and which, moreover, follows regular patterns. How is it that our non-proper behavior is patterned? When we "sin," culturally speaking, how is it that our "sins" are generally much like the sins of others? The obvious answer has some truth to it: "There is safety in numbers." However, there is more to this matter than copying each other. There are rules for the patterned improper: there are rules for the smart, which I call "social rules." In short, human life is governed by at least two rule systems:

FIGURE 5: Culture, Social Rules, and Behavior

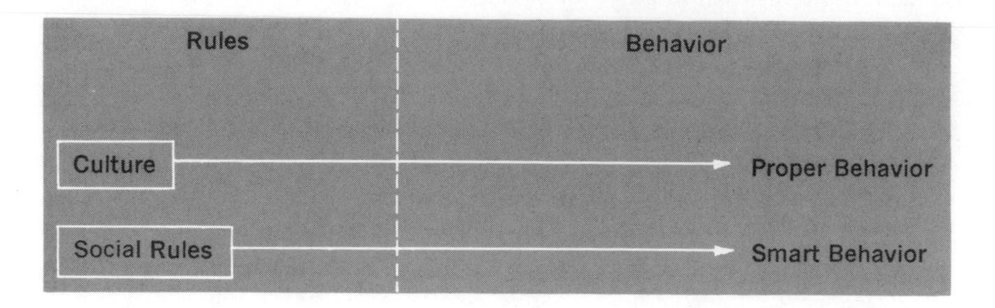

cultural rules which lead to *proper behavior* and *social rules* which lead to *smart behavior* (see Figure 5).[58]

Man is clearly not a cultural puppet, since he often behaves "smartly" rather than "properly." However, because man is often a cultural deviant does not mean that he is generally a *nonconformist;* for man often conforms to or follows social rules. The word "conformity" is more complex than we think, for it relates two distinct sets of rules: the cultural and the social. Differently put, when discussing conformity we must always ask "To what kind of custom is man conforming, the cultural or the social?" Since man's behavior in this social (or patterned improper) realm is often misunderstood, a brief analysis of pertinent writings is necessary.

Describing the patterns of behavior in American society, Robbin Williams, in a now classic text (*American Society: A Sociological Interpretation*), writes of a critical problem in American life.[59] Namely, American culture is success-centered (i.e. in the United States it is very good and very proper to be very successful); thus, many Americans are willing to break culturally appropriate rules to reach success. Differently put, the pressure in America to reach the cultural goals of wealth, power, and prestige are so great that people tend to use *any means* to be successful: those which are culturally proper and those which are culturally improper. The culturally improper behaviors, Williams tells us, are generally patterned and he calls such patterned ways of avoiding the proper, "patterned evasion." Dr. Williams provides extensive examples of patterned evasion in America.[60]

1. Prohibition vs. the bootlegging and speakeasy prior to the repeal of the Eighteenth Amendment.

---

[58] As will be clear later (see Figure 8) human life is governed by many and varied systems. The systems upon which this chapter focuses are guides and rules for the proper (culture), and guides and rules for the smart (social information).

[59] Robbin M. Williams, Jr., *American Society: A Sociological Interpretation,* N.Y.: Knopf, 1951.

[60] Williams, p. 382.

2. Impersonal, disinterested governmental service vs. political graft, "fixing," "status justice."
3. Family mores vs. prostitution.
4. Classroom honesty vs. accepted patterns of "cribbing."
5. Promotion by technical competence vs. nepotism, racial discrimination, etc.
6. Universalistic legal justice vs. white-collar crime, the public defender system, bias in jury selection.
7. Prescribed patterns of sexual behavior vs. patterns revealed by the Kinsey Report.
8. Legal ruling regarding divorce vs. actual court practice (void divorces, the "alimony racket").
9. Professional codes vs. such practices as fee-splitting among doctors, ambulance-chasing among lawyers.
10. Ethical concepts of truth vs. some advertising, financial transactions, etc. ("business is business").

Again (as with the data provided by anthropologists) it is clear that non-cultural rules do form a system. It is also demonstrable that this system goes far beyond setting up ways of *avoiding* cultural rules. Novel situations occur for which no well-defined cultural rules exist. What do people do on such occasions? They work out some solutions which appear "smart" in terms of the joint goals of the personnel involved. Such "smart" solutions do not avoid cultural rules, they are but novel ways which assist man in adapting to a relatively new environment. If successful (i.e. if these solutions are "really smart") they will tend to be repeated when the same situation recurs.[61]

In describing his experiences in the U. S. Navy, Charles Page discusses social information (he calls it "informal structure") which at times is used to avoid cultural information (he calls this "formal structure"), and which at times is used for other reasons:[62]

> The Navy is a bureaucratic structure. . . . As a complex association it is therefore an instrumental organization designed to fulfill specific goals. The latter are established in the laws of the land and receive extensive written

---

[61] The ingenious studies of "small-group" researchers contain a wealth of data to document this point. See, for example, A. P. Hare, E. F. Borgatta and R. F. Bales, *Small Group Studies in Social Interaction,* New York: Knopf, 1955. At times the "smart" solutions of a given interactional set have such wide applicability that they are independently "discovered" in dozens of historically distinct societies. For example, dozens of societies develop triadic structures which include (1) *A High-Status Authority*—a leader, a "boss," an "in-charge" person, (2) *A High-Status Friend*—a therapeutic figure with power, a chaplin, a friendly uncle, a mother's brother, and (3) *A Low-Status Subordinate*—the person who does the dirty work of the system. See Morris Freilich, "The Natural Triad in Kinship and Complex Systems," *American Sociological Review,* 1964, Vol. 29, pp. 529–540.

[62] Charles Page, "Bureaucracy's Other Face," *Social Forces,* 1946–47, Vol. 25, pp. 88–94. Reprinted in Peter I. Rose, *The Study of Society,* New York: Random House, 1967 (Italics mine).

expression in codes which govern the Navy's operation to the most detailed activities. . . . All this constitutes the *formal* structure of the Navy . . . [a complete study of this formal structure, while important] would fail to include a very significant part of the organization which is vital in any functional analysis. This aspect shall be termed the *informal structure.* Like the formal it consists of rules, groupings, and sanctioned systems of procedure. They are informal because they are never recorded in the codes or official blueprints and because they are generated and maintained with a degree of spontaneity always lacking in the activities which make up the formal structure. These rules, groupings and procedures do, nevertheless, form a structure, for though not officially recognized, they are clearly and semi-permanently established, they are just as "real" and just as compelling on the membership as the elements of the official structure, and they maintain their existence and social significance throughout many changes of personnel. . . . The informal structure may be viewed as a part of the "culture" created within the organization . . . shaped, *to some extent,* as a method of circumventing the formal structure.

Social information "told" Page when to follow official rules, procedures, and codes, and when not to follow such. Social information "told" him what to do instead of the official—that which, for his system, was culturally proper. In situations not well covered by navy regulations, social information helped Page make the "smart move."

The pervasiveness of "the smart" in American society has been most persuasively described by David Wilson. In an essay entitled "Fudge Mixed with Politics Leaves Bad Taste" (reproduced in its entirety below), Wilson shows how fudge ("the smart") is used by senators, mayors, welfare commissioners, and big-business moguls.[63]

It is probably unrealistic to call for the elimination of the "fudge factor" in government, but something really ought to be done about bringing it under control.

This increasingly current term refers to the practice of exaggeration and minimization in the interest of enhancing the acceptability of a future fact.

In politics, it is most often utilized in the pessimistic prediction of the candidate's margin of victory. Thus, in 1970, Sen. Kennedy's people talked about winning by, maybe, 400,000 votes, thereby inviting interpretation of his margin of almost 500,000 as a triumph exceeding expectations or at least a respectable run.

Given the registration figures and an even split of the unenrolled, and leaving out less arithmetical factors, you could have made a good case for a 2–1 Kennedy victory. The fudge factor tends to render such observations suspect.

Similarly, the politician who modestly insists his contest is about even often

---

[63] I am most grateful to both David Wilson and the *Boston Globe* for permission to reproduce Wilson's "Fudge Mixed with Politics Leaves Bad Taste," *Boston Globe,* January 23, 1971.

has in his coat pocket a poll showing he is either unbeatably ahead or down the drain. This kind of fudge is relatively harmless.

In government, however, it is quite another matter.

The steel price contretemps is a classic example of high-level, star quality use of the fudge factor. Bethlehem asked for the moon, knowing the White House would explode. US Steel then announced a substantial price increase, and everybody fell into line.

Result: Bethlehem and US Steel got a price increase and President Nixon won some Brownie points in the press for fighting inflation.

Closer to home, the Massachusetts mayors, fully aware that they would be shot down, proposed a one-shot, $200 million bond issue to bail them out of their financial difficulties.

But, having proposed that the state go into hock for $200 million, the city fathers have made it a bit easier for the state to borrow an "emergency" $100 million for local aid, a pernicious practice resembling the proverbial camel's nose in the entrance to the tent. Barring that expedient, the mayors have at least asked for about twice as much as they realistically expect to get in new state aid, or, in other words, fudge.

It is impossible to determine at this point how much the fudge factor is involved in Welfare Comr. Steven A. Minter's $929 million budget request. But woe be unto the welfare commissioner who ignores the fudge at budget making time.

Ideally, of course, the $929 million contains about $100 million for Governor Sargent to "slash" as evidence of his distaste for fraud and "chiselers" and at least as much for the legislature to "slash" to enhance its reputation for economizing.

That would leave $729 million, or a mere $90 million increase over the previous year's figures. The fact that $729 million won't pay the bills is beside the point. That problem can be solved in politically neuter deficiency and supplementary budgets.

Meanwhile, the commissioner gets a chance to demonstrate to the poor and their sponsors, with whom he has to deal directly, the awesome dimensions of his heart. The budgeting and appropriating authorities, i.e., the governor and Legislature are enabled to demonstrate their concern for the hard-pressed taxpayer.

In government, the fudge factor is used negatively prior to authorization and positively prior to appropriation. Before a program is authorized it is advertised as costing taxpayers little or nothing, or, indeed, saving money through such ephemeral advantages as "streamlining," "rationalizing" and "restructuring." Afterwards, of course, the program is represented as unable to do its job without large numbers of, preferably, "Professional" personnel, most of whom are otherwise unemployable and for whom the whole thing was organized in the first place.

The fudge factor is when you say you absolutely have to have it by Monday in hopes of obtaining it the following Friday. Conversely, it is when you say you might be able to deliver it by Wednesday when you already have it in hand.

> Fudge obviously has its uses. But there is so much stuff around these days that the average man ought to be forgiven a sense of surfeit and an increasingly cynical distrust of his government.

The budgeting system, so nicely described by Wilson, almost necessitates that those who "supervise" or otherwise control the flow of monies know the rules of fudge, or the smart. Supervisors and controllers assume that their "subordinates" (there is humor in considering Bethlehem Steel and U. S. Steel as subordinates to the President of the United States) are really padding their requests. Controllers therefore routinely subtract X percent of monies requested. The fact that controllers will assume that fudge is there forces those who make requests or demands to ask for much more than they need. It is most reasonable to see this whole matter as "a system." Systems, we know, often maintain themselves almost automatically, and it is instructive to see how the "automaticness" of these money-flow systems works. What if the money-requestor were completely "honest" and only requested funds which were completely necessary? Such a *Schlemiel* would quickly lose his job, and in addition help many others to lose theirs. The controllers must assume that the Schlemiel, like all others occupying the status "junior, money-distributor," has requested far more than what was really needed. His request, his budget, or what have you, will therefore receive the X percent cut which is routine. The "program" run by the Schlemiel must fold. Since he requested only what he really needed and since he was cut X percent, he cannot run his outfit. Soon, needed personnel must be fired; and soon, needed equipment cannot be purchased. Soon it will be noticed that the system had its Schlemiel. If possible he will be fired; otherwise, he will be pushed up higher in the organization where he can do no harm.

"Fudge," says Wilson, "clearly has its uses." We now understand precisely what he means. Used within manageable limits, fudge or "the smart strategy" provides humans some elbow room within which they can act as humans; "play" with their environment rather than bow low before its demands. When overused, the fudge game gets sticky and messy, and large-scale distrust enters the system, with possibilities of serious consequences. However, it is almost equally disastrous to have people in decision-making positions acting as if the smart did not exist; as if fudge were not a factor in social existence. I describe these "only-think-proper-thoughts" people as "Schlemiels"; and I am concerned about the harm such humans do to others around them. Professor Williams, in a discussion which follows similar lines, has described the harm that "Schlemiels" do to themselves:

> (People are often punished) precisely because they fully carry out the prescriptions of a moral code—even when that code is nominally and publicly placed at the apex of publicly approved values. Sometimes these heroic individuals are

> regarded as "saints;" but they are also regarded in certain circumstances as "fanatics," "troublemakers," "subversives"—the person who takes literally religious injunctions against killing, for instance, or the zealous injunctions proponent of absolute truth who refuses to tell conventional "white lies," or the minister who insists on a literal implementation of brotherly love in intercultural and interracial relations.[64]

Social information, the smart, can be misused or used to the system's advantage. To better understand "the smart" let me list some examples from North America. Most drivers know that the smart way to travel is in "convoys." When travelling in little convoys we are forced to travel above the speed limit. However this type of patterned speeding is probably the safest way to drive. Money situations frequently include smart strategies. These include ways of completing an income tax form, ways of purchasing expensive items (houses, cars, etc.), and ways of creating a "reasonable" budget. The smart instructs workers how to follow orders from superiors selectively, helping subordinates both to keep their jobs and to maintain positive relations with fellow employees.[65] The smart is used by managerial staff in order to maintain the right balance between *discipline*—following organizational rules—and *esprit de corps*. The smart is a guide for talking and for dressing. When used well it narrows the generation gap (between parents and children, between teachers and students) and the status gap (between order-givers of all types and order-receivers). The smart "tells" us to focus on *operational control* in organization life. The strategy here is "friendliness" toward low-status subordinates—janitors, parking lot attendants, ward aides, and secretaries—actors whose powers to infuriate are inversely proportional to their status. In short, the smart can always save us from rigidity: from being too proper, too formal, and too righteous.

Unlike social scientists, novelists and moralists frequently and eloquently discuss man's two realities. And implicit in the language of social science is a two-reality world: society and culture, custom and community, social behavior and tradition, and—that king of conceptual enigmas—"socio-cultural." No one doubts that "socio-cultural" identifies two realities because the hyphen "tells" us so. The hyphen functions as a bridge between the social and the cultural. However, few scholars have dared to study this bridge carefully, or very precisely to describe the two realities which it joins. Perhaps flight—running from deep involvement with the meaning of "socio-cultural"—is more prudent than valor. For those who have stood and "fought" have, more often

---

[64] Williams, p. 380. The Schlemiel, as here described, is one type of a larger category (too often found in our society) who have reached their "level of inefficiency." This matter is very cleverly and humorously discussed in a book that should be part of everyone's required reading: *The Peter Principle,* by Dr. Laurence J. Peter and R. Hull, New York: Bantam Books, 1970.

[65] George Homans, *The Human Group,* New York: Harcourt Brace, 1950.

than not, received little reward for their pains. For example, one of the most famous, misunderstood, papers in social science is the one in which two world-renowned scholars attempted to distinguish between that which is "social" and that which is "cultural."[66]

Like the unclimbed peak for mountaineers, the problem of what "socio-cultural" *means* is for me its own reason for study and conquest. That this problem is large and complex accounts in part for resistance to it. However, the problem is more than just "large." Science, we are assured, simplifies and orders that which appears complex and intellectually chaotic. To stipulate a two-reality human existence—to distinguish between "the social" and "the cultural," between "the smart" and "the proper," *seems* to create greater complexity. Further, the term "two realities" is reminiscent of something not "normal": the thinking processes of psychotics. Finally, by postulating a reality which we share with the animal world—the reality of the social—we *uncover* that which humans everywhere attempt to hide: their close kinship to other animals.

To preview a later discussion, man hides "the smart"—the "second" reality—for the same reason that he often hides his body with clothes; "hides" the basic character of his food by cooking and roasting, etc.; "hides" his dependence on nature by table manners and other types of etiquette. Like the anti-Darwinians of Victorian England, we all find it hard to accept our animal ancestry and its current consequences—animal needs, animal passions, and *the* animal goal of survival. It is to the great credit of Claude Lévi-Strauss that he has accepted the challenge of analyzing man the concealer by uncovering "the hidden" through analysis of myth.[67] The human animal, like the green algae often seen in stagnant ponds, and like other bacteria called *Chlamydomonas,* is a "half-way creature."[68] Green algae, being neither wholly animal nor wholly vegetable, live in two realities and, I would bet, tend to favor one of them. Human animals, being neither wholly animal nor wholly human, also live in two realities, and very clearly the reality created by the "big brain" is favored. The "big brain" provides an arbitrary reality called "culture," where everything important—beliefs, values, goals—is true by definition. Big-brain reality or culture has a major problem to solve: What shall we do with "the animal." Being so proud to be human our key question is not "To be or not to be?" Rather we ask "What shall I hide?" and "How shall I hide it?"

---

[66] See Talcott Parsons and A. L. Kroeber, "The Concepts of Culture and Social Structure," *American Sociological Review*, 1958, Vol. 23, pp. 582–583.

[67] See Edmund Leach, "Mythical Inequalities," *New York Review of Books,* January 1971, Vol. 16, p. 4.

[68] See John N. Bleibtrau's widely acclaimed book, *The Parable of the Beast,* Toronto: Collier Books, 1969; Roger Stanier, Michael Doudoroff and Edward A. Adelberg, *The Microbial World,* 3rd ed., Englewood Cliffs, N.J.: Prentice-Hall, 1970; and Lynn Margulis, "Symbiosis and Evolution," *Scientific American,* August 1971, Vol. 225, No. 2, pp. 49–57.

In short, as half-way creatures, humans have two histories, two "natures," and two realities. By describing man's two worlds as *the smart* and *the proper,* I only give old ideas new labels. For example, let us examine the most misunderstood conversation in history—Adam rapping with God in Eden. In answering God's question "Where are you?" Adam says, "I am hiding because I am an animal." That Adam knows his "animality" is clear from the Hebrew word used, *AROM*. *AROM* means both "naked" and "smart," the situation of all animals. The faulty translation of *AROM* in English versions of the Old Testament has impeded our understanding of man's two-reality world (Genesis 3:10). Having eaten from that famous tree, Adam discovered the proper; he tasted the bittersweet reality we call "culture." Like all men after him, Adam had trouble knowing what to do with "the animal," so he ran away and hid. Two-reality living is difficult, often creating the animal versus man conflict which is so well depicted in *Dr. Jekyll and Mr. Hyde.*

The Social and the Cultural—The Smart and the Proper

We play games to get something. In "fun" games we go after an ego recharge. In serious games we want more, much more—we want security, power, prestige, love, and sex. In any game a strategy which leads to a win is smart. Smart strategies may not be proper; they may not strictly adhere to the rules of the game. Irrespective of its properness index ("100" or completely correct culturally, or "0"—very much not-cricket), the smart strategy is not easily discovered. Many games, such as the ever popular "War," have temporary wins and losses (in battles) and often it is unclear whether a strategy which wins a battle is really smart. This is precisely the point made by Jean-Claude Pomonti pertaining to U. S. involvement in Vietnam.[69]

Smart strategies must therefore be identified in ways other than "always leading to wins." This can be done by concentrating on two variables which loom large in all games: risks and rewards. In focusing on "risks" we think about the range of the probable costs of a given strategy. Colloquially, with a risk emphasis we look at a strategy and worry about the "price" and whether we can afford to pay it. If the price is too high, immediate wins are simply not worth it; in the end "the war" will be lost. In focusing on rewards we think mainly about how much "loot" winning will bring, and tend to minimize the costs involved in winning. These two approaches to gaming provide us with two types of smartness: high-risk and low-risk. High-risk or *speculative smartness,* often leads to big gains; but the high-risk strategy can also lead to catastrophic losses—as the United States is slowly but surely discovering in

[69] Jean-Claude Pomonti, "While the U.S. is Winning the Battles, Who is Winning the War," *Atlas,* August 1970, pp. 28–29, reprinted from *Le Monde,* Paris.

Southeast Asia. Low-risk or *operational smartness,* by limiting the chances taken, often leads to but small rewards; however almost invariably, losses too are small. Hence this is a strategy generally used by small-scale, self employed people such as peasant farmers.[70]

In sum, we now have identified two kinds of smartness: operational and speculative. Given that there is also a proper or cultural strategy to living, man appears to have three modes of existence open to him: the cultural, the operational, and the speculative. Common experience will attest to the fact that few people *always* live in one mode. However, as the word "personality" tells us, people *generally* utilize a fairly consistent style in their problem-solving behavior. It is reasonable to suggest therefore that people could be identified as being one of three possible types: *traditionalists*—those who generally follow cultural guides; *operators*—those who generally follow the low-risk smart; and *speculators*—those who generally follow the high-risk smart (see Figure 6).

FIGURE 6: Action Guides, Risks, and Actor Types

Types of Guides to Action	Essential Qualities	"Size" or Kind of Risk Assumed	Name of the System	Name of the actor who generally uses the system
Cultural	"Properness" (Propriety)	Low	Culture	Traditionalist
Social	"Smartness"	Reasonable ("Minimax" Strategy)	Operational Information	Operator
		High	Speculative Information	Speculator

The model being developed seems to present man as he is: an information-hungry animal, a playful animal, and a being who uses a personal style or personality to set boundaries between himself and his friends and neighbors.

[70] Operators use what game theorists call the "minimax" strategy; they try to minimize the maximal costs inherent in a given situation. No attempt is here made to strictly adhere to game-theory models in very formal ways. However the final model presented (see below) should provide a useful mechanism in aiding in the utilization of game theory for anthropological purposes. For those who would like to know more about the utility of considering life problems as "games," I suggest Anatole Rapoport, "The Use and Misuse of Game Theory," *Scientific American*, December 1962, Vol. 207, No. 6, pp. 108–118; and J. C. C. McKinsey, *Introduction to the Theory of Games,* The Rand Corporation: McGraw-Hill, 1952.

Man the big-brained animal does not only *use* information in order to adapt to an external environment; he plays with information. And such playfulness represents a very personal adaptation to an internal environment—the introspective self. In playing with information, man is yet limited by his external environment, which in effect "allows" him three styles of presentation-of-self, here referred to respectively as "traditionalist," "operator," and "speculator."

As information collectors the man in the street and the anthropologist are very much alike. The former, I call him APO—adaptive-participant-observer—collects information in order to survive, and because information collection and analysis is fun. The latter, I call him SPO—scientific-participant-observer—collects information in order to formulate laws of human existence. APO is constantly hungry for information because, like a successful journalist, the more valid news the better his adaptation. SPO is information-hungry, idealistically because the more valid data he has, the more likely laws will be forthcoming; and practically, the more data, the more publications. In a very real sense "the name of the game" for both APO in the street and SPO in the university is *Publish-or-perish.* APO "publishes" by word of mouth: he gives others information, gets information from them in return, and thereby adapts better. SPO publishes in print: he gives information, gets fame, and often lives better.

For APO, collecting social information is a simple task; it is part of normal living in society. Irrespective of what we call information-collecting situations—conversations, bull sessions, get-togethers, rapping—the sequence is the same, the process identical. We bring information into an interactional setting, and pool it by "putting" it into each other's memory banks. The information gets tested for reliability and validity (see below) and analyzed into functional categories. Since memory constantly plays tricks on APO, his social system would seem to need some *information-storage bins* to help the average APO keep his "records" straight. Somehow or other most communities develop information-storage bins: we call them *gossips.* Whether for business or for pleasure, role-players exist who find it useful and pleasurable to keep repeating community information. Bartenders, barbers, shopkeepers, old women, and "retired" men keep the information flow circulating from one community member to another. As these gossips keep "replaying" community-information "tapes" such information becomes well recorded in the minds of some people, including most of the gossips.

Informational analysis takes place as some bits of information are questioned as to their validity and meaning. Arguments take place as to whether Jones is the real father of his wife's latest child; over the wisdom of Smith's purchase of government trees to build his own house; over the meaning of government bulletins on how to plant bananas; over the way to handle the latest change in income tax regulations; over the smartness of building a brick house (like the one going up on "The Junction") as against a traditional, cool, mud-plastered, thatched-roof hut. Argumentation, hot and cold, leads to the formation of friendship groups, cliques, and political groups; this is quite well known. Not so well understood is the fact that such "debates" provide APO with *information summaries:* conclusions as to the meaning of the latest bits of community information. Such *information summaries* function as future guides to action; and such information summaries are the "raw material" out of which future culture will be manufactured.

For example, a group of APOs may decide jointly that Jones is not the father of the child; Rodger the handsome lodger is. The conclusion (quite obvious to an APO, although not necessarily so for an SPO) is that wise husbands do not allow their wives to take in lodgers; at least not handsome ones. Further, it may be concluded that the wise thing to do is buy government trees, cut them up yourself, and greatly reduce the cost of putting up a new house. Slowly a "tree-purchasing and tree-handling" culture will develop out of this summary (as it did in Trinidad) which instructs community members on *the proper way* of cutting trees in government forests; *the proper way* of trimming trees to assist their transportation to the house site; *the proper way* of transporting such trees (use of local oxen); and *the proper way* of transforming a tree into lumber useful for house construction.[71]

Tree-purchasing and tree-handling culture developed in Anamat, Trinidad, out of the purchase of trees by some men and out of a conclusion reached by the community that such behavior was smart. In similar ways most aspects of all cultures develop. That is, acts considered by the community as "smart" are transformed into culture, the proper. It is interesting and instructive to note that APO, the man in the street practicing adaptive-participant observation, is *not* a simple-minded conformist. APO, in his own way, is a scientist, practicing science the best way he knows how. Like all scientists, APO has a constant hunger for information and like all scientists APO does not accept every bit of information he is given as being true. Interestingly enough, APO and the professional scientist use very similar ways to check on the truth of their information.

Man the Scientist

In testing for truth[72] scientists use three strategies, known respectively as *content validation, predictive validation,* and *construct validation.*[73] Something

---

[71] This example comes from my field notes on research completed in 1958 in Anamat, Eastern Trinidad. A fuller description of this work can be found in Freilich (1970).

[72] Scientists are uncomfortable with soft, "mushy," romantic words like "truth." They like tough words like "validity."

[73] Fred N. Kerlinger, *Foundations of Behavioral Research,* New York: Holt, Rinehart and Winston, 1964.

is true in terms of a content validity test, when a group of judges have examined and given it their stamp of approval. The judges selected should be expert in the subject they are studying, and the more expert the judges the more likely it is that "X" is really true. Truth by content validation is actually truth based on *expert authority.* The expert authorities in society are man's ancestors. They, through their living representatives—often called "the establishment"—tell us all what is true, and we all ("the tellers" and "the tellees") call such truth "culture." In different language, when we accept cultural information as "true" we use a truth-test that scientists call *content validation.*

Predictive validation is based on the simple idea that a bit of information "C" is true if it successfully predicts something else. Differently put, conviction as to the truth of C is here based on C's predictive powers. Now "to predict" does not just mean "to know something that will happen *in the future.*" Just as usefully one can predict *the past.* For example, if I "know" that *three-eyed people always insult fat women,* I can test my "knowledge" in at least two ways: (1) by waiting until I run into a three-eyed person talking to a fat woman, i.e. testing by predicting the future; or (2) by asking people if in their *past experience* they have noticed that whenever a three-eyed person met a fat woman an insult followed. If the latter information becomes available, my "knowledge" has been validated.[74] Strangely enough, many APOs use predictive validity testing; they take a piece of new information "*i*" and analyze it in terms of its ability to predict some of *their past experiences.* Operators, that is, are constantly checking whether a piece of new information *i* "makes sense" in terms of their past experience. If it does then *i* gets added to the operational rules they use to solve life problems.

Construct validity testing is based on the following type of reasoning: "Q is true if it is consistent with my theoretical understandings which pertain to things like Q." Construct validity testing uses "theory" to test the truth of something. Theory, in essence, is a set of speculative sentences which attempt to explain reality. Strangely enough, some APOs are constantly doing construct validity testing: they constantly use speculative, community theory as guides to action. I call these APOs speculators.

In sum, the traditionalist does content validity testing; the operator does predictive validity testing; and the speculator does consruct validity testing. Since it is reasonable to assume (and congruent with empirical findings) that most communities contain some traditionalists, some operators, and some speculators, then it seems that most communities, as communities, do validity testing by following the three basic procedures used by scientists. APO then, strangely enough, is far more of a scientist that scientists might like to believe.

[74] It is for this reason that Kerlinger speaks of prediction to "an outside source," rather than prediction of the future.

Is all this really so strange? I say no, for several reasons: first, science is basically an adaptive strategy for the survival of humanity. Since humanity has so far survived, humans must be practicing some form of science.[75] Second, every scientist of today using the scientific method for the advancement of "knowledge" is the APO of yesterday doing pseudo-science in order to survive. Science, in other words, grows out of the normal, everyday gropings of APOs everywhere. The scientist gets his passions (information needs; truth hunger; predictability thirst; and control desires) from passions already built into the average man in the street: the so-called conformist, whom I call a pseudo-scientist.

The analysis thus far presented shows that the trichotomy presented—cultural rules, versus operational rules, versus speculative rules—is *not arbitrary.* Rather this model—that I call "V-R Guidance System"—shows man as he really is: a quasi-scientist doing science as well as he can in order to survive. The model is evolutionary in nature, since rules for the smart (operational rules and speculative rules) are regularly transformed into rules for the proper (culture). Man, willy-nilly, is constantly involved in the manufacture of culture, and such culture, over time, keeps getting smarter (read, "more adaptive").

Man the pseudo-scientist, the validity tester, the cultural manufacturer, is still more like a real scientist than has so far been shown. For in man's arguments over the truth of a given piece of information, he often seeks consensus: APOs often argue with each other to gain agreed-upon views concerning a new piece of information "*i*." Such consensus-seeking arguments are, essentially, APO's attempts at reliability testing.

When a scientist does reliability testing, he questions the instrument used to collect the information. If the instrument is precise, the scientist assumes that the information is reliable, since he assumes that the same information would be obtained again and again by anyone using the same instrument under the same environmental conditions. When an APO wants to know whether a piece of information is correct, he is not overly concerned with the instrument used (generally the ears and eyes of other APOs), but rather with (1) how well the instrument was used, and (2) how accurately the results of using it are being reported. These latter concerns disappear when a large proportion of fellow

---

[75] Essentially the same message is to be found in Claude Lévi-Strauss, *The Savage Mind,* Chicago: University of Chicago Press, 1969. Illustrative passages follow:

> Neolithic, or early historical, man was therefore the heir of a long scientific tradition. (p. 15)

> The entire process of human knowledge thus assumes the character of a closed system. And we therefore remain faithful to the inspiration of the savage mind when we recognize that, by an encounter it alone could have foreseen, the scientific spirit in its most modern form will have contributed to legitimize the principles of savage thought and to re-establish it in its rightful place. (p. 269)

APOs accept a given set of information as being correct; as being reliable. In short, when the man in the street is concerned with seeking consensus about information considered important (i.e. potentially adaptive information) and, when he translates his consensus interests into consensus-seeking debates, then such a person is doing the equivalent of reliability testing.

FIGURE 7: V-R Guidance Systems

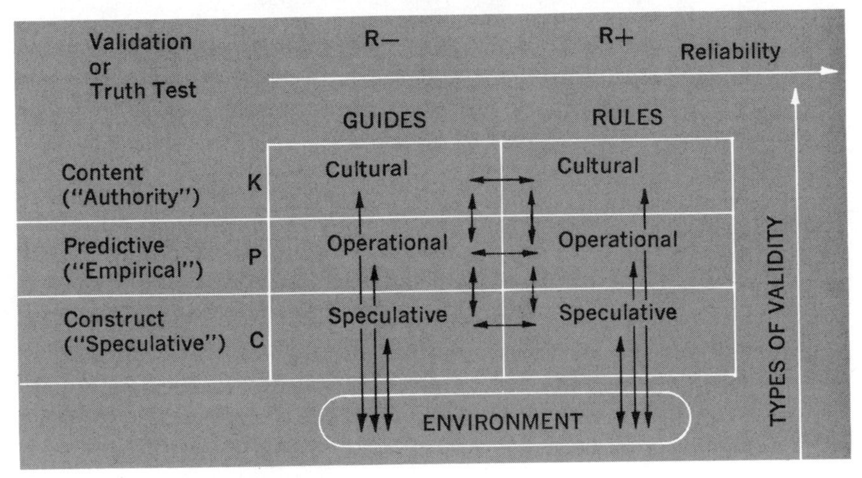

Key:
→ — reliability axis
R+ — "reliable"
R— — "non-reliable"
↑ — validity axis
K — content validation
P — predictive validation
C — construct validation

Since the average APO is both a validity tester and a reliability tester, the simplistic model used to describe him (see Figure 6) must now be dubbed "inadequate." The more complete model here developed, *V-R Guidance Systems* (see Figure 7), includes the following ideas: (1) man is an information-hungry animal; (2) his passions include needs for properness and truth; (3) his consensus strivings lead him to accumulate information he considers reliable. *"Reliable" information that is used to influence behavior is here called "Rules";* (4) some information collected does not have consensus as to accuracy; it is "non-reliable." *"Non-reliable" information that is used to influence action is here called "Guides";* (5) a constant flow of information exists in a community and it has the following characteristics: first, guides tend to become rules. Second, guides that do not become rules in time "die"—they disappear as guides and are replaced by new guides. Third, speculative rules and guides tend to become operational; or after not making this "climb" in time T they "die"—they disappear as action influences and are replaced by new speculative rules and guides. Fourth, operational rules and guides tend to become cultural

FIGURE 8: The "Logic" of Culture as a Guidance System

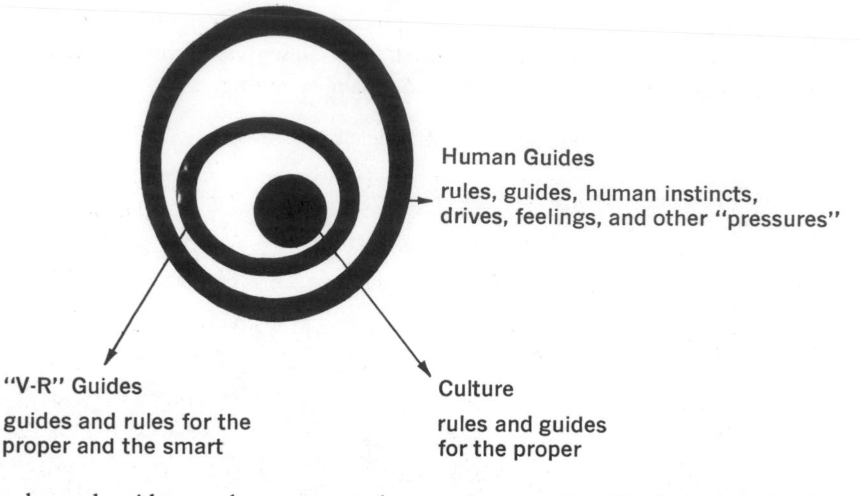

rules and guides; or they revert to the speculative realm. Finally, cultural rules and cultural guides are in constant competition with operational rules and operational guides.

Summary, Utility, and Conclusions

The question "What does culture mean?" has been examined in terms of a number of frameworks. My integration of these various viewpoints follows. Culture belongs within the family *Guidance Systems*. Culture is also a member of a subset I call *V-R Guidance Systems* (see Figure 8). Culture's central purpose is to help man solve everyday problems of existence; it does so by providing general answers (rules and guides) for the question "What is the proper way to ———?" Cultural information is almost invariably in competition with social information. Social information, like the information of culture, helps man solve everyday problems of existence. However, it provides answers to the question "What is the smart way to ———?" Essentially these "smart" solutions are information summaries of what people are currently doing to solve life problems. Members of a community (1) act in various ways, (2) observe each other's activities and talk about them, (3) conclude that some activities summarized by information (S_1 to S_n) are "smart" and worthy of emulation, (4) send (S_1 to S_n) information to community members, and (5) "store" such information in the heads of local "gossips" and others who function as "community information-storage bins."[76] Some smart solutions are

[76] See Morris Freilich, "Toward an Operational Definition of Community," *Rural Sociology,* 1963, Vol. 28, pp. 117–127.

"smart" because they provide answers which will *probably* lead to success, and because they involve the actor in reasonable risk-taking. I call these smart solutions *operational rules* and *operational guides*. Other "smart" solutions include high risks and, generally, high gains. I call these smart solutions *speculative rules* and *speculative guides*. Smart solutions which prove their worth over time (i.e. which have demonstrated their adaptive nature after being used for time T), become "raised in rank"—they become "culture." This manufacturing process, which transforms social information (the smart) into cultural information (the proper) is called "institutionalization."

V-R Guidance Systems appears to be logical and aesthetic, two qualities a model needs to be persuasive. However, beauty and logic alone do not a great model make. Scholars want more: they want practicality. What, then, are the practical or utilitarian benefits which come from using this model? First, since the model was built by means of an integrational approach to culture (ideas of many theorists were woven into each other), of necessity its focus is on ideas that many scholars share. The model thus has a *mediation function:* it creates some harmony where previously there was some conflict. Second, "V-R" sheds light and helps to resolve analytical problems found in other theories of man, society, and culture: it has a *theory explication function*. Third, following in the path mapped out by Tylor in his "creativity focus" and continuing in the trail of such anthropologists and philosophers as Edward Sapir, Morris Opler, Jean-Paul Sartre, and Albert Camus, the model stresses human dignity and human worth; "V-R," that is, has a *humanistic function*.

The mediation function of V-R Guidance Systems is quite simply demonstrated. Most anthropologists would agree that the essential ingredients of culture were very well isolated by Melville Herskovits in his classic book, *Man and His Works*. Herskovits's eight propositions which follow (H.1 through H.8) are almost completely consistent with the "V-R" model.[77]

H.1 Culture is learned;
H.2 Culture derives from the biological, environmental, psychological, and historical components of human existence;
H.3 Culture is structured;
H.4 Culture is divided into aspects;
H.5 Culture is dynamic;
H.6 Culture is variable;
H.7 Culture exhibits regularities that permit its analysis by the methods of science;

[77] Melville J. Herskovits, *Man and his Works,* New York: Knopf, 1948, p. 625. In commenting on the many definitions which exist for culture (and before listing these eight propositions developed by Herskovits) Kluckhohn wrote: "Most American anthropologists would agree substantially with the following propositions of Herskovits on the theory of culture." See Clyde Kluckhohn, "The Study of Culture," *The Policy Sciences,* ed. Daniel Lerner and Harold D. Lasswell, Stanford: Stanford University Press, 1951.

H.8 Culture is the instrument whereby the individual adjusts to his total setting and gains the means for creative expression.

As rules and guides for the proper, culture is clearly *learned*. Its relationships—in very basic ways—to *biological, environmental, psychological, and historical components of human existence* have been fully spelled out. Culture as a system is *structured* and *divided into aspects*. In most general terms I divide culture into *guides*—information lacking consensus—and *rules*—information with considerable consensus as to its reliability. In very specific terms culture can be divided up into thousands of bits of information which function as usable "programs" for the decision-maker we call *Homo sapiens*. Since social information—operational rules, operational guides, speculative rules, and speculative guides—are constantly competing with culture; and since social information in time becomes culture, *culture is dynamic* and *variable*. The *regularities of culture* are the regularities inherent in any kind of program and guide-to-action system. And rules for the proper can be studied scientifically by a combination of methods: participation and observation, focused interviews, formal questionnaires, and so on. Most of the time a simple question will bring to light the bit or bits of culture which pertain to a given situation: "What is the proper way to ———?" However, it will take more complex work to check on the accuracy of the answer and the population to which the answer applies.

It is only in the eighth proposition that "V-R" slightly strays from Herskovitsian views. Instead of using his words, I would say, "Culture is an *important* instrument whereby the individual adjusts to his total setting and gains the means for creative expression." I say "an important instrument" rather than "the instrument" because culture is but *one* of several guides which monitor our behavior.

The theory explication function of the "V-R" model will be briefly discussed in reference to some theoretical issues raised, respectively, by Bronislaw Malinowski and Claude Lévi-Strauss. A discussion of the humanistic function and some of its consequences will conclude this chapter.

Custom, Function, and Freedom: Some Malinowskian Dilemmas

Malinowski's valuable ideas concerning custom have been presented in his own words in Chapter 4. By presenting "custom" as a utilitarian system—by showing how "strange" and "exotic" behaviors are really quite functional, Malinowski kept anthropology in the mainstream of science. However, like many other powerful systems, Malinowskian theory has an Achilles heel; "custom" is overloaded with meaning, almost to the breaking point. "Custom" has several quite different connotations, including (1) behavior, what people do, (2) rules, the "customary," (3) decisions freely made by man, who is "not a slave of custom," and (4) activities which are utilitarian or functional. The semantic problems which develop when a concept is so endomorphic—so overweighted with meaning[78]—have been presented by Edmund Leach with his typical precision:

> Despite the underlying assumption that every custom has a utilitarian purpose and the emphatic assertion that the individual is not a "slave of custom," no clear cut distinction ever emerges between customary behaviour on the one hand and individual behaviour on the other.[79]

For Malinowski it was important to emphasize that man is not a "slave of custom." Indeed he wrote a complete book, *Crime and Custom in Savage Society,* whose central purpose is to show man's independence from custom. The fact that this point needs making suggests that custom can subjugate; that the concept includes "something" with powers to enslave. Custom therefore cannot mean behavior, for it is nonsensical to say "behavior could enslave man." Custom must mean *rules* and other *guides to action.* Rules, when taken too seriously, do indeed make of man but a puppet. Malinowski's insistence that generally man is not a slave of custom allows us to assume two things: first, that by "custom" he does actually mean "rules." Second, that most of the time, most men do not take their social rules too seriously; they avoid the slavery trap. But we are not yet out of the woods. Malinowski also teaches that custom is utilitarian; it has functions which are valuable. If custom or rules are functional, then it appears wise to follow them all the time. Logically, we are forced into a conclusion that Malinowski would find embarrassing: *The wise man must be a slave of custom; only the fool is free!*

Through lenses provided by V-R Guidance Systems these problems are seen for what they really are: more apparent than real. The "customary" includes at least two types of rules and guides: respectively, the ones which identify the proper way to do things ("culture") and those which direct us toward the smart way to accomplish our objectives ("social information"). For any given problem man chooses which rules to follow. Moreover, when he selects the smart as his "leader" he can then choose again: either the small-risk and small-gain smart ("the operational") or the large-risk and large-gain smart ("the speculative"). Given such choices man can hardly be described as an automaton or a slave of custom. Yet man is even more free than thus far indicated. When man finds that his rules do not satisfy biological, psychic, or

[78] Neither individuals nor concepts can work well if they are "overweighted." The person who is overly endomorphic—overstuffed with fat—has trouble staying alive: the heart is overworked by too much mass. The concept which is overly endomorphic—overstuffed with meaning—has trouble communicating: the structure is overtaxed with too many connotations.

[79] Edmund R. Leach, *Pul Eliya, A Village in Ceylon,* Cambridge, England: Cambridge University Press, 1961, p. 298.

social needs, he develops new rules. Man is a creator of his own custom; man creates the information which he uses for everyday living. As a rule-creator, and as a rule-follower under conditions of choice, man must be considered as a reasonably free animal.[80]

The explication of Malinowskian "custom" by means of the central model of this book—V-R Guidance Systems—has led to a completely unexpected conclusion: when carefully analyzed, Malinowski's "custom" is actually synonymous with *V-R Guidance Systems*! Malinowski's insistence that man does not succumb to slavery—that though man follows custom, man is yet "free"—is nicely explicated in the "V-R" model since new information is shown to constantly compete with the old (see Figure 7) and it is man who is the judge as to which information is superior. The "judge" can hardly be described as "a slave." However, these discussions of human pulls toward "freedom" do raise a question, not yet fully analyzed in terms of "V-R": Why does man follow rules and guides? What is the magnet that pulls us into doing that which we "should-do?" The words "should-do" seem to have two dimensions: time and function. The time-should-do persuades us with the message: "Do it this way; it's always been done this way." The functional-should-do persuades us with the message: "Do it that way because that way works." As Arthur Koestler teaches in his brilliant book, *The Ghost in the Machine,*[81] everything which relates to humans must become ranked. Given two types of should-do, and given that we are "forced," being human, to set one ahead of the other, which should-do is to have rank 1? It is to the great credit of human genius everywhere that each should-do can be given rank 1, under different conditions. When man wants to be proper, he ranks the time-should-do first; when he wants to be smart, he ranks the function-should-do first.

When man follows "culture" his primary focus is on time; and only secondarily does he think about utility. Better put, when "tradition" is emphasized, function is assumed. We tell ourselves, so to speak, "Tradition must work, else it would not have lasted so long." With culture, man rationalizes utility because he wants to do the traditional; he gets self-respect that way. In actuality, when man follows tradition or culture he "gives" respect to his past, to his ancestors; in exchange, so to speak, he receives respect for himself—his behavior is made legitimate.

---

[80] Clearly "freedom" is not inconsistent with guidance systems which we follow and which make our behavior, somewhat predictable. If freedom meant otherwise, if it meant everyone being able to do that which they felt "free" to do at any moment, we would live in a chaotic world; one yet more chaotic than "World 1971." In such total social chaos we would not be "free" to make rational decisions, because we would have little reliable information by which to decide. Clearly "freedom" is synonymous with "rational choice"; and *rational* choice implies some restrictions on our ability to do everything that is doable.

[81] Koestler (1967).

When man follows the smart he puts function first, and only secondarily is he concerned with time. When basic problems demand a solution which must work, when the consequences of a functional breakdown are serious, then history must be sacrificed for effectiveness. Colloquially, when the chips are down we cannot afford the luxury of tradition. Yet the smart does not completely escape the time factor. In order to know whether a bit of the smart, "*s*," actually does work well, we must look back in time. We must study *s* from a historical perspective, and discover whether it worked in the past. The time perspective is here, generally short, and it may refer to one's own experience just yesterday.

FIGURE 9: The Anatomy of Malinowski's "Custom"

"Custom" as Function	"Custom" as History	
	History is **Primary**	History is **Secondary**
Function is **Primary**		Social Information "the smart"
Function is **Secondary**	Culture "the proper"	

"V-R" seems to have "helped" Malinowskian custom (see Figure 9) and received some aid in return. Let us see what occurs with Lévi-Straussian structuralism.

Claude Lévi-Strauss, Structuralist

Structure is a motley category; it groups together people of such diverse areas of scholarship as Child Development, Mathematics, History, Linguistics, Folklore, Political Theory, and Anthropology. However, beneath their differences structuralists share some important beliefs and work practices. They believe that the whole is *more than* the sum of its parts, and has logical and analytical priority over its parts. These beliefs as to the nature of wholes are held by many scientists. Structuralists, however, take these views very seriously: they regularly and systematically (1) study the relationships which exist between the parts that constitute a whole, (2) investigate the "cement" that keeps wholes *together*,[82] and (3) try to discover how one kind of whole becomes *transformed* into another kind of whole.

Claude Lévi-Strauss, French intellectual giant and leader of structuralist thought, is concerned with a whole known as human social life. In the past his work has focused on language, family, kinship, and religion; currently his major concern is with myth and its meaning. Like all structuralists, Lévi-Strauss believes that empirical reality—phenomena that we get to know by one or more of our five senses—is the superficial stuff of human existence. The "real action" lies hidden far beneath the level of "the obvious"; far beneath the surface. Therefore, like all structuralists, Lévi-Strauss must perforce be a semantic archaeologist: he must dig around and underneath visible reality in order to uncover the "real truth": the fundamental reality which he calls the "truth of reason."[83] Unlike regular archaeology, semantic archaeology digs inward, rather than downward. The goal here is to grasp the basic nature of the human mind. For a human to use his own mind to understand "mind" appears to be an impossible task; somewhat like trying to see oneself without the use of mirrors. But structuralists like Lévi-Strauss believe it can be done—if we use the right strategy. And the right strategy, we are told, is *model-building*. In brief, the path that leads to the truth of reason starts with the empirical, goes on to models, and finally brings us to "the mind."

In discussing the nature of models Lévi-Strauss makes two pairs of distinctions: (1) between mechanical models and statistical models, and (2) between conscious models and unconscious models. The distinction between "mechanical" and "statistical" models parallels Ralph Linton's distinction between "ideal culture" and "real culture." Mechanical models ("ideal culture") are rules of ideal behavior—what should be done. Statistical models ("real culture") are summaries of what is actually done, by whom and how frequently. These meanings of mechanical models and statistical models respectively, come through clearly in an example Lévi-Strauss provides:

> A society which recommends cross-cousin marriage but where this ideal marriage type occurs only with limited frequency needs, in order that the system be properly understood, both a mechanical model [rules describing the ideal] and a statistical model [summaries of the actual].[84]

---

[82] The modern answer to the question "How are you?"—"I'm together" indicates that young people are similarly interested in keeping their various "parts" properly cemented to each other. They believe that a person with a unity of purpose manages to meaningfully relate the diverse aspects of his life. For structuralists, identifying the underlying unity of a whole is a central purpose of research.

[83] Claude Lévi-Strauss, *The Scope of Anthropology,* trans. Sherry Ortner and Robert A. Paul, London: Grossman Publishers, 1969, p. 34. The great popularity currently enjoyed by structuralism (Lévi-Strauss, for example, is a kind of national hero in France) is in part due to the fascination humans have with the hidden. We seem to find uncovering the hidden great fun, almost as enchanting as *hiding* (see below).

[84] Claude Lévi-Strauss, "Social Structure," *Anthropology Today,* ed. A. L. Kroeber, Chicago: University of Chicago Press, 1953, p. 528.

Conscious, or "home-made" models are the norms the natives identify, their own explanations of why they live the way they do. Unconscious models, on the other hand, are built by anthropologists; they are the explanations of strangers as to why the natives behave as they do. In attempting to uncover the underlying reality of human life, Lévi-Strauss is forced to evaluate native productions; he must decide what to do with native "home-made" models. This task puts Lévi-Strauss into a quandary. Deeply involved with questions concerning the quality of modern existence and a strong believer in the lessons "primitives" can teach "moderns" about the meaning of life, Lévi-Strauss's gut reaction is to say: The average native is as bright as the average anthropologist:

> As a matter of fact, many "primitive" cultures have built models of their marriage regulations which are more to the point than models built by professional anthropologists. Thus one cannot dispense with studying a culture's "home-made" models . . . after all each culture has its own theoreticians whose contributions deserve the same attention as that which the anthropologist gives his colleagues.[85]

This gut reaction, where affection conquers reason, has little staying power. The role of Brutus, "I come to praise native models," is quickly shed and replaced by that of an intellectual undertaker. As an icy-cold burial orator, Lévi-Strauss proclaims the inherent inferiority of native models and the natural superiority of anthropological ones. Conscious models, he claims, are "by very definition poor ones since they are not intended to explain phenomena but to perpetuate them." Moreover, such "home-made" models *hide reality* rather than explicate it; that is, native norms act as a screen which covers the true nature of their society. Finally comes the *coup de grace,* as Lévi-Strauss implies that native models really do not merit the term "model" since the natives do not build "structures."[86]

Linking all of Lévi-Strauss's theory with the "V-R" model, and using all of the latter to explicate all of the former, is an impossible task in a necessarily short discussion. Instead I will pick a small subject, the value of models which the natives build, give a "V-R" interpretation of it, and show why the latter (Lévi-Strauss to the contrary) is correct.

From a "V-R" perspective *all men are scientists;* therefore, intellectual productions of the man in the street deserve considerable respect and attention. Differently put, "V-R" applauds Lévi-Strauss's gut reaction and proclaims it "intellectually correct." Hence "V-R" would have us carefully examine his "burial oration" for possible flaws in logic and in fact. *A priori* "V-R" would have us reject what could be referred to as the *law of the natural superiority of anthropological models* (LONSAM). Is LONSAM worthy of lengthy analysis, irrespective of the outcome of such labors? I believe it is. Careful

---

[85] Lévi-Strauss (1953), p. 527.

[86] This rather unfriendly burial oration can be found in Lévi-Strauss (1953), pp. 526–528.

analysis of this "law" permits us to quickly grasp some fundamental Lévi-Straussian views concerning (1) man's involvement with "the hidden," (2) why man "hides things," and (3) the different levels of the hidden, including that deep layer called "structure."

LONSAM stands or falls on the strength of three arguments or "proofs" and these must be examined one by one. Proof 1 is: Native models perpetuate a way of life; they do not *explain reality*. The argument here hinges on the opposition between *perpetuation* and *explanation*. Now while it is true that native models (cultural norms) really do perpetuate a way of life, it is not correct to argue that *therefore* such models are necessarily inferior. "Perpetuation" and "explanation" are not mutually exclusive processes. Indeed, all models both perpetuate something and explain something. Anthropological models—the maps, images, and analogies which anthropologists use in order to explain what is basic in human life—attempt to perpetuate anthropological theory *and* they attempt to explain native life. That native models "perpetuate" is then no devastating attack; it is but part of the nature of the "beast" we call a model to do something "selfish" (perpetuate) while doing something "noble" (explain).

Proof 2 is: Native models hide reality rather than make it more understandable. With their "home-made" models, natives place a screen, so to speak, between their real existence and themselves. The screening function of native models is more than an attack on the natives as model-builders; it is a fundamental proposition about man and social life. As such this idea merits considerable analysis and a good place to start is with the puzzlement it has caused many anthropologists. Voicing the wonders of many, Nutini asks: Why do "societies try to hide their fundamental structure by screen type models, figuratively speaking, with little to no functional value?"[87] It is man, not society, that hides things. We must stop speaking figuratively and ask instead: Why do natives hide their social structure? Put this way the answer is not difficult to discover: natives hide their social structure because they hide almost everything else. Let me explain.

In most human societies some parts of the body are hidden for a multitude of purposes. "Hide-the-body" is a game which develops enormous complications in the so-called "advanced" societies. Here much of the body is hidden much of the time, from all but a few "intimates." Whether to screen body parts considered "private," or to hide physical characteristics considered "ugly," or to exaggerate sexual appeal, or to conceal the aging process, clothes and related paraphernalia leave only a small proportion of our total mass uncovered.

---

[87] Hugo G. Nutini, "Some Considerations on the Nature of Social Structure and Model Building: A Critique of Claude Lévi-Strauss and Edmund Leach," *American Anthropologist*, 1965, Vol. 67, pp. 707–731.

Since the human body is knowable in ways other than sight, the expert player of "hide-the-body" takes great pains to keep other senses far from the discovery process. For example, soaps, perfumes, oils, and powders are part of a growing technology aimed at transforming the body and its natural odors into a rose garden. In actuality, hide-the-body is but one game of a larger set I call "hide-reality." "Hide-reality," contrary to popular opinion, is not a game limited to psychotics and similar psychological invalids; it is something we all are involved with by nature of our very humanity. To be human is to utilize language, and linguistic symbols put a blanket of meaning between us and what is "out there." As soon as we gain some expertise in talking, everything we can see, touch, feel, smell, and hear gets one or more words attached to it. In addition we quickly develop the ability to talk about "invisible reality": phenomena such as "angels," "beauty," and "hope." In brief, everything "out there" gets its own symbol, and symbols, much like sponges on a wet surface, keep soaking up more and more meaning. Because we are humans, meaning stands between us and "reality." Differently put, "meaning" hides one kind of reality, and provides us with another kind we call "culture."

The hiding function of language and other forms of communication is well known to the human animal, for it is utilized in that popular game, "hide-the-intention." From the clever little false signals which lead to the long pass in American football; to bluffing in poker; to the faking seen in fencing, boxing, and bullfighting; to the many and ingenious misrepresentations in advertising and war—from these and related games humans receive regular sources of deep satisfaction. More to the point of my argument, in these and related ways the human animal is constantly hiding something.

"To hide" seems to be synonymous with "to be human." Therefore the fact that natives hide some of their reality by means of their models should neither surprise us nor cause us any concern. Nor does this fact make their models necessarily inferior. We are led by this analysis to wonder what kinds of information anthropological models hide. We should be quick to investigate situations where hiding does not exist. For example, how does the prophet manage to stay alive, and yet regularly "tell it like it is"? And, how does the stripper survive, and yet regularly "show it like it is"?[88]

[88] These and related questions on non-hiding cannot be further discussed here; however they highlight the fact that to hide, to cover, to screen, is not strange. Rather it is strange not to hide ("to parade," to be "indecently exposed") and it is strange to hinder the hiding efforts of others (to pry into "secrets," to be a "peeping Tom"). Hermann Hesse seems to have had ideas closely allied to these, for he once told Miguel Serrano: "Words are really a mask. They rarely express the true meaning; in fact they tend to hide it." Miguel Serrano, *C. G. Jung and Hermann Hesse, A Record of Two Friendships,* New York: Schocken Books, 1970, p. 22. This analysis, obviously, can help those interested in becoming strippers or prophets. To the former I say: Keep something on; allow something, no matter how small, to stay hidden! To the latter my message is: Speak in parables; keep some ideas screened. The

Proof 3, Lévi-Strauss's final "proof" of LONSAM, is that native models are not really models since models are structures, and the cultural norms of the natives are not structures. This "attack" on native models, while unfair, is fortuitous for it helps to focus more on that tricky word "structure." What, precisely, does Lévi-Strauss mean when he uses "structure"?

> That arrangement alone is structured which meets two conditions: that it be a system, ruled by internal cohesiveness; and that this cohesiveness, inaccessible to observation in an isolated system, be revealed in the study of transformations, through which similar properties in apparently different systems are brought to light.[89]

A structure, then, is a system whose parts are held together by an invisible cement: a cohesive which is "inaccessible to observation." Since structural analysis focuses on relationships, and since "relationships" really means "the way *parts stick together,*" the structuralist must identify this cement. How is this to be done? Simple, says Lévi-Strauss: by looking at several systems at the same time and noting *transformations,* the ways by which "things" once the same are made different. With a focus on transformations we will discover the "similar properties in apparently different systems." When we finally discover that which is "similar" in two or more systems, we will have identified "structure." A *structure,* therefore, is that which we discover when (1) we compare two superficially different systems, and (2) we concentrate on their similarities. And the fruits of such a discovery of structure are finding a hidden law:

> All forms are similar and none are the same, so that their chorus points the way to a hidden law.[90]

Now, it is often the case that when an anthropologist builds a statistical model or a mechanical model he is only working with *one society, one system.* By definition, work with one system *does not* lead to the isolation of *a structure.* Hence it is often true that anthropological models—both "statistical" and "mechanical"—are *not* structures. Why then single out native models as inferior because they are not structures? In sum, any model which focuses on one society and its culture is, by Lévi-Strauss's own definition of structure, not "a structure." We must conclude then that, first, all models (anthropological or "native") are not necessarily "structures." Second, that it is unfair to attack native models for not being structures.

---

importance of "the hidden" in social life was better understood in a previous, more sophisticated era in the Western world. People such as "sweater girls," although lacking formal training in structural analysis, somehow knew the value of "suggestive" hiding. The current value of this information, particularly among powerful figures of the Western entertainment world, is less than zero.

[89] Lévi-Strauss (1969), p. 31.

[90] Lévi-Strauss quoting Goethe (1969), p. 31.

By stipulating *the natural equality of native models,* "V-R" has helped us to dig deeply and well into Lévi-Straussian theory. And having got this far one is encouraged to push on a little further. The fact that humans hide so many things forces the question of: Why? What is it that humans are trying to hide, by hiding? In pointing to the central focus of Lévi-Strauss's recent work, Leach tells us the answer: *Man is trying to hide the fact that he is an animal!* As Leach puts it, Lévi-Strauss wants to discover, by means of the study of myth:

> How is it, and why is it that men, who are a part of Nature, manage to see themselves as "other than" Nature even though, in order to subsist, they constantly must maintain "relations with" Nature.[91]

Lévi-Strauss is telling us—using words that often hide triple meanings—that *the* major game of humanity is *hide-the-animal.* To uncover that which all natives are hiding, we must get at the structure of myth. Once the structure has been laid bare to the probing mind of science we will truly understand why man—a part of nature—manages to see himself as something *other than nature.* In terms of "V-R," hiding human animality often takes the form of hiding "the smart"—a guidance system which we inherited from our animal ancestors. In short, given that the human game is hide-the-animal, then the human strategy is *hide-the-smart.* For *Homo sapiens* to be able to maintain the illusion of separateness from animal life and destiny, he must present himself as having but *one* guide for living, a guide other animals do not have, a guide called "culture."[92]

A major job of culture is to hide-the-animal and particularly to hide animal-like guides such as "the smart." What of structure? Does it hide things, and why is structure itself "hidden"? Structure, Lévi-Strauss teaches, lies at the

---

[91] Leach (1971), p. 45. Among other fascinating writings on myth by Claude Lévi-Strauss, see *The Raw and the Cooked: Introduction to a Science of Mythology,* trans. John and Doreen Weightman, New York: Harper and Row, 1969; *Mythologiques II, Du miel aux cendres* (The Honey and the Cinder), Paris, 1966; *Mythologiques III, L'origine des manières de table* ("The Origin of Table Manners"), Paris, 1968.

[92] As previously indicated, the human embarrassment with the animal self is nicely described to us in Genesis 3. Adam, having eaten the forbidden fruit, discovers he is human but also knows how much of an animal he is. Being ashamed of his animality he hides, embarrassed to face God, the king of all that is proper, the Supreme non-animal. He thus tells God, "I hid because I was naked." That "naked" here does not mean "without clothing" is quite clear for two reasons: first, after Adam ate of the tree, he and Eve made themselves clothes out of leaves. Second, the Hebrew word for naked (ORAM) also means "smart." Adam is unfortunately misunderstood in most translations of the Hebrew Bible I have seen, as being guilty for having eaten that which was forbidden. How could an animal who knows nothing about good and evil be guilty for disobeying an order concerning good and evil? No. Adam, a human after eating of the tree, says, "I am naked-smart like all other animals; how can I deal with the king of the proper?" Thereafter, according to the theory which has been developed, man has continued to have problems accepting his animalness. One of the solutions he hit upon was to hide the animal (the smart) with the proper. This matter is dealt with at great length in my paper "Myth, Method and Madness," *Relevant Anthropology,* ed. Morris Freilich, Chicago: Aldine, in press.

FIGURE 10: Hiding Reality

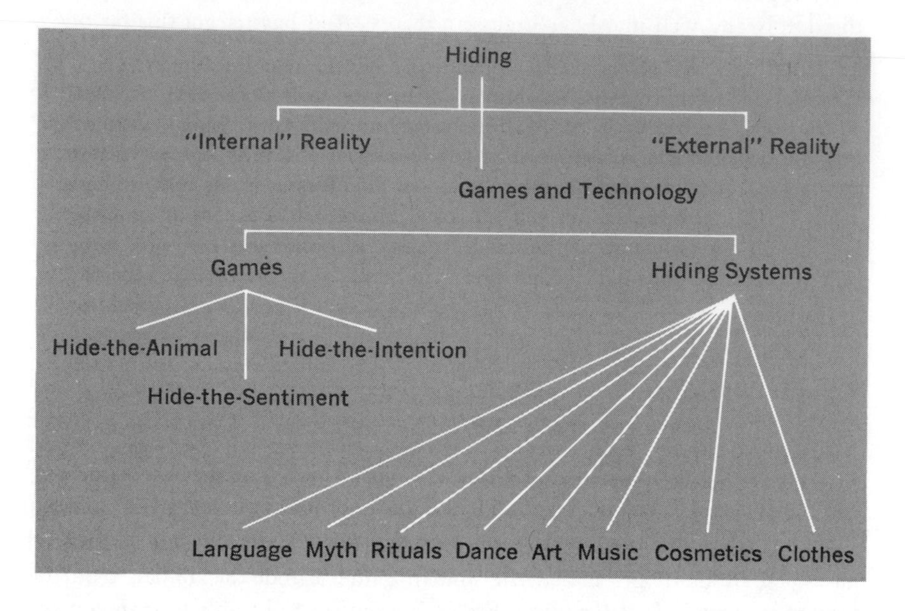

deepest level of consciousness. Structure is to society what the unconscious is to the individual. When an individual wants to keep uncomfortable information "out of sight" he "forgets." When a society wants to erase uncomfortable information it "socializes." In the socialization process we teach our young to forget they are animals, and to learn what it means to be human. Learning to be human and "forgetting" to be animals means forgetting such things as the immediacy of hunger, sex, and bowel-movement needs. We learn instead to eat when it is proper to eat, with those who are proper eating companions, in ways proper for a human. Similarly, other body functions are given their own particular human ritual which makes human life both *aesthetic*—a thing of beauty—and *unreal*—an escape from nature and from the animal that is 99 percent of man's history. In short, underneath daily behavior, and underneath the two guidance systems which account for most of it—the smart and the proper—lies a system of information Lévi-Strauss calls "structure." Differently put, like a precious letter which lies beneath "junk" mail, structure lies beneath *behavior, culture, and social information.* What is structure doing, deep down in society's shared unconscious? Following the master structuralist, we must say: *Structure is hiding the mind* (see Figures 10 and 11).

Throughout their glorious and tragic history humans have managed to "mess up" whatever they touched. Currently we are over-populating a small planet, polluting its environment, and preparing instruments for mass extermination of complete societies. It may be therefore, that hiding the mind—

FIGURE 11: Levels of Hiding and Hiding the Mind

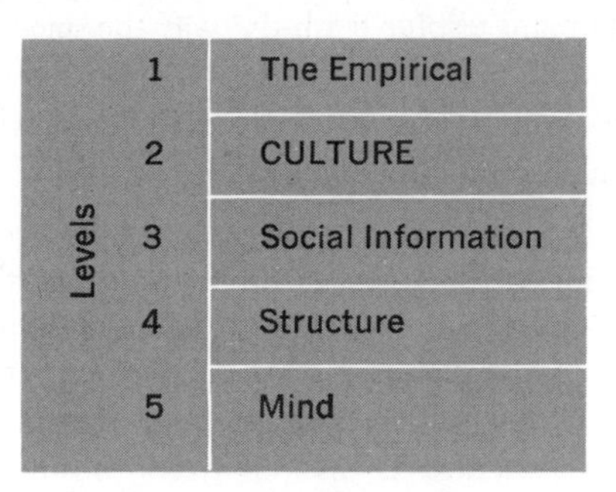

keeping it out of reach of Man, the smart spoiler—is the sanest thing to do. Like all revolutionary philosophers, Lévi-Strauss seems to be leading us along a road marked Heaven and Hell. Those who truly seek "truth" will need to muster all their energy and courage to follow.

V-R Guidance Systems, Men-in-the-Street, and Men-in-the-Bush

The insignificance of man is one of history's magnificent misrepresentations. Scholars of all kinds have taken great pains to *hide* the average human. Human history is presented full of heroes and villains. Fashions and fads led to great discoveries, and one invention inevitably led to new advances. The typical native, his talents, visions, and struggles, have been passed over. The V-R model focuses thinking on man, the creator of things magnificent and things trivial, who has the humor to call them both "my culture." Man constantly creates new social information—"the smart." Man processes constantly and transforms the smart into the proper—"culture." Man is a manufacturer and processor of information. Man is a scientist. In doing science, he utilizes several strategies. Some humans follow agreed-upon information: information that is "correct by consensus." Such "reliability testers" follow "rules" rather than "guides." Some humans are more "individualistic": if a *guide* seems correct to them, they will follow it. All humans, like all good scientists, worry about *validity*—about what is "really true." Like professional scientists, humans use three kinds of truth-tests. Professional scientists call these tests *content validation, predictive validation,* and *construct validation*. The man in the street and the man in the bush use similar but simpler words such as "tradition," "common sense," and "speculation." Irrespective of what words are used, in essence all humans test for truth the way the scientists do.

That man is a scientist should not surprise us, particularly if we understand anthropological field work. The anthropologist is successful in field work because he has emulated and formalized the behavior of the people being studied (participation and observation). The average man is a scientist because survival is not a matter of luck or chance. Survival requires the regular and systematic utilization of science: careful observation of critical environmental information, careful processing of such information, and the careful development of correct conclusions. The "primitive" hunter of large mammals in Africa is as much a scientist as his "civilized" brother hunting for wealth and power in a modern metropolis. The game is different, but the informational problems and the useful strategies are, in all essentials, the same.[93]

Given that man is a scientist it is the job of society to allow him the freedom to act out his socio-cultural and bio-psychological nature. That is, his passion for data collecting, data analyzing, and data synthesizing must be supported by society. Man is, and must be permitted to be, a decision-maker, not a puppet of the power-hungry, not a machine for political programmers. Man as a scientist is hungry for information: irrespective of what his "rulers" say, he will therefore be constantly probing for more knowledge. Freedom to travel the path of self-enlightenment is then more than a gift of a "liberal" government; it is a basic need for this big-brained animal we call *Homo sapiens.*

The glorification of science in the Western world makes "man, the scientist" sound strange. It helps to remember that the professional scientist of today receives his basic scientific passion (information hunger) and his scientific styles (traditional, operational, and speculative) from the man in the street of yesterday. Unfortunately the same source also provides the professional scientist with an important conflict: the need to be proper often interferes with desires to be smart.

Man as a scientist must somehow handle his dual nature. Man is stuck with the human dilemma—he must be proper and he must be smart. His answer, to date, is brilliant but imperfect: the smart is constantly transformed into the proper. This transformational process has a major flaw; the smart (and particularly operational rules) is adaptive but is not proper. Since the smart (and

---

[93] Lévi-Strauss has recently made a very similar statement:

> This thirst for objective knowledge is one of the most neglected aspects of the thought of people we call "primitive." Even if it is rarely directed towards facts of the same level as those with which modern science is concerned, it implies comparable intellectual application and methods of observation. In both cases the universe is an object of thought at least as much as it is a means of satisfying needs.

Lévi-Strauss (1969).

particularly operational rules) is adaptive it must be used; however since the smart is not proper it must be hidden. Moreover, and more seriously, by the time "the smart" becomes "the proper" *much of its adaptiveness has disappeared!* Let us ask again: Why is that? Because, currently, we manufacture properness too slowly; *institutionalization takes too long!* If properness could be manufactured quickly we could be proper and smart at the same time. A major problem for us all is to discover (1) what institutionalization really means,[94] (2) why institutionalization takes so long, and (3) how to speed up this manufacture-of-culture process.

Man's big brain, it has been suggested, is a two-edged sword: a razor-sharp mind which attacks problems with gusto and a psychic need, which demands properness. The need to be proper cannot be tampered with successfully; it is a function of man's big brain. However, smart strategies, developed in response to adaptational problems, can be linked more quickly to properness rules. We have learned to do many things quickly—from food preparation to travel to mass destruction. Why should institutionalization still take so long? This problem demands immediate attention, for if we falter, then big-brained man, with his passions, pressures to be smart, and needs to be proper will disappear—in about the time it takes to press a button or two.

B C D E F G H I J 9 8 7 6 5 4 3 2

[94] The word that sociologists have been concerned with is not "institutionalization," which represents a process, but "institution," which represents the end result of this process. In attempting to discover what "institution" means, Harold Smith found seventy *different* definitions! See Smith (1964).